T0134934

Big Data Management

Editor-in-Chief

Xiaofeng Meng, School of Information, Renmin University of China, Beijing, Beijing, China

Editorial Board Members

Daniel Dajun Zeng, University of Arizona, Tucson, AZ, USA

Hai Jin, School of Computer Science and Technology, Huazhong University of Science and Technology, Wuhan, Hubei, China

Haixun Wang, Facebook Research, USA

Huan Liu, Arizona State University, Tempe, AZ, USA

X. Sean Wang, Fudan University, Shanghai, Shanghai, China

Weiyi Meng, Binghamton University, Binghamton, NY, USA

Advisory Editors

Jiawei Han, Department of Computer Science, University Illinois at Urbana-Champaign, Urbana, IL, USA

Masaru Kitsuregawa, National Institute of Informatics, University of Tokyo, Chiyoda, Tokyo, Japan

Philip S. Yu, University of Illinois at Chicago, Chicago, IL, USA

Tieniu Tan, Chiense Academy of Sciences, Beijing, Beijing, China

Wen Gao, Room 2615, Science Buildings, Peking University, Beijing, Beijing, China

The big data paradigm presents a number of challenges for university curricula on big data or data science related topics. On the one hand, new research, tools and technologies are currently being developed to harness the increasingly large quantities of data being generated within our society. On the other, big data curricula at universities are still based on the computer science knowledge systems established in the 1960s and 70s. The gap between the theories and applications is becoming larger, as a result of which current education programs cannot meet the industry's demands for big data talents.

This series aims to refresh and complement the theory and knowledge framework for data management and analytics, reflect the latest research and applications in big data, and highlight key computational tools and techniques currently in development. Its goal is to publish a broad range of textbooks, research monographs, and edited volumes that will:

– Present a systematic and comprehensive knowledge structure for big data and data science research and education
– Supply lectures on big data and data science education with timely and practical reference materials to be used in courses
– Provide introductory and advanced instructional and reference material for students and professionals in computational science and big data
– Familiarize researchers with the latest discoveries and resources they need to advance the field
– Offer assistance to interdisciplinary researchers and practitioners seeking to learn more about big data

The scope of the series includes, but is not limited to, titles in the areas of database management, data mining, data analytics, search engines, data integration, NLP, knowledge graphs, information retrieval, social networks, etc. Other relevant topics will also be considered.

More information about this series at https://link.springer.com/bookseries/15869

Lizhen Wang • Yuan Fang • Lihua Zhou

Preference-based Spatial Co-location Pattern Mining

 Science Press
Beijing

Lizhen Wang
School of Information Science and
Engineering
Yunnan University
Kunming, China

Yuan Fang
School of Information Science and
Engineering
Yunnan University
Kunming, China

Lihua Zhou
School of Information Science and
Engineering
Yunnan University
Kunming, China

ISSN 2522-0179 ISSN 2522-0187 (electronic)
Big Data Management
ISBN 978-981-16-7568-3 ISBN 978-981-16-7566-9 (eBook)
https://doi.org/10.1007/978-981-16-7566-9

Jointly published with Science Press
The print edition is not for sale in China (Mainland). Customers from China (Mainland) please order the
print book from Science Press.

© China Science Publishing & Media Ltd (Science Press) 2022
This work is subject to copyright. All rights are solely and exclusively licensed by the Publisher, whether
the whole or part of the material is concerned, specifically the rights of translation, reprinting, reuse of
illustrations, recitation, broadcasting, reproduction on microfilms or in any other physical way, and
transmission or information storage and retrieval, electronic adaptation, computer software, or by
similar or dissimilar methodology now known or hereafter developed.
The use of general descriptive names, registered names, trademarks, service marks, etc. in this publication
does not imply, even in the absence of a specific statement, that such names are exempt from the relevant
protective laws and regulations and therefore free for general use.
The publishers, the authors, and the editors are safe to assume that the advice and information in this
book are believed to be true and accurate at the date of publication. Neither the publishers nor the
authors or the editors give a warranty, expressed or implied, with respect to the material contained
herein or for any errors or omissions that may have been made. The publishers remain neutral with
regard to jurisdictional claims in published maps and institutional affiliations.

This Springer imprint is published by the registered company Springer Nature Singapore Pte Ltd.
The registered company address is: 152 Beach Road, #21-01/04 Gateway East, Singapore 189721,
Singapore

Foreword

With the continuous improvement in Global Positioning System (GPS) accuracy, our location-based services have already gone deeply into all aspects of people's life, and the data containing spatial location information is increasing. In the face of the continuous growth of massive spatial data, people are finding it difficult to fully understand the data without knowledge assistance, and so spatial data mining technology has emerged. Spatial co-location pattern mining is an important branch of the field of spatial data mining. By mining the spatial co-location patterns, we can find interesting relationships between spatial features and play a positive guiding role in various location-based application domains.

Massive spatial data brings new challenges to spatial co-location pattern mining. How can we find the compressed or condensed representation of spatial patterns from a large number of mining results? How can we design appropriate preference constraints for users in spatial co-location pattern mining? How do we derive some pruning strategies from the preference constraints to improve the efficiency of the preference-based mining algorithms? This monograph answers these questions quite well.

Professor Wang's research team has systematically and continuously researched spatial co-location pattern mining since 2008. In particular, fruitful and pioneering research on preference-based spatial co-location pattern mining has been conducted. Many of their results have been published in internationally renowned journals and conferences and have been accepted by the scholars in the world, of course, including myself.

This monograph studies a series of preference-based pattern mining techniques, including: maximal prevalent co-location pattern mining, maximal sub-prevalent co-location pattern mining, SPI-closed co-location pattern mining, top-k prevalent co-location pattern mining, dominant co-location pattern mining, non-redundant co-location pattern mining, high-utility co-location pattern mining, interactive mining, the similarity measurement between spatial co-location patterns, etc. The research results are systematic and promising.

Throughout the monograph, the author gives a clear explanation of the motivation for the research, the definition of the problem, the key research, the statement and analysis of the method, and the application evaluation, etc. It is believed that this monograph may serve researchers and application developers in spatial data mining technology and related fields and may help them explore this exciting field and develop new methods and applications. It may also provide the current status of this promising latest research theme, both for graduate students and other interested readers.

I find the monograph is enjoyable to read and fully recommend this monograph to you.

Renmin University of China, Beijing,   Xiaofeng Meng
China
July, 2021

Preface

The development of information technology has enabled many different technologies to collect large amounts of spatial data every day. It is of very great significance to discover implicit, non-trivial, and potentially valuable information from this spatial data. Spatial co-location patterns expose the distribution rules of spatial features, and their discovery can be of great value to application users. This book is intended to provide commercial software developers with proven and effective algorithms for detecting and filtering these implicit patterns, and easily-implemented pseudocode is provided for all our algorithms. The book is also intended to provide a base for further research in such a promising field. We take the demand from user applications and provide a mathematical and systematic study of preference-based spatial co-location pattern mining.

Spatial co-location pattern mining has broad prospects for spatial data owners. Potential economic value has been found in mining the data from Earth science, public safety, biological information processing, location-based personalized recommendation, geo-information system (GIS), and military strategy planning. We know it has aroused strong interest amongst researchers, both at research institutions (Google, Microsoft, IBM, etc.) and at universities (Stanford University, University of Washington, University of Minnesota, Hong Kong University of Science and Technology, etc.). High-level research results have emerged in authoritative international data engineering journals such as "IEEE Transactions on Knowledge and Data Engineering (TKDE)" and at top academic conferences such as "ACM SIGSPATIAL, ACM SIGKDD, and IEEE ICDE."

The authors' research team began conducting research on spatial pattern mining in 2008. Since then it has been involved with 5 National Natural Science Fund projects on spatial co-location pattern mining, has trained 7 doctoral students and over 80 master students, and has published more than 90 relevant academic papers. We have been given prizes from the Yunnan Science and Technology Award. The research team led by the first author is called the innovation team of the "Yunnan Province Spatial Big Data Mining and Decision Support Research Group," the first provincial innovation team of our college.

Similar to frequent item set mining in transaction databases, spatial co-location pattern mining often generates a huge number of prevalent co-location patterns, but only a few of them satisfy user interests. User preferences are often subjective, and a pattern preferred by one user may not be favored by another, and so cannot be measured by objective-oriented *prevalence* measures. Therefore, the following challenges and/or issues will be answered in this book:

- What is a natural criterion for ranking patterns and presenting the "best" patterns?
- How to find a condensed representation of spatial patterns from a huge number of mined results.
- How to enable a user to have proper constraints/preferences in spatial co-location pattern mining.
- How to derive pruning properties from the constraints which improve the efficiency of the corresponding preference-based mining.

It is essential to study the theories and algorithms of preference-based co-location pattern mining in order to solve these challenges and issues. Preference-based co-location pattern mining refers to mining *constrained* or *condensed* co-location patterns instead of mining *all* prevalent co-location patterns. Specifically, this book includes problems such as *maximal* co-location pattern mining, *closed* co-location pattern mining, *top-k* co-location pattern mining, *non-redundant* co-location pattern mining, *dominant* co-location pattern mining, *high utility* co-location pattern mining, and *user-preferred* co-location pattern mining.

For the above problem areas, this book details the relevant research, the basic concepts, the resulting algorithms and their analysis, with experimental evaluation of each algorithm. These techniques come from the latest results of our research in recent years. For the convenience of readers, the chapters of this book are as integrated as possible, so the reading order of each chapter is quite flexible. You can find the corresponding chapter reading according to your interest. Of course, if you read the book from beginning to end, you will find a small amount of repetitive information intended to guarantee the relative independence of each chapter, but absolutely not information redundancy, as we describe the same content in different forms if possible. Indeed, readers are encouraged to read and study this book in order.

This book can be used both as a textbook for learners and as a good reference for professionals.

Although many people have contributed to this book, we first express our gratitude to our families. Without their encouragement and support, it would have been impossible to finish this book, and so this book is dedicated to them.

Secondly, we should sincerely thank Roger England, a colleague who helped correct the English of the book and gave a lot of valuable comments. We would also particularly like to thank Professor Xiaofeng Meng of Renmin University of China for his guidance and help. After reading the first draft of the book, he not only gave specific comments, but also gladly provided a foreword for the book; we would also like to thank Ms. Xin Li of Science Press of China and Mr. Wei Zhu of Springer. Their efforts have facilitated the smooth publication of the book.

Thanks must also go to the National Natural Science Foundation Committee and the Yunnan Provincial Department of Science and Technology for their long-term project funding (Nos.: 61966036, 61472346, 61272126, 61662086, 61762090, 2018HC019). Without their funding for specific research objectives, it would have been difficult to construct the systematic and forward-looking research results which this book conveys.

This book involves an academic discipline frontier, so numerous references have been given in the various chapters, but here we would like to particularly thank S. Shekhar, Y. Huang, and J.S. Yoo for their pioneering work in the relevant fields.

In the research work, although the authors invested a lot of effort, and in the writing of the book each chapter and every sentence has been carefully checked, although limited to our research depth and knowledge level, errors in the book are probably inevitable and we welcome the reader's criticisms and corrections.

Kunming, China   Lizhen Wang
July 2021   Yuan Fang
                                                                                     Lihua Zhou

Contents

Chapter 1
Introduction

As application areas such as earth science, public health, public transportation, environmental management, social media services, location services, multimedia, and so on started to produce large and rich datasets, it quickly became clear that there was potentially valuable knowledge embedded in this data in the form of various spatial features. *Spatial co-location pattern mining* developed to identify these interesting but hidden relationships between spatial features (Shekhar & Huang, 2001; Huang et al., 2004; Shekhar et al., 2015).

Spatial co-location patterns (SCPs) represent subsets of spatial features (spatial objects, events, or attributes), and SCP mining is essential to reveal the frequent co-occurrence patterns among spatial features in various applications. For example, these techniques can show that West Nile virus usually appears in areas where mosquitoes are abundant and poultry are kept; or that botanists discover that 80% of sub-humid evergreen broadleaved forests grow with orchid plants (Wang et al., 2009b).

In this chapter, we first briefly look at the emergence, evolution, and development of SCP mining; summarize the current major challenges and issues troubling SCP mining techniques; and indicate how preference-based SCP mining may be the future. Finally, an overview picture of the related content of the book is given and the topics that will be covered in each chapter are briefly introduced.

1.1 The Background and Applications

The emergence of SCP mining techniques has been driven by three forces:

- First, with the development of general data mining techniques, the mined objects extended from the initial relational and transactional data to spatial data. Spatial data has become important and widely used data, containing richer and more complex information than the traditional relation-based or transaction-based data.

© The Author(s), under exclusive license to Springer Nature Singapore Pte Ltd. 2022
L. Wang et al., *Preference-based Spatial Co-location Pattern Mining*, Big Data Management, https://doi.org/10.1007/978-981-16-7566-9_1

Although general data mining originated in relational and transactional databases, the rich knowledge discovery from spatial databases has brought attention to the available research on SCP data mining.

- Second, areas such as mobile computing, scientific simulations, business science, environmental observation, climate measurements, geographic search logs, and so on are continually producing enormous quantities of rich spatial data. Manual analysis of these large spatial datasets is impractical, and there is a consequent need for efficient computational analysis techniques for the automatic extraction of the potentially valuable information. The emergence of data mining and knowledge discovery would have been very constrained without the development of geo-spatial data analysis.

- Third, differently to traditional data, spatial data is often inherently related, so the closer is the location of two spatial objects, the more likely they are to have similar properties. For example, the closer the geographical locations of cities are, the more similar they are in natural resources, climate, temperature, and economic status. However, because spatial data is combined with other characteristics in massive, multi-dimension databases, possibly with uncertainty, it is necessary to use specific and targeted techniques. At its simplest, spatial co-location pattern discovery is directed toward processing data with spatial contexts to find subsets of spatial features that are frequently located together.

Spatial co-location pattern (SCP) mining, as one important area in spatial data mining, has been extensively researched for the past twenty years (Shekhar & Huang, 2001; Huang et al., 2004; Huang et al., 2008; Yoo et al., 2004, Yoo & Shekhar, 2006; Celik et al., 2007; Lin and Lim, 2008; Xiao et al., 2008; Wang et al., 2008; Wang et al., 2009a, b; Yoo & Bow, 2011a, b, 2012, 2019; Wang et al., 2013a, b; Barua & Sander, 2014; Qian et al., 2014; Andrzejewski & Boinski, 2015; Li et al., 2016; Zhao et al., 2016; Ouyang et al., 2017; Wang et al., 2018a, 2018b, c; Yao et al., 2018; Bao & Wang, 2019; Ge et al., 2021; Yoo et al., 2014, 2020; Liu et al., 2020; Yao et al., 2021). An early paper described "a set of spatial features (spatial objects, events, or attributes) which are frequently observed together in a spatial proximity." They also defined a distance-based interest measure called the *participation index* to assess the prevalence of a co-location and some of the basic nomenclature which has been used ever since.

Let F be the set of spatial features, S be the set of spatial instances. For a feature $f \in F$, the set of all instances of f is denoted as $N(f)$. Let R be a *neighbor relationship* over pairwise instances. Given two instances $i \in S$, $i' \in S$, we say they have neighbor relationship if the distance between them is no larger than a user-specified distance threshold d, i.e., $R(i, io') \Leftrightarrow distance(i, i') \leq d$. A *co-location* c is a subset of the feature set F, $c \subseteq F$. The number of features in c is called the *size* of c. A set of instances RI is a *row instance* of c, if it satisfies the following two constraints, (1) RI covers all features of c and no proper subset of RI does so, (2) $R(o_i, o_j)$ holds for every pairwise instances $i_i \in RI$, $i_j \in RI$, i.e., instances in RI form a clique.

Given a co-location $c = \{f_1, f_2, ..., f_k\}$, $k \geq 2$, where f_i $(1 \leq i \leq k)$ is a spatial feature, the *participation ratio* of feature f_i in c, denoted as $PR(c, f_i)$, is calculated by

Fig. 1.1 An example of
spatial co-location patterns

$PR(c, f_i) = |N(c, f_i)|/|N(f_i)|$, where $|N(c, f_i)|$ is the number of instances of f_i occurring in row instances of c, $|N(f_i)|$ is the total number of instances of f_i; the *participation index* of c, denoted as $PI(c)$, is the minimum participation ratio of all features in c.

A co-location is *prevalent* if its participation index is no less than a specific prevalence threshold *min_prev*, often user-supplied. The role of research, and the subject of this book, is to establish reliable techniques for finding SCPs, and validating the implications.

Example 1.1 Figure 1.1 is a simple example of a spatial data set. Different icons represent different spatial features, such as "🏠" for house. In this figure there are five spatial features, and four instances of each spatial feature. From the figure, we can see that there are two SCPs { 🌲 , 🔥 } and { 🏠 , 🐦 } whose instances frequently appear adjacent. The intuitive implications are that "frequent forest fires are associated with a large number of dead trees," and that "houses and birds often appear together, possibly indicating that people's living environment has improved."

Since the 2001 start there have been many useful applications.

- **Ecology and environment**: SCP mining techniques have helped answer the following questions: "Which animals (plants) living (growing) spaces overlap?", "What is the link between epidemic generation and environmental pollution?", and "How does the introduction of new species affect biodiversity?" The data sources for answering these questions have been GPS based sensors continually collecting ecology and environmental data, so the answers typically came from mining co-location patterns of these data.
- **Biology and medicine:** SCPs discovered in biologic and medical data can help researchers to gain insights into the association between species or diseases in spatial environments. For example, the SCP of "poor mosquito control site and the presence of birds imply human cases of West Nile disease" was discovered by analyzing a dataset of medical data records.

- **Transportation**: SCPs have been used to analyze the spatio-temporal correlation between congested highway sections, used to identify the spatio-temporal distribution patterns of congestion, or used to discover congestion propagation patterns etc., where the congestion has spatio-temporal relevance and transitivity. The propagation rule of traffic congestion is an important basis for formulating targeted traffic management. In traffic congestion events, different treatment schemes for traffic congestion will produce different congestion propagation effects. Therefore, identifying the propagation path that plays a key role in congestion propagation and effective management of relevant roads is an effective way to alleviate the urban traffic congestion.
- **Business**: Store-location planners would like to know the different types of neighboring spatial objects (features) frequently appearing together. With this knowledge, the planners can determine the expected profitability of similar stores and its surrounding synergistic objects, and so make better decisions relating to investment in new stores.
- **Facilities search:** Co-located searches from geographic search logs help search suggestion. For example, popular hotel chains are good suggestions for a simple search such as "hotel," where the popular element is based on patterns mined from logs. Learning the patterns may help with searches on a different space. Thus, a popular casino-themed hotel "MGM Grand" may be returned for people searching for Las Vegas hotels, because {"hotel", "MGM Grand"} is a co-located query pattern in Las Vegas, whereas "Ilikai hotel" may be suggested for people searching for a hotel in the Hawaii area because {"hotel", "Ilikai hotel"} is a co-located query pattern in Hawaii, and the search strategies can be taken from one to the other.
- **User modeling and user experience:** Like facilities search, SCPs discovered from GPS logs can be used for user modeling. We can identify users sharing co-located trajectories as a group of users having similar interests. Then, point of interests (POIs) can be recommended to a user based on the historical trajectories of other users in the same group.
- **Mobile Apps**: A mobile app developer may well be interested in knowing about requested services ordered by users located close to one another in neighboring areas. The knowledge of which services are frequently requested nearby areas can be used for providing location-based services. It can also be used for providing suitable location-sensitive advertisements, recommendations, and so on.
- **Urban planning**: SCPs are essential to the full consideration of the direction of urban development, providing the basis for the balanced and reasonable layout of urban residence, transportation, medical, education, and other infrastructure. For example, the co-location patterns, "there are no postal services and telecoms near to 60% of schools and residences" or "there are 49% of schools and pharmacies occurring together, but no banks," discovered from urban planning data indicate that the planning of the postal services, telecoms, and banks may need to be rethought, in order to reduce the radius of population flow, and further reduce the traffic pressure of cities.

- **Others:** Geologists and ecologists are typical, established users of SCP discovery, and the techniques are rapidly spreading to other application areas. Some are non-GPS applications, e.g., web page navigation, but spatially distributed data remain at the core of the applications relevant to this book.

1.2   The Evolution and Development

Originally, spatial co-location pattern (SCP) mining was regarded as a special case of spatial data mining, but SCPs turned out to present special challenges, in turn attracting a lot of academic research (Morimoto, 2001; Huang et al., 2004; Zhang et al., 2004; Yoo & Shekhar, 2006; Wang et al., 2008; Yao et al., 2016; and so on). The following is the main line of development in the SCP mining field.

- Morimoto (2001) first defined the problem of finding frequent neighboring co-locations in spatial databases. They used *support*, that is, the number of instances of a co-location, to measure the degree of interest of a co-location. Their approach uses a non-overlapping space partitioning scheme and identifies instances of a size-$k + 1$ co-locations by grouping instances of a size-k co-locations with instances of another feature. This early space partitioning approach may miss co-location instances across partitions and therefore might not find all patterns.
- Shekhar and Huang (2001) re-formulated the SCP mining problem, and Huang et al. (2004) proposed a general framework for the SCP mining. They defined the *participation index*, which is more statistically meaningful than support, to measure the degree of interest of an SCP. The participation index not only has statistical significance, but also satisfies the anti-monotone property which can be employed to enhance algorithmic efficiency. Utilizing the anti-monotone property, an Apriori-like search approach was proposed, called the join-based algorithm (Huang et al., 2004). Multiple studies were later presented to further improve the efficiency of SCP mining, such as the join-less approach (Yoo & Shekhar, 2006), tree-based approaches (Wang et al., 2008), and clique-based approaches (Yao et al., 2016; Bao & Wang, 2019; Tran et al., 2019a). In addition, some parallel algorithms were designed for massive spatial data analysis, such as MapReduce-based algorithms (Yang et al., 2018b, c, 2020; Yoo et al., 2020) and GPU-based (Andrzejewski & Boinski, 2018; Andrzejewski & Boinski, 2019).
- Utilizing the basic participation index measure, some variants were proposed to process different types of data or achieve different mining objectives. Xiao et al. (2008) proposed a density-based approach to identifying co-location instances. They divide spatial instances into partitions and identify co-location instances in dense partitions first. Ge et al. (2021) addressed the problem of discovering co-locations from extended spatial objects. Yang et al. (2019, 2021) proposed a weighted participation index to discover SCPs from spatial data with rare features. Hu et al. (2020) studied how to discover co-locations from dynamic spatial

data. Wang et al. (2013a) proposed the discovery of SCPs from uncertain data. Lu et al. (2018) further researched some interesting relationships among features in a co-location, such as symbiotic, competitive, and causal relationships. Yao et al. (2017) presented a kernel-density-estimation-based model to discover co-locations by considering the distance decay effect. Tran et al. (2019b, c), Tran and Wang 2020 and Wang et al. (2019a) studied ways to automatically determine the neighbor relationship between spatial instances in spatial co-location pattern mining. Fang et al. (2017) proposed dominant-feature co-location mining to consider those features playing a dominant role in an SCP. Wang et al. (2019b) studied sub-prevalent co-location mining to address the issue that the participation index only considers clique instances and may overlook some important spatial correlations. Chan et al. (2019) adapted the participation index to a novel interest measure called *Fraction-Score*, which calculated the contribution of objects in the form of a fraction, so that it could alleviate the problem that the contribution of objects may be over-counted by the participation index when multiple objects overlap.

- In addition to apriori-gen-based approaches, there are clustering-based SCP discovery methods (Estivill-Castro and Murray, 1998; Estivill-Castro and Lee, 2001; Huang et al., 2005; Huang & Zhang, 2006). The method proposed by Estivill-Castro and Murray (1998), Estivill-Castro and Lee (2001) first clusters the objects of a class and approximates each cluster by a polygon, the method then overlays the polygons of all classes together. The overlapping area of polygons are used to measure how frequently different classes are neighbors. A method proposed by Huang and Zhang (2006) constructs a proximity matrix and applies existing clustering methods to find co-location class clusters. By introducing fuzzy set theory, Lei et al. (2019) and Wang et al. (2021) defined the fuzzy proximity between features based on the fuzzy proximity relation between instances, and developed a fuzzy C-medoids clustering algorithm to cluster the features for mining the SCPs. The common problem of the clustering based methods is that the resulting patterns are not fixed. When different clustering methods or parameters are used, the resulting patterns may be quite different.

- Researchers have studied the problem of *maximal SCP* mining (Wang et al., 2009b; Yoo & Bow, 2011b; Yao et al., 2016; Yoo & Bow, 2019; Tran et al., 2021). The concept of maximal SCPs is based on a lossy condensed representation, which infers the original collection of interesting co-locations but not their participation index (PI) values. The introduction of *closed SCPs* creates a lossless condensed representation (Yoo & Bow, 2011a, 2012; Wang et al., 2018b), which can infer not only the original collection of prevalent SCPs but also their PI values. The redundancy reduction problem of prevalent SCPs has been studied (Wang et al., 2018a).

- Bao et al. (2016, 2021), Bao and Wang (2017) proposed an interactive approach, OICM (ontology-based interesting co-location miner), to find interesting co-location patterns, but the ontology-based method requires users to explicitly construct a reasonably precise background knowledge, which is found to be difficult in many real applications. To overcome this drawback, an interactive probabilistic post-mining method to discover user-preferred co-location patterns is proposed in Wang et al. (2018c).

- Because different features may have different "value," Yang et al. (2015) introduced the concept of *utility* in SCP mining, defining the concepts of pattern utility and pattern utility rate, and putting forward an efficient high utility SCP mining method with appropriate algorithm. As the utility between different instances under the same features may also be different, Wang et al. (2017a) extend "utility" to the spatial instance level, define the internal utility rate and the inter-utility rate to capture the global impact of each feature in the pattern, and propose utility participation index as a measure of interest to mine high utility SCPs from the spatial data sets with instance-specific utilities.

1.3 The Challenges and Issues

Faced with different spatial data, different objectives and different applications, traditional SCP mining often encounters challenges and issues. We sum up the current main challenges and issues as follows.

Too many mining results. Traditional algorithms for mining SCPs find **all** prevalent SCPs. Often, in order not to lose interesting SCPs, the user sets a small prevalence threshold, which will mine a large number of results in which only a small proportion are interesting. This problem is further exacerbated by the *downward closure* property that holds for the *prevalence* measure (the PI) in SCP mining, whereby all of the 2^l subsets of each l-size prevalent SCP are included in the result set. In this book, we tackle the problem of *too many mining results* by answering the following questions:

- How to find a condensed representation of SCPs from a huge number of mined results?
- How to design a proper constraint/preference for the user in SCP mining?
- What is a natural criterion for ranking patterns and presenting the "best" SCPs?
- How can we derive some pruning properties from the constraints to improve the efficiency of the corresponding preference-based mining?

Serviceability. SCP mining aims to guide applications and aid decision-making, but the existing SCP mining methods rarely consider domain knowledge, application background, or constraints, so they mine countless unrelated, incomprehensible, and even abnormal SCPs. We need to know how to introduce constraints, background, and domain knowledge into SCP mining so as to improve the serviceability of mining results.

Dependability. When we face a massive spatial database, the SCP mining technology should not only consider the appropriateness of mining algorithms, but also consider their scalability. By *dependability* we mean appropriateness and scalability. The dependability issue is not only a difficult problem in this book, but also a continual challenge for researchers in the field of data mining technology.

Gaps between the transaction pattern and the spatial pattern. Although SCP mining is often compared to classical association rule mining, it is a more difficult process to mine SCPs. Firstly, there is no concept of transaction or similar transaction in spatial data. This leads not only to the difficulty of SCP mining, but also to the challenge of mining preference-based SCPs. In association rule mining, transactions are used to calculate the distance between two patterns P_1 and P_2, $(D(P_1, P_2) = 1 - \frac{T(P_1) \cap T(P_2)}{T(P_1) \cup T(P_2)}$, where $T(P)$ is the set of transactions containing pattern P). Note that the distance measure between two SCPs is not a straightforward problem. Secondly, different instance distributions and different feature distributions of spatial data are continuous and gradually changing, and there is not necessarily any clear dividing line. For example, there is no obvious dividing line between different natural geographical zones, such as different climatic zones or different plant zones. Therefore, the neighbor measure of the instances becomes very important and, depending on its choice, the pattern space searching requires much more time and space.

1.4   Content and Organization of the Book

It is essential to study the theories and algorithms of preference-based SCP mining in order to solve the challenges and issues mentioned in the previous section. Preference-based SCP mining refers to mining *constrained* or *condensed* SCPs instead of mining *all* prevalent SCPs. Specifically, this book includes problems such as maximal SCP mining, closed SCP mining, top-k SCP mining, non-redundant SCP mining, dominant SCP mining, high utility SCP mining, and interactive SCP mining. The book's organization is shown in Fig. 1.2 and below is a brief introduction to the topics that will be covered in each chapter.

Chapters 2, 3, and 4: Based on the anti-monotonic constraint of the SCP prevalence measure (the participation index (PI)), Chapters 2, 3, and 4 outline "natural preference" or "best" SCPs. Chapter 2 presents a novel maximal SCP mining framework based on maximal cliques and hash tables. In Chapter 3, a new concept of the maximal sub-prevalent SCPs is given which replaces traditional clique instances with star participation instances, and two efficient algorithms for mining the maximal sub-prevalent SCPs are also presented. Chapter 4 proposes a novel *lossless condensed representation* of prevalent SCPs, *super participation index-closed (SPI-closed) SCPs*. An efficient *SPI-closed Miner* is designed to effectively capture the SPI-closed SCPs.

Chapter 5: Setting suitable prevalence thresholds is an issue in SCP mining. One effective way is to mine top-k SCPs, and Chapter 5 studies the top-k probabilistic prevalent SCPs based on a possible world model. We find that top-k probabilistic prevalent SCP mining can be regarded as a convenient alternative to the uncertainties of mining all co-locations with a prevalence probability above a fixed threshold, since the parameter k allows, in practice, for a better control on the size of output.

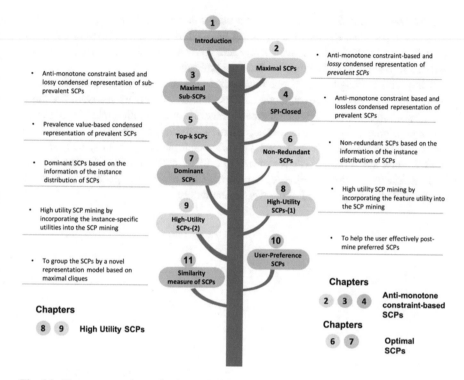

Fig. 1.2 The content and organization of the book

Chapters 6 and 7: The prevalence of an SCP is determined by the spatial distribution of its instances. Based on the information of the instance distribution of the pattern, new concepts of non-redundant SCPs and dominant SCPs are shown to mine *optimized SCPs*. Chapter 6 develops two algorithms to perform the redundancy reduction of prevalent SCPs. The concept of dominant SCPs, where an SCP is dominant if it is not dominated by another, is outlined in Chapter 7. An algorithm called DCPMA (dominant co-location pattern mining algorithm) is presented to implement the dominant SCP mining technique.

Chapters 8 and 9: In traditional SCP mining, the selection of result patterns is generally based on a frequency framework, ignoring some interesting but low frequency patterns, and mining a lot of frequent but uninteresting patterns. Chapters 8 and 9 therefore discuss the problem of high utility SCP mining. Chapter 8 studies and resolves the problem of high utility SCP mining from spatial databases which emphasize features, and chapter 9 studies the mining problem of spatial databases which emphasize instances.

Chapter 10: All SCP mining is instigated by a user and the user rarely wants a black-box process. To satisfy user preferences, Chapter 10 proposes an interactive probabilistic post-mining method to discover user-preferred SCPs by iteratively involving user feedback and probabilistically refining user-preferred patterns. The goal of this chapter is to show how the user can effectively post-mine preferred co-location patterns. Rather than requiring the user to explicitly construct the entire prior knowledge beforehand, we merely ask them to choose preferred co-location patterns in a small set of sample co-location patterns.

Chapter 11: Chapters 2–10 we have developed several similarity measures for co-location patterns. However, none of these can quantitatively measure the similarity between *any* two SCPs. In Chapter 11, a new representation of SCPs based on *maximal cliques* in spatial data sets is presented, whereby the spatial information of the co-location instance can be saved without loss. A general similarity measure that can calculate the similarity degree of *any* two SCPs without adding further domain information is developed. Finally, a hierarchical clustering algorithm is used to group SCPs by the proposed similarity measurement.

Chapter 2
Maximal Prevalent Co-location Patterns

2.1 Introduction

In spatial co-location pattern mining, we use the participation index (PI) as a prevalence measure, which satisfies the *downward inclusion property* (Huang et al., 2004). That is, if a co-location pattern is prevalent with respect to a threshold of PI, then all of its subsets will be found to be prevalent co-location patterns. Unfortunately, as the number of spatial features increases, the search space of co-location mining algorithms exponentially increases. This exponential complexity increases the computational time of mining *all* prevalent co-location patterns and can restrict the related algorithms to mine only spatial data sets of limited size.

In fact, the traditional Apriori-like method to generate size-k prevalence co-locations after size-$(k-1)$ prevalence co-locations have been established generally suffers from the following two non-trivial costs:

1. It is costly to handle a huge number of candidate co-locations. For example, if there are 10^3 spatial features, the Apriori-like algorithms will need to generate more than 10^5 size-2 candidates and test their prevalence. If the user wants to discover a prevalent co-location of size-100, such as $\{f_1, \ldots, f_{100}\}$, about 10^{30} candidates must be generated in total. This is an inherent cost of generating the set of all prevalent co-location patterns, no matter what implementation technique is applied.
2. It is wasteful to store excessive table instances of co-location patterns, especially so when the number of table instances is very large.

From Tran, V., Wang, L.*, Chen, H., Xiao, Q.: MCHT: A maximal clique and hash table-based maximal prevalent co-location pattern mining algorithm. *Expert Systems With Applications* 175 (2021) 114830.

© The Author(s), under exclusive license to Springer Nature Singapore Pte Ltd. 2022
L. Wang et al., *Preference-based Spatial Co-location Pattern Mining*, Big Data
Management, https://doi.org/10.1007/978-981-16-7566-9_2

Can the number of co-location patterns generated in *all* prevalent co-location pattern mining be substantially reduced while preserving the complete information regarding the set of prevalent co-location patterns?

This question motivates this chapter's study, how to mine only *maximal* prevalent co-location patterns (MPCPs). Of course, a co-location pattern is maximal if and only if it is prevalent and it does not have any prevalent super-set.

A novel MPCP mining framework based on maximal cliques and hash tables (MCHT for short) is developed in this chapter. The MCHT algorithm first materializes neighbor relationships of instances into a set of maximal cliques. By employing maximal cliques, it not only ensures that no neighboring instances are lost, but it is also a compact storage strategy that reduces the memory space cost. To accelerate the speed of enumeration of maximal cliques, the advantages of bit string operations are fully utilized. Once obtained, these cliques are then converted to a participating instance hash table structure which is carefully designed to efficiently query and gather information about the participating instances of co-location patterns. Finally, based on the hash table structure, the prevalence of each pattern can be calculated and MPCPs quickly filtered.

This chapter proceeds as follows:

1. A novel MPCP mining framework is put forward to eliminate the shortcomings of existing algorithms which follow the conventional generate-test-candidate model.
2. The proposed mining framework makes full use of the advantages of various data structures, e.g., maximal cliques compress neighboring instances compactly, and hash tables accelerate queries so that computational time and memory space costs are efficiently reduced.
3. Bit string operations are adopted to improve the speed of enumerating maximal cliques.
4. A series of experiments is designed to determine whether the proposed mining framework can efficiently discover all MPCPs.

Figure 2.1 presents the organization of this chapter. Section 2.2 discusses why MCHT is proposed for mining MPCPs. Section 2.3 gives a clear problem statement and the consequent mining framework. Section 2.4 presents the proposed algorithm in detail, and the time and space complexities of our algorithm are also analyzed here. The performance of our algorithm is evaluated by a set of experiments described in Sect. 2.5. Section 2.6 concludes this chapter.

2.2   Why the MCHT Method Is Proposed for Mining MPCPs

Chapter 1 indicated some of the sources of spatially located information, and more data and more sources appear every day. Prevalent spatial co-location pattern mining, which refers to discovering a set of Boolean spatial features whose instances

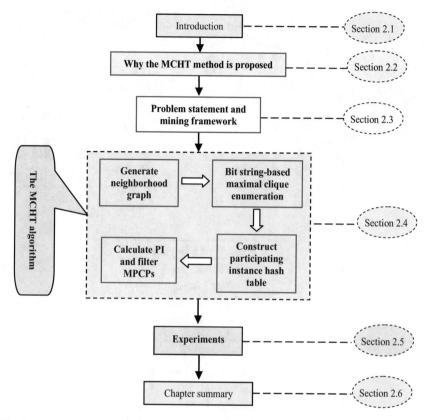

Fig. 2.1 The organization of Chap. 2

frequently occur in close proximity to each other, is an important branch of spatial data mining. Co-location pattern mining technology has become a powerful tool to expose relationships and distribution rules of spatial features in geographic space and the technology is widely applied in many domains such as urban planning (Yu et al., 2017), location-based services (Yu, 2016), ecology (Cai et al., 2018; Deng et al., 2017), criminology (Li & Shekhar, 2018; Mohan et al., 2011; Phillips & Lee, 2012), environmental management (Akbari et al., 2015), and social science (Sierra & Stephens, 2012).

For example, Fig. 2.2(a) shows a distribution of a set of facility points in a Californian city. There are four different facility types (spatial feature types) of these points, i.e., hotel, restaurant, bank, and bus stop. Each point (spatial instance) describes the position where an object of a particular facility type is set; e.g., A.1 is a specific hotel with its location (x_1, y_1). Intuitively, if it is the case that in the nearby geographic space of a hotel (e.g., A.2), a restaurant is usually observed (e.g., B.2), then {hotel, restaurant} could be called a prevalent co-location pattern. After performing a rigorous co-location pattern mining analysis, a list of frequent facility groups (each frequent facility group will be a prevalent co-location pattern) is

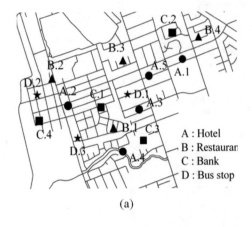

Facility type	ID	Location
	1	(x1, y1)
Hotel	...	...
	5	(x5, y5)
	1	(x6, y6)
Restaurant	...	...
	4	(x10, y10)
	1	(x11, y11)
Bank	...	...
	4	(x15, y15)
	1	(x16, y16)
Bus stop	...	...
	3	(x19, y19)

A : Hotel
B : Restauran
C : Bank
D : Bus stop

(a)   (b)

Frequent facility group
{hotel, restaurant}
{hotel, bank}
{hotel, bus stop}
{restaurant, bank}
{restaurant, bus stop}
{bank, bus stop}
{hotel, restaurant, bus stop}
{hotel, bank, bus stop}
{restaurant, bank, bus stop}
{hotel, restaurant, bank, bus stop}

(c)

Fig. 2.2 An example of spatial co-location patterns: (**a**) distribution, (**b**) facility point, and (**c**) patterns

produced, such as the one listed in Fig. 2.2(c), and these are given to users, very often for decision support. For example, a restaurant investor seeking to expand operations may be interested in the particular pattern {hotel, restaurant, bank}. He or she may suspect that a new restaurant should be located in the neighborhood of hotels and banks for maximizing their profit, but wishes to investigate more fully the spatial relationships and the distribution rule relevant to hotels, restaurants, and banks. If they do decide to open a new restaurant, the pattern {hotel, restaurant, bank, bus stop} may then be useful to transportation planners so that bus stops could be set up in close proximity to clusters of hotels, restaurants, and banks where the visitor flow rate is high, with the possible benefit of increasing the passenger load factor of urban public transport.

Spatial co-location pattern mining typically generates large numbers of redundant patterns, making it difficult to draw meaningful inferences. Thus the notion of

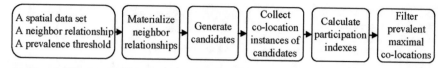

Fig. 2.3 A common framework of mining maximal PCPs

maximal prevalent co-location patterns was proposed (Wang et al., 2009b) whereby, if a prevalent co-location pattern does not have any prevalent super-patterns, the pattern is maximal. Maximal prevalent co-location patterns are a condensed and concise representation of all the prevalent co-location patterns contained in the mined results. An example is in Fig. 2.2(c), where {hotel, restaurant, bank, bus stop} is a maximal prevalent co-location pattern because it does not have any prevalent super-patterns. This pattern is considered the most concise description of the total mining result and so only it is given to users, instead of the confusing set of all 11 prevalent co-location patterns.

Many MPCP mining algorithms have been developed (Wang et al., 2009b; Yoo & Bow, 2011b; Yao et al., 2016; Yoo & Bow, 2019). All these algorithms are based on a candidate-generation-and-test mining framework (Huang et al., 2004) that employs a size-wise search model as shown in Fig. 2.3. In practice, users supply a spatial data set which includes instances of the characteristics of interest to the user, where these instances may belong to different feature types. Very often they are also asked to supply a neighbor relationship and a prevalence threshold. Then the neighboring instances are calculated by the given neighbor relationship and candidate sets are generated. Next, co-location instances of each candidate are collected. A co-location instance is a set of instances that belong to different feature types and both of them satisfy the neighbor relationship. After that, the participation indexes of the candidates are calculated, to measure its prevalence. Finally, the candidates become prevalent co-location patterns if their participation index is not smaller than the prevalence threshold. Furthermore, if the patterns have no super-patterns, they are marked as maximal PCPs and they are given to the user.

Although algorithms of this kind can discover MPCPs correctly and completely there are some shortcomings:

1. As indicated in the introduction to this chapter the number of candidates grows exponentially as features are included (Mohan et al., 2011; Wang et al., 2009b). Suppose that m is the number of feature types, then in the worst case, $(2^m - 1)$ candidates will be generated. For realistic data sets, the computational time of processing such a huge number of candidates is prohibitive.
2. Collecting co-location instances of candidates is the heaviest task and it takes up the bulk of the execution time of the mining process. Figure 2.4 shows the execution time of each phase in two typical algorithms, the joinless algorithm (Yoo & Shekhar, 2006) and the improved co-location pattern instance tree algorithm (iCPI-tree) (Wang et al., 2009a). Both of these two algorithms follow the candidate-generate-test mining framework shown in Fig. 2.3.

Fig. 2.4 The execution time devoted to each phase in (**a**) the joinless algorithm and (**b**) the iCPI-tree algorithm

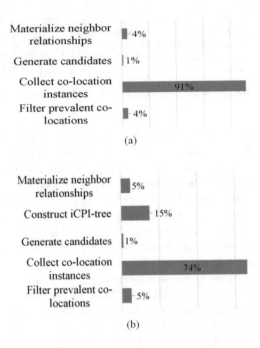

3. The flexibility of these algorithms is relatively poor. When users alter minimum prevalence thresholds and/or distance thresholds in order to meet their application needs, the candidate-generate-test framework has to be run again from the start meaning that these algorithms must re-generate candidates, re-collect co-location instances, and re-filter prevalent patterns. Since collecting co-location instances is a very time-consuming task, users can be deterred from experimenting with their input.

To eliminate these shortcomings, a novel MPCP mining framework based on maximal cliques and hash tables (MCHT for short) is developed in this chapter. The candidate-generate-test mining framework is completely abolished in the MCHT framework. Our algorithm first materializes neighbor relationships of instances into a set of maximal cliques. By employing maximal cliques, it not only ensures that no neighboring instances are lost, but it is also a compact storage strategy that reduces the memory consumption. In order to accelerate the speed of enumerating maximal cliques, the advantages of bit string operations are utilized. These cliques are then converted to a participating instance hash table structure which is designed to efficiently query and gather information about participating instances of maximal co-location patterns. Each key and each value of the hash table are the set of features and instances of objects in maximal cliques, respectively. Finally, based on the hash table structure, the participation index of each candidate pattern can be efficiently calculated, and MPCPs are quickly filtered.

2.3   Formal Problem Statement and Appropriate Mining Framework

In this section, the concepts of spatial co-location pattern mining are described briefly, but formally, and then the problem of maximal prevalent co-location pattern (MPCP) discovering is defined formally.

2.3.1   Co-Location Patterns

Definition 2.1 (Spatial feature and spatial instance) A spatial feature f is a type of spatial data contained in a dataset. A spatial instance o is an object of a spatial feature represented by a triple vector $<$spatial feature type, instance ID, location $(x, y) >$ and we use $o._f$ to represent that instance o belongs to spatial feature type f.

In different domains, particular spatial features and particular spatial instances depend on their context. In the ecology domain (Cai et al., 2018; Deng et al., 2017), spatial instances are wetland species, e.g., Calamagrostis angustifolia, Carex lasiocarpa, and each wetland species in a specific location refers to a spatial instance, e.g., a piece of Calamagrostis angustifolia, a piece of Carex lasiocarpa.

In Fig. 2.2(a), we have Point of Interest (POI) data, whereby any points of interest with a specific location such as a hotel, a restaurant, a bank, or a bus stop would be considered as spatial instances. Each spatial instance belongs to different spatial feature types; e.g., hotel A.1 belongs to the hotel spatial feature. There are four different spatial feature types in Fig. 2.2(a): hotel (A), restaurant (B), bank (C), and bus stop (D).

Definition 2.2 (Neighbor relationship) Given a set of spatial instances S, the neighbor $N(o_i)$ of an instance $o_i \in S$ is a set of instances that satisfy the distance threshold d determined in advance by the user, i.e., $N(o_i) = \{o_j \mid dist(o_i, o_j) \leq d \wedge o_{i._f} \neq o_{j._f}\}$, where $dist(o_i, o_j)$ is the distance between instances o_i and o_j.

For example, Fig. 2.5 shows the result after materializing neighbor relationships of instances with a distance threshold d, for example, $d = 200$ m. If two instances have a neighbor relationship, they are connected by a solid line. Note that, according to Definition 2.2 and the definition of a spatial co-location pattern (given in Definition 2.3 later), only instances that belong to different feature types can have a neighbor relationship. Instances with the same feature types are not considered as having the neighbor relationship, because we are looking for the co-located relationship of different features.

Definition 2.3 (Spatial co-location pattern) Given a set of spatial instances $S = \{S_1, \ldots, S_m\}$, where $S_i = \{o_1, \ldots, o_t\}$ is a set of instances of feature type $f_i \in F = \{f_1, \ldots, f_m\}, f_i \neq f_j$, and a neighbor relationship NR, a spatial co-location pattern is a subset of Boolean feature types, $c = \{f_1, \ldots, f_k\} \in F, 1 \leq k \leq m$, whose

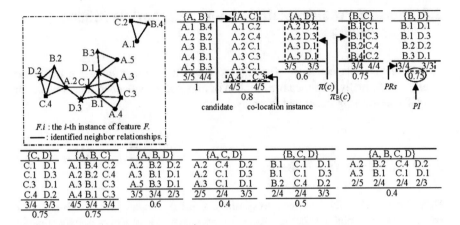

Fig. 2.5 An illustration of the spatial co-location pattern mining process

instances frequently form a clique under the neighbor relationship *NR*. The number of feature types in a spatial co-location pattern, k, is called the size of the pattern.

For example, as shown in Fig. 2.5, there are four different spatial feature types, $F = \{A, B, C, D\}$. The four feature types are combined into 11 possible feature type sets, $\{A, B\}$, $\{A, C\}$, $\{A, D\}$, $\{B, C\}$, $\{B, D\}$, $\{C, D\}$, $\{A, B, C\}$, $\{A, B, D\}$, $\{A, C, D\}$, $\{B, C, D\}$, and $\{A, B, C, D\}$. These feature type sets are called candidates. Within these candidates, the size-3 candidates are $\{A, B, C\}$, $\{A, B, D\}$, $\{A, C, D\}$, $\{B, C, D\}$.

Definition 2.4 (Co-location instance and participating instance set) A co-location instance I of a co-location pattern $c = \{f_1, \ldots, f_k\}$ is the set of spatial instances, $I = \{o_1, \ldots, o_k\} \in S$, which includes all the feature types in c and each instance pair has a neighbor relationship. The participating instance set of a pattern c is the set of all co-location instances of c, $\pi(c) = \{I_1, \ldots, I_t\}$. $\pi_f(c)$ is the set of instances of feature type f that participates in $\pi(c)$.

Definition 2.5 (Participation index) The participation index of a co-location pattern c is used to quantify the prevalence of c and is calculated as $PI(c) = \min \{\frac{|\pi_f(c)|}{|S_f|}\}$, $f \in c$, where $|\pi_f(c)|$ is the number of non-repeating instances in the participating instance set $\pi(c)$ of f in c and $|S_f|$ is the total number of instances of f in the input data set. We say an instance o of feature f participates in pattern c if there is at least one co-location instance of c involving o.

Definition 2.6 (Prevalent co-location pattern) A pattern $c = \{f_1, \ldots, f_k\} \subseteq F$, $1 \le k \le m$ is prevalent if its participation index is not smaller than the prevalence threshold μ_{prev} supplied by a user, i.e., $PI(c) \ge \mu_{prev}$.

Definition 2.7 (Maximal prevalent co-location pattern) Given that c is a prevalent co-location pattern if no super sets of c are prevalent, we say that c is a maximal prevalent co-location pattern.

As plotted in Fig. 2.5, $\{A.4, C.3\}$ is a co-location instance of pattern $\{A, C\}$. The participation instance set of $\{A, D\}$ is $\pi(\{A, D\}) = (\{A.2, D.2\}, \{A.2, D.3\}, \{A.3, D.1\}, \{A.5, D.1\})$ and thus, $\pi_A(\{A, D\}) = \{A.2, A.3, A.5\}$, $\pi_D(\{A, D\}) = \{D.2, D.3, D.1\}$. Features A and D have 5 and 3 instances, respectively. Hence, the participation index of $\{A, D\}$ is $PI(\{A, D\}) = \min(\frac{|\pi_A(\{A, D\})|}{|S_A|}, \frac{|\pi_D(\{A, D\})|}{|S_D|}) = (\frac{3}{5}, \frac{3}{3}) = 0.6$. Figure 2.5 also lists all participating instance sets of the other 10 candidates and their participation indexes. If a user set a prevalence threshold $\mu_{prev} = 0.5$, $\{A, B\}$, $\{A, C\}$, $\{A, D\}$, $\{B, C\}$, $\{B, D\}$, $\{C, D\}$, $\{A, B, C\}$, $\{A, B, D\}$, $\{B, C, D\}$ would be selected and they are prevalent co-location patterns. Furthermore, we can mark $\{A, B, C\}$, $\{A, B, D\}$, and $\{B, C, D\}$ as maximal prevalent co-location patterns since they have no super-patterns that are prevalent. While $\{A, B\}$, $\{A, C\}$, $\{B, C\}$ are also prevalent, they are subsets of pattern $\{A, B, C\}$ and, therefore, these three prevalent patterns are not maximal patterns. In the same way, $\{A, D\}$, $\{B, D\}$, $\{C, D\}$ are also not maximal patterns. Normally, only maximal prevalent co-location patterns are presented to users.

To summarize, the problem statement of discovering maximal prevalent co-location pattern is as follows: given a spatial data set S, a distance threshold d, and a prevalence threshold μ_{prev}, the requirement is to develop an algorithm to efficiently find all maximal prevalent co-location patterns (MPCPs), efficient in both the computational time and memory consumption.

2.3.2 Related Work

The concept of co-location patterns was formally presented by Huang et al. (2004) where the join-based algorithm was proposed. This algorithm uses an expensive join operation to generate co-location instances of candidates. To avoid that weakness, many other mining algorithms without join operations have been subsequently developed. The partial-join algorithm (Yoo & Shekhar, 2006) partitions neighboring instances into a set of separate cliques, all instances in a clique having a neighbor relationship with each other, and co-location instances can be directly formed based on these cliques. However, the partial-join algorithm needs to additionally maintain the instances that are cut off between cliques, and collecting co-location instances still requires the join operation. The following algorithms have all been proposed to completely eliminate join operations, the joinless (Yoo & Shekhar, 2006), the co-location pattern instance tree (CPI-tree) (Wang et al., 2008), the improved co-location pattern instance tree (iCPI-tree) (Wang et al., 2009a), and the overlap maximal clique partitioning (OMCP) (Tran et al., 2019a). In these algorithms, joinless and iCPI-tree employ the generate-test candidate mining framework, while CPI-tree and OMCP directly collect co-location instances without generating candidates. However, both of these two algorithms need a very large memory space to hold all co-location instances at the same time.

Users in different domains will have data sets with different characteristics, and some co-location pattern mining algorithms have been designed to process specific data sets, examples being interval data (Wang et al., 2010), uncertain data (Wang et al., 2013a, b), fuzzy data (Ouyang et al., 2017), and dynamic data (Duan et al., 2018; Hu et al., 2020). As these data sets carry not only spatial location information but also other data-specific attributes, it becomes harder to extract new knowledge from these data sets.

In terms of the general spatial co-location pattern mining techniques we have outlined, users need to give two thresholds, one being a distance threshold which determines the spatial neighbor relationship between instances and the other being a minimum prevalence threshold for filtering prevalent co-location patterns. However, for ordinary users, it is problematic to give appropriate values to the two thresholds, so co-location pattern mining algorithms without thresholds have been proposed, such as distance threshold-free algorithms (Qian et al., 2014; Tran & Wang, 2020) and non-minimum prevalence threshold algorithms (Barua & Sander, 2014).

So far, all of the mentioned co-location pattern mining algorithms are executed in the main memory, but if the volume of data is large, these algorithms are impossible to run because of their inability to load sufficient data into the available memory. Indeed, discovering co-location patterns in the era of big data has become a major challenge. To face this challenge, parallel co-location pattern mining algorithms have been developed and then run on different platforms such as MapReduce (Yoo et al., 2014; Yang et al., 2018b, c, 2020), Hadoop (Sheshikala et al., 2017), NoSQL (Yoo et al., 2020), and the graphic processing unit (GPU) (W. Andrzejewski & Boinski, 2018; Witold Andrzejewski & Boinski, 2015, 2019; Sainju et al., 2018).

Another major challenge is that as the mining normally results in many redundant patterns, difficult for a user to manage or utilize, so the condensed co-location pattern mining algorithms have been proposed. Yoo and Bow proposed an algorithm to discover top-k closed co-location patterns (Yoo & Bow, 2011a, 2019). Two interesting algorithms have been designed to discover condensed co-location patterns, one reducing redundancy co-location patterns (Wang et al., 2018a) and the other efficiently discovering lossless condensed prevalent co-location patterns (Wang et al., 2018b).

Another compact representation of compressed co-location patterns is *maximal* patterns. A maximal pattern is the most concise representation of the mining result with the least number of patterns. The first maximal co-location pattern mining algorithm was developed by Yoo and Bow (2011b) and named MaxColoc. This algorithm first converts a set of neighboring instance transactions (Yoo & Shekhar, 2006) to a set of feature type neighboring transactions. Then a lexicographic subset tree is constructed to prune candidates. Thus, unsatisfied prevalent candidates are deleted in advance to reduce the number of candidates. After that, co-location instances of each candidate are gathered by using the neighboring instance transactions. In the MaxColoc algorithm, although the number of candidates is reduced, it is still time-consuming to collect co-location instances of the remaining candidates, especially when the number of neighboring instances of each instance is large.

Wang et al. (2009b) proposed an order-clique-based (OCB) approach for mining maximal co-location patterns. The OCB generates a set of candidates of maximal co-location patterns by compressing the size-2 prevalent patterns (the number of features in each pattern is 2) into a prefix-tree which is called a prevalence size-2 co-location header relationship tree (P_2-tree). Then, co-location instances of each candidate are identified by constructing a co-location instance-identifying tree for each candidate (Ins-tree), where each branch of the tree is a co-location instance. The Ins-tree is built based on another tree structure, the neighbor relationship tree (Neib-tree), whose design is based on a set of ordered neighbor relationship sets of all instances of each feature type. The OCB reduces the number of candidates and does not need to store the co-location instances of size-k patterns in order to gather size-$(k + 1)$ patterns, so reducing the space required for mining maximal co-location patterns. However, the copy sub-tree operation in Neib-tree needs to construct Ins-tree for each candidate and is used very frequently. Thus, as OCB needs to hold Neib-tree in main memory, the OCB algorithm is not appropriate with dense or big data sets.

More recently, a sparse-graph and condensed tree-based maximal co-location algorithm (SGCT) has been proposed (Yao et al., 2016) to tackle the drawback of the OCB algorithm. To generate candidates of maximal co-location patterns, the SGCT algorithm treats as a sparse graph those neighboring features which are determined by the features in their size-2 prevalent patterns. A maximal co-location candidate is a maximal clique in the sparse graph. To collect co-location instances of these candidates, SGCT adopts a hierarchical verification approach to build a condensed instance tree that stores co-location instances for each candidate. Each time the co-location instances of a candidate are collected, only one condensed tree is kept in memory, and thus SGCT reduces the requirement for memory space. However, if the size of candidates is large and/or the data is dense and/or very big, the computational cost of the hierarchical verification phase becomes very expensive, so the performance of the SGCT algorithm deteriorates rapidly.

2.3.3 Contributions and Novelties

In summary, the MaxColoc, OCB, SGCT algorithms improve the efficiency of maximal co-location pattern mining from two design aspects: reducing the number of candidates and designing a data structure to store the neighbor relationships of instances enabling the quick collection of the co-location instances of these candidates. However, they still adopt the generate-test candidate mining framework, and most of the execution time is still occupied by collecting co-location instances of candidates. Thus, the improvement in the performance of these algorithms is limited, especially when dealing with large and/or dense spatial data sets. In order to remedy the shortcomings of the generate-test candidate mining framework, in this book we propose a novel maximal co-location pattern mining framework, named MCHT, which has a design based on maximal cliques and hash tables.

MCHT abolishes the candidate generation phase and the calculation of co-location instances by directly calculating the participation indexes of co-location patterns.

The main contributions of this approach to co-location mining are to be as follows:

1. To propose a novel maximal prevalent co-location pattern mining framework. Our mining framework will no longer use the generating candidate and collecting co-location instances scheme.
2. The proposed mining framework will make full use of the advantages of various data structures; e.g., maximal cliques materialize spatial neighboring instances, hash tables accelerate the queries of maximal cliques, and thereby the computational time and memory consumption are reduced.
3. Bit-string operations will be adopted to improve the speed of enumerating maximal cliques.
4. A series of experiments will be designed to demonstrate that the proposed mining framework can efficiently discover all maximal prevalent co-location patterns.

2.4 The Novel Mining Solution

2.4.1 The Overall Mining Framework

Figure 2.6 shows the MCHT mining framework proposed in this study. It has five phases, where the first and the last phases are the same as in the candidate-generate-test mining framework. Enumerating maximal cliques is performed in the second phase. The third phase compresses these maximal cliques into a participating instance hash table structure. Although the function of the fourth phase is the same as in previous algorithms, the implementation method is completely different. In MCHT, the participation index of each pattern can be calculated by querying and collecting information about participating instances from the hash table. Comparing MCHT with the candidate-generate-test framework shown in Fig. 2.3, the superiority of the MCHT framework is reflected by the two aspects: (1) it does not generate candidates and (2) it does not collect co-location instances of candidates.

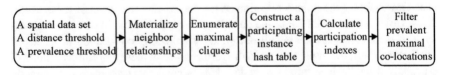

Fig. 2.6 The maximal clique and hash table–based MPCP mining framework

In essence, spatial co-location pattern mining is a statistical process: it finds a possible set of spatial features, based on the input data set and the neighbor relationship, collects the instances that belong to this feature set and forms cliques (each instance pair in a clique has to satisfy the neighbor relationship), and then counts the number of non-repeating instances under each feature type that participate in these cliques. So, in order to discover a complete result, the conventional candidate-generate-test framework needs to validate the possibility of every feature-type set. This is a mining framework from spatial feature's point of view.

The proposed mining framework shown in Fig. 2.6 differs from the above statistical method, as MCHT is designed from the viewpoint of maximal instance cliques. Looking at the data in Fig. 2.5, we find that {A.2, B.2, C.4, D.2} is a maximal clique and we can extract many co-location instances of different candidates from the maximal clique; i.e., {A.2, B.2}, {A.2, C.4}, {A.2, D.2}, {B.2, C.4}, {B.2, D.2}, {C.4, D.2}, {A.2, B.2, C.4}, {A.2, B.2, D.2}, {A.2, C.4, D.2}, {B.2, C.4, D.2}, and {A.2, B.2, C.4, D.2} are a co-location instance of {A, B}, {A, C}, {A, D}, {B, C}, {B, D}, {C, D}, {A, B, C}, {A, B, D}, {A, C, D}, {B, C, D}, and {A, B, C, D}, respectively. Clearly one maximal clique {A.2, B.2, C.4, D.2} can hold many co-location instances of candidates, so we only need to obtain and save the one maximal clique instead of generating and saving all co-location instances of candidates. Thus, we can immediately reduce storage space requirements.

After obtaining all the maximal cliques of a spatial data set, the question is raised of how to gather participating instance sets of patterns from these maximal cliques. To solve this question, we devise a participating instance hash table that compactly stores the maximal cliques. As analyzed above, it only needs to count the number of non-repeating instances under each feature type of a pattern, so the generation of all co-location instances is now redundant. We can take advantage of the efficient query of the hash table structure to get the number of participating instances in each pattern. A quick query operation replaces the collection process contained in the candidate-generate-test framework, so the efficiency of calculating participation indexes can be radically improved.

2.4.2 Bit-String-Based Maximal Clique Enumeration

In this section, we describe the method of enumerating maximal cliques after calculating neighbor relationships between instances under a distance threshold d given by a user.

Definition 2.8 A neighboring instance graph, $G(V, E)$, is an undirected graph which is constructed by considering the neighbors of instances, where $V = \{o_i\}, \forall o_i \in S$ is a set of instances of the input data set and $E = \{(o_i, o_j) \mid o_j \in N(o_i) \}$ is a set of edges that connect neighboring instances.

Taking the data set in Fig. 2.5 as an example, after executing the first phase, the neighboring instances are connected by dotted lines and a neighboring instance graph is generated.

Although the enumeration of maximal cliques is recognized as an NP-hard problem, many efficient algorithms for enumerating maximal cliques have been proposed (Cheng et al., 2012a; Eppstein et al., 2010; Eppstein & Strash, 2011; Schmidt et al., 2009; Tomita, 2017; Tomita et al., 2016). For our purposes, we utilize an efficient algorithm for listing all maximal cliques in large sparse real-world graphs in near-optimal time which was developed by Eppstein et al. (2010). Algorithm 2.1 describes the pseudocode of the basic maximal clique enumerating algorithm used in our work. Instances in graph G are sorted by their degeneracy (Step 1), where the degeneracy of a graph G is the smallest value deg such that every non-empty subgraph of G contains a vertex of degree of at most deg (Eppstein et al., 2010). P is a set of instances which have not been considered yet, and X is a set of instances that have already been considered to add to R, as R is a clique. If $P \cup X = \emptyset$, R becomes a maximal clique because there are no instances that might be considered to add into R to form a larger clique at this stage (Steps 7–9). For each instance o_t in P \\$N(o_j)$, Algorithm 2.1 makes a recursive call for $R \cup \{o_t\}$ and restricts P and X to the neighbors of o_t (Steps 11–12). Then, instance o_t is deleted from P, $P\backslash\{o_t\}$, and is appended to X, $X \cup \{o_t\}$ (Steps 13–14).

Algorithm 2.1: Enumerating maximal cliques

function BRONKERBOSCHDEG()
Input: $G(V, E)$
Output: a set of maximal cliques, MCs
1). **for** o_i in a degeneracy ordering $o_0,...,o_n$ of $G(V, E)$ **do**
2). $P \leftarrow N(o_i) \cap \{o_{i+1},...,o_n\}$
3). $X \leftarrow N(o_i) \cap \{o_0,...,o_{i-1}\}$
4).   BRONKERBOSCHPIVOT($P, \{o_i\}, X$)
5). **end for**
6). **end function**

function BRONKERBOSCHPIVOT(P, R, X)
7). **if** $P \cup X = \emptyset$ **then**
8). MCs.add(R)
9). **else**
10).   choose a pivot instance $o_j \in P \cup X$ with $P \cap N(o_j) = \max\limits_{o_t \in P \cup X} |P \cap N(o_t)|$
11).   **for** $o_t \in P \setminus N(o_j)$ **do**
12).   BRONKERBOSCHPIVOT($P \cap N(o_t), R \cup \{o_t\}, X \cap N(o_t)$)
13). $P \leftarrow P \setminus \{o_t\}$
14). $X \leftarrow X \cup \{o_t\}$
15).   **end for**
16). **end if**
17). **end function**

Table 2.1 All maximal cliques listed from Fig. 2.5

Maximal cliques	Maximal cliques
A.1, B.4, C.2	A.3, B.1, C.3
A.2, B.2, C.4, D.2	A.4, B.1, C.3
A.2, C.1, D.3	A.5, B.3, D.1
A.3, B.1, C.1, D.1	B.1, C.1, D.3

For example, Table 2.1 lists all maximal cliques yielded after performing Algorithm 2.1 on the data set shown in Fig. 2.5.

It can be seen that in Algorithm 2.1 the operations of the intersection (Steps 2, 3, 10, and 12) and the difference (Steps 11 and 13) of two sets are frequently used. If the input data set is large and/or dense, these operations become very expensive. However, we can take advantage of efficiency of bit string operations to improve the performance of Algorithm 2.1.

Definition 2.9 Given two instances o_i and o_j, o_i is smaller than o_j if one of the following conditions are satisfied:

1. The feature type of o_i is smaller than the feature type of o_j in a lexicographic order.
2. If o_i and o_j belong to the same feature type, the instance ID of o_i is smaller than the instance ID o_j.

Our bit-string-based maximal clique enumeration is designed as follows: First, all instances in S are sorted according to Definition 2.9 (see Fig. 2.7(a), Line 1). Next, these instances are represented by their indexes in a sorted list (Fig. 2.7(b), Line 1). Then neighboring instances of each instance o_i, $N(o_i)$, are also described by the indexes (Fig. 2.7(a), Line 3 and Fig. 2.7(b), Line 3). The degeneracy ordering of the neighboring instance graph (*deg_order*) is also converted to the indexes of instances (Fig. 2.7(a), Line 2 and Fig. 2.7(b), Line 2). In the same way, cliques are also represented by instance indexes, e.g., $R = \{6\}$ (Fig. 2.7(b), Line 6).

Subsequently, bit strings with their length equal to the size of S are created and the set of neighboring instances and the degeneracy ordering are all converted to bit strings. The indexes of bits in bit strings are exactly the elements in the set of neighboring instances and the degeneracy ordering, so we set these bits to 1, while all other bits are set to 0. For example, at a certain state of Algorithm 2.1, $o_i = $ B.2, its neighbor represented by indexes is $N(6) = \{1, 12, 14\}$ (Fig. 2.7(b), Line 3), so $N(6)$ is converted to the bit string, $N(o_i)_{bit\text{-}string}$ (Fig. 2.7(c), Line 1). Other instances in the degeneracy ordering are also converted to bit strings, $\{o_0,\ldots, o_{i-1}\}_{bit\text{-}string}$ and $\{o_{i+1},\ldots, o_n\}_{bit\text{-}string}$ (Fig. 2.7(c), Lines 2 and 3).

To find the intersection and difference of two sets, we simply perform (&) and (&~) operations on these bit strings, respectively. For example, for the intersection operations of Steps 2 and 3 in Algorithm 2.1, $P \leftarrow N(o_i) \cap \{o_{i+1},\ldots,o_n\} \Leftrightarrow P_{bit\text{-}string} \leftarrow N(o_i)_{bit\text{-}string}$ & $\{o_{i+1},\ldots, o_n\}_{bit\text{-}string}$ (see Fig. 2.7(c), line 4) and $X \leftarrow N(o_i) \cap \{o_0,\ldots,o_{i-1}\} \Leftrightarrow X_{bit\text{-}string} \leftarrow N(o_i)_{bit\text{-}string}$ & $\{o_1,\ldots, o_{i-1}\}_{bit\text{-}string}$ (giving Line 6 of Fig. 2.7(c)). Another example of the difference operation is in Step 11 of Algorithm

Fig. 2.7 An illustration of enumerating maximal cliques based on bit string operations, where (a) an example used to sort the instances in S; (b) an example that the instances represented by their index in the sorted list; (c) create a bit string for the instances; (d) (e) (f) examples of string operations

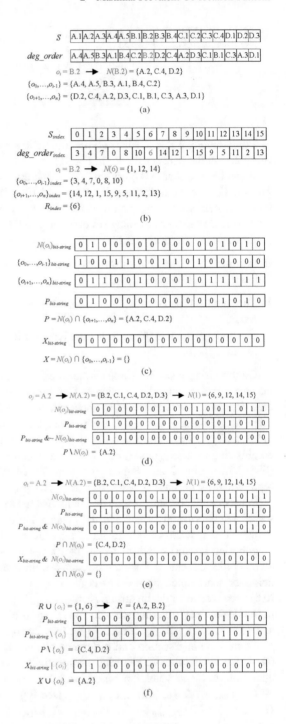

2.1, $P \setminus N(o_j) \Leftrightarrow P_{bit\text{-}string}$ & $\sim N(o_j)_{bit\text{-}string}$ (Fig. 2.7(d), Line 4). Figure 2.7(e) shows the result of the intersection operation of the two sets in Step 12 of Algorithm 2.1.

To remove an element in a set, we just reset the bit in the bit string where the index of the bit corresponds to the element. For example, in Step 13 of Algorithm 2.1, $P \setminus \{o_t\}$ is performed by setting the bit of index o_i in $P_{bit\text{-}string}$ to 0 (Fig. 2.7(f), Line 3). Adding an element to a set is performed by setting to 1 the bit of the element in the bit string equal to the index, e.g., $X \cup \{o_t\} \equiv$ sets the bit at t in $X_{bit\text{-}string}$ to 1. For our example, the result is shown in Line 5 of Fig. 2.7(f).

Finally, we can obtain maximal cliques as their instances are represented by the indexes, so we only need to map to the sorted instance list in the first step to get the instances themselves. For example, a maximal clique R is {1, 6, 12, 14} and it corresponds to {A.2, B.2, C.4, D.2} after mapping to S in Fig. 2.7(a).

Algorithm 2.2: Enumerating maximal cliques based on bit strings.

function BRONKERBOSCHDEGBIT()
Input: $G(V, E)$,
Output: a set of maximal cliques, *MCs*
1). $S_{index} \leftarrow$ sortAndConvertIndexDataset(S)
2). $deg\_order_{index} \leftarrow$ convertIndex(deg_order)
3). $N_{index} \leftarrow$ covertIndex(N)
4). **for** $i \in deg\_order_{index}$ **do**
5). $\{i+1,..., n\}_{bit\text{-}string} \leftarrow$ setBit($\{i+1,..., n\}$)
6). $\{0,..., i\text{-}1\}_{bit\text{-}string} \leftarrow$ setBit($\{0,..., i\text{-}1\}$)
7). $N(i)_{bit\text{-}string} \leftarrow$ setBit($N(i)$)
8). $P_{bit\text{-}string} \leftarrow N(i)_{bit\text{-}string}$ & $\{i+1,..., n\}_{bit\text{-}string}$
9). $X_{bit\text{-}string} \leftarrow N(i)_{bit\text{-}string}$ & $\{0,..., i\text{-}1\}_{bit\text{-}string}$
10).   BRONKERBOSCHPIVOTBIT($P_{bit\text{-}string}, \{i\}, X_{bit\text{-}string}$)
11). **end for**
12). **end function**

function BRONKERBOSCHPIVOTBIT($P_{bit\text{-}string}, R_{index}, X_{bit\text{-}string}$)
13). **if** all bits in ($P_{bit\text{-}string} \mid X_{bit\text{-}string}$) are 0 **then**
14). $R \leftarrow$ mapIndex(R_{index})
15). MCs.add(R)
16). **else**
17). $j \leftarrow$ mapIndex($\max\limits_{t \in MapIndex(P_{bit\text{-}string} \mid X_{bit\text{-}string})} |P_{bit\text{-}string}$ & $N(t)_{bit\text{-}string}|$)
18). $N(j)_{bit\text{-}string} \leftarrow$ setBit($N(j)$)
19).   **for** $t \in$ mapIndex($P_{bit\text{-}string}$ &$\sim N(j)_{bit\text{-}string}$) **do**
20). $N(t)_{bit\text{-}string} \leftarrow$ setBit($N(t)$)
21).   BRONKERBOSCHPIVOTBIT($P_{bit\text{-}string}$ & $N(t)_{bit\text{-}string}$, $R_{index} \cup \{t\}$, $X_{bit\text{-}string}$ & $N(t)_{bit\text{-}string}$)
22). $P_{bit\text{-}string}$.reset[t]
23). $X_{bit\text{-}string}$.set[t]
24).   **end for**
25). **end if**
26). **end function**

To sum up, Algorithm 2.2 describes the pseudocode of our three-phase algorithm designed to efficiently enumerate maximal cliques based on bit string operations.

The first phase is a preparation process, including sorting and representing the input data set by indexes (Step 1), and then converting the degeneracy ordering (Step 2) and neighbors (Step 3) to indexes. The second phase scans each element in the degeneracy ordering represented by indexes and converts the neighbor of the element to a bit string (Step 7). $P_{bit\text{-}string}$ and $X_{bit\text{-}string}$ are initialized by the AND (&) operation of bit strings (Steps 8–9). The third phase calls the BRONKERBOSCHPIVOTBIT function to add new elements into R_{index} to form a maximal clique (Step 10). First, the OR (|) operation of $P_{bit\text{-}string}$ and $X_{bit\text{-}string}$ is executed to validate whether R_{index} becomes a maximal clique (Step 13). If R_{index} is a maximal clique, it is mapped to S to get instances (Step 14) and added to the result (Step 15). Next, we choose a pivot instance j (Step 17) and convert the neighbor of j into a bit string, $N(j)_{bit\text{-}string}$ (Step 18). To find the difference between $P_{bit\text{-}string}$ and $N(j)_{bit\text{-}string}$, the (&~) operation is performed (Step 19). Then for each element in the resulting difference of the two bit strings (Step 19), a recursive call is made with $R_{index} \cup \{t\}$, so restricting $P_{bit\text{-}string}$ and $X_{bit\text{-}string}$ to $N(t)_{bit\text{-}string}$ (Step 21). After that, the bit with the index t is deleted from $P_{bit\text{-}string}$ (Step 22) and added to $X_{bit\text{-}string}$ (Step 23).

2.4.3   Constructing the Participating Instance Hash Table

In most situations, hash tables turn out to be more efficient than other lookup structures, so after all maximal cliques have been listed, a participating instance hash table is designed to compactly keep these cliques and accelerate queries about participating instances of patterns.

Definition 2.10 A participating instance hash table is a hash data structure where the key is a set of feature types and the value is a list of instance sets of objects in maximal cliques.

For example, from maximal clique {A.1, B.4, C.2}, an item in the participating instance hash table is constructed as shown in Fig. 2.8(a), ABC: [{1}, {4}, {2}]. Figure 2.8(b) describes the complete participating instance hash table based on all the maximal cliques listed in Table 2.1.

It is a unidirectional process to build the participating instance hash table from maximal cliques, meaning that we cannot go back to the maximal cliques from the hash table, but all the participating instances of patterns are completely retained for future computing of the participation index of patterns. Instances of a feature that participate in maximal cliques are accessed by the index of the feature in the key. For example, to obtain instances of feature A, which participated in the maximal cliques formed by feature set {A, B, C}, based on Fig. 2.8(b), the index of A in key ABC is 0, and the value corresponding to the key is $value = [\{1, 3, 4\}, \{1, 4\}, \{2, 3\}]$, and thus the participation instance of A is $value[0] = \{1, 3, 4\}$.

Algorithm 2.3 gives the pseudocode to construct the participating instance hash table. The algorithm scans each maximal clique (Step 1) and creates a key based on

Fig. 2.8 An illustration of enumerating maximal cliques based on bit string operations, where (a) an example of a maximal clique being transformed; (b) the complete participating instance hash table based on all the maximal cliques listed in Table 2.1

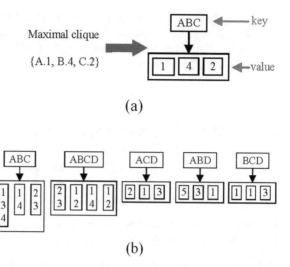

(a)

(b)

the feature types of instances in the current maximal clique (Step 2). If the key already exists in the participating instance hash table (Step 3), the value of the key is updated by putting instances of the current maximal clique into the corresponding position (Steps 4–5). Otherwise, if the clique with the key has not yet created a value in the hash table, the value of the key is built (Steps 8–9) and the key and the value are added as new items into the hash table (Step 11).

Algorithm 2.3: Constructing the participating instance hash table structure

function CONSTRUCTHASH()
Input: a set of maximal cliques, *MCs*
Output: a participating instance hash table, *CoLHT*
1). **for** $R \in MCs$ **do**
2). $key \leftarrow$ buildKey(R)
3).   **if** $\exists\ key\ \in CoLHT$ **then**
4).   **for** $o_i \in R$ **do**
5).   *CoLHT*.update(*key*, o_i)
6).   **end for**
7).   **else**
8).   **for** $o_i \in R$ **do**
9).   *value*[o_i.feature] = {o_i.ID}
10).   **end for**
11).   *CoLHT*.add(*key*, *value*)
12).   **end if**
13). **end for**
14). **end function**

It can be seen that there are two advantages to be gained by using the participating instance hash table. First, maximal cliques are compactly compressed into a hash table structure without losing any neighboring instances. Second, the high-efficiency query property of hash tables is utilized to accelerate the gathering of information about participating instances of patterns. The next section describes strategies for collecting information about participating instances, how to calculate participation indexes, and the filtering of maximal prevalent co-location patterns from the participating instance hash table.

2.4.4 Calculating Participation Indexes and Filtering MPCPs

The following two lemmas will be used to query and gather information about participating instances of patterns and to calculate their participation indexes from the participating instance hash table.

Lemma 2.1 Any maximal prevalent co-location patterns can be generated from the keys of the participating instance hash table.

Proof It is obvious that if a pattern has no co-location instances, its participation index is equal to 0 and it is not a prevalent pattern in any situation. A pattern can verify the prevalence if and only if the pattern has at least one co-location instance. Since neighbor relationships between instances are compressed to a set of maximal cliques, the co-location instance must be either a maximal clique or a subset of a maximal clique. The keys in the participating instance hash table record the feature types of maximal cliques. Thus, if the co-location instance is a maximal clique, the co-location instance must belong to the pattern represented by the key created by the feature types of the instances in the maximal clique. Alternatively, if the co-location instance is not a maximal clique, it must be a sub-clique of one or more maximal cliques, and the co-location instance belongs to the pattern that is the sub-set of the key made by the feature types of the instances in the maximal cliques. Hence, any prevalent co-location patterns can be produced from the keys of the participating instance hash table structure.

Lemma 2.2 Given a maximal co-location pattern c, the information about participating instances of c can be queried and gathered from the values of keys where these keys are c itself (if c is a key in the hash table) or c's super-keys. The participation index of pattern c is calculated as.

$$PI(c) = \min\{\frac{|\pi_f(c)|}{|S_f|}\}, f \in c,$$ where $|\pi_f(c)|$ is total number of instances of feature f in values of key c, or the keys are super-sets of c and $|S_f|$ is the total number of instances of f in the input data set.

Proof Assume that $c = \{f_1, \ldots, f_k\}$ is a pattern, then according to Lemma 2.1, c must be a key or a sub-set of the keys in the participating instance hash table. If c is a key of the hash table, the value of the key represents instances that participate in co-location instances of c. If c is not a key in the hash table, c is identified as a sub-set of the keys of the hash table. Each feature f in c that participates in the co-location instances of c has its information queried according to the corresponding part of the values of the keys. In other words, the information of participating instances of c is incorporated into all of the values of the super-keys of c, or c on its own, in the participating instance hash table.

For example, let us calculate the participation index of pattern $c = \{A, C, D\}$, supposing $I(c)$ records information about participating instances of c. Since c is a key in the participating instance hash table, the value of the key directly provides support for the participating instances of c, $I(c) = \{\{2\}, \{1\}, \{3\}\}$. The collected super-keys of c are $\{\{A, B, C, D\}\}$, so the participating instances of each feature in c are also gathered from the corresponding part of the value of key ABCD, meaning that the instances of A, B, C in the value of key ABCD are gathered to $I(c) = [\{2, 3\}, \{1, 4\}, \{1, 2, 3\}]$. Finally, the participation index of c is $PI(c) = \min\{\frac{2}{5}, \frac{2}{4}, \frac{3}{3}\} = 0.4$.

Algorithm 2.4: Calculating participation indexes and filtering maximal prevalent co-location patterns.

function CALCPISANDFILPATTERN()
Input: a participating instance hash table, *CoLHT*
       a minimum prevalence threshold, μ_{prev}
Output: a set of maximal prevalent co-location patterns, *MPCPs*
1). $keys \leftarrow CoLHT$.getKeys()
2). $keys_{sorted} \leftarrow$ sortBySizeOfKey($keys$)
3). **while** $keys_{sorted} \neq \emptyset$ **do**
4). $c \leftarrow keys_{sorted}$.popFirst()
5). $c_{super} \leftarrow$ findSuperKeys(c, *CoLHT*)
6).   **for** $f \in c$ **do**
7). $Ic[f] \leftarrow$ queryInstances(c, c_{super}, *CoLHT*)
8).   **end for**
9). $PI \leftarrow$ calculatePI(Ic)
10).   **if** $(PI \geq \mu_{prev})$ **then**
11). $MPCPs$.add(c)
12). $keys_{sorted} \leftarrow$ deleteSubPatterns(c, $keys_{sorted}$)
13).   **else**
16). $c_{sub} \leftarrow$ generateDirectSubPatterns(c)
17). $keys_{sorted} \leftarrow$ addNewPatterns(c_{sub})
18).   **end if**
19). **end while**
20). **end function**

Based on Lemmas 2.1 and 2.2, Algorithm 2.4 has been designed to gather information about participating instances of patterns, calculate participation indexes, and filter maximal prevalent co-location patterns. Algorithm 2.4 has the three requisite phases. The first phase collects all keys in the participating instance hash table (Step 1) and sorts these keys by their size (Step 2). The second phase first scans each pattern c in the sorted list of keys (Steps 3–4) and finds all super-keys of c in the participating instance hash table (Step 5). Then the information about participating instances of c is queried and gathered by the values of c and its super-keys (Steps 6–8). Variable Ic is used to record information about participating instances of a pattern. The third phase measures the prevalence of c by calculating the participation index of c, PI (Step 9). If PI is not smaller than the minimum prevalence threshold given by users, μ_{prev}, c is marked as a maximal prevalent co-location pattern and added to the mining result (Steps 10–11). Since, if c is a maximal prevalent co-location pattern it does not need to validate the prevalence of all its sub-patterns in the sorted list of keys, these sub-patterns can be deleted (Step 12). Alternatively, if c is not a maximal prevalent co-location pattern, the direct sub-sets of c will be considered, and hence all sub-sets of c are generated (Step 16) and added to the sorted list of keys as new patterns (Step 17).

2.4.5 The Analysis of Time and Space Complexities

In this section, we analyze the time and space complexities of the MCHT algorithm. The whole algorithm is divided into the following four main parts for analysis:

1. Compute the neighbor relationships of instances: Assume that the number of instances of the input data set is n and the spatial frame size is $D \times D$. We impose a grid with the cell size $d \times d$ (where d is the distance threshold) on the data set. The space of the input data set is then divided into $\left(\frac{D}{d}\right)^2$ cells, so the average number of instances in each cell is $n\left(\frac{d}{D}\right)^2$. To determine the neighbors of an instance in a cell, we only need to evaluate the distance between the instance and any other instances that fall into the nine cells around the current cell. Thus, the time complexity of this phase is about $O\left(n\left(\frac{d}{D}\right)^2 \times 9\left(\frac{D}{d}\right)^2\right) \approx O(n)$ and the space complexity is also about $O(n)$.

2. List maximal cliques: As it has been proved by (Eppstein et al., 2010), the time complexity of enumerating all maximal cliques is $O\left(deg \times n \times 3^{\frac{deg}{3}}\right)$ in the worst case, where $deg \ll n$ is the degeneracy of the neighboring instance graph obtained by Definition 2.2. Supposing that $|R|_{avg}$ is the average number of instances in a maximal clique and $|MCs|$ is the total number of maximal cliques obtained after Algorithm 2.2 is performed, then the number of recursive function calls (Line 4 of Algorithm 2.1) is equal to $|R|_{avg}$. Thus the space complexity for this part is about $O(|R|_{avg} \times |MCs|)$.

3. Construct a participating instance hash table: The time and space complexities for constructing participating instance hash tables for all maximal cliques are $O(|MCs|)$.

4. Calculating the participation indexes and filter prevalent patterns: In the worst case, a pattern (key) is not prevalent and the direct sub-sets of the pattern are considered as new patterns that need to have their participation indexes calculated. Supposing k_{avg} is the average size of keys in the participating instance hash table then the upper boundary of the number of sub-sets is $(2^{k_{avg}} - 1)$. If $|CoLHT|$ is the number of the participating instances' hash table, the upper boundary of time complexity of is $O((2^{k_{avg}} - 1) \times |CoLHT|) \leq O((2^{k_{avg}} - 1) \times |MCs|)$. The space complexity of this part is about $O(|CoLHT|) \leq O(|MCs|)$.

Combining the analysis of these four parts, the time complexity of the MCHT algorithm is about $O(n + deg \times n \times 3^{\frac{deg}{3}} + |R|_{avg} \times |MCs| + 2^{k_{avg}} \times |MCs|)$. Since after each phase is completed, memory is released immediately, we only need to consider the peak storage space. Hence, the space complexity of MCHT is about $O(|R|_{avg} \times |MCs|)$. Note that, $|R|_{avg} \ll n$ and $2^{k_{avg}} \ll n$, so the largest part of the computational time of the proposed algorithm is the enumeration of maximal cliques, which will be clearly shown in our experiments.

2.5 Experiments

In this section, we evaluate the performance of the MCHT algorithm using a series of synthetic data sets with different densities, and using the case studies relating to the point of interest (POI) data sets. MCHT is compared with all three algorithms mentioned in the related work section, including OCB (Wang et al., 2009b), SGCT (Yao et al., 2016), and MaxColoc (Yoo & Bow, 2019) to demonstrate that the performance of the MCHT algorithm is more efficient than those existing algorithms. All algorithms are coded in C++ and performed on computer running Windows 10 with Intel(R) Core(TM) i7–3770 3.4GHz CPU and 16GB of main memory.

2.5.1 Data Sets

2.5.1.1 Synthetic Data Sets

A set of synthetic data sets is generated by using a data generator developed by (Yoo & Shekhar, 2006). The parameters of these data sets are different for different experimental objectives. Table 2.2 lists these data sets in detail.

Table 2.2 Parameters of synthetic data sets

Table/ Figure no.	Spatial area size	Number of instances	Number of features	d	μ_{prev}	Clumpiness
Fig. 2.10	2 k × 2 k	*	15	20	–	1
Tables 2.4 and 2.5	1 k × 1 k	25 k, 40 k, 55 k	15	14	0.6	1
Fig. 2.11, Fig. 2.13	1 k × 1 k 10 k × 10 k	*	15	10	0.4	1
Fig. 2.12(a)	5 k × 5 k	50 k	*	30	0.3	1
Fig. 2.12 (b)	10 k × 10 k	50 k	15	10	0.25	*
Fig. 2.14(a, b)	5 k × 5 k	50 k	15	*	0.4	1
Fig. 2.15(a, b)	5 k × 5 k	50 k	15	40	*	1

*: variables, $k = 1000$, −: not applicable

Table 2.3 A summary of the real POI data sets

Name	Spatial frame size (m²)	Number of instances	Number of features	Property
Shenzhen	28,400 × 88,600	31,827	13	Dense, clustered
Guangzhou	104,000 × 113,500	45,489	15	Dense, zonal
Beijing	134,000 × 229,000	54,198	13	Dense, concentrated
Shanghai	65,500 × 115,300	66,865	15	Dense, uniform

2.5.1.2   Real Data Sets

The performance of the MCHT algorithm is also examined by using case studies of POI data sets from Shenzhen, Guangzhou, Beijing, and Shanghai. These data sets are related to facility points such as fast food outlets, parking lots, and residential areas. Table 2.3 gives a statistical summary and Fig. 2.9 is the distribution of these data sets, respectively. It can be seen that the distribution of these data sets has different properties, including clustered, zonal, concentrated, and uniform. The discovery of maximal prevalent co-location patterns from these POI data sets should provide new insights into the interaction of city facilities.

2.5.2   Experimental Objectives

To evaluate completely the performance of the proposed mining framework, we set five objectives for our experiments: (1) investigate the improvement in the enumeration of maximal cliques brought about by using bit string operations; (2) assess the improvement in the general performance of the MCHT algorithm; (3) evaluate the scalability of the proposed algorithm; (4) examine the memory consumption of the proposed framework; and (5) investigate how our algorithm responds to changes in user queries.

2.5.3   Experimental Results and Analysis

2.5.3.1   The Effect of Bit Strings on Enumerating Maximal Cliques

In the first experiment, we survey the effect on enumerating maximal cliques by utilizing bit strings. Algorithm 2.2 is named BK-Deg-Bit. Another four enumerating maximal clique algorithms are also chosen for comparison, including the Bron–Kerbosch algorithm (BK for short) (Schmidt et al., 2009), the Bron–Kerbosch pivot algorithm (BK-Pivot for short) (Eppstein & Strash, 2011), the Bron-Kerbosch degeneracy (BK-Deg for short) (Eppstein et al., 2010), and the SeqMCE algorithm (Cheng et al., 2012a, b).

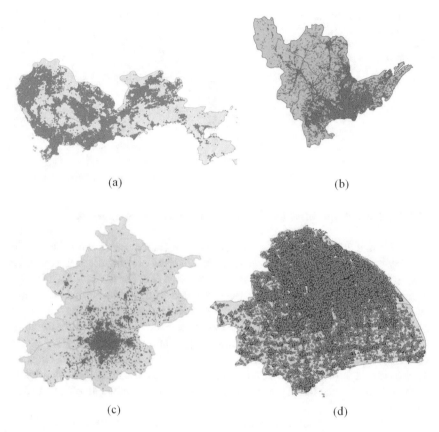

Fig. 2.9 The distributions of the real data sets used in our experiments. (**a**) Shenzhen, (**b**) Guangzhou, (**c**) Beijing, and (**d**) Shanghai

Figure 2.10 shows the execution times of these algorithms with different numbers of spatial instances. As expected, all the execution times increase with the number of instances. The BK-Pivot algorithm is a development based on the BK algorithm but using a pivoting heuristic that can reduce the number of recursive calls in BK. BK-Deg improves on BK-Pivot by utilizing the degeneracy ordering of instances, limiting the size of the set of instances which have not been considered, and so improving performance. Generally, the performance ordering is BK-Deg, BK-Pivot, BK, although when the number of instances is 150 k, the BK algorithm becomes impractical to run. SeqMCE is a variant of BK-Pivot, and is designed to deal with large data sets that cannot be fitted into limited memory. However, even when the data can be fitted in memory, SeqMCE will lose efficiency as instances increase because it has to scan the input data many times (Cheng et al., 2012a, b). Overall, BK-Deg-Bit shows better performance than the other algorithms.

Fig. 2.10 The effect of the
number of instances in the
different enumerating
maximal clique algorithms

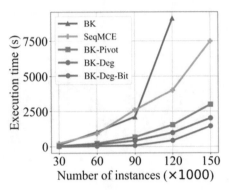

2.5.3.2 The Comparative Performance of the MCHT Algorithm

Tables 2.4 and 2.5 list the execution time taken in each phase in the OCB, SGCT, MaxColoc, and MCHT algorithms over different sizes of synthetic data sets. It can be seen that, as expected from the analysis in Sect. 2.3, for the non-MCHT algorithms the most time-consuming phase is devoted to the collection of co-location instances of candidates. In more detail, Neib- and Ins-tree construction, condensed instance tree construction, and finding co-location instances take the most execution time in the OCB, SGCT, and MaxColoc algorithms, respectively. The MCHT algorithm avoids this phase. As analyzed in Sect. 2.4, listing maximal cliques is the heaviest task for the MCHT algorithm. In all the situations provided by the synthetic data sets, the MCHT algorithm takes less computational time than the other algorithms.

We list the memory usages of the four algorithms in the last row of Tables 2.4 and 2.5. It can be seen that the MCHT algorithm takes less storage space than the other three algorithms. This is because MCHT compresses the neighbor relationship of instances into a set of maximal cliques, and these maximal cliques are then further condensed by a carefully designed hash table, so MCHT can efficiently reduce memory consumption while the OCB, SGCT, and MaxColoc algorithms need to hold all co-location instances of current candidates in memory at the same time, so needing more storage space. Moreover, OCB also has to keep the Neib- and Inst-trees in memory, where Nei-tree holds all neighboring instances and Ins-trees keeps the co-location instances of the current candidate. As shown in Table 2.4, when a data set is large and/or dense (in our experiment when the number of instances is set to 55 k the data set becomes very dense), the OCB algorithm runs out of memory.

We also evaluated the comparative improvement in the performance of the MCHT algorithm on real data sets. Tables 2.6 and 2.7 record the execution time of each phase of the OCB, SGCT, MaxColoc and MCHT algorithms on the real data sets. Clearly, the largest portion of execution time portion is still devoted to collecting co-location instances of those candidates in OCB, SGCT, and MaxColoc that belong to the candidate-generate-test mining framework. When the data set is dense and its instances form a zonal or clustered distribution, the computational

Table 2.4 The execution time of each phase of the four algorithms on different volumes of data sets (Part 1: OCB and SGCT)

Algorithm	OCB			SGCT		
	Number of instances					
Factor (s)	25 k	40 k	55 k	25 k	40 k	55 k
T_materialize_neighbors	0.3162	0.726	×	0.372	0.725	1.307
T_find_size_2_patterns	0.196	0.241	×	0.176	0.244	0.392
T_gen_candidates	0.002	0.003	×	0.001	0.001	0.002
T_constr_Neib-&Inst-tree	**1339.573**	**17354.825**	×	–	–	–
T_constr_condensed-inst-tree	–	–	–	**560.687**	**3583.39**	**19206.8**
T_find_colocation_instances	–	–	–	–	–	–
T_enum_maximal_cliques	–	–	–	–	–	–
T_constr_co-location_hashtable	–	–	–	–	–	–
T_call_PIs_filter_patterns	60.691	362.667	×	24.329	35.295	139.177
T_total	1400.778	17718.63	×	585.565	3619.655	19347.68
Memory consumption (MB)	**1942.17**	**14470.93**	**×**	**123.14**	**162.75**	**300.66**

–: not applicable, ×: unrepresentable

Table 2.5 The execution time of each phase of the four algorithms on different volumes of data sets (Part 2: MaxColoc and MHCT)

Algorithm	MaxColoc			MHCT		
	Number of instances					
Factor (s)	25 k	40 k	55 k	25 k	40 k	55 k
T_ materialize_neighbors	0.365	0.767	1.39	0.295	0.74	1.318
T_find_size_2_patterns	–	–	–	–	–	–
T_ gen_candidates	13.517	22.005	39.911	–	–	–
T_constr_Neib-&Inst-tree	–	–	–	–	–	–
T_constr_condensed-inst-tree	–	–	–	–	–	–
T_find_colocation_instances	**305.482**	**717.832**	**6730.47**	–	–	–
T_enum_maximal_cliques	–	–	–	**57.103**	**84.855**	**224.328**
T_constr_co-location_hashtable	–	–	–	5.675	7.505	20.3
T_call_PIs_filter_patterns	1.401	4.333	48.431	19.265	35.543	44.444
T_total	320.765	744.937	6820.141	82.338	128.643	289.903
Memory consumption (MB)	**260.20**	**671.57**	**6675.06**	**49.84**	**94.21**	**143.25**

–: not applicable, ×: unrepresentable

times of the OCB and SGCT algorithms increase while the performance of MaxColoc is poor when dealing with zonally distributed data. However, MCHT shows relatively stable performance on the differently distributed data sets.

Overall, MCHT, the proposed mining algorithm, efficiently reduces both the computational time and memory consumption.

2.5.3.3 The Scalability of the MCHT Algorithm

In this experiment, we evaluated the scalability of the proposed algorithm on different numbers of instances, different numbers of feature types, and different numbers of neighboring instances.

Figure 2.11 shows the effects of the number of instances on the execution times of the four algorithms on synthetic data sets. The spatial area size is fixed, so the data sets become denser when increasing the number of instances. As shown in Fig. 2.11 (b), if the data sets are sparse, the difference between the algorithms is small. However, the gap between the effects of the four algorithms becomes larger when the data sets are large as plotted in Fig. 2.11(a). As can be seen, the performance of OCB and SGCT deteriorate rapidly under large/dense data sets. In particular, when the data set is larger than 60 k, OCB cannot complete since it runs out of memory, and if the number of instances is larger than 80 k, SGCT takes too long to complete, while the execution time of MCHT rises slowly. MaxColoc shows a better performance than OCB and SCGT because it utilizes an upper participation index, whereby a candidate can be judged whether it is a prevalent pattern early in the algorithm and, if the upper participation index of a candidate is smaller than the prevalence threshold, this candidate cannot be prevalent. MaxColoc will then no

Table 2.6 The execution time of each phase of the compared algorithms on different real-world data sets (Shenzhen and Guangzhou)

Data set	Shenzhen				Guangzhou			
Algorithm								
Factor (s)	OCB	SGCT	Max Coloc	MCHT	OCB	SGCT	Max Coloc	MCHT
T_ materialize_neighbors	0.422	0.472	0.451	0.406	0.634	0.627	0.68	0.65
T_find_size_2_patterns	0.267	0.208	–	–	0.401	0.458	–	–
T_ gen_candidates	0.001	0.001	2.519	–	0.003	0.002	14.126	–
T_constr_Neib-&Inst-tree	**3547.609**	–	–	–	**3403.223**	–	–	–
T_constr_condensed-inst-tree	–	**2116.1**	–	–	–	**1048.18**	–	–
T_find_colocation_instances	–	–	**191.72**	–	–	–	**1372.17**	–
T_enum_maximal_cliques	–	–	–	**81.208**	–	–	–	**111.482**
T_constr_co-location_hashtable	–	–	–	6.806	–	–	–	7.14
T_call_PIs_filter_patterns	280.857	22.239	0.488	2.431	117.621	19.31	0.381	22.145
T_total	3829.156	2139.02	195.178	90.851	3521.882	1068.577	1387.357	141.417
Memory consumption (MB)	**11479.67**	**682.39**	**181.20**	**57.37**	**5834.043**	**385.81**	**188.66**	**88.27**

–: not applicable, ×: unrepresentable, d = 300 meters, μ_prev = 0.4 for Shenzhen; d = 300 meters, μ_prev = 0.45 for Guangzhou

Table 2.7 The execution time of each phase of the compared algorithms on different real-world data sets (Beijing and Shanghai)

Data set	Beijing				Shanghai			
	Algorithm							
Factor (s)	OCB	SGCT	Max Coloc	MCHT	OCB	SGCT	Max Coloc	MCHT
$T\_materialize\_neighbors$	0.577	0.508	0.574	0.553	0.809	0.83	0.83	0.834
$T\_find\_size\_2\_patterns$	0.366	0.326	–	–	0.485	0.414	–	–
$T\_gen\_candidates$	0.001	0.001	2.562	–	0.001	0.001	2.468	–
$T\_constr\_Neib-\&Inst-tree$	**745.028**	–	–	–	**409.45**	–	–	–
$T\_constr\_condensed-inst-tree$	–	**468.898**	–	–	–	**723.209**	–	–
$T\_find\_colocation\_instances$	–	–	**257.697**	–	–	–	**549.745**	–
$T\_enum\_maximal\_cliques$	–	–	–	**46.666**	–	–	–	**170.032**
$T\_constr\_co-location\_hashtable$	–	–	–	2.17	–	–	–	16.802
$T\_call\_PIs\_filter\_patterns$	15.736	6.519	0.392	2.537	20.327	3.805	1.248	1.567
T_total	761.708	476.252	261.225	51.926	431.072	728.259	554.291	189.235
Memory consumption (MB)	**827.95**	**197.99**	**182.11**	**79.42**	**3435.34**	**1278.87**	**696.25**	**104.80**

–: not applicable, $d = 300$ meters, $\mu_{prev} = 0.45$ for Beijing; $d = 300$ meters, $\mu_{prev} = 0.4$ for Shanghai

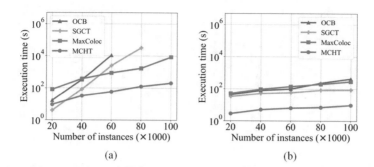

Fig. 2.11 The execution times of the four algorithms on synthetic data sets with different numbers of instances. (**a**) dense and (**b**) sparse

longer collect co-location instances of this candidate, and directly jumps to the next candidate. OCB and SGCT have to first collect all co-location instances of a candidate before judging its prevalence, and so OCB and SGCT have longer execution times.

The effects of the number of feature types on the execution times of these algorithms are plotted in Fig. 2.12(a). In this experiment, the spatial frame size, the number of instances, the distance threshold, and the prevalence threshold are fixed (as Table 2.2), while the number of feature types is increased. The plots show that the execution times of these algorithms increase with the number of feature types. This is because, first, with an increase in the number of feature types, more instances are likely to form the neighbor relationship. Second, the average number of instances for each feature decreases and, eventually the participation indexes of candidates will be larger, size-2 prevalent patterns will grow in number, and more and more long size candidates will be generated. Hence constructing Nei-tree and Ins-tree in OCB, and processing hierarchical verification needed to construct condensed instance trees in SGCT, and finding co-location instances in MaxColoc for these long-size candidates take more computational time.

Figure 2.12(b) describes the computational times of the four algorithms as a function of the number of neighboring instances. The clumpiness is a factor to control the number of neighboring instances (Huang et al., 2004); it represents the number of overlaying co-location instances within the same neighborhood area. The higher the clumpiness value, the greater the number of co-location instances. As shown in Fig. 2.12(b), the execution times increased with the number of neighboring instances, but MCHT shows better performance overall.

2.5.3.4 Memory Consumption

Figure 2.13 compares the memory usages of OCB, SGCT, MaxColoc, and MCHT as performed on synthetic data sets with different numbers of instances. On the whole, with the increase of the number of instances, the required storage spaces of the four

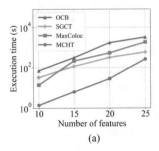 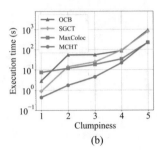

Fig. 2.12 The execution times of the four algorithms on synthetic data sets with different numbers of (**a**) feature types and (**b**) neighboring instances

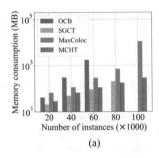 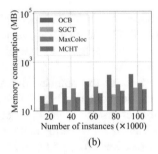

Fig. 2.13 The memory usages of the four algorithms on synthetic data sets with different numbers of instances: (**a**) dense and (**b**) sparse

algorithms also increases. For dense datasets, as can be seen in Fig. 2.13(a), the memory usage of the OCB algorithm is the highest, and when the number of instances approaches 80 k, it runs out of memory. So, when the data set is small, the required storage space of SGCT is less than that of MCHT, but as the number of instances increases, the memory usage of SGCT increases and then exceeds MCHT's. This is also the point at which the condensed instance tree in SGCT becomes more complex, so needing more storage to hold the tree. In our experiment, when the number of instances was larger than 80 k, although SGCT did not suffer memory overflow, its execution time was too long. MaxColoc, of course, required more and more storage space to hold all the co-location instances of each candidate. If data sets are sparse, the memory usage of the four algorithms increases slowly, as shown in Fig. 13(b).

2.5.3.5   The Evaluation of Response to Changing User Requests

This section examines the ability to respond to the changing requests of users, for instance, if they want to change distance and/or prevalence thresholds. At the same time, the memory consumption of MCHT is also compared with the existing algorithms.

Figure 2.14 represents the execution times and memory consumption of the OCB, SGCT, MaxColoc, and MCHT algorithms with an increase in the distance thresholds on both the synthetic and real data sets. Note that, when the distance threshold increases to a large value, OCB shows poor performance, running out of memory and failing to give mining results. We set $d \geq 40$ in Fig. 2.14(a), $d \geq 300$ m in Fig. 2.14(c), $d \geq 250$ m in Fig. 2.14(e), and $d \geq 350$ m in Fig. 2.14 (g, i).

In all the experiments, the execution time of the SGCT algorithm increases dramatically with the increase of the distance threshold. Since increasing distance thresholds makes neighborhood areas larger, more and more instances will satisfy the neighbor relationship and so SGCT requires more time to perform the necessary hierarchical validation to construct the condensed instance tree for each candidate. In addition, as shown in Fig. 2.14(b, d, f, h, j), the memory consumption of SGCT becomes larger than that of MCHT when increasing the distance threshold. With large values of the distance threshold, neighboring instances will have grown in number, and more and more instances are stored repeatedly in SGST's condensed instance tree, in requiring extensive storage space.

Similarly, as shown in Fig. 2.14(a, c, e, g, i), with an increase in the distance threshold, MaxColoc shows better performance than OCB and SGCT. This is because, if the distance threshold is made larger, size 2 prevalent patterns grow in number, and more and more longer size candidates are generated. Early in the algorithm MaxColoc uses an upper participation index to terminate the collection of the co-location instances of these candidates. However, OCB and SGCT need to collect all co-location instances of these candidates before deciding whether the candidates are prevalent, eventually making the performance of the two algorithms impractical.

Overall, the execution time and memory consumption increases for all four algorithms with an increase of the distance threshold, although MCHT shows less of an increase in both its execution time and memory usage.

The execution times and memory consumption of the four compared algorithms with changes over the prevalence threshold are shown in Fig. 2.15. As can be seen, both the execution time and memory consumption of the candidate generate-test mining framework, represented by the OCB, SGCT, and MaxColoc algorithms, decrease with an increase of the prevalence threshold. Again, our proposed algorithm, MCHT, shows a stable performance.

With smaller values of prevalence thresholds, the number of size-2 patterns becomes large, due to the formation of more long size (large cardinality) candidates. Thus, constructing Nei-tree and Inst-tree in OCB, and the hierarchical verification process of SGCT, becomes very time-consuming. Moreover, as these trees become more complex, a large amount of storage space is required. Thus, OCB and SGCT take more computational time, and have high memory consumption. As can be seen in Fig. 2.15 (a, c, e, g), when the prevalence threshold is set low, at 0.3, 0.5, and 0.55 for the synthetic, Shenzhen and Guangzhou data sets, respectively, OCB runs out of

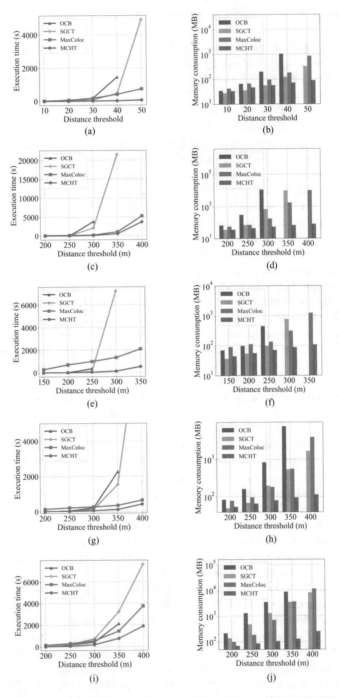

Fig. 2.14 Response of the compared algorithms in different distance thresholds. (**a**, **b**) synthetic data sets; (**c**, **d**) Shenzhen; (**e**, **f**) Guangzhou; (**g**, **h**) Beijing; (**i**, **j**) Shanghai ($\mu_{prev} = 0.4$ for all data sets)

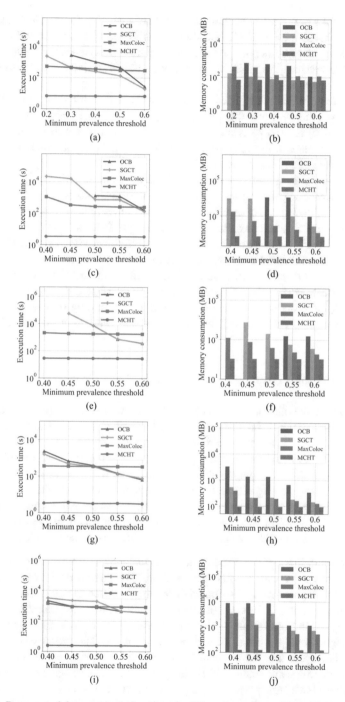

Fig. 2.15 Response of the compared algorithms in different prevalence thresholds. On synthetic data set (**a**) execution time, (**b**) memory consumption, $d = 40$; Shenzhen, $d = 350$ m, (**c**) execution time, (**d**) memory consumption; Guangzhou, $d = 350$ m, (**e**) execution time, (**f**) memory consumption; Beijing, $d = 400$ m, (**g**) execution time, (**h**) memory consumption; Shanghai, $d = 350$ m, (**i**) execution time, (**j**) memory consumption

memory. If the prevalence threshold is set smaller than 0.45 for the Guangzhou data set, the execution time of SGCT becomes impossibly long, as shown in Fig. 2.15(e).

MaxColoc also shows poor performance when the prevalence threshold is set to a small value because the utility of its upper participation index in MaxColoc will degenerate quickly.

In contrast, MCHT only needs to re-calculate and re-filter maximal prevalent co-location patterns from the participating instance hash table. As shown in Tables 2.4–2.7, its two parts only take a small portion of the execution time and so, with an increase in the value of the prevalence threshold, the execution time and memory usage of MCHT are relatively stable.

Further, the execution times of the OCB, SGCT, and MaxColoc algorithms are not only governed by their distance and prevalence thresholds but also depend on the distribution of data sets. For example, for smaller values of the prevalence threshold, if the distribution of instances is clustered (e.g., the POI data set of Shenzhen) or zonal (e.g., the POI data set of Guangzhou or Beijing), both OCB and SGCT require more execution time and more storage space than for a uniform distribution of data sets (e.g., the POI data set of Shanghai). In contrast, the MCHT algorithm shows relatively stable performance for these differently distributed data sets.

Overall, the proposed maximal co-location pattern mining framework is able to quickly respond to changes made by users, compared with conventional algorithms.

2.5.3.6 Analysis of Mining Results on the Real Data Sets

In this section, the mining results on the real data sets are also analyzed to reflect the different phenomena of facilities in these cities, using the same values of distance and minimum prevalence threshold as with the synthetic data sets. As the participation index is used to measure the prevalence of a pattern, and the higher the participation index of a pattern the more prevalent the pattern, and we sort the patterns from the mining results by their participation index, in descending order, and present the top-10 patterns in Tables 2.8 and 2.9. In the two tables, the distance threshold is set to 250 meters, and the minimum prevalence threshold is set to 0.3. From Tables 2.8 and 2.9, we can roughly draw three conclusions as follows:

1. At the same level of the distance and prevalence thresholds, the maximal prevalent co-location patterns mined on the four POI data sets are different. The same facilities are presumably distributed differently in different cities, and their spatial interaction is also different. For example, in Shenzhen city, clothing stores and training institutions frequently appear together, but not so in Guangzhou, while beverage shops are often located near schools in Guangzhou city but not in Shanghai. Note that the co-location parking lot, shopping center is a maximal prevalent co-location pattern in Beijing, but it only is a sub-pattern in Shanghai.
2. Where we have large places with high visitor flow rates such as *farmers' markets*, *furniture markets*, and *shopping centers*, the service industry appears relatively developed, e.g., fast foods, beauty salons, and convenience stores.

Table 2.8 The top-10 patterns mined in the real-world data sets of Shenzhen and Guangzhou cities

Shenzhen	Guangzhou
Clothing store, Training institution	Beverage shop, Training institution
Beauty salon, Parking lot	Residential area, Training institution
Clothing store, Farmers' market	Furniture market, Convenience store
Clothing store, Parking lot	Farmers' market, Beverage shop
Beauty salon, Farmers' market	Convenience store, Farmers' market
Fast food, Clothing store, China restaurant	Parking lot, Training institution
Fast food, Clothing store, Beauty salon	Company, Furniture market, Fast food
Fast food, Furniture market, China restaurant	Parking lot, Farmers' market
Company, Fast food, Convenience store	Furniture market, Parking lot
Residential area, Parking lot	Fast food, Beauty salon, Farmers' market

Table 2.9 The top-10 patterns mined from the real-world data sets of Beijing and Shanghai cities

Beijing	Shanghai
Parking lot, Shopping center	Residential area, Shopping center, Fast food, Local service
Shopping center, Local service	Company, Shopping center, Fast food, Local service
China restaurant, Residential area, Parking lot	Company, Residential area, Local service
Convenience store, Hotel	Company, Residential area, Shopping center
Convenience store, Furniture market	Company, Residential area, Fast food
China restaurant, Convenience store, Beauty salon	Parking lot, School
Parking lot, Hotel	Shopping, Bank
China restaurant, Local service	Local service, Parking lot
China restaurant, Residential area, Beauty salon	Fast food, Bank
China restaurant, Parking Lot, Convenience store	Shopping center, Fast food, Parking lot

3. More long-size maximal co-location patterns are discovered in Shanghai than elsewhere. That may indicate that the physical layout of facilities in Shanghai is in larger blocks and so more services are provided in one place.

2.6   Chapter Summary

In this chapter, a novel maximal prevalent co-location pattern (MPCP) mining framework, based on maximal cliques and hash tables, has been developed (called the MCHT framework). The proposed algorithm eliminates the drawbacks of existing algorithms, e.g., without generating and testing candidates, without collecting co-location instances. First, neighbor relationships of instances are divided into a set of maximal cliques. In order to accelerate enumerating maximal cliques, a bit-string based maximal clique enumerating algorithm is designed. Then, a specially designed participating instance hash table is employed to store these maximal cliques and to further condense neighbor relationships of instances. In addition, the hash table accelerates the queries information about the participating instances of patterns, so that the participation indexes of patterns can be calculated and MPCPs filtered efficiently. The performance of the proposed framework is examined on a series of both synthetic and real data sets. The experimental results show that the proposed MHCT can efficiently discover MPCPs and its time and space requirements are greatly reduced, compared to existing algorithms. Additionally, MHCT has the ability to quickly respond to user requests, for instance when they change thresholds to accommodate different application domains. Theoretical and experimental analysis of the proposed algorithm has been presented.

In Chap. 3, a new concept of *sub-prevalent* SCPs is introduced, which replaces traditional clique instances with star instances in prevalence metrics of SCPs. Because we note that in some applications, we cannot require neighbors with a spatial feature to be adjacent to each other. The *sub-prevalent* SCPs can help people to gain insight into another distribution of spatial features in space.

A traditional prevalent SCP must be a sub-prevalent SCP, but not vice versa. That is to say, the set of sub-prevalent SCP will be larger, so we plan to mining "natural preference" or "best" sub-prevalent SCPs, instead of mining *all sub-prevalent* SCPs. Fortunately, the sub-prevalence satisfies the downward inclusion property, this allows the maximum sub-prevalent SCPs mining to be studied in the next chapter.

Chapter 3
Maximal Sub-prevalent Co-location Patterns

3.1 Introduction

Spatial co-location pattern (SCP) mining is essential to reveal the frequent co-occurrence patterns among spatial features in various applications. For example, a co-location pattern may show that the region where mosquitoes are abundant and poultry are kept usually has West Nile virus around (Huang et al., 2004); or botanists discover that 80% of sub-humid evergreen broadleaved forests grow with orchid plants (Wang et al., 2009b).

The traditional model of mining prevalent SCPs was proposed by Shekhar and Huang (Shekhar & Huang, 2001; Huang et al., 2004). In this model, the prevalence measure of SCPs is defined based on *clique instances* under spatial neighbor relationships. In detail, the prevalence of a co-location c is the minimum participation ratio $Pr(f_i, c)$ among all features f_i in c. The participation ratio $Pr(f_i, c)$ of feature f_i in a co-location c is the fraction of the instances of f_i that participate in a co-location instance (a clique instance, where the set of instances has a clique relationship) of c. Figure 3.1 shows an example of data sets with three spatial features $\{A, B, C\}$ where two spatial instances are connected with a solid line if their corresponding distance is smaller than the given threshold and $A.i$ denotes the i-th instance of feature A. The co-location pattern $\{A, B, C\}$ in Fig. 3.1 is not prevalent when the minimum prevalence threshold *min_prev* is given 0.4, because there is only one clique instance $\{A.1, B.1, C.1\}$ for the pattern $\{A, B, C\}$ and the prevalence of $\{A, B, C\}$ is only 0.2. But we can see that there are three out of four instances of A which are neighbors to instances of B and C, and that B has two out of the five instances which are neighbors to instances of A and C, and C has two out of three. That is to say, at least 40% of instances of each spatial feature in $\{A, B, C\}$ are close to instances of the other

From Wang, L., Bao, X., Zhou, L., and Chen, H.: Mining Maximal Sub-prevalent Co-location Patterns. *World Wide Web* 22(5), 1971–1997 (2019).

© The Author(s), under exclusive license to Springer Nature Singapore Pte Ltd. 2022
L. Wang et al., *Preference-based Spatial Co-location Pattern Mining*, Big Data Management, https://doi.org/10.1007/978-981-16-7566-9_3

Fig. 3.1 An example of
spatial data sets

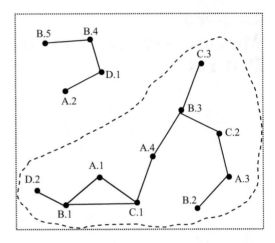

features. This implies that instances from A, B, and C are spatially correlated, which
is neglected if we only consider the clique instances.

Discovering patterns that are similar to {A, B, C} in Fig. 3.1 can help people to
gain insight into other distributions of spatial features in space. Two examples are
given here.

First, suppose pattern {A, B, C} is discovered from the distributional data set of
vegetation in a certain region, then other vegetation appears in the neighborhood of
growing any vegetation in {A, B, C}, and represents symbiotic vegetation in the
region. Such patterns can be useful in practical applications. For example, they can
help vegetation distribution analysis, or in the site selection for investigating vegetation, or in vegetation protection.

Second, and in a different context, suppose feature A represents "hospital," B is
"resident area," and C is "bus station" in Fig. 3.1. If we analyze the distribution of
instances of spatial feature set {"hospital," "resident area," "bus station"}, we can
see that the resident area "B.3" is near to the hospital "A.4" as well as the bus stations
"C.2" and "C.3", while the bus stations "C.2" and "C.3" are not in the neighborhood
of the hospital "A.4", but "A.4" is near to another bus station "C.1." The layout of
the three spatial features within the dotted line contains a co-located correlation.

Again, we can also take spatial features A, B, and C into the consideration of plant
diseases. Here, those plant diseases which coexist may not form clique instances due
to the effect of the wind and/or altitudes affecting their spatial distribution.

The problem in the traditional models of mining prevalent SCPs is that they only
choose clique instances as the measure of interests. However, the statement that "the
presence of B and C in the neighborhood of an instance of the spatial feature A"
obviously does not necessarily imply that instances of B and C are neighbors. To
tackle the problem, this chapter advocates a new concept of *sub-prevalent SCPs,* by
replacing clique instances with star participation instances.

We will see that a traditional clique-based prevalent SCP must be a sub-prevalent
SCP, but not vice versa. That is to say, the set of sub-prevalent SCPs will be larger,
and the user may face a larger number of patterns and often not know what course to

take. A key observation is that the downward inclusion property is satisfied by sub-prevalence. This enables *maximal* sub-prevalent SCP mining to be studied in this chapter.

Thus, our contributions in this chapter are as follows:

1. First, we define a new concept of *sub-prevalent* SCPs by introducing star participation instances, and the anti-monotonic property of sub-prevalent SCPs is proved. Following the maximal SCP mining of Chap. 2, instead of mining *all* sub-prevalent SCPs, we mine the *maximal* sub-prevalent SCPs in this chapter.
2. Second, we propose two novel maximal sub-prevalent SCP mining algorithms, namely, the prefix-tree-based algorithm (PTB algorithm) and the partition-based algorithm (PB algorithm). At the same time, an intersection-based method is proposed to compute the interest measures of the patterns containing star participation instances.
3. Third, the advantages and disadvantages of the two algorithms are analysed in depth, and we experimentally evaluate our works on synthetic and real data sets. The experimental results show that our algorithms are scalable and the mined patterns are longer than the traditional results and can capture the star-correlations of the spatial features.

Figure 3.2 presents the organization of this chapter. Section 3.2 defines the related concepts of sub-prevalent SCP mining and proves the *anti-monotonic property* of sub-prevalent SCPs. Two novel maximal sub-prevalent SCP mining algorithms are presented in Sections 3.3 and 3.4, respectively. In Sect. 3.5, a comparison of the two algorithms is presented. We show the experimental evaluation in Sect. 3.6 and related work in Sect. 3.7. Finally, we summarize the chapter in Sect. 3.8.

3.2   Basic Concepts and Properties

We first present the basic concepts of maximal sub-prevalent SCP mining and discuss its anti-monotonic property.

In a spatial data set, let F be a set of n *features* $F = \{f_1, f_2, \ldots f_n\}$. Let S be a set of *instances* of F. Let NR be a *neighbor relationship* over locations of instances. NR is symmetric and reflexive. We again use the Euclidean distance with a distance threshold d as a neighbor relationship in this chapter.

A co-location c is a subset of spatial features, i.e., $c \subseteq F$.

We use the star neighborhoods instance, which was introduced in the join-less algorithm (Yoo & Shekhar, 2006), as the method for materializing the neighbor relationship between spatial instances. The star neighborhoods instance is a set comprising a center instance and other instances in its neighborhood. It has a formal definition.

Definition 3.1 (Star neighborhoods instance, *SNsI*) *SNsI*$(o_i) = \{o_j | distance(o_i, o_j) \leq d$, where d is a neighbor relationship distance threshold$\}$ is the star neighborhoods instance of o_i, and o_i is the label of *SNsI*(o_i). In other words, *SNsI*(o_i) is the set

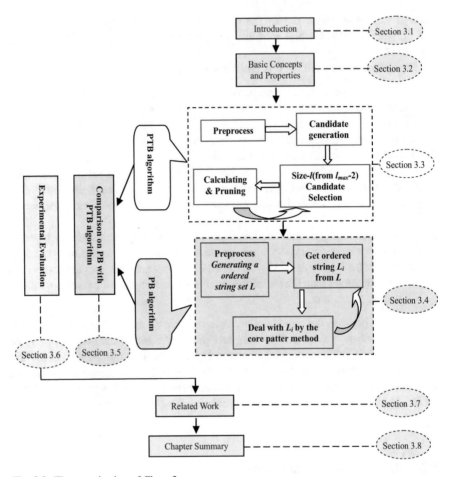

Fig. 3.2 The organization of Chap. 3

consisting of o_i and the other spatial instances located within distance d from o_i, i.e., having neighbor relationships with o_i.

In Fig. 3.1, a point represents an instance and a solid line between two points represents the neighbor relationship between two instances. $X.i$ is the i-th instance of the feature X. As can be seen in Fig. 3.1, $SNsI(A.1) = \{A.1, B.1, C.1\}$, and $SNsI(B.3) = \{A.4, B.3, C.2, C.3\}$.

Based on the concept of star neighborhoods instance, the concept of star participation instances is defined, and then we use the participation ratio and the participation index defined by Huang et al. (2004) to characterize how frequently instances of different features in a co-location pattern are neighbors.

Definition 3.2 (Star participation instance, SPIns) $SPIns(f_i, c) = \{o_i | o_i$ is an instance of feature f_i and $SNsI(o_i)$ contains instances of all features in $c\}$ is the star participation instance of feature f_i in c. In other words, $SPIns(f_i, c)$ *is the set* consisting of instances of f_i whose star neighborhoods instances contain all features in c.

Definition 3.3 (Star participation ratio, SPR) $SPR(f_i, c) = |SPIns(f_i, c)| / |S_{f_i}|$ is the star participation ratio of feature f_i in a co-location c, where S_{f_i} is the set of instances of f_i. In other words, $SPR(f_i, c)$ is the fraction of instances of f_i that occur in the star participation instance of f_i in c.

Definition 3.4 (Star participation index, SPI) $SPI(c) = \min_{f \in c} \{SPR(f, c)\}$ is the star participation index of a co-location c. In other words, $SPI(c)$ is the minimum star participation ratio $SPR(f_i, c)$ among all features f_i in c.

Definition 3.5. (Sub-prevalent SCP) A co-location c is a sub-prevalent SCP, if its star participation index is no less than a given sub-prevalence threshold *min_sprev*, that is, $SPI(c) \geq min\_sprev$.

For example, in Fig. 3.1, the star participation instance $SPIns(A, \{A, B, C\})$ of feature A in $\{A, B, C\}$ is $\{A.1, A.3, A.4\}$, $SPIns(B, \{A, B, C\}) = \{B.1, B.3\}$, and $SPIns(C, \{A, B, C\}) = \{C.1, C.2\}$. Thus, the star participation ratio $SPR(A, \{A, B, C\})$ of A in $\{A, B, C\}$ is 3/4 because 3 out of 4 instances of A occur in the star participation instance of A in $\{A, B, C\}$. Similarly, $SPR(B, \{A, B, C\}) = 2/5$, and $SPR(C, \{A, B, C\}) = 2/3$. Therefore, $SPI(\{A, B, C\}) = min\{3/4, 2/5, 2/3\} = 2/5 = 0.4$. If the sub-prevalence threshold *min_sprev* is set by the user at no more than 40%, $\{A, B, C\}$ is a sub-prevalent SCP.

Lemma 3.1 (Monotonicity of SPR and SPI) Let c and c' be two co-locations such that $c' \subseteq c$. Then, for each feature $f \in c'$, $SPR(f, c') \geq SPR(f, c)$. Furthermore, $SPI(c') \geq SPI(c)$.

Proof For the first claim in the lemma, we only need to show that for a spatial feature $f \in c'$, $|SPIns(f, c')| \geq |SPIns(f, c)|$.

Since $c' \subseteq c$, every star participation instance of feature f in c contains instances of all features in c'. Thus, the inequality holds.

The second claim follows from the fact that $SPI(c') = \min_{f \in c'} \{SPR(f, c')\} \geq \min_{f \in c} \{SPR(f, c)\} = SPI(c)$.

This lemma establishes the downward closure property of *SPR* and *SPI*.

It is obvious that we can mine longer co-location patterns after introducing the *sub-prevalent* concept. But the mined results might be massive and mutually inclusive. Maximal sub-prevalent SCP mining can resolve this problem.

Definition 3.6 (Maximal sub-prevalent SCP) Given a sub-prevalent SCP $c = \{f_l, \ldots, f_v\}$ in a set of spatial features $F = \{f_1, \ldots, f_n\}$, $l, v \in \{1, 2, \ldots, n\}$, if none of c's super-patterns are sub-prevalent, then c is called a maximal sub-prevalent SCP.

The set of maximal sub-prevalent SCPs is a compact representation of a large number of sub-prevalent SCPs. The maximal sub-prevalent SCPs form the minimal set which can lead to all the sub-prevalent SCPs.

Based on Lemma 3.1, two novel mining algorithms are proposed, respectively, presented in Sect. 3.3 and Sect. 3.4, to discover the complete set of maximal sub-prevalent SCPs from a spatial data set.

3.3   A Prefix-Tree-Based Algorithm (PTBA)

A prefix-tree-based algorithm (PTBA) is developed in this section. In PTBA, in order to efficiently perform candidate pruning, all maximal sub-prevalent candidates generated from 2-size sub-prevalent SCPs are organized into a *prefix tree*. At the same time, an *intersection-based* method to compute the SPIs of candidates is presented. Finally, the performance of PTBA is analyzed, and then a pruning lemma is given.

3.3.1   Basic Idea

First, we note that star neighborhood instances are equivalent to each other, i.e., if $o_j \in SNsI(o_i)$, then $o_i \in SNsI(o_j)$. So, our algorithm firstly collects those pair of instances which are neighbors to each other, and then selects 2-size sub-prevalent SCPs by comparison with a user-given sub-prevalence threshold *min_sprev*.

Then, due to Lemma 3.1, maximal sub-prevalent candidates can be generated from the set of 2-size sub-prevalent SCPs by detecting feature sets which can form cliques. For example, if there was a set of 2-size sub-prevalent SCPs: $SPCP_2 = \{\{A, B\}, \{A, C\}, \{A, D\}, \{B, C\}, \{B, D\}, \{C, D\}, \{C, E\}, \{D, E\}\}$, the feature set $\{A, B, C, D\}$ is a 4-size sub-prevalent candidate because it forms a clique under the 2-size sub-prevalent relationship, while the feature set $\{B, C, D, E\}$ does not belong to the 4-size candidate set because $\{B, E\}$ is not a 2-size sub-prevalent SCP.

We use a lexicographic order–based method for generating all maximal sub-prevalent candidates. In order to reduce the candidate search space dynamically in the mining process, all generated candidates are organized into a *prefix tree*. In the prefix tree, a branch is created for a candidate and a new branch shares common prefixes. For example, the prefix tree of a set of all candidates {{ABCD, ABC, ABD, ACD, AC, AD}, {BCD, BC, BD}, {CDE, CE}, {DE}} is shown in Fig. 3.3, where the candidate $\{A, B, C, D\}$ leads to the first branch of the candidate search space tree. The second candidate $\{A, B, C\}$ does not form a new branch because it shares common prefixes with the first branch, while $\{A, B, D\}$ forms a new branch because it shares two common prefixes, etc.

The feature set identifying each node will be referred to as the node's *head*, while possible extensions of the node are called the *tail*. For example, consider nodes Y' and Y'' in Fig. 3.3; their head is $\{A\}$ and $\{A, B\}$, respectively, and the tail is the set $\{B, C, D\}$ and $\{C, D\}$, respectively. The Head Union the Tail (HUT) of Y' is $\{A, B, C, D\}$.

Our mining method starts with the longest $l = l_{max}$ maximal sub-prevalent candidates in the search space and determines whether they are maximal sub-prevalent SCPs as specified in Definitions 3.5 and 3.6. Once the algorithm determines that a candidate is maximal, the algorithm can begin a pruning process. That is, the algorithm checks breadth-first whether the HUT of each node in the candidate search space tree is a subset of a current maximal set. If the HUT is a

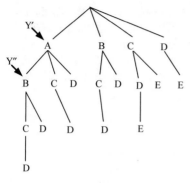 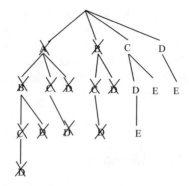

(a) A candidate search space tree   (b) After finding a {A,B,C,D} maximal set

Fig. 3.3 Candidate search space tree and pruning, where (**a**) a candidate search space tree; (**b**) after finding a {A,B,C,D} maximal set

subset of any of the maximal sub-prevalent SCPs, the sub-tree whose root is the node is pruned. For example, in Fig. 3.3(a), let's assume that {A, B, C, D} is a maximal sub-prevalent SCPs. Then the algorithm checks breadth-first for candidates to prune in the search space tree. In the first level, the HUT of node A is {A, B, C, D}. Since it is a subset of {A, B, C, D}, the algorithm prunes the sub-tree whose root is A. The next node at that level is node B whose HUT is {B, C, D}. Since this candidate is a subset of {A, B, C, D}, the algorithm prunes this sub-tree as well. The pruning continues with the rest of the nodes in the first level. Then the algorithm starts pruning the next level until the subset tree resembles Fig. 3.3(b).

Finding maximal sub-prevalent SCPs and running the pruning scheme happens at each *l*-size until there are no more candidates to process.

In the method discussed above, computing the sub-prevalence measure of a candidate c, i.e., $SPI(c)$, is a core problem. Based on the 2-size co-location instances (neighborhoods instances' pairs), we can compute the sub-prevalence measure of any k-size pattern ($k > 2$) by the following Lemma 3.2.

Lemma 3.2 (The sub-prevalence measure of k-size SCPs ($k > 2$)) Given the 2-size co-location instances of a spatial data set, the star participation index of a k-size SCP $c = \{f_1, \ldots f_k\}$ can be calculated as follows:

$$SPI(c) = \min\{|\underset{j=2,\ldots k}{\cap} SPIns(f_1, \{f_1, f_j\})|/|S_{f_1}|, \cdots |\underset{j=1,\ldots k-1}{\cap} SPIns(f_k, \{f_k, f_j\})|/|S_{f_k}|\}$$

$$(3.1)$$

Proof For $c = \{f_1, \ldots f_k\}$, according to Definition 3.2, $SPIns(f_i, c) = \underset{j=1,\ldots k, j \neq i}{\cap} SPIns(f_i, \{f_i, f_j\})$. From Definitions 3.3 and 3.4, Eq. (3.1) for calculating $SPI(c)$ is obvious.

For example, for the spatial data set in Fig. 3.1, given $c = \{A, B, C\}$, then SPI $(c) = \min\{|\{A.1, A.3, A.4\} \cap \{A.1, A.3, A.4\}|/4, |\{B.1, B.2, B.3\} \cap \{B.1, B.3\}|/5, |\{C.1, C.2\} \cap \{C.1, C.2, C.3\}|/3\} = \min\{3/4, 2/5, 2/3\} = 0.4$.

This method is a typical candidate generate-and-test method. We call it a prefix-tree-based algorithm (PTBA) due to the fundamental nature of the method's candidate search space tree.

3.3.2 Algorithm

The pseudo-code of PTBA to mine all maximal sub-prevalent SCPs is shown in Algorithm 3.1.

Algorithm 3.1 Prefix-tree-based Mining Algorithm

Input
  $F = \{f_1, f_2, \ldots, f_n\}$: a set of spatial feature types;
  S: a spatial data set;
  d: a spatial neighbor distance threshold;
  min_sprev: a minimum sub-prevalence threshold;
Output
  MSPCP: A set of all maximal sub-prevalent SCPs;
Variables
  SI_2: a set of 2-size co-location instances; l: a co-location size of interest; C: a set of all candidate sets; C_l: a set of l-size candidates; *spi*: star participation index; l_{max}: the longest size of candidate c; $MSPCP_l$: a set of size l maximal sub-prevalent SCPs; *MSPCP*: a set of all maximal sub-prevalent SCPs;
Steps
  //**Preprocess and candidate generation**
    1. SI_2=gen_2-size_co-loc_ins (S, F, d);
    2. $SPCP_2$=sel_2-size_sub-prev_co-loc (*min_sprev*, SI_2);
    3. $MSPCP$=*null*;
    4. C=gen_maxi_candi ($SPCP_2$);   //candidates are organized into a prefix tree
  //**MSPCP mining**
    5. l_{max} =longest_size(C);
    6. $l = l_{max}$;
    7. **while** ($l > 2$ or $C_l \neq \emptyset$) **do**
    8. C_l = get_l_candi (C, l);
    9.   **for** each candidate c in C_l **do**
    10.   *spi* = calculate_spi(c, SI_2);   //using Lemma 3.2
    11.   **if** *spi* $\geq$ *min_sprev*
    12.   Insert(c, $MSPCP_l$);
    13.   **end for**
    14. $MSPCP = MSPCP \cup MSPCP_l$;
    15.   Subset_Pruning($MSPCP_l$, C);
    16. $l = l - 1$;
    17. **end while**

---

1. *Preprocessing and candidate generation* (*Steps* 1–4): Given an input spatial data set S and a neighbor distance threshold d, we firstly find all neighboring instance pairs (all 2-size co-location instances) using a geometric method such as plane sweep, or a spatial query method using quaternary trees or R-Trees. We then compute their star participation index (SPI) and determine whether a 2-size co-location is sub-prevalent, by comparing its SPI to a user-defined sub-prevalence threshold *min_sprev*, and include it as the result set of $MSPCP_2$. Based on $MSPCP_2$, all maximal sub-prevalent candidates are generated using the lexicographic order method.
2. *Select l-size* (*from* l_{max} *to* 2) *co-location candidates* (*Steps* 5–8): First, the longest size of candidates is set to l_{max}. The maximal sub-prevalent SCP mining is processed starting from size $l = l_{max}$. Select l-size candidates C_l from the candidate pool.
3. *Calculate l-size sub-prevalent co-locations* (*Steps* 9–13): For each candidate c in C_l, based on the related 2-size co-location instances SI_2, SPI(c) is calculated by Lemma 3.2. If SPI(c) $\geq$ *min_sprev*, insert c into the l-size maximal sub-prevalent SCP set $MSPCP_l$.
4. *Update result set and prune the subsets* (*Steps* 14–15): Update the maximal sub-prevalent result set $MSPCP$, and all subsets of the maximal set $MSPCP_l$ are pruned.
5. *Return the final result set* (*Steps* 16–17): The procedure from Step 7 to Step 17 is repeated continually until $l = 3$ or the candidate set is empty. The final result can then be returned.

3.3.3   Analysis and Pruning

The main cost of performing the prefix-tree-based algorithm (PTBA) occurs with procedures *gen_2-size_co-loc_ins*, *gen_max_candi*, and the loop of Step 7. Suppose the total number of spatial instances is m, the number of features is n, and A^m denotes the average number of instances in all features. Then the cost of procedure *gen_2-size_co-loc_ins* is at most $O(m^2 \log_2 m)$, and procedure *gen_max_candi* is at most $O(n^2)$ if we suppose that computing an order string needs only a unit time by the lexicographic order method.

For the loop of Step 7, the procedures *calculate_spi* and *Subset_Pruning* are the dominant costs. If we calculate the SPI of candidates using Lemma 3.2, the procedure *calculate_spi* would cost at most $O\left(\sum_{k=3}^{l_{max}} |C_k| \cdot k^2 \cdot A^m\right)$, where $|C_k|$ is the number of k-size candidates. The computational complexity of procedure *Subset_Pruning* is related to the number of candidates, and the effects of pruning. The smaller is the size of maximal sub-prevalent SCPs, the fewer is the number to be pruned, and so higher is the cost of *Subset_Pruning*.

The number of candidates may become exponential 2^n, and if the longest size of maximal sub-prevalent SCPs is not long enough, the effect of the procedure *Subset_Pruning* would not be ideal. As an improvement, we propose the following pruning lemma to prune sub-trees or nodes in a candidate search space tree when a candidate is **not** a maximal sub-prevalent SCP.

Lemma 3.3 (Depth-First Pruning) If a candidate $c = c' \cup \{X\} \cup \{Y\}$ is not maximal sub-prevalent, then

1. The node "Y" can be pruned;
2. If $SPI(c' \cup \{X\} \cup \{Y\}) = SPI(c' \cup \{X\})$, then the sub-tree whose root is node "X" can be pruned;
3. If $SPI(c') = SPI(c' \cup \{X\})$, then the node "$Y$" which is a brother of the node "X" can be pruned.

Proof Case (1) is obvious because the candidate c is not a maximal sub-prevalent SCPs; For case (2) $SPI(c' \cup \{X\} \cup \{Y\}) = SPI(c' \cup \{X\})$, because $SPI(c' \cup \{X\}) = SPI(c' \cup \{X\} \cup \{Y\}) < min\_sprev$, according to case (1), the sub-tree whose root is "X" can be pruned; For case (3) $SPI(c') = SPI(c' \cup \{X\})$, because $SPI(c' \cup \{Y\}) = SPI(c' \cup \{X\} \cup \{Y\}) < min\_sprev$, according to case (1), the node "Y" in $c' \cup \{Y\}$ can also be pruned.

For example, Figs. 3.4(a) and (b), respectively, show the pruning results of cases (2) and (3) in Lemma 3.3 after finding {A, C, D, E} is not a maximal sub-prevalent SCP.

We have presented a PBTA for mining all maximal sub-prevalent SCPs, but the large number of candidates in the candidate search space tree and the computational complexity of sub-prevalence measures for long patterns limit the scale of spatial data sets that can be handled. In the next section, a novel partitioning technique is proposed that can resolve these problems efficiently.

3.4 A Partition-Based Algorithm (PBA)

3.4.1 Basic Idea

This section presents an interesting method called partition-based algorithm (PBA), which adopts a divide-and-conquer strategy as follows. First, it divides the set of 2-size sub-prevalent SCPs into the set of lexicographic order strings by the relation $=_{head}$. It then mines each string separately based on a *core pattern method*. We first define the related concepts as follows.

Definition 3.7 (Partition pattern (PP) and core pattern (CP)) A 2-size pattern contained in a SCP c is called a ***partition pattern (PP)*** of c, if its star participation

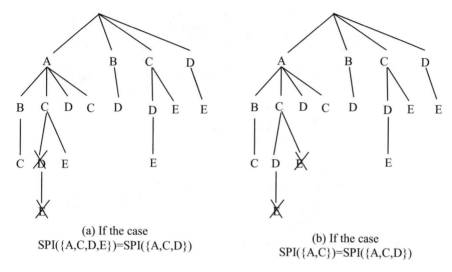

(a) If the case
SPI({A,C,D,E})=SPI({A,C,D})

(b) If the case
SPI({A,C})=SPI({A,C,D})

Fig. 3.4 Pruning results after finding {A, C, D, E} is not maximally sub-prevalent, where (**a**) if SPI ({A,C,D,E})=SPI({A,C,D}); (**b**) if SPI({A,C})=SPI({A,C,D})

index (SPI) is the largest of all the 2-size co-locations of c. The two sub-patterns of c, which are divided by the *PP*, are called ***core patterns (CPs)*** of c.

For example, if the PP of $c = \{A, B, C, D, G\}$ is $\{C, D\}$, then CPs of c are $\{A, B, C, G\}$ and $\{A, B, D, G\}$. Because the SPI of PP is the largest of the 2-size co-locations of c, the CPs of c may be key patterns deciding on whether c is sub-prevalent or not.

Lemma 3.4 Given a l-size co-location $c = \{f_1, f_2, \ldots f_l\}$ and its PP $\{f_{l-1}, f_l\}$, we divide c into two $(l-1)$-size CPs $\{f_1, \ldots, f_{l-2}, f_{l-1}\}$ and $\{f_1, \ldots, f_{l-2}, f_l\}$ by $\{f_{l-1}, f_l\}$. If two CPs $\{f_1, \ldots, f_{l-2}, f_{l-1}\}$ and $\{f_1, \ldots, f_{l-2}, f_l\}$ are sub-prevalent, and the two additional conditions shown below are also satisfied, then it can be determined that c is a sub-prevalent SCP.

The additional *condition (1)*: $|SPIns(f_{l-1}, \{f_1, \ldots, f_{l-2}, f_{l-1}\}) \cap SPIns(f_{l-1}, \{f_{l-1}, f_l\})| / |S_{fl-1}| \geq min\_sprev$ and $|SPIns(f_l, \{f_1, \ldots, f_{l-2}, f_l\}) \cap SPIns(f_l, \{f_{l-1}, f_l\})| / |S_{fl}| \geq min\_sprev$.

The additional condition (2): $\min\{|SPIns(f_1, \{f_1, \ldots, f_{l-2}, f_{l-1}\}) \cap SPIns(f_1, \{f_1, \ldots, f_{l-2}, f_l\})| / |S_{fl}|, \ldots |SPIns(f_{l-2}, \{f_1, \ldots, f_{l-2}, f_{l-1}\}) \cap SPIns(f_{l-2}, \{f_1, \ldots, f_{l-2}, f_l\})| / |S_{fl-2}|\} \geq min\_sprev$.

Proof By Definitions 3.3 and 3.4, $SPI(c) = \min\{|SPIns(f_1, \{f_1, \ldots, f_{l-2}, f_{l-1}\}) \cap SPIns(f_1, \{f_1, \ldots, f_{l-2}, f_l\})| / |S_{f1}|, \ldots |SPIns(f_{l-2}, \{f_1, \ldots, f_{l-2}, f_{l-1}\}) \cap SPIns(f_{l-2}, \{f_1, \ldots, f_{l-2}, f_l\})| / |S_{fl-2}|, |SPIns(f_{l-1}, \{f_1, \ldots, f_{l-2}, f_{l-1}\}) \cap SPIns(f_{l-1}, \{f_{l-1}, f_l\})| / |S_{fl-1}|, |SPIns(f_l, \{f_1, \ldots, f_{l-2}, f_l\}) \cap SPIns(f_l, \{f_{l-1}, f_l\})| / |S_{fl}|\}$.

The idea of Lemma 3.4 is shown in Fig. 3.5 visually.

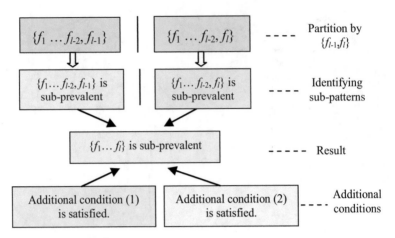

Fig. 3.5 The idea of the core pattern method

To identify the two CPs $\{f_1,\ldots,f_{l-2}, f_{l-1}\}$ and $\{f_1,\ldots,f_{l-2}, f_l\}$, we deal with them recursively using the core pattern method. In fact, the core pattern method employs a bottom-up iteration strategy, which starts from identifying 3-size core patterns, then to 4-size core patterns,...up to the l-size pattern.

With the following example, we will illustrate how the PB method works in detail.

Suppose there is the set of 2-size sub-prevalent SCPs: $SPCP_2 = \{\{A, B\}, \{A, C\},$ $\{A, D\}, \{A, F\}, \{A, G\}, \{B, C\}, \{B, D\}, \{B, G\}, \{C, D\}, \{C, F\}, \{C, G\}, \{D, E\},$ $\{D, F\}, \{D, G\}, \{E, F\}\}$ in a certain spatial data set whose feature set is $\{A, B, C, D,$ $E, F, G\}$.

We first partition $SPCP_2$ into the set of lexicographically ordered strings under the relation $=_{head}$. This resulting set is denoted L_1. Thus, we have $L_1 = \{\delta_{head}(A) = ABCDFG, \delta_{head}(B) = BCDG, \delta_{head}(C) = CDFG, \delta_{head}(D) = DEFG, \delta_{head}(E) = EF, \delta_{head}(F) = F, \delta_{head}(G) = G\}$. We call this partition **Partition_1**.

Then, according to 2-size non-sub-prevalent SCPs, the ordered strings in L_1 are divided further. In our example, there are 2-size non-sub-prevalent SCPs $\overline{SPCP_2} = \{AE, BE, BF, CE, EG\}$. So, the ordered string $\delta_{head}(A) = ABCDFG$ is further divided into two strings ABCDG and ACDFG by BF. We continue to divide these sub-strings, respectively, until there exists no 2-size non-SPCP in them or their size is less than 2. Thus, L_1 is replaced with $L = \{ABCDG, ACDFG, BCDG, CDFG, DEF, DFG, EF\}$. The non-sub-prevalent-based partition is called **Partition_2**.

Next, we deal with strings in L, one by one, using the core pattern method to obtain whole maximal sub-prevalent SCPs. For our example, we first consider the ordered string "ABCDG." Suppose $\{C, D\}$ is the PP of $c = \{A, B, C, D, G\}$, then the

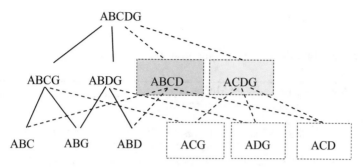

Fig. 3.6 {A, B, C, D, G} and its sub-sets with head of "A"

CPs of c are {A, B, C, G} and {A, B, D, G}. Continuing to partition, we may get 3-size CPs {A, B, C} and {A, B, G} for {A, B, C, G}, and {A, B, D} and {A, B, G} for {A, B, D, G}. We call **Partition_3** the partition obtaining CPs based on PP. The solid line part in Fig. 3.6 is the result of partitioning {A, B, C, D, G} by Partition_3.

We can directly compute the SPI values of 3-size core patterns using Lemma 3.2, using the results of 3-size core patterns to identify the related 4-size core patterns by Lemma 3.4, and then 5-size patterns. For our example:

If two 3-size core patterns {A, B, C} and {A, B, G} are sub-prevalent, and their additional conditions (1) and (2) are satisfied, then we can determine that the 4-size co-location {A, B, C, G} is sub-prevalent. Similarly, we can identify {A, B, D, G}, and then identify {A, B, C, D, G}.

Once the 5-size pattern {A, B, C, D, G} is not a sub-prevalent SCP, the rest of the 4-size patterns with the same head (beside two CPs) {A, B, C, D} and {A, C, D, G} (see the dotted line part in Fig. 3.6) need to be identified. From Fig. 3.6, we note that there are common patterns for identifying higher-size patterns. For example, {A, B, G} is common for identifying {A, B, C, G} and {A, B, D, G}, and {A, B, C} is common for identifying {A, B, C, G} and {A, B, C, D}. Thus it is better to store the results of lower-size patterns. In addition, if the 5-size pattern {A, B, C, D, G} is sub-prevalent, then the remaining 4-size patterns need not be identified.

When finishing the processing of judging the prevalence of ordered string "ABCDG," the next ordered string "ACDFG" in $\delta_{\text{head}}(A)$ is dealt with. Then we obtain the set $MSPCP_A$ of maximal sub-prevalent SCPs with the head of "A," and then prune all subsets of $MSPCP_A$ in L. In the following, the ordered strings with a head of "B" in L are handled.

3.4.2 Algorithm

Algorithm 3.2 summarizes this mining process.

Algorithm 3.2 Partition-Based Mining Algorithm

Input and Output is the same as Algorithm 3.1

Variables

   SI_2: a set of 2-size co-location instances; $SPCP_2$: a set of 2-size sub-prevalent SCPs; L: a set of ordered strings of $SPCP_2$ under Partition_1and Partition_2; L_i: a set of ordered strings with the head "i" in L; $MSPCP_i$: a set of maximal sub-prevalent SCPs with the head of "i"; B: a mark array to indicate whether a pattern has been identified or not; $MSPCP$: a set of all maximal sub-prevalent SCPs;

Steps

   //**Preprocessing**

      1. SI_2=gen_2-size_co-loc_ins (S, F, d);
      2. $SPCP_2$=sel_2-size_sub-prev_co-loc (min_sprev, SI_2);
      3. $MSPCP$=null;
      4. L=Partitioning_1_2($SPCP_2$);   //by Partition_1 and Partition_2

   //**Main program**

      5. **for** i=1 **to** m //m features corresponding to digits 1-m
      6. L_i =get_head_i(L);   //L_i is the set with the head of "i" in L
      7. $MSPCP_i$=null;
      8.   mark array B is set to initial value 0;
      9.   **while** $(L_i \neq \phi)$ **do**
      10.   get a pattern c from L_i;
      11. HS_c =null;   //HS_c is the set of all maximal sub-prevalent SCPs of c
      12.   CPD(c, $|c|$);
      13. $HS_c \leftarrow$ Deal with the results of c;
      14. $MSPCP_i = MSPCP_i$ merge HS_c;
      15.   **endwhile**
      16. $MSPCP = MSPCP \cup MSPCP_i$;
      17.   Subset_Pruning($MSPCP_i, L$);
      18. **endfor**

Preprocessing (*Steps* 1–4): First, compute the instances set SI_2 of 2-size co-locations, and select all 2-size $SPCP_2$. Then, based on Partition_1 and Partition_2, we obtain a set L of ordered strings.

Get the ordered strings with the head of "i" (*Steps* 5–8): First, the set of ordered strings with the head of "i" in L is put to L_i. The set $MSPCP_i$ of all maximal sub-prevalent SCPs with the head of "i" is set to "*null*". The mark array B is initialized to 0 (B prevents repeat computation), and the value of B is 1 if the corresponding pattern is sub-prevalent, otherwise −1. "i" runs from the first feature to the last feature.

Deal with ordered strings in L_i by the core pattern method (*Steps* 9–15): For each ordered string c in L_i, compute the set HS_c of all maximal sub-prevalent SCPs in c by the recursive procedure CPD(c, |c|). The design of the recursive procedure is based on the core pattern method. For Step 13, according to the computational results of

CPD(c, |c|), we can obtain maximal sub-prevalent SCPs of c. For example, if B(Hash (c)) = 1 then $c \to HS_c$. *Either c is a unique maximal sub-prevalent SCP in c, or else we have to check the two core patterns c' and c'' of c*. Next, we merge the computational result HS_c into the result set $MSPCP_i$ with the head of "i". In the merging operation of Step 14, we need to delete patterns which are the sub-sets of other patterns. Then the next ordered string in L_i is dealt with until there are no ordered strings left.

Update result set and prune the subsets (Steps 16–17): Update maximal sub-prevalent result set $MSPCP$, and all subsets of $MSPCP_i$ in L are also pruned.

Return the final result set (Step 18): The set of ordered strings with the head of the next feature is dealt with until there are no ordered strings left in L. Finally, return the final result set $MSPCP$ of maximal sub-prevalent SCPs.

The recursive procedure CPD(c, |c|) in Algorithm 3.2 is shown below.

Procedure CPD(c, k)
  1. **if** B(Hash(c))$\diamond$0 **then** Return;   //c has been identified
  2. **if** k=3 **then**
  3.   directly calculate SPI(c) by Lemma 3.2;
  4.   **if** SPI(c)$\geq$*min_sprev* **then** B(Hash(c))=1;
  5.   **else** B(Hash(c))=-1;
  6. **else** CPD(c', k-1);   //c' and c'' are two CPs of c
  7.   CPD(c'', k-1);
  8.   **if** B(Hash(c'))=1 and B(Hash(c''))=1 **then**
  9.   calculate SPI(c) by core pattern method;
  10.   **if** SPI(c)$\geq$*min_sprev* **then** B(Hash(c))=1
  11.   **else** B(Hash(c))=-1;
  12.   **for** each rest (k-1)-size c''' with the head of "i" in c
  13.   CPD(c''', k-1);
  14. HS_c ← Deal with the results of c'''
  15.   **endfor**
  16.   **else** B(Hash(c))=-1;
  17.   **for** each rest (k-1)-size c''' with the head of "i" in c
  18.   CPD(c''', k-1);
  19. HS_c ←Deal with the results of c'''
  20.   **endfor**
  21.   **endif**
  22. **endif**

In CPD, if c has been identified (i.e., c is a common pattern), then return; Steps 2–5 exit the recursive procedure; Steps 6 and 7 recursively call CPD with the two core patterns c' and c'' of c; Steps 8–15 are for dealing with the case that two core patterns c' and c'' of c are sub-prevalent, while Steps 16–20 deal with the case that c' and c'' are not all sub-prevalent, whereas Steps 12–14 and Steps 17–19 are for dealing with patterns other than the two core patterns, marked as dotted lines in Fig. 3.6.

3.4.3   Analysis of Computational Complexity

The main cost of Algorithm 3.2 comes from performing Partition_1, Partition_2 and the recursive procedure CPD. The cost of Partition_1 + Partition_2 is about $O(n^2)$ because we scan all 2-size sub-prevalent patterns in Partition_1, and because all 2-size non-sub-prevalent patterns are scanned in Partition_2, the total number of 2-size patterns is $n(n - 1)/2$, where n is the number of spatial features.

For the cost of recursive procedure CPD, if we suppose the worst cost of computing a k-size pattern c is $T(k)$, then $T(k)$ satisfies: $T(k) =$

$$\begin{cases} 3 & k = 3 \\ (k - 1)T(k - 1) & k > 3 \end{cases}.$$

A 3-size pattern needs 3 times the intersection operations, and when $k > 3$, in the worst case, all $(k - 1)$-size sub-patterns are recursively called in CPD, and for a k-size pattern c, there are $k - 1$ sub-patterns which are of $(k - 1)$-size and with the same head of c.

Thus $T(k)$ is about $\prod_{i=3}^{k-1} 3 \cdot i$. This is the worst case and includes large amounts of repeated computation. Fortunately, repeated computation has been avoided in the core pattern method.

3.5   Comparison of PBA and PTBA

The core problems of the PTBA presented in Sect. 3.3 are: (1) the candidate search space tree might be too large to store and search when we confront a data set which has a large number of features; (2) the total cost to compute the SPIs of candidate patterns by Lemma 3.2 might be too expensive due to a large number of intersection operations. The PBA is aimed to relieve these two problems.

First, we divide candidates into equivalent classes by Partition_1 and Partition_2, and deal with a pattern in an equivalent class which has the same head each time, so as to resolve the problem of the candidate search space tree being too large.

Second, differing from the PTBA which starts with the identification of the longest patterns, the PBA is performed step by step from 3-size core patterns. With regard to the expected cost of the intersection operations as a whole, the core pattern method is better than the PTBA. For example, for a 6-size pattern $c = \{A, B, C, D, E, F\}$, the cost of directly computing SPI(c) by Lemma 3.2 is 24 intersection operations. Because computing the star participation instance SPIns(A, c) of feature A in c needs 4 times the intersection operations, if c is not sub-prevalent, then the cost of computing a 5-size sub-set of c is 15, and the cost of a 4-size is 8. But if we use PBA, then a 3-size pattern costs 3. To compute a 4-size pattern based on two 3-size core patterns needs 4 times the intersection operations. Similarly, the cost of a 5-size is 5 and 6-size's is 6. Thus, the expected cost of the PTBA for a 6-size pattern

c is $(24 + 54 + 78 + 90)/4 = 61.5$, while the expected cost by the PBA is $(12 + 24 + 34 + 40)/4 = 27.5$. In fact, we have the following Lemma 3.5.

Lemma 3.5 The expected cost ratio of the core pattern method versus the PTB method in identifying a size k ($k > 2$) co-location pattern is about $\frac{2}{k-1}$.

Proof In the following proof, we only consider the computational cost of the two methods where their computational volume is similar to Fig. 3.7, where a 6-size pattern contains 2 size-5 sub-patterns, 3 size-4 sub-patterns, and 4 size-3 sub-patterns.

For the PBA, the total cost of a k-size pattern is $\left(\sum_{i=3}^{k} i \cdot (k - i + 1)^2 \right)$. For example, with a 6-size pattern c, it is $(3 \cdot 4^2 + 4 \cdot 3^2 + 5 \cdot 2^2 + 6 \cdot 1^2) = 110$. So, the expected cost of identifying c is $\left(\sum_{i=3}^{k} i \cdot (k - i + 1)^2 \right) / (k - 2)$.

For the PTBA, the expected cost of a k-size pattern is $\left(\sum_{i=3}^{k} i \cdot (i - 2)^2 \cdot (k - i + 1) \right) / (k - 2)$. For example, with a 6-size pattern c, it is $(3 \cdot 1^2 \cdot 4 + 4 \cdot 2^2 \cdot 3 + 5 \cdot 3^2 \cdot 2 + 6 \cdot 4^2 \cdot 1)/4 = 246/4 = 61.5$.

Consequently, the expected cost ratio τ of two methods is

$$\frac{\left(\sum_{i=3}^{k} i \cdot (k-i+1)^2 \right) / (k-2)}{\left(\sum_{i=3}^{k} i \cdot (i-2)^2 \cdot (k-i+1) \right) / (k-2)} = \frac{\sum_{i=3}^{k} i \cdot (k-i+1)^2}{\sum_{i=3}^{k} i \cdot (i-2)^2 \cdot (k-i+1)}.$$ We note that τ is approximately equal

to the ratio of their medoids. That is $\tau \approx \dfrac{\frac{k+3}{2} \cdot \left(k - \frac{k+3}{2} + 1 \right)^2}{\frac{k+3}{2} \cdot \left(\frac{k+3}{2} - 2 \right)^2 \cdot \left(k - \frac{k+3}{2} + 1 \right)} = \dfrac{\left(k - \frac{k+3}{2} + 1 \right)}{\left(\frac{k+3}{2} - 2 \right)^2} = \dfrac{2(k-1)}{(k-1)^2} = \dfrac{2}{k-1}$.

The explanation of formula $\left(\sum_{i=3}^{k} i \cdot (k - i + 1)^2 \right)$: In the core pattern method, for a k-size pattern c, we need to compute 3 patterns of $k - 2$ size and, at least, 4 patterns of $k - 3$ size. In general, i patterns of $(k - i + 1)$ size need to be computed, until we get a k-size pattern c. Furthermore, the computational cost of a size i pattern is i, and the computation of a size i pattern is based on size $i - 1$ core patterns. So, the cost i of a size i pattern is repeatedly counted $(k - i + 1)$ times.

The explanation of formula $\left(\sum_{i=3}^{k} i \cdot (i - 2)^2 \cdot (k - i + 1) \right)$: In the prefix-tree-based method, for a k-size pattern c, we also need to compute i patterns $(i = 3, \ldots k)$ of $(k - i + 1)$ size where the computational cost of a size i pattern is $i \cdot (i - 2)$ in the prefix-tree-based method. When we compute a size i pattern, we must have already computed all higher patterns, so the cost $i \cdot (i - 2)$ of a size i pattern is repeatedly counted $(i - 2)$ times.

Third, if a pattern considered is not sub-prevalent, PBA could find it sooner because Partition_3 is based on a partition pattern in which SPI is the biggest in all

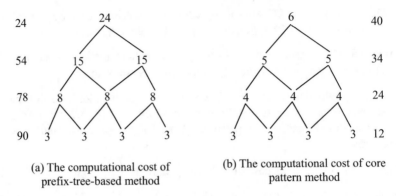

(a) The computational cost of
prefix-tree-based method

(b) The computational cost of core
pattern method

Fig. 3.7 The comparison of a 6-size pattern's computation cost, where (**a**) the PTBA; (**b**) the PBA

the 2-size co-locations with respect to it. In addition, the middle computational results could either be maximal sub-prevalent SCPs or be used in the computation of other corresponding patterns. For example, in Fig. 3.6, if the computation comes to 5-size {A, B, C, D, G} (i.e., its two 4-size core patterns are sub-prevalent), and that it is not sub-prevalent has been determined, then we can declare that the two core patterns {A, B, C, G} and {A, B, D, G} are maximally sub-prevalent up to now. At the same time, the computational results of 3-size patterns {A, B, C} and {A, B, D} could also be used to identify the remaining 4-size patterns marked by dotted lines in Fig. 3.6.

3.6   Experimental Evaluation

In this section, we evaluate the performance of the proposed two algorithms and analyze the difference in the results from the traditional maximal prevalent SCP mining. To aid analysis, we have improved the join-less algorithm (Yoo & Shekhar, 2006) so as to mine all maximal prevalent SCPs. The improved algorithm is called the M-join-less algorithm. We have optimized the implementation of M-join-less and, compared with other algorithms for mining maximal prevalent SCPs, it seems M-join-less can deal with more data for the same run-time.

All algorithms are memory-based and implemented using C# with Intel i3–3240 @3.4 GHz CPU and 4GB of memory. As these are experiments, we have manually verified that the results of all algorithms presented in this section are the expected results.

3.6.1 Synthetic Data Generation

Synthetic data sets were generated using a spatial data generator similar to (Huang et al., 2004; Yoo & Shekhar, 2006). Synthetic data sets allow greater control over studying the effects of interesting parameters.

Table 3.1 describes the parameters used for our data generation. First, we generated F features, and then generated R 2-size core patterns, where the feature types of each 2-size core pattern were randomly chosen from F features. Next, the average number of P 2-size co-location instances per 2-size core pattern was generated. The total number of instances was N. For locating 2-size instances, we randomly chose S 2-size core patterns as a 2-size cluster, and then chose a point randomly in the spatial frame $(D \times D)$, and located a cluster instance within an area $(d \times d)$ whose center is the chosen point, and where cluster instances are united by 2-size co-location instances in a cluster.

To generate our specialized data sets, first, the spatial frame size $D \times D$ controls overall data density. For a fixed total number of instances N, the smaller D was, the denser the data was. Second, the data density in neighborhood areas was controlled by a parameter *clumpy*. When a point was randomly chosen for locating a 2-size cluster instances, a *clumpy* number of cluster instances were generated in the $d \times d$ area. The default *clumpy* value is 1. Finally, the number of instances overlapped in different cluster instances was controlled by the parameter *overlap*, and $N \times overlap$ instances were randomly selected. The parameter values for the synthetic data set used in each experiment are described in Table 3.1.

3.6.2 Comparison of Computational Complexity Factors

We examined the **costs** of the computational complexity factors using 3 synthetic data sets of different density. A sparse data set generated 6-size maximal sub-prevalent SCPs out of 20 features while a dense data set generated 9-size maximal sub-prevalent SCPs out of 20 features. In order to observe the advantage of PTBA compared with PBA, a dense* (see Table 3.2) data set was generated which generated 13 maximal sub-prevalent SCPs out of 15 features. In Table 3.2, all data values except total execution time represent percent values. Overall, we can see that M-join-less algorithm is always slower than our two algorithms, because M-join-less computes prevalence measures of candidates by identifying clique instances, and the cost of computing clique instances is more expensive than that of intersection operations. Thus we discarded M-join-less and only discuss PBA and PTBA in our later comparisons.

With a very dense data set like dense*, PTBA shows much better performance than PBA, but in both sparse and dense data, PBA shows better performance than PTBA. This is because PBA is a bottom-up method and, if a data set is sparse, it will stop more quickly than PTBA, while PTBA is a top-down method, and it can find long maximal sub-prevalent SCPs more quickly. Also we see that in the PTBA, the denser a data set is, the more the percentage $T_{prunning}$ costs. Similarly, the better performance PTBA shows, the worse PBA shows. In addition, we notice that T_{gen_mspcp} and $T_{pruning}$ take a much bigger portion of total costs than any other costs. Clearly, the different candidate identification methods are the core distinction between two algorithms. Note that the factor $T_{order\_features}$ is merely for selecting the core patterns of candidates in PBA.

Table 3.1 Experimental parameters and their values in each experiment

| Parameter | Definition | Experiment tables or figs. | | | | | | |
		T.3.2/F3.8	F.3.9	F.3.10	F.3.11 (a)	F.3.11 (b)	F.3.11 (c)	F.3.11 (d)
R	Number of 2-size core co-locations	60	60	60	60	60	60	60
S	Size of a cluster formed by 2-size core co-locations	6	6	6	6	6	6	6
P	Average number of 2-size instances in 2-size core co-locations	200	200	200	N/100	200	200	200
N	Number of instances	20 K,15 K	20 K	20 K	*	20 K	20 K	20 K
F	Number of features	20,15	20	20	*	20	20	20
D	Spatial frame size($D \times D$)	*	1 K	2 K	2 K	2 K	5 K	1 K
d	Neighborhood distance threshold	15	15	15	15	15	*	15
Min_sprev	Sub-prevalence threshold	0.3	0.2	0.3	0.3	0.3	0.3	*
$Clumpy$	Number of cluster instances generated in a same neighborhood area	1	1	*	1	1	1	1
$Overlap$	Ratio of points overlapped in different cluster instances over all points	0	*	0	0	0	0	0

*Variable values

3.6.3 Comparison of Expected Costs Involved in Identifying Candidates

From Table 3.2, we saw that no one method has the absolute advantage in the two candidate identification methods, so we compared the expected costs of identifying candidates in PBA with those in PTBA.

We used a dense data set and a sparse data set to evaluate the expected performance ratio. The spatial frame size $D \times D$ is chosen as 1000×1000 and 5000×5000 for the dense and sparse data sets, respectively. We selected all k-size candidates for each data set, where size k is 6, 8, 10, 12, 14, 16, and 18. Then, we set *min_sprev* as 0.2, 0.4, 0.6, and 0.8, respectively, obtained each candidate's execution time, and then calculated the average execution time per size for all *min_sprev*. In Fig. 3.8, the y-axis represents the ratio of the average execute time of PBA to the average execute time of PTBA. The results show that, as the size of candidate increases, the expected cost ratio is reduced overall, especially for the sparse data set. At the same time, we also note that the experimental results are basically consistent with the analysis in Sect. 3.5.

3.6.4 Comparison of Candidate Pruning Ratio

We studied the effect of candidate pruning ratios with the overlap ratio, which controls the false maximal sub-prevalent candidates generated from our 2-size sub-prevalent SCPs. In order to make our results more efficient, we reduced the range D and *min_sprev* in order to make sure that the candidate sets are dense enough to perform our experiments.

As Fig. 3.9 shows, as the overlap ratio increases, the pruning ratio also increases in both PTBA and PBA, but PTBA can do better pruning than PBA although PBA

Table 3.2 Comparison of computational complexity factors

Method	M-join-less		PTBA			PBA		
	Data type							
Factor (%)	Sparse	Dense	Sparse	Dense	Dense*	Sparse	Dense	Dense*
$T_{gen\_2\_prev\_col}$	6.12	0.6	0.2	0.001	3.40	16.25	0.9	1.87
T_{gen_candi}	2.58	3.85	1.96	0.29	0.44	–	–	–
$T_{gen\_candi-tree}$	–	–	6.49	0.74	0.74	–	–	–
$T_{gen\_2-non\_prev\_col}$	–	–	–	–	–	2.52	0.001	0.001
$T_{order\_features}$	–	–	–	–	–	13.89	0.002	0.001
$T_{Part\_1 + Part\_2}$	–	–	–	–	–	1.77	0.002	0.002
$T_{Pruning}$	–	–	3.12	39.21	61.53	8.59	4.16	0.26
T_{gen_mspcp}	91.29	95.64	88.19	59.76	33.88	56.89	94.94	97.88
Total execution time (s)	3.03	108.36	0.65	102.17	1.32	0.48	7.23	9.17

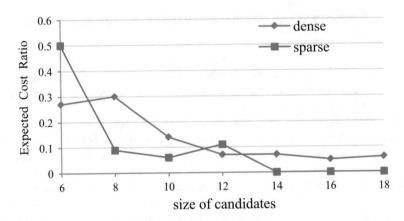

Fig. 3.8 Comparison of the expected cost of identifying candidates

algorithm has a good performance too. This is explained by the fact that when all the 2-size patterns are all sub-prevalent, the PTBA has $2^{\wedge}|F| - (|F| + 1)$ candidates while PBA only has $|F|$ candidates, and if the longest candidate from a prefix-tree generated in PTBA is prevalent, it will prune the whole tree because the remaining candidates are subsets of this candidate. We can also see that the candidate pruning ratio of PTBA is over 90% when the degree of overlap is bigger than 15%, and that of PBA is also over 90% when the degree of overlap is 20%.

3.6.5   Effects of the Parameter Clumpy

We examined the effects of the parameter *clumpy* for PTBA and PBA. *Clumpy* shows the number of cluster instances generated in a same neighborhood area. The bigger the clumpy degree is, the more cluster instances gather in the same neighborhood area. As Fig. 3.10 shows, as *clumpy* increases, PTBA and PBA all increase very slowly. In fact, their $T_{gen\_max\_prev\_coloc}$ is almost the same for different *clumpy* values. Only $T_{gen\_2-prev\_coloc}$ is affected as the clumpy degree increases. So, both PTBA and PBA have good robustness with respect to the parameter *clumpy*.

3.6.6   Scalability Tests

We examined the scalability of PTBA and PBA with several workloads, e.g., different numbers of instances, numbers of features, neighbor distance thresholds, and sub-prevalence thresholds. We compared the total computation time for finding all maximal sub-prevalent SCPs.

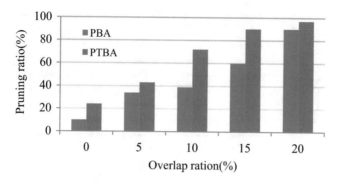

Fig. 3.9 Comparison of candidate pruning ratios

Effect of the number of instances. First, we compared the effect of the number of instances in PTBA and PBA. In order to ensure that each data set generates around 10-size prevalent patterns, we increased P (the average number of 2-size instances in 2-size core co-locations, see Table 3.1) with the increase of the number of instances. As shown in Fig. 3.11(a), when the number of instances is fewer, PBA shows better time performance than PTBA, but as the data set grows denser and denser, PBA spends more and more time on calculation while PTBA drops after 80 K (80,000) instances. When the number of instances reaches 120 K, the data set is dense enough that the longest candidate pattern is sub-prevalent, so PTBA and PBA stop quickly, having spent most time on generating 2-size prevalent patterns. Because PTBA costs more time on creating the prefix tree than PBA costs on Partition_1 and Partition_2, PTBA costs a little more than PBA. The space costs of both algorithms increase as the number of instances increases, and the main reason why PTBA costs much more than PBA when the number of instances is over 100 K is that the data set gets dense enough that PTBA may generate many long-size non-prevalent candidates to be checked while PBA can discard them by checking lower-size subsets. Figure 3.11(a) shows that both algorithms scale to large dense data sets.

Effect of the number of features. In the second experiment, we compared the performance of PTBA and PBA as a function of the number of features. Figure 3.11 (b) shows the results. PTBA is better than PBA on running time when the number of features is over 30. As the number of features increased, the execution time of PTBA decreased, while that of PBA increased. The reason is that, under the same number of instances, the increase of features causes the number of instances per feature to be decreased, which in turn may lead to a decrease in the number of instances per 2-size pattern. PBA spends much more time on Partition_2 and obtains more shorter-size candidates, because the number of non-prevalent 2-size patterns becomes larger. The space costs of the two algorithms are much the same because the data set is sparse and the average size of result co-locations and the average number of row-instances per co-location are quite low, which means that the main space cost of both algorithms is the storage of row-instances. In sparse data sets, PBA may cost more space than PTBA mainly because of the recursive process. Overall, the two

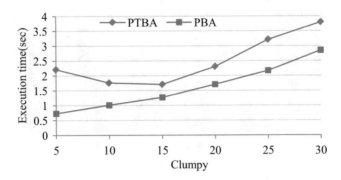

Fig. 3.10 Effects of the parameter clumpy

algorithms both show good performance even if the number of features reaches 50. It needs to be said that when $N > 300{,}000$ and the number of features reaches 40, a memory overflow occurred in the implementation of PTBA.

Effect of neighbor distances. The third experiment examined the effect of different neighbor distances. As Fig. 3.11(c) shows, when the distance threshold is below 100, the time costs of PTBA and PBA both increase quickly because the increase of neighbor distance makes the neighborhood areas larger and increases the number of size-2 co-location instances, although PBA performs better than PTBA. When the distance reaches 120, PTBA becomes a little better than PBA because the neighborhood area is large enough that PTBA can stop earlier than PBA. The space costs of the two algorithms increase as the neighbor distances increase, because a denser data set makes longer size candidates and a larger count of row-instances, and in dense data, PBA performs much better than PTBA.

Effect of sub-prevalence threshold. In the final scalability experiment, we examined the performance effect of different sub-prevalence threshold *min_sprev*. Overall, the execution time decreases for both algorithms as the sub-prevalence threshold increases, as shown in Fig. 3.11(d). However, the PBA method reduces the computation time by a larger magnitude for lower threshold values. With the increase of thresholds, the space costs decrease because a higher threshold may cause fewer candidates with less size and row-instances. When the threshold is low, PTBA will generate much more long candidates than PBA; thus, PBA performs better than PTBA.

3.6.7 Evaluation with Real Data Sets

The experimental real data sets come from the rare plant distribution data sets of the "Three Parallel Rivers of Yunnan Protected Areas." Figure 3.12 gives the distribution of plant data in two-dimensional space, where the X and Y coordinates represent the instances' locations. We can see that this is a zonal plant distribution data,

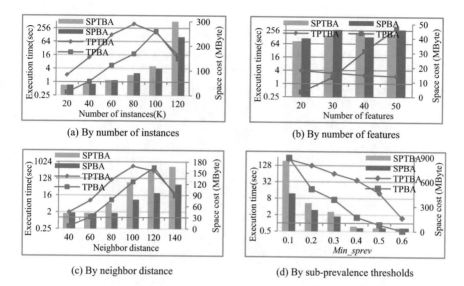

Fig. 3.11 Evaluation and comparison of the two algorithms, where (**a**) by number of instances; (**b**) by number of features; (**c**) by neighbor distance; (**d**) by sub-prevalence thresholds

because plants are affected by the effects of altitude or river formations. Zonal data are common in natural ecological studies.

First, we tested the mining result difference between maximal sub-prevalent SCPs with star participation instances and maximal prevalent SCPs with clique instances. In the experiment, the rare plant distribution data set in Fig. 3.12 was chosen, where the number of features (plants) is 31 and the number of instances is 336. We used a rectangular spatial framework of size 130 K × 130 K, a neighbor distance threshold $d = 12,000$ m, and prevalence thresholds $min\_sprev = min\_prev = 0.3$. Table 3.3 shows the number of maximal sub-prevalent SCPs/maximal prevalent SCPs with different lengths.

From Table 3.3 we can see that, with the same data set and parameter settings, the maximal sub-prevalent SCP mining method can generate longer patterns than the maximal prevalent SCP mining method. This is because, if an instance occurs in a clique instance, it must be in a star participation instance, but a star neighbor relationship may not be a clique relationship. From the table, we also found that the percentage of long patterns in maximal sub-prevalent SCPs is greater than that in maximal prevalent SCPs. There are 15.5% maximal sub-prevalent SCPs whose size is over 7, compared to only 4.1% maximal prevalent SCPs. Generally, users are more interested in long patterns, because long patterns contain more interesting information and short patterns usually are obvious.

Let us take some mined results to analyze in detail. Three mined 11-size maximal sub-prevalent SCPs are {B, G, J, O, Q, R, T, V, W, c, e}, {G, J, O, Q, R, T, V, W, a, c, e}, and {G, H, J, O, Q, R, V, W, a, c, e}, while three mined 10-size maximal prevalent SCPs are {G, J, O, R, T, V, W, a, c, e}, {G, J, Q, R, T, V, W, a, c, e}, and

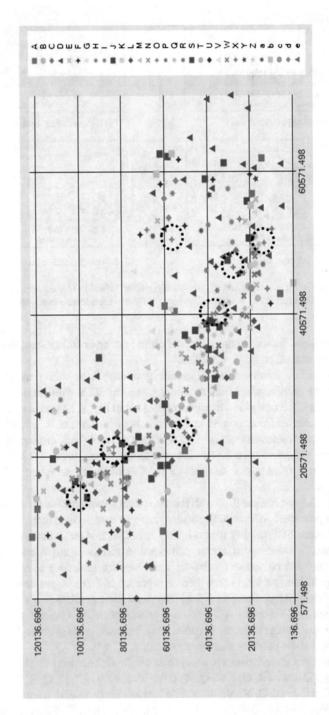

Fig. 3.12 The distribution of a certain plant data

{J, O, Q, R, T, V, W, a, c, e}. We note that each 10-size maximal prevalent SCP is a sub-set of one of the 11-size maximal sub-prevalent SCPs. We mark the rare plant "O" with dashed circles in Fig. 3.12, and we can see that it is basically distributed in an axial line which is the focus area of growing plants. That is why it occurs in three mined 11-size maximal sub-prevalent SCPs, and similarly the plants "G" and "Q."

Second, we used a large-scale vegetation distribution data set in the "Three Parallel Rivers of Yunnan Protected Area" to examine the efficiency of the PBA method. In this data set, the total number of features is 15, and the total number of instances is 487,857. We used 0.3 as *min_sprev*, and 1000, 3000, and 5000 m as the neighborhood distance thresholds, respectively. The running time of PBA is respectively 148.26 (sec), 1967.84 (sec), and 7906.74 (sec).

3.7 Related Work

Koperski and Han (1995) first proposed the problem of mining association rules based on spatial relationships. The work discovers the subsets of spatial features frequently associated with a specific *reference feature*. A set of neighboring objects of each reference object is converted to a transaction. A top-down, progressive refinement method to discover all rules from the transactions was presented in Koperski and Han (1995), and Wang et al. (2005) proposed a novel method based on the partition of spatial relationships for mining multilevel spatial association rules from the transactions. In this method, the introduction of an equivalence partition tree method makes the discovery of rules efficient.

Morimoto (2001) discovered frequent co-located features sets using a *support count* measure. This approach uses a space partitioning and non-overlap grouping scheme for identifying co-located instances. However, the explicit space partitioning approach may miss co-location instances across partitions. Shekhar and Huang (2001) and Huang et al. (2004) proposed the *minimum participation ratio* based on *clique instances* to measure the frequency of a co-location pattern. This is a statistically meaningful interest measure for spatial co-location pattern mining. Based on the interest measure, many mining algorithms were proposed (Huang et al., 2004, 2005, 2006; Wang et al., 2008, 2009a, b, 2013a, 2018a, Xiao et al., 2008; Yao et al., 2016, 2017, 2021; Yoo & Shekhar, 2006; Yoo & Bow, 2011a, 2012, 2019; Li & Shekhar, 2018; Bao & Wang, 2019; Li et al., 2020). Specifically, Huang et al. (2004) presented a classic *join-based* mining algorithm. The core idea of this approach is to find size k clique instances by joining the instances of its size $k - 1$ co-locations where the first $k - 2$ objects are common and then checking the neighbor relationship between the $k - 1$th objects. Yoo and Shekhar (2006) proposed a star-neighborhood-based *joinless* algorithm. The joinless method uses an instance-lookup scheme instead of the instance join operation as used in the join-based method for identifying clique instances. Wang et al. (2008) put forward a *CPI-tree* algorithm which uses a tree-structure to store the neighbor relationships between spatial instances, with the benefit that the clique instances of candidate patterns can be quickly generated by CPI-tree.

Table 3.3 Mining results on the plant data set in Fig. 3.12

Size	No. of MSPCPs	No. of MPCPs	Size	No. of MSPCPs	No. of MPCPs
2	5	15	7	23	31
3	41	70	8	35	9
4	64	115	9	10	5
5	95	98	10	7	3
6	72	73	11	3	–

In terms of uncertain data, Liu and Huang (2013) utilized a probability density function to describe the uncertainty of spatial instances' locations, defined as the expected distance between instances and proposed the UJoin-based algorithm. Based on the concept of semantic proximity neighborhoods under the fuzzy equivalent classes of instances, Wang et al. (2010) studied the problem of discovering co-location patterns from interval data. Wang et al. (2013a, b) considered the uncertainty of spatial instances' existence, defined a prevalence probability and expected participation index based on a possible world model, and then provided exact and approximation algorithms that mine probabilistic prevalent co-location patterns. Ouyang et al. (2017) proposed two new kinds of co-location pattern mining for *fuzzy objects*, single co-location pattern mining (SCP) and range co-location pattern mining (RCP), for mining co-location patterns at a membership threshold or within a membership range.

To deal with the situation where there exists a rare feature in the data sets (i.e., the number of instances with this feature is significantly smaller than those with other features), Huang et al. (2006) proposed a *maximal participation ratio* (maxPR) interest measure and a *maxPrune* algorithm based on a weak monotonicity property of the maxPR measure, and Yang et al. (2019, 2021) defined a *minimum weighted participation ratio* interest measure and gave a mining algorithm based on this ratio, which can not only mine the prevalent co-location patterns with rare features, but also exclude the non-prevalent patterns.

In some cases, co-location patterns are not prevalent globally, or some low participation index patterns are still prevalent in a specific region. Therefore, regional co-location pattern mining has become a research focus (Akbari et al., 2015; Celik et al., 2007). Clearly, the huge size of prevalent co-location patterns does not help the user easily retrieve relevant information, and this observation leads to various definitions of redundancy in order to limit the number of spatial prevalent co-location patterns (Wang et al., 2009b, 2018a, b; Yoo & Bow, 2011a, b, 2012). Recently domain-driven spatial co-location pattern discovery has been attracting more researchers (Fang et al., 2017; Lu et al., 2017, 2018; Wang et al., 2017a).

Although there has been a lot of research about the spatial co-location pattern mining, the problem of sub-prevalent co-location pattern mining was first tackled by us in Wang et al. (2017b), and the enlarged work was then published in Wang et al. (2019b).

Our work on the interest measure lies between the *reference object* model of Koperski and Han (1995) and the *minimum participation ratio* measure of Shekhar and Huang (2001, 2004). With no specific reference feature, directly applying the model of Koperski and Han (1995) for co-location mining may not capture the co-locations found by the techniques in this chapter, while the measure in Shekhar and Huang (2001, 2004) may miss some reasonable and useful co-located patterns in practical applications due to its requirement of clique instances. In the designs of the algorithms for mining maximal sub-prevalent SCPs, the idea of using a prefix-tree structure to store all maximal candidates comes from the work presented in Wang et al. (2009b); the idea of pruning breadth-first in candidate space search tree can be traced back to Yoo and Bow (2011a) and Yoo and Bow (2012). In the literature we have found no mention of his chapter's core pattern method based on partitions.

3.8 Chapter Summary

In this chapter, we have analyzed the limit of the traditional *clique instances*–based measure in some practical applications. A new concept of *sub-prevalent* co-location patterns based on *star participation instances* has been defined. It was especially important to show that the proposed star participation ratio (SPR) and star participation index (SPI) obey the downward closure property, thus allowing maximal sub-prevalent SCP mining and interactive pruning.

The sub-prevalent co-location miner, which contains two novel algorithms (PTBA and PBA) for mining maximal sub-prevalent SCPs, was presented. PTBA adopts a typical candidate generate-and-test method starting from candidates with the longest pattern-size, while PBA is performed step by step from 3-size core patterns.

The proposed algorithms were evaluated using theoretical and experimental methods. Empirical evaluation shows that the PBA performs much better than the PTBA when we confront sparse data sets but it becomes slower in very dense data sets. Compared with the M-join-less algorithm for mining maximal prevalent SCPs, our miner is more efficient.

The concept of *maximal prevalent SCPs* discussed in Chaps. 2 and 3 is based on a lossy condensed representation, which can infer the original collection of prevalent SCPs but not their PI values. Similar to the *closed frequent itemsets* in transactional data sets, Yoo and Bow (2011b) define a prevalent co-location c as *closed* if there exists no proper prevalent co-location c' such that $c \subset c'$ and $PI(c) = PI(c')$. The introduction of *closed prevalent SCPs* creates a lossless condensed representation, which can infer not only the original collection of prevalent SCPs but also their PI values.

In Chap. 4, we will discuss a novel method of mining closed prevalent SCPs which effectively has a lossless condensed representation of all prevalent SCPs.

Chapter 4
SPI-Closed Prevalent Co-location Patterns

4.1 Introduction

A spatial co-location pattern is a set of spatial features frequently co-occuring in nearby geographic spaces. Similar to *closed frequent itemset mining, closed co-location pattern (CCP) mining* was proposed for lossless condensed collections of all prevalent co-location patterns. However, the state-of-the-art methods for mining condensed CCPs are derived from closed frequent itemset mining and do not consider the intrinsic characteristics of spatial co-location patterns, e.g., the spatial feature interactions in the prevalence metrics of co-location patterns, thus causing serious inclusion issues in CCP mining.

This problem drives the content of this chapter. The main contributions of this chapter to spatial co-location patterns mining will be:

(1) A novel *losslessly condensed representation* of spatially prevalent co-location patterns, *super participation index-closed (SPI-closed)* is proposed.
(2) An efficient *SPI-closed Miner* is designed to effectively capture the SPI-closed prevalent co-locations, alongside the development of three additional pruning strategies to make the SPI-closed Miner more efficient. This method captures richer feature interactions in spatial co-locations and solves the inclusion issue found in existing CCP methods.
(3) A performance evaluation conducted on both synthetic and real-life data sets shows that SPI-closed Miner reduces the number of CCPs by up to 50%, and runs much faster than the baseline CCP mining algorithm described in Yoo and Bow (2011a).

Figure 4.1 presents the organization of this chapter. Section 4.2 discusses why the SPI-closed prevalent co-location is developed for mining lossless co-locations.

From Wang, L., Bao, X., Chen, H. and Cao L.: Effective Lossless Condensed Representation and Discovery of Spatial Co-location Patterns, *Information Sciences* 436 (2018), 197–213.

© The Author(s), under exclusive license to Springer Nature Singapore Pte Ltd. 2022
L. Wang et al., *Preference-based Spatial Co-location Pattern Mining*, Big Data Management, https://doi.org/10.1007/978-981-16-7566-9_4

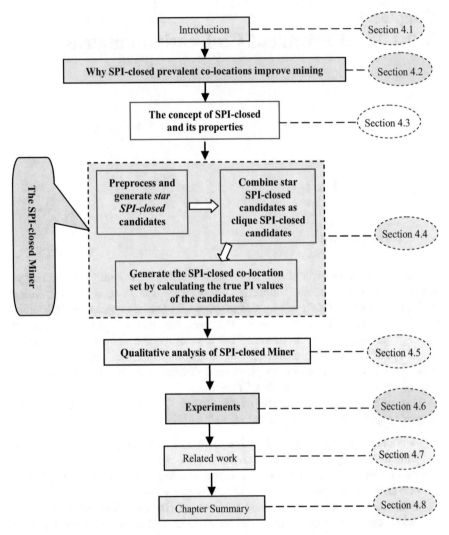

Fig. 4.1 The organization of Chap. 4

Section 4.3 defines the concept of *super participation index-closed* (SPI-closed) and analyzes its properties. In Sect. 4.4, a SPI-closed Miner is presented and three pruning strategies to make SPI-closed Miner efficient are introduced. Section 4.5 carries out the qualitative analysis of the SPI-closed Miner. Section 4.6 presents the work related to the high-quality representation of the prevalent co-location patterns. The experimental results are presented in Sect. 4.7. Section 4.8 summarizes the chapter.

4.2 Why SPI-Closed Prevalent Co-locations Improve Mining

Application areas such as earth science (Verhein & Al-Naymat, 2007), public health (Li et al., 2016), public transportation (An et al., 2016; Yu, 2016; Moosavi et al., 2019; Yang & Wang, 2020; Wang et al., 2020), environmental management (Akbari et al., 2015), social media services (Song et al., 2015; Zhang et al., 2016), location services (Chang et al., 2017; Wang et al., 2015b; Yang et al., 2018a), multimedia (Chang et al., 2016; Ma et al., 2017; Zhu et al., 2015a, b, 2016, 2017), and so on produce large and rich spatial data. Potentially valuable knowledge is embedded in such data in various spatial features, and spatial co-location pattern mining has been developed to identify interesting but hidden relationships between spatial features (Shekhar & Huang, 2001; Huang et al., 2004).

A spatial co-location pattern (co-location) represents a set of spatial features that frequently co-occur in spatial proximity (Shekhar & Huang, 2001). For example, West Nile Virus often appears in the regions with poor mosquito control and the presence of birds. Spatial co-location patterns yield an important insight for various applications such as urban facility distribution analysis (Yu, 2016), e-commerce (Zhang et al., 2004), and ecology (Wang et al., 2013b). A common framework of spatial co-location pattern mining uses the frequencies of a set of spatial features participating in a co-location to measure the prevalence (known as participation index (Huang et al., 2004), or PI for short) and requires a user-specified minimum PI threshold M to find interesting co-locations. M determines the level of prevalence of identified co-locations and M may have to be small to avoid overlooking co-locations. However, a small M might induce a larger number of co-locations with lower actionability (Cao, 2010; Cao, 2015; Khan et al., 2017), so it is difficult for a user to determine a suitable value for M.

Figure 4.2(a) shows an example spatial data set. There are four different spatial features $F = \{A, B, C, D\}$ with each instance denoted by a feature type and a numeric ID value, e.g., A.1. Edges among the instances indicate spatial neighboring relationships. Feature A has four instances, B has five instances, C has three instances, and D has four instances in the data set. Figure 4.2(b) lists all possible co-locations in F, and their *co-location instances* and their corresponding *PI* (the definitions of *co-location instances* and *PI* are provided in Sect. 4.3). If M is given as 0.3, we can see that the prevalent co-location set of this data set is $\{\{A, B, C, D\}, \{A, B, C\}, \{A, B, D\}, \{A, C, D\}, \{B, C, D\}, \{A, B\}, \{A, C\}, \{A, D\}, \{B, C\}, \{B, D\}, \{C, D\}\}$ since all their PI values are no less than 0.3.

Condensed representations describe small collections of prevalent co-locations such that it is possible to infer the original collection of prevalent co-locations. The concept of *maximal co-locations* (Wang et al., 2009b; Yoo & Bow, 2011b) is based on a lossy condensed representation, which infers the original collection of prevalent co-locations but not their PI values. The introduction of *closed prevalent co-location patterns (CCPs)* creates a lossless condensed representation (Yoo & Bow, 2011a, 2012), which can infer not only the original collection of prevalent co-locations but

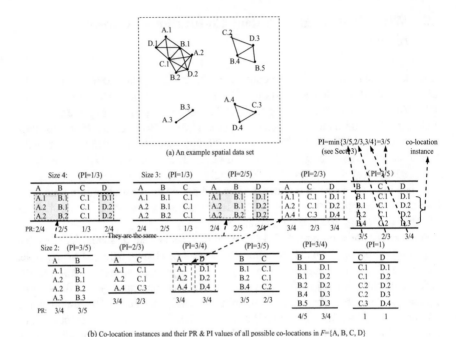

(a) An example spatial data set

PI=min{3/5,2/3,3/4}=3/5 (see Sect.3)   co-location instance

Size 4: (PI=1/3)

A	B	C	D
A.1	B.1	C.1	D.1
A.2	B.1	C.1	D.2
A.2	B.2	C.1	D.2
PR: 2/4	2/5	1/3	2/4

Size 3: (PI=1/3)

A	B	C
A.1	B.1	C.1
A.2	B.1	C.1
A.2	B.2	C.1
2/4	2/5	1/3

(PI=2/5)

A	B	D
A.1	B.1	D.1
A.2	B.1	D.2
A.2	B.2	D.2
2/4	2/5	2/4

(PI=2/3)

A	C	D
A.1	C.1	D.1
A.2	C.1	D.2
A.4	C.3	D.4
3/4	2/3	3/4

(PI=3/5)

B	C	D
B.1	C.1	D.1
B.1	C.1	D.2
B.2	C.1	D.2
B.4	C.2	D.3
3/5	2/3	3/4

They are the same

Size 2: (PI=3/5)

A	B
A.1	B.1
A.2	B.1
A.2	B.2
A.3	B.3
PR: 3/4	3/5

(PI=2/3)

A	C
A.1	C.1
A.2	C.1
A.4	C.3
3/4	2/3

(PI=3/4)

A	D
A.1	D.1
A.2	D.2
A.4	D.4
3/4	3/4

(PI=3/5)

B	C
B.1	C.1
B.2	C.1
B.4	C.2
3/5	2/3

(PI=3/4)

B	D
B.1	D.1
B.1	D.2
B.2	D.2
B.4	D.3
B.5	D.3
4/5	3/4

(PI=1)

C	D
C.1	D.1
C.1	D.2
C.2	D.2
C.2	D.3
C.3	D.4
1	1

(b) Co-location instances and their PR & PI values of all possible co-locations in F={A, B, C, D}

Fig. 4.2 An illustrative example, where (**a**) an example spatial data set; (**b**) co-location instances and their PR & PI values

also their PI values. A prevalent co-location c is *closed* if there exists no proper prevalent co-location c' such that $c \subset c'$ and PI$(c) = $ PI(c') (Yoo & Bow, 2011a). This concept is similar to the *closed frequent itemsets* found in transactional data sets (Pei et al., 2000; Wang et al., 2003; Zaki & Hsiao, 2002). For example, the CCPs of the data set in Fig. 4.2(a) are {A, B, C, D}, {A, B, D}, {A, C, D}, {B, C, D}, {A, B}, {A, D}, {B, D}, and {C, D} because PI({A, B, C, D }) = PI({A, B, C}), PI({A, C, D }) = PI({A, C}) and PI({B, C, D }) = PI({B, C}).

Nevertheless, the above methods can cause serious confusion in mining CCPs as illustrated by the problem in Fig. 4.2(b). The co-location instance of measuring the PI value of pattern {A, B, D} is contained by the co-location instance of its super-pattern {A, B, C, D} (as shown in the dotted boxes in the co-location instances of {A, B, C, D} and {A, B, D}). The same situation occurs in the co-location instances of {A, C, D} and {A, D}. That means the PI values of {A, B, D} and {A, D} can be inferred from their super-pattern {A, B, C, D} and {A, C, D}, respectively. However, PI({A, B, D}) $\neq$ PI({A, B, C, D}) and PI({A, D}) $\neq$ PI({A, C, D}), so {A, B, C, D}, {A, B, D}, {A, C, D}, and {A, D} are all in the set of CCPs.

The above confusion is essentially caused by the direct transplant to CCP mining of the concept of *closed frequent itemsets* used in transactional data, where the CCP mining is a lossless condensed representation of the prevalent co-locations. However, spatial feature interactions are different from the feature relations in transactional data, and spatial co-location pattern mining is different from frequent itemset mining. CCP involves not only a *participation index* to measure the prevalence of co-locations but also a *participation ratio* to measure the prevalence of spatial features in co-locations, and so differs from the support/confidence measures of frequent itemset mining.

To address the intrinsic characteristics of spatial feature interactions and CCP mining in spatial co-locations, we first define the concept of a *super participation index* SPI($c|c'$), which is the participation index of the co-location pattern c in its super-pattern c'. The concept of *SPI-closed* is then introduced to more effectively and losslessly condense the collections of prevalent co-location patterns. We show that the *SPI-covered* relationship (see Definition 4.7) is a pseudo partial order in the prevalent co-location set. A theoretical analysis is provided which shows that SPI-closed reduces the number of closed co-locations by up to 50% compared to existing methods when the number of spatial features is sufficiently large. Lastly, an efficient *SPI-closed Miner* is proposed to mine SPI-closed prevalent co-locations, and three pruning strategies are developed to make the SPI-closed Miner more efficient.

Our experimental evaluation shows that SPI-closed Miner runs much faster than the closed prevalent co-location pattern mining algorithm in Yoo and Bow (2011a), which itself is a very fast closed prevalent co-location mining method and also the only one available in current literature. This is because our method manages to capture richer information in spatial feature interactions and spatial co-locations.

4.3   The Concept of SPI-Closed and Its Properties

The definitions related to classic co-location pattern mining are first reviewed; then the concept of *super participation index-closed (SPI-closed)* is defined and its properties are analyzed.

4.3.1   Classic Co-location Pattern Mining

A spatial feature f_i represents a specific aspect of information in a spatial region. For example, the species of a plant in a geographical area is a feature. An occurrence of f_i at a location is called an *instance* of f_i. For example, a plant of certain species is an instance. The *spatial neighbor relationship NR* describes the relationships between spatial feature instances. Two spatial feature instances i_1 and i_2 form an *NR*, denoted as $NR(i_1, i_2)$, if *distance*$(i_1, i_2) \leq d$, where d is a distance threshold to determine how close the neighbors are.

Given a spatial feature set F, a *spatial co-location pattern c* is a subset of the feature set F. The number of features in c is called the size of c. For example, if $F = \{A, B, C\}$, and $\{A, B\}$ co-occurs more than a threshold M, then it is a prevalent co-location with size 2. The spatial prevalent co-location pattern (PCP) mining problem can be formulated as follows.

Definition 4.1 (PCP mining) Given a co-location pattern set *CP* and a *quality predicate* (or a *prevalence predicate*) q ($q \rightarrow \{0, 1\}$, where 0 refers to non-prevalent, and 1 indicates prevalent) that measures the quality of *CP*, PCP mining discovers all prevalent co-location patterns $\{c_1, c_2, \ldots c_n\}$, which have $q(c_i) = 1$.

In practice, to make the predicate q more flexible and applicable for real-life applications, q is usually defined by a quality measure $\partial: CP \rightarrow [0, 1]$ in terms of a domain-specific threshold value $M \in [0, 1]$:

$$q(c) = \begin{cases} 1 & if\ \partial(c) \geq M \\ 0 & otherwise \end{cases} \tag{4.1}$$

The *minimum participation ratio (PR)* (renamed the *participation index (PI)*) is a frequently used quality measure, as in (Huang et al., 2004; Wang et al., 2008; etc.). Before defining PR and PI, we define the concepts of *row instance* and *co-location instance*. If there is a set of instances $I = \{i_1, i_2, \ldots, i_m\}$ such that $\{NR(i_j, i_k)\ |\ 1 \leq j \leq m,\ 1 \leq k \leq m\}$, then I is called an *NR clique*. If an *NR* clique I contains all the features in a co-location pattern c, but there is not a proper subset of I containing all the features in c, then I is called a *row instance* of c. The set of all row instances of c is called a *co-location instance* (or more often called a *table instance*) of c, denoted as $T(c)$.

Definition 4.2 (Participation ratio) The *participation ratio* $PR(c, f_i)$ of feature f_i in a co-location c is the fraction of instances of f_i that occur in $T(c)$, i.e.,

$$PR(c, f_i) = \frac{Number\ of\ distinct\ instances\ of\ f_i\ in\ T(c)}{Number\ of\ instances\ of\ f_i} \tag{4.2}$$

Definition 4.3 (Participation index) The *participation index* $PI(c)$ of a co-location pattern c is the minimum participation ratio $PR(c, f_i)$ among all features $\{f_i\}$ in c, *i.e.*,

$$PI(c) = \min_{f_i \in c}\{PR(c, f_i)\} \tag{4.3}$$

A co-location c is considered *prevalent* if $PI(c) \geq M$, where M is a user-specified prevalence threshold.

For example, for the pattern $c = \{A, B, C, D\}$ in Fig. 4.2, the co-location instance $T(c) = \{\{A.1, B.1, C.1, D.1\}, \{A.2, B.1, C.1, D.2\}, \{A.2, B.2, C.1, D.2\}\}$. Feature A has a participation ratio $PR(c, A)$ of 2/4 since only A.1 and A.2 among the four instances participate in its co-location instance, and $PR(c, B)$, $PR(c, C)$ and $PR(c, D)$ are 2/5, 1/3 and 2/4, respectively. The participation index of c is the minimum of these four participation ratios, i.e., $PI(c) = 1/3$.

The PR measures the prevalence strength of a feature in a co-location pattern, and the PI measures the prevalence strength of a co-location pattern. Wherever a feature in a co-location pattern c is observed, all other features in c can be observed in the feature's neighborhood with a probability of $PI(c) \geq M$. The PI and PR measures satisfy the *anti-monotonicity* property (a *downward closure property*, i.e., $PI(c) \geq PI$ (c') for any $c \subset c'$), which enables level-wise search (like Apriori) (Huang et al., 2004). This kind of search method has good performance when a given threshold M is high and the neighborhood relations of spatial data are sparse. Unfortunately, an Apriori-based co-location discovery algorithm not only examines all of the 2^k subsets of each size k feature set but also generates numerous irrelevant patterns.

Lossless condensed representations are the diminished descriptions of the prevalent co-location collections such that it is possible to infer the original collection of prevalent co-locations and their PI values by inference methods. The introduction of *closed co-location patterns* (CCP) creates a lossless condensed representation (Yoo & Bow, 2011a), which can not only infer the original collection of PCPs but their PI values as well. However, the condensing power of CCP mining methods is quite limited.

4.3.2 The Concept of SPI-Closed

By analyzing the properties of the PR and PI measures of spatial co-location patterns, such as their anti-monotonicity, we introduce a new lossless condensed representation method of PCPs, i.e., *super participation index closed* (*SPI-closed*) *co-locations*, which effectively improves the condensing power when mining CCPs. The related definitions are as follows.

Definition 4.4 (The super participation index SPI(c|c')) Let c and c' be two co-locations, and $c \subset c'$. The super participation index $SPI(c|c')$ of c in super-pattern c' is defined as the minimum $PR(c', f_i)$ among all features $\{f_i\}$ in c, *i.e.*,

$$SPI(c|c') = min\{PR(c', f_i), f_i \in c\} \tag{4.4}$$

Example 4.1 In the data set of Fig. 4.2(a), $SPI(\{A, C, D\}|\{A, B, C, D\})=min\{PR(\{A, B, C, D\}, A)=2/4, PR(\{A, B, C, D\}, C)=1/3, PR(\{A, B, C, D\}, D) = 2/4\} = 1/3$. Similarly, $SPI(\{A, B, D\}|\{A, B, C, D\})=2/5$.

Definition 4.5 (SPI-closed co-location) A co-location c is *SPI-closed* if and only if its PI value is greater than the SPI value of c in any of its super-patterns c' which are *SPI-closed*, i.e., if and only if

$$(c \subset c') \text{ and } (c' \text{ is } SPI - closed \rightarrow PI(c) > SPI(c|c')) \tag{4.5}$$

The *SPI-closed* definition is recursive in this presented form. This is to ensure that an *SPI-closed* co-location set not only can infer the original collection of prevalent co-locations but their PI values as well. Accordingly, the discovery of *SPI-closed* co-locations has to progress from the largest size to size 2.

Recall the traditional concept of *closed* co-location defined in Yoo and Bow (2011a): A co-location c is *closed* if and only if its PI value is greater than the PI value of any of its super-patterns c', i.e., if and only if

$$c \subset c' \rightarrow \text{PI}(c) > \text{PI}(c') \tag{4.6}$$

In the remainder of this chapter, we call such closed co-locations *PI-closed co-locations* to distinguish the classic closed co-locations from our defined *SPI-closed* co-locations.

Example 4.2 Taking the example data set in Fig. 4.2(a), if $M = 0.3$, then {A, B, C, D} is an *SPI-closed* co-location since PI({A, B, C}) = SPI({A, B, C}|{A, B, C, D}) = PI({A, B, C, D}) and PI({A, B, D}) = SPI({A, B, D}|{A, B, C, D}) > PI ({A, B, C, D}), so {A, B, C} and {A, B, D} are both *non-SPI-closed* co-locations, but {A, B, D} is *PI-closed*.

Definition 4.6 (SPI-closed prevalent co-location) An *SPI-closed* co-location c is an *SPI-closed* prevalent co-location if c is *SPI-closed* and PI(c) $\geq M$, where M is a user-specified threshold.

For simplicity, we use *SPI-closed* co-locations to represent *SPI-closed* prevalent co-location patterns.

4.3.3   The Properties of SPI-Closed

In this sub-section, we analyze the properties of SPI-closed.

Definition 4.7 (SPI-covered (or PI-covered)) For a co-location c, if there is a co-location c' such that $c \subset c'$ and PI(c) = SPI($c|c'$) (PI(c) = PI(c')), we say c is *SPI-covered* (or *PI-covered*) by c'.

Lemma 4.1 If $c \subset c'$ and c is *PI-covered* by c', then c must be *SPI-covered* by c'.

Proof If c' PI-covers c, then PI(c) = PI(c'). According to the anti-monotonicity of PR and PI, PI(c) $\geq$ SPI($c|c'$) $\geq$ PI(c'). Therefore, PI(c) = SPI($c|c'$) holds, i.e., c' SPI-covers c.

Lemma 4.2 The *SPI-covered* relationship is a pseudo partial order in the prevalent co-location pattern set, such that:

(1) c is *SPI*-covered by c itself. (reflexivity).
(2) if c is *SPI-covered* by c' and c' is *SPI-covered* by c, then $c = c'$ (anti-symmetry).
(3) if $c \subset c' \subset c''$, PI(c) = PI(c') and c' is *SPI-covered* by c'', then c must be *SPI-covered* by c'' (pseudo-transitivity).

Proof By the concept of *SPI-covered*, it is easy to verify that the first two properties are true. We prove the third statement below.

According to the conditions of the third statement and related definitions, if c is not *SPI-covered* by c'', then

$PI(c) > min\{PR(c'', f_i), f_i \in c\}$

$\geq min\{PR(c'', f_i), f_i \in c'\}$ $(c \subset c')$

$= min\{PR(c', f_i), f_i \in c'\}$ (by c' is *SPI-covered* by c'')

$= PI(c')$ (by the PI definition)

$\Rightarrow PI(c) > PI(c')$, contradiction.

Hence, c must be *SPI-covered* by c''.

We note that the *PI-covered* relationship satisfies transitivity, but the *SPI-covered* relationship does not. That is why the condition "c' is *SPI-closed*" is put into Definition 4.5. Otherwise, the main point of the closure, which is able to deduce the prevalence of deleted patterns by looking at the remaining patterns, will be lost. The process of discovering *SPI-closed* co-locations still has to progress from the largest size down to size 2, but our new *SPI-closed* outperforms the traditional concept of *PI-closed* defined in Yoo and Bow (2011a), i.e., the set of *SPI-closed* co-locations $S_{SPI\text{-}closed}$ is smaller than the set of *PI-closed* co-locations $S_{PI\text{-}closed}$.

Lemma 4.3 If $c \in S_{SPI\text{-}closed}$, then $c \in S_{PI\text{-}closed}$. However, $c \in S_{SPI\text{-}closed}$ might not hold when $c \in S_{PI\text{-}closed}$.

Proof If $c \in S_{SPI\text{-}closed}$, for any of c's super-patterns c' which are in $S_{SPI\text{-}closed}$, we have $PI(c) > SPI(c|c')$. According to the anti-monotonicity of PR and PI, $SPI(c| c') \geq PI(c')$. Therefore, $PI(c) > PI(c')$. For any of c's super-patterns c'' which comes from $S_{SPI\text{-}closed}$, if $PI(c) = PI(c'')$ then there exists c'''s super-pattern c''' which is in $S_{SPI\text{-}closed}$, and c is *SPI-covered* by c''' (by Lemma 4.2(3)), so we infer $c \notin S_{SPI\text{-}closed}$ (contradiction). Thus, $PI(c) > PI(c'')$. In summary, $c \in S_{PI\text{-}closed}$.

Conversely, we give a counter example: $\{A, B, D\}$ is a *PI-closed* co-location in the data set of Fig. 4.2(a), i.e., $\{A, B, D\} \in S_{PI\text{-}closed}$, but it is not *SPI-closed*, i.e., $\{A, B, D\} \notin S_{SPI\text{-}closed}$.

Accordingly, can we estimate how many fewer co-locations are in $S_{SPI\text{-}closed}$ than in $S_{PI\text{-}closed}$. For a k-size co-location c, if $PI(c) = min\{PR(c, f_i), f_i \in c\} = PR(c, f_s)$, there are $k - 1$ $(k - 1)$-size co-locations containing feature f_s but only one $(k - 1)$-size co-location that does not contain it. We call co-locations that do not contain the minimum PR feature of their super-patterns *should-be-closed* co-locations since the probability that they are *PI-closed* is generally higher. Other co-locations are called *might-be-closed* co-locations. For the data set in Fig. 4.2(a) where $PI(\{A, B, C, D\}) = PR(\{A, B, C, D\}, C)$, C is the minimum PR feature of the 4-size co-location $\{A, B, C, D\}$. Thus 3-size co-locations $\{A, B, C\}$, $\{A, C, D\}$ and $\{B, C, D\}$ containing C are *might-be-closed*, and $\{A, B, D\}$, which does not contain C, is a 3-size *should-be-closed* co-location.

Some of the *should-be-closed* co-locations might be non-SPI-closed. We denote them as *not-SPI-closed*. It may be that the fraction of *should-be-closed* co-locations compared to *not-SPI-closed* co-locations (denoted as *FR(should-be-closed, not-SPI-*

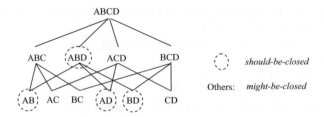

Fig. 4.3 The should-be-closed and might-be-closed patterns of the data set in Fig. 4.2(a)

closed)) is almost equal to *FR*(*should-be-closed + might-be-closed, not-PI-closed*), when the following lemma is useful.

Lemma 4.4 If $|F| = n$ and *FR*(*should-be-closed, not-SPI-closed*) $\approx$ *FR* (*should-be-closed + might-be-closed, not-PI-closed*), then $(|S_{PI\text{-}closed}| - |S_{SPI\text{-}closed}|)/|S_{PI\text{-}closed}| \approx (2^{n-1} - n)/(2^n - (n + 1))$.

Proof
(1) If $|F| = n$, there are $2^n - (n + 1)$ possible co-locations in F. For example, if $n=4$, there are 11 possible co-locations (*should-be-closed + might-be-closed*) in $F = \{A, B, C, D\}$.
(2) There are at most $2^{n-1} - n$ *should-be-closed* co-locations in $2^n - (n + 1)$ possible co-locations. For example, if $F = \{A, B, C, D\}$, there is one 3-size *should-be-closed* co-location and three 2-size *should-be-closed* co-locations in 11 possible co-locations (see Fig. 4.3).

Combining (1) with (2), under the condition that *FR*(*should-be-closed, not-SPI-closed*) $\approx$ *FR*(*should-be-closed + might-be-closed, not-PI-closed*), we have $(|S_{PI\text{-}closed}| - |S_{SPI\text{-}closed}|)/|S_{PI\text{-}closed}| \approx (2^{n-1} - n)/(2^n - (n + 1))$.

In general, *FR*(*should-be-closed, not-SPI-closed*) $\leq$ *FR* (*should-be-closed + might-be-closed, not-PI-closed*), hence, $(|S_{PI\text{-}closed}| - |S_{SPI\text{-}closed}|)/|S_{PI\text{-}closed}| \leq (2^{n-1} - n)/(2^n - (n + 1))$ holds.

For example, in Fig. 4.2(a), $|F| = 4$, accordingly, $(2^{n-1} - n)/(2^n - (n + 1)) = 4/11 = 0.36$. If $M = 0.3$, $(|S_{PI\text{-}closed}| - |S_{SPI\text{-}closed}|)/|S_{PI\text{-}closed}| = (8 - 6)/8 = 0.25$ (see Fig. 4.2(b)).

We note that $(2^{n-1} - n)/(2^n - (n + 1)) \approx 1/2$ when n is large enough. It means that the introduction of *SPI-closed* can reduce the number of *PI-closed* co-locations by about 50% under the conditions that *FR*(*should-be-closed, not-SPI-closed*) $\approx$ *FR* (*should-be-closed + might-be-closed, not-PI-closed*) and that the number of spatial features n is large enough.

Distinct from the discovery of frequent itemsets in transactional databases, we can obtain not only PI(c) for a spatial co-location pattern c, but $\{PR(c, f_i), f_i \in c\}$ as well. However, the concept of the traditional *PI-closed* co-locations as in Yoo and Bow (2011a) only applies to the PI values. The proposed concept of *SPI-closed* co-locations in Definitions 4.5 and 4.6 includes information from both PI and PR, and hence the power of the corresponding lossless condensing approach to prevalent co-location collection is effectively strengthened.

4.4 SPI-Closed Miner

Based on Lemmas 4.1, 4.2, and 4.3, a direct approach to discovering all SPI-closed co-locations involves the identification of all PI-closed co-locations and then the pruning of non-SPI-closed co-locations. This approach first has to compute the PI-closed co-location set, which is larger than the SPI-closed co-location set. We introduce *SPI-closed Miner*, which adopts an FP-growth-like method for directly mining SPI-closed co-locations, and we then develop three pruning strategies to make SPI-closed Miner efficient.

4.4.1 Preprocessing and Candidate Generation

To generate the smallest possible candidate set of SPI-closed co-locations, the input spatial data set will undergo the following preprocessing: converting the input data to neighborhood transactions, and then extracting features in the converted neighborhood transactions. We explain these stages below.

(1) *Converting the input data to neighborhood transactions*

Given a spatial instance $f.i \in S$, the *neighborhood transaction* of $f.i$ is defined as a set that consists of $f.i$ and all other spatial instances having neighborhood relationships with $f.i$, i.e., $NT(f.i) = \{f.i, g.j \in S \mid NR(f.i, g.j) = true$ and $f \neq g\}$, where NR is a neighborhood relationship.

For example, the neighborhood transaction of A.1 in Fig. 4.2(a) is {A.1, B.1, C.1, D.1}. Fig. 4.4(a) shows the neighborhood transactions of the data in Fig. 4.2 (a). Each instance in the transaction has a neighborhood relationship with the first instance, which is called a *reference* instance.

The data structure for storing the neighborhood information was first introduced in Yoo and Shekhar (2006). It has several advantages for SPI-closed co-location mining. First, neighborhood transactions do not lose any instances, nor do any neighborhood relationships of the original data. Second, neighborhood transactions can be easily constructed from the paired neighboring instances in the input data. Third, they can be used to filter the SPI-closed candidate set.

(2) *Extracting features in neighborhood transactions*

We name the lexicographic set of distinct features in the neighborhood transactions, *neighborhood transaction features*. For example, Fig. 4.4(b) shows the neighborhood transaction features of the neighborhood transactions shown in Fig. 4.4(a).

Trans. No.	Neighborhood instances	
1	A.1	B.1,C.1,D.1
2	A.2	B.1,B.2,C.1,D.2
3	A.3	B.3
4	A.4	C.3,D.4
5	B.1	A.1,A.2,C.1,D.1,D.2
6	B.2	A.2,C.1,D.2
7	B.3	A.3
8	B.4	C.2,D.3
9	B.5	D.3
10	C.1	A.1,A.2,B.1,B.2,D.1,D2
11	C.2	B.4,D.3
12	C.3	A.4,D.4
13	D.1	A.1,B.1,C.1
14	D.2	A.2,B.1,B.2,C.1
15	D.3	B.4,B.5,C.2
16	D.4	A.4,C.3

(a) Neighborhood transactions

extract
→

Trans. No.	Neighborhood features	
1	A	B,C,D
2	A	B,C,D
3	A	B
4	A	C,D
5	B	A,C,D
6	B	A,C,D
7	B	A
8	B	C,D
9	B	D
10	C	A,B,D
11	C	B,D
12	C	A,D
13	D	A,B,C
14	D	A,B,C
15	D	B,C
16	D	A,C

(b) Neighborhood transaction features

Fig. 4.4 Neighborhood transactions and neighborhood transaction features of the data set in Fig. 4.2(a), where (**a**) neighborhood transactions; (**b**) neighborhood transaction features

We generate the feature sets for SPI-closed candidates based on these neighborhood transaction features. For the convenience of generating and pruning the SPI-closed candidates, we use a lexicographic prefix-tree structure to store the neighborhood transaction features. This kind of data structure was also used in Yoo and Bow (2011a) to generate top-k PI-closed co-location candidates. Here, we revise the process that Yoo and Bow (2011a) employed to generate SPI-closed candidates. Our process for generating and pruning the SPI-closed candidates is described below.

First, the lexicographic prefix-tree structure is described as follows:

(1) It consists of a root, labeled the *reference feature*, and a set of feature neighborhood relationships as the children of the root.
(2) Each node consists of three fields: feature-type, count, and node-link, where feature-type denotes a feature this node represents, count records the number of neighborhood transaction features represented by the portion of the path reaching this node, and node-link holds the link to the next node in the tree carrying the same feature-type.

For example, the lexicographic prefix-tree constructed from the neighborhood transaction features in Fig. 4.4(b) is shown in Fig. 4.5(a). We can see that one prefix-tree is built for each reference feature.

Second, all feature sets having a neighborhood relationship with the root node (reference feature) are generated. We call the generated feature sets *star SPI-closed candidates* since all features in a set have neighborhood relationships with their first feature. The output also includes the prevalence information, which indicates the likelihood of its first feature having a neighborhood relationship with all other features in the set. This represents the *upper bound of the participation ratio* (upper PR, or UPR for short). If the UPR of a star SPI-closed candidate is equal to

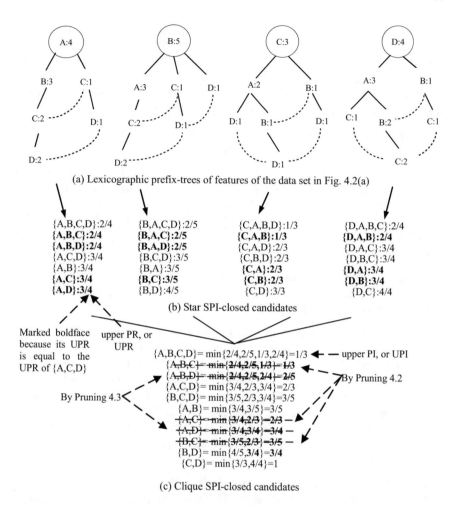

(a) Lexicographic prefix-trees of features of the data set in Fig. 4.2(a)

{A,B,C,D}:2/4   {B,A,C,D}:2/5   {C,A,B,D}:1/3   {D,A,B,C}:2/4
{A,B,C}:2/4   **{B,A,C}:2/5**   **{C,A,B}:1/3**   **{D,A,B}:2/4**
{A,B,D}:2/4   **{B,A,D}:2/5**   {C,A,D}:2/3   {D,A,C}:3/4
{A,C,D}:3/4   {B,C,D}:3/5   {C,B,D}:2/3   {D,B,C}:3/4
{A,B}:3/4   {B,A}:3/5   **{C,A}:2/3**   **{D,A}:3/4**
{A,C}:3/4   **{B,C}:3/5**   **{C,B}:2/3**   **{D,B}:3/4**
{A,D}:3/4   {B,D}:4/5   {C,D}:3/3   {D,C}:4/4

(b) Star SPI-closed candidates

Marked boldface   upper PR, or
because its UPR   UPR
is equal to the   {A,B,C,D}= min{2/4,2/5,1/3,2/4}=1/3 ◀— — upper PI, or UPI
UPR of {A,C,D}   {A,B,C}= min{2/4,2/5,1/3}=1/3 ◀——
                              {A,B,D}= min{2/4,2/5,2/4}=2/5 ◀——
                              {A,C,D}= min{3/4,2/3,3/4}=2/3   By Pruning 4.2
           By Pruning 4.3◀   {B,C,D}= min{3/5,2/3,3/4}=3/5
                              {A,B}= min{3/4,3/5}=3/5
                              {A,C}= min{3/4,2/3}=2/3 —▶
                              {A,D}= min{3/4,3/4}=3/4 —
                              {B,C}= min{3/5,2/3}=3/5 —
                              {B,D}= min{4/5,3/4}=3/4
                              {C,D}= min{3/3,4/4}=1

(c) Clique SPI-closed candidates

Fig. 4.5 Candidate generation, where (**a**) the lexicographic prefix-tree structure; (**b**) star SPI-closed candidates; (**c**) clique SPI-closed candidates

the UPR of any super star SPI-closed candidate in the same reference feature set, we mark it in *boldface*. If the UPR of a star SPI-closed candidate is smaller than M, we delete it from the set of star SPI-closed candidates.

For example, in the prefix-tree of feature A of Fig. 4.5(a), we generate all feature sets having a relationship with A and their UPR values: {A, B, C, D}: 2/4, {A, B, C}: 2/4, {A, B, D}: 2/4, {A, C, D}: 3/4, {A, B}: 3/4, {A, C}: 3/4, {A, D}: 3/4. If $M = 0.3$, no star SPI-closed candidates can be pruned. The feature sets marked in boldface are **{A, B, C}: 2/4, {A, B, D}: 2/4, {A, C}: 3/4** and **{A, D}: 3/4**. The star SPI-closed candidates generated by prefix-trees in Fig. 4.4(a) are shown in Fig. 4.5 (b) (assuming $M = 0.3$).

Third, the star SPI-closed candidates are combined to filter *clique SPI-closed candidates*. This is done as follows. First, k star SPI-closed candidates are combined to a k-size clique SPI-closed candidate, and the minimum value of k UPR values forms the *upper participation index* (upper PI, or UPI) of this clique SPI-closed candidate. The super participation index SPI($c|c'$) ($c \subset c'$), which is calculated from UPRs, is called *upper SPI($c|c'$)* (or *USPI($c|c'$)*).

Three pruning strategies are incorporated into the above combination process: non-prevalent pruning and two strategies for non-SPI-closed pruning.

Pruning 4.1 (Non-prevalent pruning) If a co-location c is not the star SPI-closed candidate of a certain prefix-tree f_i ($f_i \in c$), c can be pruned.

Proof For a spatial feature $f_i \in c$, if c is not in the set of star SPI-closed candidates of the prefix-tree f_i, then UPR(c, f_i) < M. We have PI(c) < UPI(c) < UPR(c, f_i) < M. Hence, c can be pruned.

For example, if $M = 0.4$, co-locations {C, A, B, D} and {C, A, B} in the prefix-tree C are not star SPI-closed candidates. Then {A, B, C, D} and {A, B, C} cannot be combined in the clique SPI-closed candidate generation.

Pruning 4.2 (Non-SPI-closed pruning strategy 1) If the UPI value of a clique SPI-closed candidate c is marked in boldface, and UPI(c) = UPI(c') ($c \subset c'$, where c' is a clique SPI-closed candidate), then c can be pruned.

Proof In the process of generating star SPI-closed candidates, a candidate c is marked in boldface when its UPR is equal to that of its certain super star SPI-closed candidate in the same reference feature set. Therefore, if and only if UPI(c) is marked in boldface, the value of UPI(c) might be equal to that of its super-patterns. When UPI(c) = UPI(c') ($c \subset c'$, c' is a clique SPI-closed candidate), c is not a clique SPI-closed candidate, then c can be pruned.

For example, in Fig. 4.5(c), UPI({A, B, C}) = UPI({A, B, C, D}), if {A, B, C, D} is a clique SPI-closed candidate, so {A, B, C} can be pruned, and the same applies to {A, C} and {B, C}.

Pruning 4.3 (Non-SPI-closed pruning strategy 2) If the UPI value of a clique SPI-closed candidate c is in boldface, and UPI(c) = USPI($c|c'$) ($c \subset c'$, c' is a clique SPI-closed candidate), then c can be pruned.

Proof First, if UPI(c) is not in boldface, it is not possible that UPI(c) = USPI($c|c'$) ($c \subset c'$). Then, if UPI(c) = USPI($c|c'$) ($c \subset c'$), according to Definitions 4.5 and 4.6 c is a non-SPI-closed pattern when c' is an SPI-closed pattern. Therefore, c can be pruned if c' has already been a candidate. □

For example, in Fig. 4.5(c), UPI({A, B, D}) = USPI({A, B, D}|{A, B, C, D}) = 2/5, and if {A, B, C, D} is a clique SPI-closed candidate, then {A, B, D} can be pruned, and the same applies for {A, D}. However, {B, D} cannot be pruned since UPI({B, D}) $\neq$ USPI({B, D}|{B, C, D}).

As shown in Fig. 4.5(c), if $M = 0.3$, the generated clique SPI-closed candidates and their UPI values are {A, B, C, D}: 1/3, {A, C, D}: 2/3, {B, C, D}: 2/3}, {A, B}: 3/5, {B, D}: 3/4 and {C, D}: 1. We note that all non-SPI-closed co-locations have been pruned in the combination phase for the data set in Fig. 4.2(a).

In addition, we note that the Pruning 4.3 strategy contains the Pruning 4.2 strategy, i.e., the co-locations pruned by the Pruning 4.2 strategy will always be pruned by the Pruning 4.3 strategy. The reasons for keeping Pruning 4.2 are: (1) the computational complexity of Pruning 4.2 is lower than that of Pruning 4.3 because we can use a value search strategy in Pruning 4.2; (2) there are generally more co-locations satisfying Pruning 4.2.

4.4.2 Computing Co-location Instances and Their PI Values

Once the clique SPI-closed candidates have been generated, the co-location instances of each clique SPI-closed candidate and their true PI values need to be computed. The computation process starts from the largest size candidates.

The *candidate co-location instances* of clique SPI-closed candidates are gathered by scanning neighborhood transactions (e.g., Fig. 4.4(a)). They are not the true co-location instances. True co-location instances can be filtered from the candidate co-location instances by examining a clique relationship between other instances, except for the first instance of the candidate co-location instance. For example, in Fig. 4.4(a), {A.2, B.2, C.1, D.2} is a true co-location instance of candidate {A, B, C, D}, but {A.2, B.1, C.1, D.2} is not.

For a k-size candidate c, if $PI(c) = UPI(c)$ then c must be an SPI-closed co-location. Otherwise, we first need to generate all pruned $(k - 1)$-size sub-sets of c. Next, if $PI(c) < M$ then c can be pruned; otherwise, we need to check whether c is an SPI-closed co-location according to Definitions 4.5 and 4.6.

Note that the UPI values of size 2 co-locations are their true PI values.

4.4.3 The SPI-Closed Miner

We propose the *SPI-closed Miner* to enable the above process. The pseudocode below describes its main process.

Algorithm 4.1 SPI-closed Miner

Inputs:

(1) A feature set, $F=\{f_1, f_2, ..., f_n\}$;

(2) A spatial data set, D;

(3) A spatial neighborhood distance threshold, d; and

(4) A minimum participation index threshold, M.

Output:

The SPI-closed co-location set Ω.

Method:

// Preprocess and generate star SPI-closed candidates

1) NP =find_neighbor_pairs(D,d);

2) (NT,ENT)=gen_neighbor_transactions(NP);

3) **for** i=1 to n

4) $Tree_i$=build_prefix-tree(f_i,ENT);

5) $SNCC_i$=gen_candi_and_cal_upr ($Tree_i$,M); *//Generating the star SPI-closed candi-*
      dates of $Tree_i$ and calculate their UPR

6)   **if** $UPR(c, f_i)$<M *//$c \in SNCC_i$*
      then c is pruned from $SNCC_i$;

7)   **if** $UPR(c, f_i)$=$UPR(c', f_i)$ *//c, $c' \in SNCC_i$ and $c \subset c'$*
      then c is marked in *boldface*;

//Filter clique SPI-closed candidates by combining star SPI-closed candidates

8) z=1;

9) **While** z<n **do**

10) l = largest size of $SNCC_z$

11)   **while** (l>1 and $SNCC_z \neq \phi$) **do**

12)   **for** each l-size candidate c in $SNCC_z$;

13) $CNCC$←combine_and_cal_upi ($SNCC_{z+1}$, ..., $SNCC_n$); *//CNCC is the set of*
           clique SPI-closed candidates

14)   **if** $UPI(c)$ is *boldface* **and** $UPI(c)$=$USPI(c|c')$)   *//$c' \in CNCC$ and $c \subset c'$*
           then c is pruned from $CNCC$;

15) l=l-1;

16) z=z+1;

//Calculate true PIs of candidates and obtain the SPI-closed set Ω

17) Ω←size 2 candidates in $CNCC$;

18) l=largest size of $CNCC$;

19) **while** (l>2 and $CNCC \neq \phi$) **do**

20)   **for** each l-size candidate c in $CNCC$;

21) SI_c=find_star_instances(c, NT);

22) CI_c=filter_clique_instances(SI_c, NT);

23) $PI(c)$=calculate_true_pi(CI_c);

24)   **if** $PI(c)$=$UPI(c)$
        then move c from $CNCC$ into Ω

25)   **else** $CNCC$ ← gen_pruned_(l-1)-sub-sets(c, $CNCC$);

26)   **if** $PI(c)$<M or non-SPI-closed(c)   *//per Definitions 4.5 & 4.6*
           then prune c from $CNCC$

27)   **else** move c from $CNCC$ into Ω

28) l=l-1;

29) **Output** Ω

The algorithm *SPI-closed Miner* contains three phases. The first one preprocesses and generates *star SPI-closed* candidates, the second combines star SPI-closed candidates as clique SPI-closed candidates, and the third generates the SPI-closed co-location set Ω by calculating the true PI values of the candidates.

In the first phase, we find all neighboring instance pairs for a given input spatial data set and a neighborhood distance threshold d. The instance neighborhood transactions NT are generated by grouping the neighboring instances for each instance. The feature neighborhood transactions ENT are then obtained from NT. Next, a prefix-tree $Tree_i$ of the feature f_i is built based on the neighborhood transaction features of the feature f_i in ENT, where $i = 1,2,\ldots,n$. Lastly, the set of star SPI-closed candidates $SNCC_i$ is generated by using $Tree_i$, and their UPR values are calculated at the same time. For a candidate c in $SNCC_i$, if $UPR(c, f_i) < M$, then c cannot be prevalent, and we can prune c from $SNCC_i$. If $UPR(c, f_i) = UPR(c', f_i)$ for c, $c' \in SNCC_i$ *and* $c \subset c'$, c is marked in boldface.

In the second phase, the set of clique SPI-closed candidates $CNCC$ is filtered by combining the star SPI-closed candidates in $SNCC_1, SNCC_2,\ldots, SNCC_n$. The UPI of each candidate in $CNCC$ is computed at the same time. The boldface marks of UPRs are maintained in the combination process. The combination process starts from the largest size of $SNCC_1$, and ends when no patterns in $SNCC_1, SNCC_2,\ldots, SNCC_n$ can be combined. If the minimum UPR value (i.e., UPI) is a boldface one for a candidate c in $CNCC$, and $UPI(c) = USPI(c|c')$ (where $c' \in CNCC$ *and* $c \subset c'$), c can be pruned from $CNCC$ by pruning strategies Pruning 4.2 and Pruning 4.3.

The third phase calculates the true PI values of candidates in $CNCC$ and discovers the SPI-closed prevalent co-location set Ω. First, the star co-location instances of a candidate are found by scanning NT. The clique co-location instances can then be filtered from the star co-location instances by examining a clique relationship among other instances except for the first instance of the star instance. Next, the true PIs can be calculated based on the clique co-location instances of candidates. For a candidate c, if $PI(c) = UPI(c)$, then the candidate can be moved from $CNCC$ to the SPI-closed co-location set Ω. However, if $PI(c) \neq UPI(c)$, we have to take a number of further steps, as shown in SPI-closed Miner (Steps 25–27). For a l-size co-location c, if PI $(c) \neq UPI(c)$ then all those $l - 1$-size co-locations which were pruned by Pruning strategies 2 or 3 need to be recovered. If $PI(c) < M$ or $PI(c) = SPI(c|c')$ ($c \subset c'$ and c' is SPI-closed), c can be pruned since it is not prevalent or SPI-closed per Definitions 4.5 and 4.6; otherwise, c must be a prevalent SPI-closed co-location.

4.5 Qualitative Analysis of the SPI-Closed Miner

Below, we provide a qualitative analysis of the ability of SPI-closed Miner to accurately discover SPI-closed co-locations.

4.5.1 Discovering the Correct SPI-Closed Co-location Set Ω

SPI-closed Miner can discover the correct SPI-closed co-location set Ω. First, a co-location instance must be a star neighborhood instance and correspond to a neighborhood transaction feature in Miner. Thus, the star SPI-closed candidates and clique SPI-closed candidates can be introduced into SPI-closed Miner, as shown in Step 6 and Step 14.

Second, in the case of PI(c) $\neq$ UPI(c), we first generate all pruned $(l-1)$-size-candidates of c in CNCC in Step 25, following which c is checked and then dealt with based on Definitions 4.5 and 4.6 in Steps 26–27. In addition, the process of the third phase starts from the largest size of CNCC.

Third, to avoid duplicative combination, we adopt a backward combination of SNCC (the star candidates of feature z) at Step 13. Step 9 guarantees the correctness of the combination phase.

4.5.2 The Running Time of SPI-Closed Miner

The running time of SPI-closed Miner is much faster than that of traditional PI-closed co-location mining methods. First, the SPI-closed condition is stronger than the PI-closed condition. Accordingly the candidate set generated in SPI-closed Miner must be smaller than that mined by classic PI-closed co-location mining methods.

Second, the majority of the running time in spatial co-location mining is consumed during the generation of co-location instances and in calculating the PI values. Hence, it is preferable to prune non-SPI-closed patterns when generating candidates as far as possible. This is the method adopted in SPI-closed Miner and the top-k closed co-location mining (Yoo & Bow, 2011a). For the data set in Fig. 4.2(a), all non-SPI-closed co-locations have been pruned in the combination step.

Third, when there are many star co-location instances that are not true co-location instances, the work of generating and checking their sub-sets is time-consuming. However, a corresponding problem is also evident in PI-closed co-location mining. Therefore in this case, the running time of SPI-closed Miner is still faster than that of PI-closed co-location mining methods.

4.6 Experimental Evaluation

Various experiments are conducted to verify the effectiveness and efficiency of the proposed SPI-closed concept and SPI-closed Miner on both synthetic and real data sets. All algorithms are implemented in Visual C++ in a computer with Intel Core i5 3337U @ 1.80GHz, 2GB RAM, and in Microsoft Windows 7.

To the best of our knowledge, the only algorithm to identify closed co-location patterns, as discussed in this paper, is the Top-k closed co-location mining algorithm presented in Yoo and Bow (2011a). Accordingly, we create PI-closed Miner based on the Top-k CCP mining algorithm presented in Yoo and Bow (2011a) as follows. First, top-k Miner finds k CCPs with the highest prevalence values, so it has no prevalence threshold, while PI-closed Miner finds all CCPs with PI values not less than a given threshold. PI-closed Miner can therefore prune candidate CCPs according to the given threshold. Second, top-k Miner traverses the candidate subset tree in a breadth-first manner by raising an internal prevalence threshold to prune candidate co-locations, as it has no pre-determined prevalence threshold, whereas PI-closed Miner uses the depth-first search strategy to discover all CCPs, saving considerable time and space.

4.6.1 Experiments on Real-life Data Sets

This section examines the performance of the proposed algorithms on three real-life data sets. A summary of the three real data sets is presented in Table 4.1. The data set Real-1 concerns the rare plant data of the Three Parallel Rivers of Reserved Areas in Yunnan Province, China. It contains 32 features and only 355 instances with a zonal distribution in a 130,000 m × 80,000 m area as shown in Fig. 4.6(a). Real-2 is a spatial distribution data set with urban elements, which has more instances than Real-1; the distribution of its instances is even and dense in a 50,000 m × 80,000 m area as shown in Fig. 4.6(b). Real-3 is a vegetation distribution data set of the Three Parallel Rivers of Reserved Areas in Yunnan Province, China. It has the least number of features and the largest number of instances, and its instance distribution is both scattered and clustered in an area of 110 000 m × 160,000 m as shown in Fig. 4.6(c).

Table 4.1 A summary of the three real data sets

Name	Number of features	Number of instances	(Max, min)	The distribution area of spatial instances (m²)
Real-1	32	335	(63, 3)	130,000 × 80,000
Real-2	20	377,834	(60000, 347)	50,000 × 80,000
Real-3	15	501,046	(55646, 8706)	110,000 × 160,000

(Max, Min): The maximum and minimum number respectively of the feature's instances in the data sets

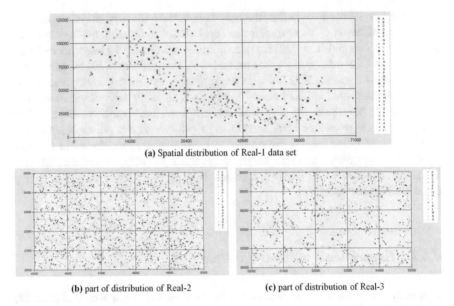

(a) Spatial distribution of Real-1 data set

(b) part of distribution of Real-2   (c) part of distribution of Real-3

Fig. 4.6 Spatial distribution of the three real data sets, where (**a**) Real-1; (**b**) Real-2; (**c**) Real-3

4.6.1.1   The Effectiveness of SPI-Closed Miner

For each real data set, we vary the values of parameters M (the minimum participation index threshold) and d (the spatial neighbor distance threshold) to verify the condensation power of the SPI-closed co-location mining relative to the result of PI-closed co-location mining using Formula (4.7):

$$(|S_{PI-closed}| - |S_{SPI-closed}|)/ \ |S_{PI-closed}| \qquad (4.7)$$

where $S_{PI-closed}$ is the set of PI-closed co-locations and $S_{SPI-closed}$ is the set of SPI-closed co-locations. The larger the condensation power given by Formula (4.7), the better is the performance of SPI-closed Miner. The experimental results are shown in Figs. 4.7(a, b). In this experiment, we set the default d value of Real-1 as 10,000, Real-2 as 4000, and Real-3 as 10,000. The default M value is 0.3 for all three real data sets.

We make the following observations from our experiments. First, on all three real data sets, the condensation power is between 10% and 50%, and the mean value is about 30%. The condensation power is highest on the Real-2 data set, and the mean condensation power almost reaches 40%. This is because Real-2 is an even distribution data set. Second, the condensation power increases when M becomes smaller or d becomes larger. This was anticipated, because there are more prevalent co-locations mined under lower M or larger d. Third, when M or d changes, Real-3 faces fewer changes than Real-2. This is because Real-3 is a clustered distribution data set.

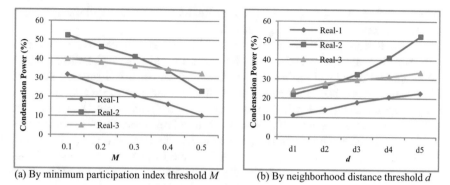

(a) By minimum participation index threshold M (b) By neighborhood distance threshold d

Fig. 4.7 Analysis of the effectiveness of SPI-closed Miner over the three real data sets, where (**a**) vary the minimum participation index threshold M; (**b**) vary the spatial neighbor distance threshold d (In (b), $di = 10,000–1000*(4 - i)$ for Real-1, $di = 4000 - 1000*(4 - i)$ for Real-2, and $di = 11,000 - 2000*(4 - i)$ for Real-3)

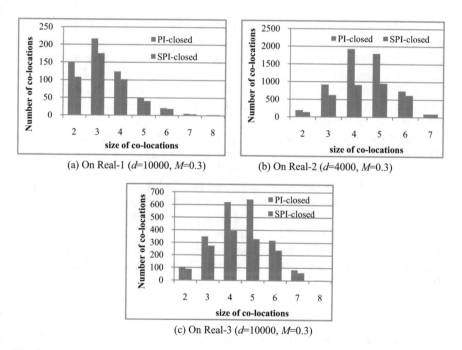

(a) On Real-1 (d=10000, M=0.3)   (b) On Real-2 (d=4000, M=0.3)

(c) On Real-3 (d=10000, M=0.3)

Fig. 4.8 Comparison of the mined results w.r.t. co-location sizes, where (**a**) on Real-1; (**b**) on Real-2; (**c**) on Real-3

Figs. 4.8(a)–(c) shows the number of mined SPI-closed co-locations compared with the number of PI-closed co-locations by co-location size on the three real data sets using default parameter values. As can be seen, the number of SPI-closed co-locations is less, sometimes much less, than the number of PI-closed co-locations. The largest difference appears in the middle sizes for Real-2 and Real-3, e.g., size

4 and size 5 in Figs. 4.8(b, c), whereas for Real-1 with zonal distribution, there is little difference when size is bigger than 5.

We can find some intuitive insights obtained from the experiments over the real data sets. For example, in the results of Real-2 data set of urban facilities, there are both co-location {Educational institution, bus station, snack bar, small supermarket} and {bus station, snack bar, small supermarket} in the set of PI-closed co-locations, but only {Educational institution, bus station, snack bar, small supermarket} appears in the set of SPI-closed co-locations. This is because the all row instances of the 3-size {bus station, snack bar, small supermarket} appear in that of 4-size {educational institution, bus station, snack bar, small supermarket}. This means that the occurrence of {bus station, snack bar, small supermarket} is due to the occurrence of educational institution in the data set. In other words, the feature "educational institution" is the key feature in co-location {educational institution, bus station, snack bar, small supermarket}.

4.6.1.2   The Efficiency of SPI-Closed Miner

The running time of SPI-closed Miner and PI-closed Miner is shown in Figs. 4.9(a)–(f). Figure 4.9 shows that SPI-closed Miner runs much faster than PI-closed Miner when M is small and d is large. We also observe that SPI-closed Miner runs twice as fast as PI-closed Miner in Real-2 when $M = 0.1$ and $M = 0.2$ in Fig. 4.9(b) or $d = 5000$ in Fig. 4.9(e), and three times faster in Real-3 when $M = 0.1$ in Fig. 4.9(c) or $d = 13,000$ in Fig. 4.9(f). In addition, SPI-closed Miner is also more space efficient because it avoids the checking of many candidates.

Table 4.2 compares the number of generated candidates and final results over different sizes by the two algorithms when parameters are set as the default values. For example, the pair value (165/149, 134/108) of size 2 in Table 4.2 indicates that the number of PI-closed candidates is 165 and the number of PI-closed co-locations is 149, and the related number of SPI-closed is 134 and 108, respectively. As can be seen, the number of SPI-closed Miner candidates is much smaller than the number of PI-closed Miner candidates. Further, we can see that as the size of the candidates grows, the number of SPI-closed Miner-identified candidates is close to the final number in the results. We know that checking a long pattern costs much more time than checking a short one.

4.6.2   Experiments with Synthetic Data Sets

This section examines the scalability of SPI-closed Miner and PI-closed Miner in several scenarios, i.e., different numbers of spatial instances, numbers of spatial features, neighbor distance thresholds, and prevalence thresholds. Synthetic data sets were generated using a spatial data generator (Huang et al., 2004; Yoo & Shekhar, 2006). Such synthetic data sets allow greater control in studying the effect of corresponding parameters.

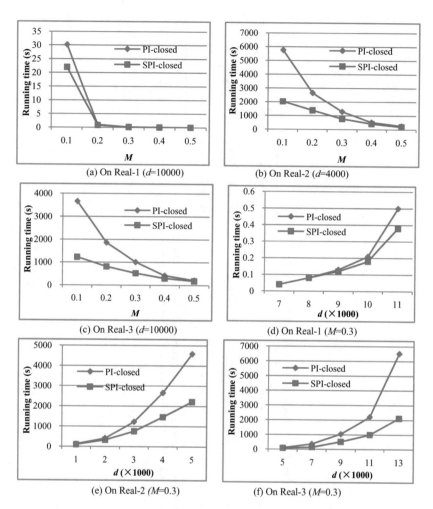

Fig. 4.9 Running time of SPI-closed Miner and PI-closed Miner over three real data sets, where (**a**) vary M on Real-1; (**b**) vary M on Real-2; (**c**) vary M on Real-3; (**d**) vary d on Real-1; (**e**) vary d on Real-2; (**f**) vary d on Real-3

The running time of PI-closed Miner exceeds the time limit (20 ks (kiloseconds) > 5 h) when the number of spatial instances is 600,000, as shown in Fig. 4.10(a), and when the distance threshold is 10,000, as shown in Fig. 4.9(c). As shown in Figs. 4.10(a)–(d), SPI-closed Miner is scalable to large dense data sets, lower M, and larger d. It performs better than PI-closed Miner in all the experiments. This is because the set of PI-closed co-locations is larger than that of the SPI-closed co-locations and the SPI-closed candidates set is smaller than that of the PI-closed candidates due to the application of the Pruning 4.3.

Figure 4.10(b) shows interesting cost information: both algorithms cost more time until they reach a peak time cost as the number of features increases, then

Table 4.2. Comparison of generated candidates and mined results by SPI-closed Miner and PI-closed Miner

Size	2	3	4	5	6	7	8	9	10
Real-1	(165/149, 134/108)	(328/217, 254/175)	(194/124, 135/102)	(148/50, 102/41)	(37/21, 34/19)	(9/5, 8/4)	(7/2, 5/2)	(2/0, 2/0)	(1/0, 1/0)
Real-2	(190/190, 154/132)	(1594/923, 664/626)	(2714/1932, 1108/914)	(1974/1799, 688/956)	(847/744, 41/621)	(107/95, 84/95)	(6/0, 4/0)	(1/0, 1/0)	
Real-3	(105/105, 74/88)	(789/348, 358/275)	(921/621, 547/394)	(1229/643, 448/329)	(384/318, 298/238)	(105/84, 88/62)	(7/4, 3/4)	(1/0, 1/0)	

The two pair values in the entries are PI-closed candidates/PI-closed co-locations and SPI-closed candidates/SPI-closed co-locations

In these experiments, we set $d = 10,000$, $M = 0.3$ for Real-1, $d = 4000$, $M = 0.3$ for Real-2 and $d = 10,000$, $M = 0.3$ for Real-3

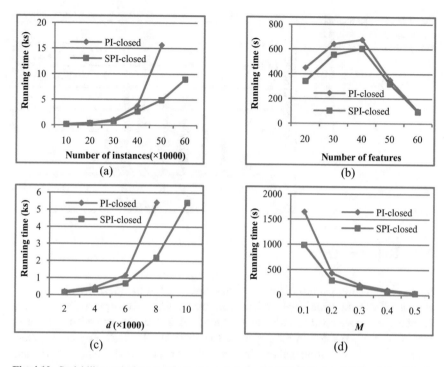

Fig. 4.10 Scalability analysis on synthetic data sets (where (**a**) $|F| = 20$, $d = 1000$ and $M = 0.2$; (**b**) $|S| = 200,000$, $d = 1000$ and $M = 0.2$; (**c**) $|F|=20$, $|S| = 200,000$ and $M = 0$; (**d**) $|F| = 20$, $|S| = 200,000$ and $d = 1000$)

running time is reduced when the number of features increases further. This is because, as the number of features grows, more time is spent on the prefix-trees of features; when the number of features reaches 40, it drops because the data set is too sparse to have longer prevalent patterns when the total number of spatial instances is fixed. In addition, we can see that the cost difference between the two algorithms in Fig. 4.10(b) is the smallest of all the figures. This is because the prefix-tree operation becomes a major factor in SPI-closed Miner when the number of features grows but the total number of spatial instances is fixed.

We also note that, when the number of spatial instances is 500,000 in Fig. 4.10(a), SPI-closed Miner runs almost three times faster than PI-closed Miner. At that point, if we compare the number of SPI-closed candidates with the number of PI-closed candidates w.r.t. the co-location size, as shown in Fig. 4.11, we can see that the number of SPI-closed candidates is far fewer than the number of PI-closed candidates at all sizes, which is why our SPI-closed Miner is so efficient in such situations.

Fig. 4.11 Further analysis
on the 500,000 instances in
Fig. 4.10(a)

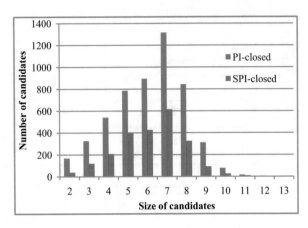

4.7   Related Work

Spatial co-location pattern mining was first discussed in the paper by Shekhar and
Huang (2001), in which the authors formulated the co-location pattern mining
problem and developed a co-location mining algorithm. An extended version of
the work was presented in the paper by Huang et al. (2004). Zhang et al. (2004)
enhanced the co-location pattern in the paper Shekhar and Huang (2001) and
proposed an approach to find spatial star, clique, and generic patterns. Approaches
to reduce expensive join operations used for finding co-location instances in papers
by Shekhar and Huang (2001) and Huang et al. (2004) were proposed in papers by
Yoo and Shekhar (2006), Wang et al. (2008), and Xiao et al. (2008). The work in
papers by Wang et al. (2009b) and Yoo and Bow (2011b) studied the problem of
maximal co-location pattern mining. The problem of co-location pattern mining with
spatially uncertain data sets was presented in papers by Wang et al. (2013a, b), Liu
and Huang (2013), Wang et al. (2016a), and Ouyang et al. (2017). The spatial
instance distribution information was integrated into prevalence metrics in the
paper by Sengstock et al. (2012). The incremental mining and competitive pairs
mining of co-location patterns were studied in papers by Lu et al. (2015, 2017). The
concept and mining methods of spatial high utility co-location patterns were
presented in Wang et al. (2017a) and Yang et al. (2015). Prevalent co-location
redundancy reduction problem was studied in Wang et al. (2018a). Considering
the spatial auto-correlation property in co-location pattern detection approaches,
Barua and Sander (2011) studied the problem of discovering statistically significant
co-location patterns, and Yao et al. (2017) studied the problem of co-location pattern
mining considering detailed relationships of instances in a continuous space.

Limited work is available on closed co-location pattern mining. By contrast,
many algorithms were proposed for finding closed frequent itemsets, such as
CLOSET (Pei et al., 2000), CLOSET+ (Wang et al., 2003), and CHARM (Zaki &
Hsiao, 2002). However, to the best of our knowledge, only the top-k closed
co-location pattern mining method is presented by Yoo and Bow (2011a), which

identifies closed co-location patterns as focused on in this paper. Although their algorithm is very efficient for mining closed co-locations, it was essentially built on extending the concept of closed frequent itemsets and so leads to a lossy condensed representation of spatial co-locations by the proposed top-k *PI-closed* co-location mining. The algorithms for mining closed frequent itemsets cannot be directly used to mine closed co-location patterns because, in contrast to closed frequent itemset mining in transactional data, spatial objects are embedded in a continuous space without transactional information. Our proposed *SPI-closed* co-location Miner captures spatial feature interactions and co-locations by introducing a lossless condensed representation and an efficient discovery process.

4.8   Chapter Summary

This paper presents a new lossless condensed representation of all prevalent co-location collections and an efficient algorithm *super participation index-closed* (SPI-closed) *Miner*. Both theoretical and experimental analyses show that the proposed SPI-closed concept and its corresponding SPI-closed Miner significantly improve the lossless condensation power of identified spatial co-locations and the efficiency of its execution.

We note that the first k most probabilistically prevalent co-location mining problem is meaningful in the context of uncertain data sets because they have particular semantics. In other words, the top-k probabilistically prevalent co-location mining problem can be regarded as an ideal alternative to computing all probabilistically prevalent co-locations with prevalence probability above a fixed threshold, since the parameter k allows, in practice, for a better control on the output size.

In the next chapter, we will study the extraction of the **top-k** probabilistically prevalent co-locations to present the "*best*" set of all probabilistically prevalent co-location patterns. This is an important part of preference-based spatial co-location pattern mining.

Chapter 5
Top-k Probabilistically Prevalent Co-location Patterns

5.1 Introduction

We note that top-k problems, including top-k queries and top-k frequent itemset mining, are meaningful in the context of uncertain data sets, because of their particular semantics. For the spatial co-location mining problem, finding the first k most probabilistically prevalent co-locations is even more meaningful. In this chapter, we focus on mining top-k probabilistically prevalent co-location patterns (PPCPs) and make the following contributions:

(1) The concept of the top-k PPCPs based on a possible world model is defined.
(2) A framework for discovering the top-k PPCPs is set up.
(3) A matrix method is proposed to improve the computation of the prevalence probability of a top-k candidate, and two pruning rules of the matrix block are given to accelerate the search for exact solutions.
(4) A polynomial matrix is developed to further speed up the top-k candidate refinement process.
(5) An approximate algorithm with compensation factor is introduced so that a relatively big data can be processed quickly.

Figure 5.1 presents the organization of this chapter. Section 5.2 discusses why we consider the top-k PPCP mining. Section 5.3 gives the related definitions for the top-k PPCP mining problem. A framework of mining top-k PPCPs is presented in Sect. 5.4. The basic matrix method and polynomial matrix method for top-k PPCP mining appear in Sect. 5.5. Section 5.6 gives an approximate algorithm to deal with larger data sets. An experimental study is performed in Sect. 5.7. Section 5.8 ends this chapter with some conclusive remarks.

From Wang, L., Han, J., Chen, H., and Lu, J.: Top-k Probabilistic Prevalent Co-location Mining in Spatially Uncertain Data Sets. *Frontiers of Computer Science* 10(3), 488-503 (2016).

© The Author(s), under exclusive license to Springer Nature Singapore Pte Ltd. 2022
L. Wang et al., *Preference-based Spatial Co-location Pattern Mining*, Big Data Management, https://doi.org/10.1007/978-981-16-7566-9_5

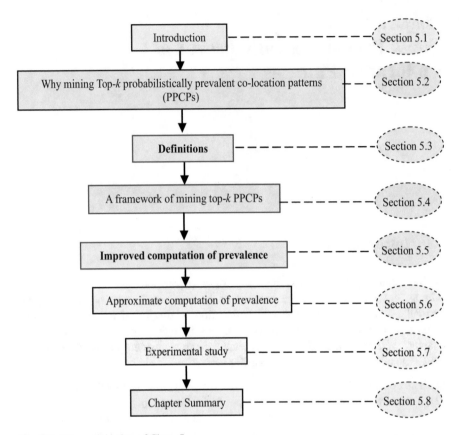

Fig. 5.1 The organization of Chap. 5

5.2 Why Mining Top-k Probabilistically Prevalent Co-location Patterns (Top-k PPCPs)

Finding spatial co-location patterns (SCPs) is an important spatial data mining task. SCPs represent subsets of spatial features whose instances are frequently located in spatial neighborhoods. For example, the symbiotic plant species "Picea Brachytyla," "Picea Likiangensis," and "Tsuga Dumosa" grow frequently in an alpine terrain of the "Three Parallel Rivers of Yunnan Protected Areas." Co-location rules "Picea Brachytyla → Picea Likiangensis and Tsuga Dumosa" can be obtained and used to predict that "Picea Likiangensis" and "Tsuga Dumosa" probably appear in areas where "Picea Brachytyla" exists. Application domains of mining SCPs include Earth science, public health, public transportation, biological information processing, GIS, individual market strategies, military system engineering, and so on.

Due to its importance in a wide range of spatial applications, the topic of finding SCPs has been extensively studied (Huang et al., 2004; Yoo & Shekhar, 2006, Wang et al., 2008; Yao et al., 2016; and so on). Shekhar and Huang (2001) proposed statistically meaningful interest measures for SCPs and a join-based algorithm (Huang et al., 2004), the FP-CM algorithm (Huang et al., 2005), the clustering-based mining algorithm (Huang & Zhang, 2006), and the mining of SCPs with rare features based on introducing the maxPR measure (Huang et al., 2006). Yoo and Shekhar (2006) thoroughly studied the theories and algorithms of SCP mining over spatially precise data sets. They proposed the partial-join method (Yoo et al., 2004), the join-less method (Yoo & Shekhar, 2006), the top-*k* closed SCPs mining algorithm (Yoo & Bow, 2011a), the maximally prevalent SCP mining algorithm (Yoo & Bow, 2011b), and the first *N* most prevalent SCP mining algorithm (Yoo & Bow, 2012). Wang et al. (2009b, 2013a, 2013b, 2018a) comprehensively studied SCP mining on precise and uncertain data sets. They proposed three prefix-tree-based SCP mining algorithms on precise data sets: the CPI-tree (co-location pattern instances tree) method (Wang et al., 2008), the iCPI-tree (improved co-location pattern instances tree) method (Wang et al., 2009a), and the order-clique-based method (Wang et al., 2009b). They also studied SCP mining over *uncertain* data sets, including SCP mining on interval data (Wang et al., 2010), probabilistically prevalent co-location mining (Wang et al., 2013a), and expected prevalent co-location mining (Lu et al., 2009; Lu et al., 2010). Notably, Wang et al. (2013a) presented a dynamic programming algorithm and pruning strategies to find all PPCPs. Considering the exponential complexity problem under a possible world model, an approximate computation method was developed in the paper of Wang et al. (2013a).

We note that top-*k* problems, including top-*k* queries and top-*k* frequent itemset mining, are meaningful in the context of uncertain data sets, because of their particular semantics (Yi et al., 2008; Beskales et al., 2008; Hua et al., 2008; Liu et al., 2010; Pietracaprina et al., 2010; Wu et al., 2012; Zhu et al., 2011). For the SCP mining problem, finding the first *k* most probabilistically prevalent SCPs is even more meaningful. Let us consider a co-location candidate *c* which contains 10 features and 100 spatial instances with existential probabilities. If the occurrence of instances is independent, there would be 2^{100} possible worlds in the candidate *c*. Then the probability of a possible world in all possible worlds of *c* would be a tiny value, and so setting a prevalence probability threshold to mine PPCPs becomes troublesome. Small changes in setting the thresholds may change the number of mined results, and hence many different thresholds may need to be explored in order to mine the appropriate number of PPCPs. In other words, the top-*k* PPCP mining problem can be regarded as a convenient alternative to the uncertain SCP mining problem of computing all SCPs with prevalence probability above a fixed threshold, since the parameter *k* allows, in practice, for a better control on the output size.

A threshold-based PPCP mining is addressed in the paper of Wang et al. (2013a), where a dynamic programming algorithm to compute the prevalence probability of a candidate is proposed. The computation in threshold-based mining will be determined once the sum of prevalence probabilities exceeds the given threshold. So, the exponential possible worlds do not need to be scanned in the most time. But when we use the method of Wang et al. (2013a) in the top-*k* PPCP mining, the effect is not just as one wish. The method proposed in this chapter groups the exponential of possible worlds by using matrix. This method not only makes us could prune some matrix, but also combines the computation of the same columns (the possible worlds of having the same results). Based on the basic matrix method with pruning strategies, a polynomial matrix and an approximate algorithm could be presented. Compared with studying in Wang et al. (2013a), the method proposed in this chapter is a novel and more efficient method.

5.3 Definitions

This section defines the spatially uncertain data sets formally, and then under the possible worlds semantic, the prevalent co-locations, prevalence probabilities, and top-k probabilistic prevalent co-location patterns (top-k PPCPs) are defined.

5.3.1 Spatially Uncertain Data

When compared with spatially precise data set, each spatially uncertain data set contains uncertain features, while an uncertain feature contains spatial instances and their *existential probabilities*. The existential probability $P(T.i)$ of the i-th instance of the feature T indicates the likelihood of the instance $T.i$ appearing in a certain given location. We use a vector <*instance-id, spatial feature, location, existential probability*> to describe a spatially uncertain instance.

Figure 5.2 is an example of the spatially uncertain data sets. As can be seen, the locations of instances are depicted in Fig. 5.2(a). In this figure, a point represents a spatial instance and each instance is uniquely identified by $T.i$, where T is the feature and i is the unique id inside each feature. For example, A.2 represents the second instance of the feature A. A solid line between two points represents the neighbor relationship between two instances.

The neighbor relationship in SCP mining is an important concept. Given a reflexive and symmetric neighbor relationship NR over a set S of spatial instances,

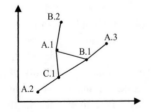

Instance-id	Spatial feature	location	$P(T.i)$
1	A	in Fig. 5.2(a)	0.5
2	A	...	0.4
3	A	...	0.9
1	B	...	0.1
2	B	...	1
1	C	...	0.1

(a) Spatial instances' distribution

(b) The uncertain data set of the corresponding spatial instances in (a)

Fig. 5.2 An example of the spatially uncertain data sets, where (**a**) spatial instances' distribution; (**b**) the corresponding uncertain data set

a *NR-proximity neighborhood* is a set $I \subseteq S$ of instances that form a clique under the relation *NR*. The relation *NR* should be defined based on the semantics of the application domains. For example, the *NR* may be defined using spatial relationships (e.g., connected, adjacent), metric relationships (e.g., Euclidean distance), or a combination (e.g., shortest-path distance in a graph such as a roadmap).

This kind of spatially uncertain data set can be observed over many real applications. For example, epiphytology experts may highly suspect (but cannot guarantee) that a plant growing in a certain location suffers from mildew (a plant disease). It is obvious that the uncertainty attached to such suspicion can be expressed by an existential probability. Here is another example, the heavy metal pollution data in a city can be obtained by sampling, but pollution information at a sampling point is associated with a likelihood measure or an existential probability due to measurement error or noise.

Using the "*possible world*" interpretation of spatially uncertain data, there are two worlds for a spatial instance $T.i$ in a set c of features: (a) the possible world w_1 where $T.i$ is an instance of c and (b) the possible world w_2 where $T.i$ is not an instance of c. Although it is uncertain which of two worlds is the true world, the probability of w_1 being the true world is $P(T.i)$ and that of w_2 is $1 - P(T.i)$. Take a set $c = \{f_1, \ldots f_z\}$ of features, and a set $S = \{S_{f_1}, S_{f_2}, \ldots, S_{f_z}\}$ of their instances, where S_{f_i} $(1 \leq i \leq z)$ is the set of all instances of feature f_i. If we assume that instances are independent, each world is a combination of instances in c and there are $2^{|S|} = 2^{|S_{f_1}| + \ldots |S_{f_z}|}$ possible worlds at most. Each possible world w is associated with a probability $P(w)$, where a possible world is called the true world if its probability is larger than 0, and $P(w)$ can be computed by:

$$P(w) = \prod_{i=1}^{z} \left(\prod_{e \in S_{f_i}, e \in w} P(e) \times \prod_{e \in S_{f_i}, e \notin w} (1 - P(e)) \right) \quad (5.1)$$

Example 5.1 For the feature set $\{A, B\}$ in Fig. 5.2, its instance set is $\{A.1, A.2, A.3, B.1, B.2\}$. There are 2^5 combinations of instances, but there are only 2^4 combinations whose probability is larger than 0 as the probability of instance B.2 is 1. So there are 2^4 true worlds corresponding to $\{A, B\}$. These worlds and their probabilities are shown in Table 5.1. For a possible world $w = \{A.1, A.3, B.2\}$, $P(w) = P(A.1) \times P(A.3) \times P(B.2) \times (1 - P(A.2)) \times (1 - P(B.1)) = 0.243$.

In the general case, the existence of instances may be mutually dependent. If the dependency is known, it can also be used in the possible world model (Hua et al., 2008; Liu et al., 2010; Bartolini et al., 2012) For example, if instances A.1 and A.2 are mutually exclusive, the feature set $\{A, B\}$ in Fig. 5.2 will be instantiated into 12 possible worlds, because the worlds $\{A1, A2, B2\}$, $\{A2, A2, A3, B2\}$, $\{A1, A2, B1, B2\}$, and $\{A1, A2, A3, B1, B2\}$ in Table 5.1 will not be possible worlds. In this paper, we only consider the case that the occurrence of instances is independent.

Table 5.1 The 16 possible worlds of the feature set {A, B} and their probabilities

w	$P(w)$	w	$P(w)$	w	$P(w)$	w	$P(w)$
{B2}	0.027	{A1,A2,B2}	0.018	{B1,B2}	0.003	{A1,A2,B1,B2}	0.002
{A1, B2}	0.027	{A1,A3,B2}	0.243	{A1,B1, B2}	0.003	{A1,A3,B1,B2}	0.027
{A2, B2}	0.018	{A2,A3,B2}	0.162	{A2,B1, B2}	0.002	{A2,A3,B1,B2}	0.018
{A3, B2}	0.243	{A1,A2,A3, B2}	0.162	{A3,B1, B2}	0.027	{A1,A2,A3,B1, B2}	0.018

5.3.2 Prevalent Co-locations

Given a spatially uncertain data set D, where F is a set of features, and S is a set of instances of F, let NR be a neighbor relationship between instances. A *co-location c* is a subset of features, $c \subseteq F$. The *size* of c is the number of features in c. Under the possible worlds semantic, a possible world instantiated from instances' set S_c of all features in c is called a *possible world of c*. Let W be the set of all possible worlds of c.

We first define row instance and table instance of c in a possible world; then the participation ratio and participation index in a possible world are defined to characterize the prevalence of a co-location in a possible world of c.

Definition 5.1 For a possible world $w \in W$, a set of instances $I \subseteq S_c$ is called a *row instance* of c, if (1) I contains instances of all features in c and no proper subset of I does so, and (2) I is a NR-proximity neighborhood. The *table instance*, *table_instance$_w$(c)*, of c in the possible world w is the collection of all row instances of c.

Definition 5.2 In a possible world $w \in W$, the *participation ratio* $\mathrm{PR}_w(c, f_i)$ of the feature f_i in a z-size co-location $c = \{f_1, f_2 \ldots, f_z\}$ is defined as:

$$\mathrm{PR}_w(c, f_i) = \begin{cases} 1 & \text{if } |\text{ table\_instance}_w(\{ f_i\}) | = 0 \\[2mm] \dfrac{|\ \pi_{f_i}(\text{table\_instance}_w(c))\ |}{|\ \text{table\_instance}_w(\{ f_i\})\ |} & \text{otherwise} \end{cases}$$

(5.2)

where π is the relational projection operation with duplication elimination.

Definition 5.3 The *participation index* $\mathrm{PI}_w(c)$ of a z-size co-location $c = \{f_1, \ldots, f_z\}$ in a possible world $w \in W$ is defined as:

$$\mathrm{PI}_w(c) = \min_{i=1}^{z}(\mathrm{PR}_w(c, f_i))$$

(5.3)

Definition 5.4 For a user-specified prevalence threshold *min_PI*, a co-location *c* is called a *min_PI-prevalent co-location* in a possible world $w \in W$ if

$$\text{PI}_w(c) \geq min\_PI \tag{5.4}$$

Example 5.2 For Fig. 5.2, given $c = \{A, B\}$, $w = \{A.1, A.2, A.3, B.2\}$, then *table_instance*$_w(\{A, B\}) = \{\{A.1, B.2\}\}$, $\text{PR}_w(c, A) = 0.333$ because 1 instance out of 3 instances participates in table instances of *c* in *w*. Similarly, $\text{PR}_w(c, B) = 1$ because all of B's instances participate in the table instances of *c*. Therefore, $\text{PI}_w(c) = \min(0.333, 1) = 0.333$. If the user-specified prevalence threshold *min_PI* is 0.4, then *c* is not a 0.4-prevalent co-location in *w*.

5.3.3   Prevalence Probability

We introduce the *prevalence probability* to further characterize the prevalence degree of a co-location *c* in all possible worlds *W* of *c*.

Definition 5.5 Given a prevalence value *prev*, the *prevalence probability* $P(c, prev)$ of a co-location *c* is the probability that the participation index (PI) of *c* is *prev* in all worlds *W*, defined as:

$$P(c, prev) = \sum_{w \in W, \text{PI}_w(c) = prev} P(w) \tag{5.5}$$

Intuitively, $P(c, prev)$ denotes the probability that the prevalence of *c* is exactly *prev* in *W*. The prevalence probabilities associated with a co-location *c* for different prevalence values form the *prevalence probability distribution* of *c*. It satisfies the following statement:

$$\sum_{0 \leq prev \leq 1} P(c, prev) = 1 \tag{5.6}$$

Example 5.3 Again consider Fig. 5.2. For the co-location $c = \{A, B\}$, $P(c, 0.5) = 0.308$ as $\text{PI}_{\{A1,A2,B2\}}(c) = 0.5$, $\text{PI}_{\{A1,A3,B2\}}(c) = 0.5$, $\text{PI}_{\{A3,B1,B2\}}(c) = 0.5$ and $\text{PI}_{\{A1,A2,B1,B2\}}(c) = 0.5$. Using similar calculations Fig. 5.3 shows the prevalence probability distribution of *c*.

If a co-location $c = \{f_1, f_2, \ldots, f_z\}$ and a related uncertain instance set $S = \{S_{f_1}, S_{f_2}, \ldots, S_{f_z}\}$, where S_{f_i} $(1 \leq i \leq z)$ is a set of instances of feature f_i, then the number of possible worlds is $|W|$ that need to be considered for the computation of $P(c, prev)$ is $O\left(2^{\sum_{i=1}^{z} |S_{f_i}|}\right)$. It is extremely large.

Fig. 5.3 The prevalence
probability distribution of
{A, B}

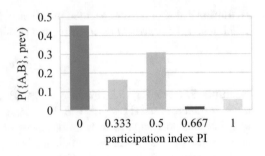

Fig. 5.4 The *min_PI*-
prevalence probabilities of
{A, B}

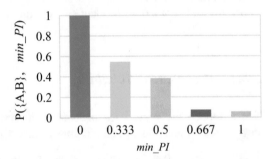

5.3.4 Min_PI-*Prevalence Probabilities*

We are interested in the probability that the prevalence of a co-location is at least
min_PI. We have the following definition.

Definition 5.6 Given a co-location c and a user specified prevalence threshold
min_PI, P(c, $\geq min\_PI$) denotes the probability that the PI of c is at least *min_PI*,
that is:

$$P(c, \geq min\_PI) = \sum_{min\_PI \leq prev \leq 1} P(c, prev) \tag{5.7}$$

We call the probability P(c, $\geq min\_PI$) the *min_PI-prevalence probability* of c.

Example 5.4 Again considering the spatially uncertain data set shown in Fig. 5.2,
the *min_PI*-prevalence probabilities of $c = \{A, B\}$ are shown in Fig. 5.4. From
Fig. 5.4, we can see that the 0.5-prevalence probability of c is 0.383, and its 0.667-
prevalence probability is 0.075.

5.3.5 Top-k PPCPs

After introducing the *min_PI*-prevalence probability of a co-location, we introduce the concept of top-k PPCPs, which can effectively avoid the specification of *min_PI*-prevalence probability thresholds.

Definition 5.7 (Top-k PPCP mining) For a given prevalence threshold *min_PI*, return the k co-locations whose prevalence is at least *min_PI* and that have highest *min_PI*-prevalence probability, where k is specified by the user.

Thus the top-k mining not only makes the approach free of the parameter *min_PI*-prevalence probability threshold and ensures that co-locations with the highest probability of being prevalent are output first, but also enables the design of more efficient algorithms to mine PPCPs.

5.4 A Framework of Mining Top-k PPCPs

In this section, we present a basic mining algorithm to find top-k PPCPs over spatially uncertain data sets, and then analyze its performance and give a pruning lemma.

5.4.1 Basic Algorithm

We now give a lemma for dynamically finding the top-k PPCPs.

Lemma 5.1 $\forall c' \subseteq c : P(c', \geq min\_PI) \geq P(c, \geq min\_PI)$.

Proof Firstly, based on Definitions 5.5 and 5.6, we have $P(c', \geq min\_PI) =$
$\sum_{i=1}^{|W_{c'}|} P(w_i) \times I_{\mathrm{PI}_{w_i}(c') \geq min\_PI}$, where $W_{c'}$ is the set of all possible worlds of c', and I_p is an indicator variable that is 1 when $p = true$ and 0 otherwise.

Secondly, for $\forall c' \subseteq c$, according to Definitions 5.2 and 5.3, we have $\mathrm{PI}_{w_i}(c') \geq \mathrm{PI}_{w_i}(c)$ in a possible world w_i. Therefore, $I_{\mathrm{PI}_{w_i}(c') \geq min\_PI} \geq I_{\mathrm{PI}_{w_i}(c) \geq min\_PI}$ holds in w_i.

Thirdly, for $\forall c' \subseteq c$, the set of all possible worlds of c contains the set of all possible worlds of c', i.e., $W_{c'} \subseteq W_c$. For a possible world $w' \in W_{c'}$, if $\mathrm{PI}_{w'}(c') \geq min\_PI$, then there are a group of possible worlds $w_i \in W_c$ ($1 \leq i \leq l, l \geq 0$) satisfy $w' \subseteq w_i$ and $\mathrm{PI}_{w_i}(c) \geq min\_PI$. Thus,

$$P(w') = P(w') \times 1 = P(w') \times P_{all}\left(\bigcup_{i=1}^{l} w_i - w'\right),$$ where $P_{all}(S)$ denotes the sum of probabilities of all possible worlds of the set S, it is one.

The set of $w_i \in W_c$ ($1 \leq i \leq l, l \geq 0$) is the subset of the combination of w' and the power set $\bigcup_{i=1}^{l} w_i - w'$, so we have $P(w') \times P_{all}\left(\bigcup_{i=1}^{l} w_i - w'\right) \geq \sum_{i=1}^{l} P(w_i)$.

In summary, $\forall c' \subseteq c : P(c', \geq min\_PI) \geq P(c, \geq min\_PI)$. $\square$

Using Lemma 5.1, we can design a basic algorithm (Algorithm 5.1) to mine top-k PPCPs. In Algorithm 5.1, we keep an *Active Co-locations Queue* (*ACQ*) and constrain the length of the *ACQ* to k. The *ACQ* is sorted by *min_PI*-prevalence probability in descending order. Without the loss of generality, co-locations are represented in lexicographical order to conveniently perform the joining operation in generating candidates. In a z-size iteration of the algorithm (z is started from 2, since all singleton co-location patterns have both participation index and prevalence probability equal to 1, and do not need to be checked.), the z-size candidates are inserted into the *ACQ* after their related *min_PI*-prevalence probabilities are computed, and then the ($z + 1$)-size candidates are generated based on z-size co-locations in *ACQ*. Any co-locations for which their subsets do not exist in *ACQ* can safely be ignored. The rationale behind this approach is that if a co-location c does not belong in the results of top-k, then all supersets of c cannot belong in the top-k's results either, i.e., Lemma 5.1. Consequently, Algorithm 5.1 will correctly return top-k PPCPs.

Algorithm 5.1 Basic Mining Algorithm

//initialize

1) *ACQ*=A new Priority Queue with Size k;

2) Gen_2-Size_Candidates C_2; *//C_2 is all pairs of features*

3) z=2

//iteratively generate k highest PPCPs

4) **WHILE** C_z not empty DO

5) **FOR** each c in C_z

6)   *ACQ*.insert([c, P(c, $\geq min\_PI$)]); *//Insert c and its min_PI-prevalence probability into ACQ*

7) z=z+1

8) Gen_z-Size_Candidates C_z based on *ACQ*;

9) **ENDWHILE**

10) RETURN *ACQ*

5.4.2 Analysis and Pruning of Algorithm 5.1

The main cost of performing Algorithm 5.1 is the computation of the value $P(c, \geq min\_PI)$. Due to the design of Algorithm 5.1, at least the 2-size candidates need to be computed. The number of 2-size candidates is $\frac{|F|(|F|-1)}{2}$, where $|F|$ is the number of features in the uncertain data set D. If we denote the average number of instances of all features in D as A^m, a 2-size candidate has 2^{2A^m} possible worlds on average. So, at least $O\left(\frac{|F|(|F|-1)}{2} 2^{2A^m}\right)$ time needs to be spent in mining the top-k PPCPs.

We note that some k-size candidates could be generated for $k \geq 3$ and that the computational complexity of Algorithm 5.1 is then much greater than the value $O\left(\frac{|F|(|F|-1)}{2} 2^{2A^m}\right)$. But by using the following pruning lemma, some candidates' computation may be avoided.

Lemma 5.2 (Pruning candidates) For a candidate c, if $(1 - P(c,0)) < ACQ[k].$ *Prob*, where $ACQ[k].Prob$ is the *min_PI*-prevalence probability of the k-th item in ACQ, then the candidate c cannot be a top-k PPCP under a *min_PI* > 0.

Proof Because $P(c, \geq min\_PI) \leq (1 - P(c,0)) < ACQ[k].prob$, and $ACQ[k].Prob$ is the k-th *min_PI*-prevalence probability in ACQ, it is impossible to insert c into ACQ. □

We can order all z-size candidates with the value $P(c, 0)$, i.e., the probability that the prevalence of c is exactly *zero* in all possible worlds. Once one candidate satisfies the condition of Lemma 5.2, the remaining z-size candidates can be pruned.

Example 5.5 For the uncertain data set in Fig. 5.2, the 2-size candidates are $\{A, B\}$ $(P(\{A, B\}, 0) = 0.455)$, $\{A, C\}$ $(P(\{A, C\}, 0) = 0.903)$, and $\{B, C\}$ $(P(\{B, C\}, 0) = 0.99)$. If $k = 2$ and *min_PI* $= 0.5$, after calculating $P(\{A, B\}, \geq 0.5) = 0.383$ and $P(\{A, C\}, \geq 0.5) = 0.097$, the candidate $\{B, C\}$ may be pruned due to $(1 - P(\{B, C\}, 0)) < 0.097$.

The pruning of Lemma 5.2 is significant, because we observe that the cost of computing $P(c, \geq min\_PI)$ is exponential and increases further as the number of instances of features in c increases.

5.5   Improved Computation of $P(c, \geq min\_PI)$

To compute $P(c, \geq min\_PI)$ in Algorithm 5.1, we can sum all possible worlds satisfying the *min_PI* condition. This naïve method is very inefficient, however, and we can speed this up significantly by the following techniques.

5.5.1   0-1-Optimization

First, we do not need to consider the spatial instances which have a probability of 0 because the corresponding worlds' probability will be 0. Note that if $P(T.i) = 1$, we do not need to compute any possible worlds that the instance $T.i$ is absent.

Second, if there is not certain feature's instance in a possible w of c, then w can be ignored due to $\text{PI}_w(c) = 0$. For example, considering $\text{PI}_w(\{A, B\})$ of the data set shown in Fig. 5.1, if $w = \{B2\}$ or $w = \{A1, A2\}\ldots$, then $\text{PI}_w(\{A, B\}) = 0$.

Beside 0-1-optimization, a matrix method is introduced for further improving the computation of $P(c, \geq min\_PI)$.

5.5.2 The Matrix Method

In computing $P(c, \geq min\_PI)$, we need to identify $\text{PI}_w(c) \geq min\_PI$ for each $w \in W$. According to Definitions 5.2 and 5.3, the value $\text{PI}_w(c)$ can be obtained based on $table\_instance_w(c)$. We know that the problem of computing table instances is troublesome in the SCP mining. A matrix method is introduced in this subsection to solve this problem.

First, a z-dimension matrix of a z-size co-location c's instance relationship is computed, called **basic matrix** and denoted M_b. As shown in Fig. 5.5, M_b of co-location $\{A, B\}$ for the uncertain data set in Fig. 5.2 is a 3×2 2-d matrix. In the basic matrix, there is information about all possible worlds only containing one instance for each feature in c and their corresponding prevalence values. For example, in M_b shown in Fig. 5.5, the value "1" in the row $\{A1\}$ and the column $\{B2\}$ represents $\text{PI}_{w=\{A1,B2\}}(\{A, B\}) = 1$. Therefore, by scanning this matrix we can compute the probabilities of these possible worlds w_i in which $\text{PI}_{w_i}(c) \geq min\_PI$.

Second, we combine instances of the dimension in M_b to compute $\text{PI}_w(c)$ of the other possible world w. For convenience, features (dimensions) are represented in lexicographical order to avoid dealing with them more than once. The character "f_i^x" means x-instances' combination in feature f_i. For example, "A^3" means the combination of three instances pertaining to feature A. Matrices are used to store the types of combinations. As shown in Fig. 5.5, the matrix M_{A^2B} is the combination in which feature A has two instances and B has one instance. According to the prevalence definition (i.e., Definitions 5.4 and 5.5), by Lemma 5.3 we can compute new values in new matrices from the basic matrix M_b.

Lemma 5.3 A value of the new matrix $M_{f_1^{x_1}\ldots f_z^{x_z}}\left[S_{f_1^{x_1}}, \ldots S_{f_z^{x_z}}\right]$ for a z-size co-location c can be calculated as follows:

$$M_{f_1^{x_1}\ldots f_z^{x_z}}\left[S_{f_1^{x_1}}, \ldots S_{f_z^{x_z}}\right] = \min_{i=1}^{z}\left(\sum_{int \in S_{f_i^{x_i}}} (\Omega M_b[\ldots, int, \ldots])/|S_{f_i^{x_i}}|\right)$$

where the operation "Ω" is defined as: $\Omega_{i=1}^{m} A_i = \begin{cases} 1 & \text{if any } A_i = 1 \ (1 \leq i \leq m) \\ 0 & \text{otherwise} \end{cases}$

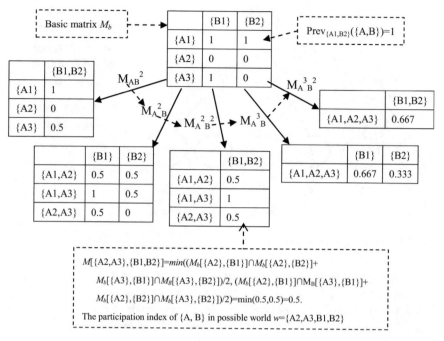

Fig. 5.5 Illustration of the matrix method

Proof Based on Definition 5.4, it is easy to verify that the value $\sum_{int \in S_{f_i^{x_i}}} (\Omega M_b[\ldots, int, \ldots])/ \mid S_{f_i^{x_i}} \mid$ in Lemma 5.3 is the value $PR_{\left\{ S_{f_1^{x_1}}, \ldots S_{f_z^{x_z}} \right\}} (c, f_i)$, which is the participation ratio of feature f_i in c in a possible world $w = S_{f_1^{x_1}} \cup \ldots \cup S_{f_z^{x_z}}$. According to Definition 5.5, we have $PI_w(c) = \min_{i=1}^{z} (PR(c, f_i))$.

So Lemma 5.3 is correct. $\square$

Example 5.6 Considering the uncertain data set in Fig. 5.2, Fig. 5.5 depicts the computation process of the value $P(\{A, B\}, \geq min\_PI)$ by using the matrix method. As shown in Fig. 5.5,

$$M_{A^2B^2}[\{A2, A3\}, \{B1, B2\}]$$
$$= \min((M_b[A2, B1] \Omega M_b[A2, B2])$$

$$+ \left(\frac{(M_b[A3, B1] \Omega M_b[A3, B2])}{2 \frac{(M_b[A2, B1] \Omega M_b[A3, B1]) + (M_b[A2, B2] \Omega M_b[A3, B2])}{2}} \right) = \min(0.5, 0.5) = 0.5$$

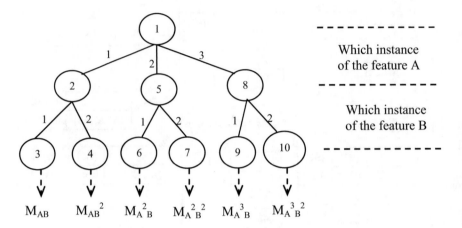

Fig. 5.6 The solution space tree of $\{A, B\}$

Third, we adopt a **backtracking method** to generate all matrices in order to perform pruning by virtue of Lemma 5.4 and Lemma 5.5. For the example in Fig. 5.5, the solution space tree of using backtracking method to generate all matrices is shown in Fig. 5.6. So, the matrices in Fig. 5.5 are calculated in the order AB, AB^2, A^2B, A^2B^2, A^3B, A^3B^2.

Lemma 5.4 (Pruning matrix 1) For a z-size co-location c, if

$$\text{PI}_{\left\{ f_1^1,...f_i^{x_i}...f_z^1 \right\}}(c) < min\_PI, \text{ then PI}_{\left\{ f_1^1,...f_i^{x_i+l}...f_z^1 \right\}}(c) < min\_PI (l \geq 1).$$

Proof We note that a spatial instance of feature f_i that participates in a row instance of c under $f_i^{x_i+l}$ also participates in a row instance of c under $f_i^{x_i}$. So, if $\text{PI}_{\left\{ f_1^1,...f_i^{x_i+l}...f_z^1 \right\}}(c) \geq min\_PI \ (l \geq 1)$, then $\text{PI}_{\left\{ f_1^1,...f_i^{x_i}...f_z^1 \right\}}(c) \geq min\_PI$. $\square$

From Lemma 5.4, if the maximum value in M_{A^2B} is smaller than min_PI, the matrix M_{A^3B}, M_{A^4B} can be pruned.

Lemma 5.5 (Pruning matrix 2) For a z-size co-location c, if certain $x_i > \frac{|table\_instance(c)|}{min\_PI}$ $(1 \leq i \leq z)$, then matrix $M_{f_1^{x_1}...f_z^{x_z}}$ can be pruned.

Proof According to Definition 5.2, in any a possible world w combined by $f_1^{x_1}, ... f_z^{x_z}$, $PR_w(c, f_i) \leq \frac{|table\_instance(c)|}{x_i}$. If $x_i > \frac{|table\_instance(c)|}{min\_PI}$, then $PR_w(c, f_i) < min\_PI$. Therefore, $\text{PI}_{\left\{ f_1^{x_1}...f_z^{x_z} \right\}}(c) < min\_PI$ holds. $\square$

For example, let $c = \{A, B, C\}$, where the feature A has 30 instances, B has 20, and C has 25. Min_PI is specified as 0.5. If we suppose that there are 8 row instances in c, then because 8/0.5=16, matrix $A^{17}B^3C^2$, $A^5B^{17}C^{13}$, ... can be pruned.

Based on the discussion above, a procedure for computing $P(c, \geq min\_PI)$ of z-size candidate c using the matrix method is presented.

Procedure Computing $P(c, \geq min\_PI)$

//initialize
1) M_b= The basic matrix of c;
2) P= 0; t=1; $x[t]$=0;   // $x[t]$ is the value x in f_t^x (f_t=t)
   // Backtracking-based generating all matrices to compute $P(c, \geq min\_PI)$
3) **WHILE** (t>=1) **DO**
4)   { $x[t]$=$x[t]$+1;
5)   **if** ($x[t]$<=l_t) **then**   // l_t is the number of instances of feature t
6)   **if** (t=z) **then** //the last feature, X=($x[1]$,...$x[z]$) implies a matrix $M_{f_1^{x[1]},...f_z^{x[z]}}$
7)   { **if** M_X is not M_b and M_X cannot be pruned by Lemmas 5.4 and 5.5
8)   **then** M=Gen_M(M_b,X);   //by Lemma 5.3
9) P=P+cal_P(M, min_PI); //the procedure cal_P computes prevalence probability based on M }
10)   **else if** (t<z) **then** { t=t+1; $x[t]$=0 }
11)   **else** t=t-1
12)   };
13) **RETURN** P

The key idea in the matrix method is to group all the possible worlds for the computation of $P(c, \geq min\_PI)$. For example, there are 6 groups (matrices) in the example of Fig. 5.5. Note that for computing $P(c, \geq min\_PI)$ of a z-size co-location c, the number of matrices is $\prod_{i=1}^{z} l_i$, where l_i is the number of instances in the i-th dimension. So we have Lemma 5.6 for the complexity of the matrix method.

Lemma 5.6 The computation of $P(c, \geq min\_PI)$ by the matrix method requires at most $O\left(\prod_{i=1}^{z} (2^{l_i} - 1) \right)$ time and at most $\prod_{i=1}^{z} l_i$ space.

Proof Using the matrix method as shown in Fig. 5.5, the computational complexity of $P(c, \geq min\_PI)$ is bounded by the number and size of the matrices. If a value in a matrix computed by Lemma 5.3 is performed in $O(1)$ time, the computational complexity of computing $P(c, \geq min\_PI)$ is at most $O\left(\prod_{i=1}^{z} (2^{l_i} - 1) \right)$, where $2^{l_i} - 1$ is the number of ways of combining the dimension i in all the matrices. The computation of each matrix only requires information of the basic matrix. Therefore, only the basic matrix needs to be preserved requiring at most $\prod_{i=1}^{z} l_i$ space. $\square$

In the computation of Example 5.6, the matrix method needs 21 computational time units including basic matrix M_b as there exist 21 values in 6 matrices for co-location {A, B}. Note that the matrix method can efficiently compute the prevalence $PI_w(c)$ of a co-location c, but suffers from the exponential possible worlds of c. To further improve the run time of the algorithm so that it can be processed quickly, we further combine matrices in the matrix method by a polynomial matrix.

5.5.3 Polynomial Matrices

A polynomial method to further efficiently compute $P(c, \geq min\_PI)$ is presented in this section. This method is based on constructing a polynomial matrix that enables efficient computing the value of $P(c, \geq min\_PI)$ over relatively larger data sets. We first introduce the polynomial matrix concept.

Definition 5.8 The basic matrix M_b represented by polynomials is called a *polynomial basic matrix* PM_b, where a value in basic matrix M_b is represented by a polynomial $F_e(x)$:

$$F_e(x) = \begin{cases} P(e)x + (1 - P(e)) & M_b[\{e\}, \ldots] = 1 \\ P(e)x^{-1} + (1 - P(e)) & M_b[\{e\}, \ldots] = 0 \end{cases} \quad (5.8)$$

where e is an instance of feature f_1 in a top-k candidate $c = \{f_1, \ldots f_z\}$, $P(e)$ is the existential probability of e.

Based on Definition 5.8, the basic matrix M_b of the example in Fig. 5.5 is changed into polynomial basic matrix PM_b in Fig. 5.7. Each value in PM_b is a polynomial which contains the existential probability of an instance of f_1 in c and also its prevalence. For example, the polynomial "$0.9x + 0.1$" in the row $\{A3\}$ and the column $\{B1\}$ of PM_b indicates that A3 participates in *table_instance(c)* with its existential probability of 0.9, while its absence probability is 0.1.

After obtaining PM_b represented by polynomials, the multiplication of two polynomials in the same column represents the combinations' probabilities and their prevalence of the two instances in f_1. In Fig. 5.7, the multiplication of the three polynomials in column $\{B1\}$ contains the information of matrices AB, A^2B, and A^3B in the example of Fig. 5.5. This result is denoted as A^*B in Fig. 5.7.

By multiplying polynomials directly, the computational complexity of our algorithm cannot be reduced. However, for a z-size co-location $c = \{f_1, \ldots f_z\}$, let W' be the set of possible worlds of $\{f_2, \ldots f_z\}$. The method of multiplying polynomials can then be discussed as follows.

(1) Consider the case A^*B in example of Fig. 5.7, i.e., the case in which each feature in the possible world $w \in W'$ only contains one spatial instance.

We note that there are only two kinds of polynomials in this case. One is "$ax + b$" when there is neighbor relationship between instances, and the other is "$ax^{-1} + b$" when there is not. For example, the polynomials of Column $\{B1\}$ in PM_b can be divided into $R^+ = \{\text{Row } \{A1\}, \text{Row } \{A3\}\}$ and $R^- = \{\text{Row } \{A2\}\}$.

Multiplying polynomials in R^+ can be computed efficiently by using the following iterated procedure. It costs at most $O(|R^+|^2)$. The result is denoted MPr^+.

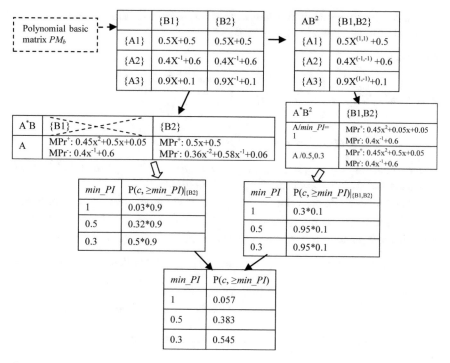

Fig. 5.7 Illustration of the polynomial matrix

//Multiplying polynomials in R^+
$MPr^+[0]=P(R^+[0]); MPr^+[1]=1- P(R^+[0]);$ //$R^+[0]$ is the first instance in R^+
For i=1 **to** $|R^+|$-1 **Do**
  { $T= MPr^+[i]$
  For j=1 **to** i **Do**
    $MPr^+[j]= MPr^+[j$-1$] \times (1- P(R^+[i])) + MPr^+[j] \times P(R^+[i]);$
  $MPr^+[0]= MPr^+[0] \times P(R^+[i]);$
  $MPr^+[i$+1$]=T \times (1-P(R^+[i]));$
  }

Example 5.7 Suppose there are three polynomials in R^+: $a_1x + b_1$, $a_2x + b_2$ and $a_3x + b_3$. The iterated result is $MPr^+ = MPr^+[0]x^3 + MPr^+[1]x^2 + MPr^+[2] x^1 + MPr^+[3]$, where $MPr^+[0] = a_1a_2a_3$, $MPr^+[1] = a_1b_2a_3 + a_1a_2b_3 + b_1a_2a_3$, $MPr^+[2] = b_1b_2a_3 + a_1b_2b_3 + b_1a_2b_3$, $MPr^+[3] = b_1b_2b_3$.

The polynomials in R^- may be computed similarly in polynomial time $O(|R^-|^2)$. The result is MPr^-. We can combine the two polynomials MPr^+ and MPr^- into MPr in polynomial time. But by using Lemma 5.7, the value of $P(c, \geq min\_PI)|_w$ can be computed directly based on the two polynomials MPr^+ and MPr^-, where $w \in W'$, W' is the set of possible worlds of $\{f_2, \ldots f_z\}$.

Lemma 5.7

$$P(c, \geq min\_PI)|_w = \left(\sum_{i=1}^{l_1^+} MPr^+ \left[l_1^+ - i \right] \times \sum_{j=0}^{min\left(\left\lfloor \frac{1-min\_PI}{min\_PI} \times i \right\rfloor, l_1^- \right)} MPr^- \left[l_1^- - j \right] \right) \times P(w),$$ where $l_1^{+/-} = |R^{+/-}|$.

Proof First, if $l_1^+ = |R^+| = 0$, then $P(c, \geq min\_PI)|_w = 0$. In general, $|R^+| \neq 0$ is supposed and so $PI(c)|_w = PR(c, f_1)|_w$ (by Definition 5.3)

Then, we note that the value $MPr^+ \left[l_1^+ - i \right]$ is the probability of i instances of f_1 appearing in $table\_instance(c)|_w$ and $MPr^- \left[l_1^- - j \right]$ is that of j instances of f_1 not being in $table\_instance(c)|_w$. According to Definition 5.2, $PR(c, f_1)|_w = \frac{i}{i+j}$. If $PR(c, f_1)|_w \geq min\_PI$, then $j \leq min\left(\left\lfloor \frac{1-min\_PI}{min\_PI} \times i \right\rfloor, l_1^- \right)$. Note that we do not need to compute the inner sum $\sum_{j=0}^{min\left(\left\lfloor \frac{1-min\_PI}{min\_PI} \times i \right\rfloor, l_1^- \right)} MPr^- \left[l_1^- - j \right]$ in Lemma 5.7 from scratch for each i. As i increases, this sum can be calculated incrementally, taking $O(l_1^+)$ time in total. $\square$

Example 5.8 As shown in Fig. 5.7, if $min\_PI = 0.3$, then

$$P(c = \{A, B\}, \geq 0.3)|_{\{B2\}} = \left(\sum_{i=1}^{z} MPr^+ [1 - i] \times \sum_{j=0}^{min\left(\left\lfloor \frac{1-0.5}{0.5} \times i \right\rfloor, 2 \right)} MPr^- [2 - j] \right) \cdot$$

$\times P(w) = 0.5 \times (0.06 + 0.58 + 0.36) \times P(w) = 0.5 \times 0.9$, where $P(w = \{B2\}) = 0.9$, MPr^+: $0.5x + 0.5$, MPr^-: $0.36x^{-2} + 0.58x^{-1} + 0.06$.

(2) Consider the case A^*B^2 in example of Fig. 5.7, a complex general case where there are more than one spatial instances in each feature of the possible world $w \in W'$.

Firstly we can divide instances of f_1 into two groups. One is the instances where all polynomials are of the type "x^1", and the other is the remainder. For example, to compute A^*B^2, the instances of f_1 are divided into $R^+ = \{A1, A3\}$ and $R^- = \{A2\}$.

Secondly, instances in R^+ need to be partitioned further. The first class contains such instances as e where $min_{i=2}^{z} (PR_{\{e\} \cup w}(c, f_i)) \geq min\_PI$. For example, the "A1" in R^+ belongs to this class when $min\_PI > 0.5$. The second class contains the instances that cannot appear in a possible world alone. For example, when computing A^*B^2, the "A3" in R^+ cannot alone appear in a possible world when $min\_PI > 0.5$ because $PI_{w = \{A3, B1, B2\}}(c) = min (PR_w(c, A), PR_w(c, B)) = 0.5$. A third class contains instances where their appearance is mutually inclusive. For example, if the polynomial of row $\{A1\}$ of "AB^2" in Fig. 5.7 was "$0.5x^{(-1,1)} + 0.5$", then "A1" also could not appear alone, but at that time "A1" and "A3" can appear together since $PI_{w = \{A1, A3, B1, B2\}}(c) = 1$.

Thirdly, we can compute MPr^+ and MPr^- similarly, but we compute MPr^+ with constraints because of the above discussion.

Therefore, the multiplying operation in the polynomial matrix method can be performed in polynomial time. At the same time, we note that if the values in Column {B2} are same as in Column {B1}, then the results of multiplying polynomials in Column {B2} and in Column {B1, B2} will be same as in Column {B1}.

As shown in Fig. 5.7, for computing $P(\{A, B\}, \geq min\_PI)$, three columns (three combinations of feature B) need be performed. But Column {B1} can be pruned since $P(B2) = 1$.

From the process of multiplying polynomials in R^+, we can see that the polynomials need not actually be preserved. They are just conceptual and the values stored in PM_b are still 1 or 0. So the polynomial method can save computational time but at no more space cost. In fact, we have Lemma 5.8 for the complexity of the polynomial matrix.

Lemma 5.8 Computing the value $P(c, \geq min\_PI)$ by the polynomial matrix method requires at most $O\left(\prod_{i=2}^{z} (2^{l_i} - 1)\right)$ time and at most $\prod_{i=1}^{z} l_i$ space.

Proof Using the polynomial matrix as shown in Fig. 5.7, the computational complexity of computing $P(c, \geq min\_PI)$ is bounded by the number of the columns. We note that the multiplying operation in the polynomial method can be completed in *polynomial* time. So the computational complexity of $P(c, \geq min\_PI)$ is at most $O\left(\prod_{i=2}^{z} (2^{l_i} - 1)\right)$, where $2^{l_i} - 1$ is the number of combinations of the dimension i. The computation of each new column only requires information from the polynomial basic matrix. Therefore, only $O\left(\prod_{i=1}^{z} l_i\right)$ polynomial space is required in our polynomial matrix method. $\square$

Compared to Lemma 5.6, the new method seems cut down one dimension only. This is significant. Firstly, due to Lemma 5.1, the top-k mining can deal with greater sizes in the least time. Secondly, once there are columns in a polynomial basic matrix with the same value, the computational complexity of the polynomial method will be reduced significantly.

5.6   Approximate Computation of $P(c, \geq min\_PI)$

The polynomial matrix gives us a chance to approximately compute the value $P(c, \geq min\_PI)$ using a similar approach presented in Wang et al. (2013a). At first, we note that the polynomial method has reduced the problem of one dimension (a feature), but suffers from an exponentially increasing number $|W'|$, where W' is the set of possible worlds of $\{f_2, \ldots f_z\}$. Then we settle for an approximate value of the $P(c,$

$\geq$*min_PI*) by using an error threshold ε to control the number of possible worlds selected from W'. This has an impact on the method's accuracy, that is, on its possible error bound.

Take a z-size candidate $c=\{f_1,\ldots,f_z\}$ with its a prevalence threshold *min_PI* and the prevalence probability *ACQ*[k].*Prob* of the k-th result in *ACQ*. In the computation of the P(c, $\geq$*min_PI*), we only generate $l = 3\ln\left(\frac{1}{\varepsilon}\right)/\left(min\_PI^2 \times ACQ[k].Prob^2\right)$ possible worlds from W', say w_1, w_2, ..., w_l. For convenient analysis, let $Y_i^c = P(c,\geq min\_PI)\big|_{w_i}$ and $G^c = \sum_{i=1}^{l} Y_i^c$. If $G^c > ACQ$ [k]. *Prob*, we can insert the candidate c into the top-k queue *ACQ*; otherwise we assert that c does not belong to the top-k probabilistic prevalent co-locations. We now prove that for any candidate c, the approximate method incorrectly selects it with probability at most ε.

Lemma 5.9 For any candidate c, if $P(c, \geq min\_PI) > ACQ[k].Prob$, then $G^c > ACQ$ [k]. *Prob* with probability at least $1 - \varepsilon$.

Proof First, let $\mu = \mathrm{E}\left[Y_i^c\right]$ for $1 \leq i \leq l$. According to the Chernoff inequality, we have

$$P(G^c \leq ACQ[k].Prob) = P(|G^c - l \cdot \mu| \geq (l \cdot \mu - ACQ[k].Prob))$$

$$\leq e^{4 \cdot \left(\frac{l \cdot \mu - ACQ[k].Prob}{l}\right)} \tag{5.9}$$

Second, we use *RW* to denote a *random possible world* instantiated from the instances of features in a z-size c. Since $\mathrm{PI}^{RW}(c)$ is a random variable, we have:

$$P(c, \geq min\_PI) = P\left(\mathrm{PI}^{RW}(c) \geq min\_PI\right)$$

$P(\mathrm{PI}^{RW}(c) \geq min\_PI) \leq P(\mathrm{PR}^{RW}(c, f_i) \geq min\_PI)$ for $1 \leq i \leq z$ (Definition 5.3)

$\mathrm{PR}^{RW}(c, f_i) = \frac{|\pi_{f_i}\left(table\_instance^{RW}(c)\right)|}{|table\_instance^{RW}(\{f_i\})|}$ (Definition 5.2)

We denote $table\_instance^{RW}(\{f_i\})$ as f_i^{RW} and $\pi_{f_i}(table\_instance^{RW}(c))$ as $f_i^{RW}(c)$ for short, then

$$P(c, \geq min\_PI) \leq P\left(|f_i^{RW}(c)| \geq min\_PI|f_i^{RW}|\right)$$

We decompose the event $|f_i^{RW}(c)| \geq min\_PI |f_i^{RW}|$ into two disjoint events, where $0 < t < 1$ is an arbitrary constant:

$\left(|f_i^{RW}(c)| \geq min\_PI|f_i^{RW}|\right) \cap \left(|f_i^{RW}| \geq (1-t)\mathrm{E}\left[|f_i^{RW}|\right]\right)$ and
$\left(|f_i^{RW}(c)| \geq min\_PI|f_i^{RW}|\right) \cap \left(|f_i^{RW}| < (1-t)\mathrm{E}\left[|f_i^{RW}|\right]\right)$

We then bound their probabilities, respectively.

(1) $P\left(\left(|f_i^{RW}(c)| \geq min\_PI|f_i^{RW}|\right) \cap \left(|f_i^{RW}| \geq (1-t)\mathrm{E}\left[|f_i^{RW}|\right]\right)\right)$

$$\leq P\left(|f_i^{RW}(c)| \geq min\_PI \times (1-t) \times \mathrm{E}\left[|f_i^{RW}|\right]\right)$$

$$\leq \frac{\mathrm{E}\left[|f_i^{RW}|\right]}{min\_PI \times (1-t) \times \mathrm{E}\left[|f_i^{RW}|\right]} \ (Markov \ inequality)$$

(2) $P\left(\left(|f_i^{RW}(c)| \geq min\_PI|f_i^{RW}|\right) \cap \left(|f_i^{RW}| < (1-t)\mathrm{E}\left[|f_i^{RW}|\right]\right)\right)$

$$< P\left(|f_i^{RW}| < (1-t)\mathrm{E}\left[|f_i^{RW}|\right]\right)$$

$$\leq e^{-\frac{t^2}{2}\mathrm{E}\left[|f_i^{RW}|\right]} \ (Chernoff \ inequality)$$

Therefore, $P(c, \geq min\_PI) < \frac{\mathrm{E}\left[|f_i^{RW}(c)|\right]}{min\_PI \times (1-t) \times \mathrm{E}\left[|f_i^{RW}|\right]} + e^{-\frac{t^2}{2}\mathrm{E}\left[|f_i^{RW}|\right]}$.

With no loss generally, $t=1/2$ can be chosen. If $\mathrm{E}\left[|f_i^{RW}|\right]$ is large enough, $e^{-\mathrm{E}\left[|f_i^{RW}|\right]} \leq 1/\mathrm{E}\left[|f_i^{RW}|\right]$ is satisfied. So, we obtain that $P(c, \geq min\_PI) < \frac{3 \times \mathrm{E}\left[|f_i^{RW}(c)|\right]}{min\_PI \times \mathrm{E}\left[|f_i^{RW}|\right]}$ for $1 \leq i \leq z$.

If $P(c, \geq min\_PI) > ACQ[k].Prob$, we obtain

$$\mu > \frac{min\_PI \times ACQ[k].Prob}{3} \tag{5.10}$$

If we plug $l = 3\ln\left(\frac{1}{\varepsilon}\right)/\left(min\_PI^2 \times ACQ[k].Prob^2\right)$ and inequality (5.10) into inequality (5.9), we then get

$$P(G^c \leq ACQ[k].Prob) < \varepsilon$$

Therefore, we have $G^c > ACQ[k].Prob$ with probability at least $1 - \varepsilon$ when P $(c, \geq min\_PI) > ACQ[k].Prob$. □

Lemma 5.9 tells us that if we choose $l = 3\ln\left(\frac{1}{\varepsilon}\right)/\left(min\_PI^2 \times ACQ[k].Prob^2\right)$, the overall error as to whether a candidate could be inserted into the top-k queue would be bounded by ε. So we have Lemma 5.10 for the computational complexity of the approximate algorithm.

Lemma 5.10 The approximate algorithm spends at most $O\left(l_1^2 \times \left(3\ln\left(\frac{1}{\varepsilon}\right)/\left(min\_PI^2 \times ACQ[k].Prob^2\right)\right)\right)$ time to compute the P $(c, \geq min\_prev)$ for a candidate $c = \{f_1, \ldots f_z\}$, where l_1 is the number of instances of the feature f_1.

Proof For a possible world generated by instances of features $f_2, \ldots f_z$, the polynomial method costs at most $O\left(l_1^2\right)$. The approximate algorithm only generates $l = 3\ln\left(\frac{1}{\varepsilon}\right)/\left(min\_PI^2 \times ACQ[k].Prob^2\right)$ possible worlds. □

In the approximate computation of $P(c, \geq min\_PI)$, the approximate value $P'(c, \geq min\_PI)$ is always less than the original value. We have, though, $P'(c, \geq min\_PI) > ACQ[k].Prob$ with probability at least $1-\varepsilon$ when P-$(c, \geq min\_PI) > ACQ[k].Prob$. To advance the approximation quality, we can introduce a ***compensation factor*** δ to amend the value $P'(c, \geq min\_PI)$ by the value $P'(c, \geq min\_PI) + P'(c, \geq min\_PI) \times \delta$.

5.7   Experimental Evaluations

In this section, we attempt to evaluate the performance of the basic top-*k* mining algorithm (BA) against its competitors, namely, the matrix method (MA), the polynomial method (PA), and the proximate method (PPA) through a series of experiments on both real and synthetic data sets. All algorithms are implemented and compiled by Microsoft's Visual Studio C# 2008 and run on a normal PC with Intel Core i3-2100 @ 3.1 GHz CPU, 4GB of memory and Microsoft Windows 7.

5.7.1   Evaluation on Synthetic Data Sets

Table 5.2 shows the characteristics of the randomly synthesized three uncertain data sets used in experimental evaluations. From our theoretical analysis of Lemmas 5.6, 5.8, and 5.9, we note that the number of instances of features in candidates is a primary factor in determining the algorithms' running time. So, the experimental synthetic data sets consider mainly the population distribution of spatial instances. The population distribution is either "not skewed" or "skewed." The distribution area of spatial instances is in a 1000×1000 area.

data-1: The instances' population distribution is not skewed, and it has a maximum number of 12 instances and a minimum of seven instances. For each feature, the number of instances follows a normal distribution with mean $A^m = 10$. The probability values of instances lie in [0, 1] randomly.

data-2: This data set has an average number of 10 instances, a maximum number of 20 instances and a minimum of three instances. To generate a much skewed data set, we divide the 20 features into two parts. One part contains 15 features and the other 5. The part with 15 features has an average number of seven instances, while the part with five features has an average number of 18. The probability values of instances are also generated randomly.

data-3: This is a relatively larger synthetic data set. Its average number of instances is 20. The maximum number of instances is 26, and the minimum is 13. In selecting the number of instances, an average number of 17 instances are given to

Table 5.2 Characteristics of the three synthetic data sets

Name	|*F*|	A^m	(Max, Min)	Popul distr
data-1	20	10	(12, 7)	Not skew
data-2	20	10	(20,3)	Strong skew
data-3	20	20	(26,13)	Skew

Table 5.3 Parameter settings in experimental evaluations

Parameters	Default values in Section 5.7.1.1–5.7.1.2 / 5.7.1.3 / 5.7.1.4
Neighbor distance d	120 / 150 / 150
Number of results k	40 / 80 / 70
Minimum prevalence Min_PI	0.4 / 0.4 / 0.3
Possible error threshold ε	0.0001 / 0.0001 / 0.0001
Compensation factor δ	0.02 / 0.02 / 0.02
Neighbor distance d	120 / 150 / 150

15 features, and an average number of 24 for the other five features. The probability values of instances are also generated randomly.

The sparseness or denseness of data sets will be regulated by the parameter d, which is a distance threshold that is used when determining neighbor relationships between spatial instances in experiments. Besides the parameter d, there is either the parameter k for the top-k or the minimum prevalence threshold min_PI. For the approximation algorithm, there are also parameters for the possible error threshold ε and the compensation factor δ. Considering the efficiency of polynomial matrix method and approximation algorithm compared to the basic algorithm and matrix method, the default values of d, k and min_PI are respectively changed in the experiments. Table 5.3 summarizes the parameters' default values used in experiments.

5.7.1.1 Main Memory Cost of Algorithms

First, we run all algorithms on three synthetic data sets to see their memory cost using the default parameter settings. The results are shown in Fig. 5.8. As expected, the memory cost of the four algorithms only slightly differs. MA, PA, and PPA can avoid storing table instances above 3-size. On the other hand, MA reduces some calculations of possible worlds by grouping and pruning, PA further combines possible worlds, and PPA directly cuts out some possible worlds. So, in relatively larger data sets, MA is superior to BA, but MA is the loser if compared to PA. Moreover PPA spends the least among the four algorithms.

5.7.1.2 Running Time of Algorithms

We now study the running time of algorithms on the three synthetic data sets. Figure 5.9 shows all the results with an exponential scale. Figure 5.9(a)–(c) are the results of the four algorithms obtained by varying d from 80 to 160 in data-1, data-2 and data-3, respectively. Figure 5.9(d)–8(f) are the results of varying k from 10 to 50, and Fig. 5.9(g)–(i) show the results by varying min_PI from 0.8 to 0.3. We can

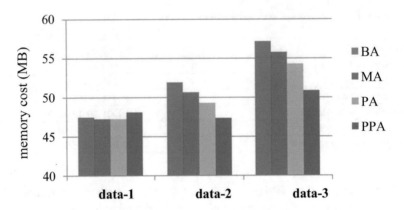

Fig. 5.8 Memory cost analysis

observe that PA is always the fastest in the three exact algorithms, but compared to PPA, it is a loser. The superiority of PPA is more obvious in the larger data set *data*-3. From Fig. 5.9(a), (d), and (g), we can see that the running time of four algorithms does not exceed 3 hours in *data*-1. But in *data*-2, as shown in Fig. 5.9(b), (e), and (h), the running time of BA has exceeded 30 hours with the same parameters settings. At the same time, the running time of BA and MA exceeds 30 hours in *data*-3 even on the lowest parameter settings.

Effect of d. From Fig. 5.9(a)–(c), we can observe that the running time of the algorithms basically goes up when d increases, but PA and PPA do not always go up. This is because increasing d makes the neighbor areas larger, so increasing the number of row instances in the candidates' table instances. But in the top-k mining, a situation may occur where the number of candidates goes down when d increases, because candidates are generated from the top-k queue. This is a difference between top-k co-location mining and prevalent co-location mining. In addition, we find that the matrix method based on the table instances is sensitive to d in the strong skew data sets (see Fig. 5.9(b)). Moreover, we observe that the advantages of PA and PPA become more obvious as d increases.

Effect of k. According to Fig. 5.9(d)–(f), the performance of all algorithms deteriorate as k increases. This is due to the fact that the number of above 3-size candidates increases as k increases. On the other hand, MA and PA are less sensitive to variations of k in the relatively smaller data sets *data*-1 and *data*-2. The pruning of Lemma 5.5 makes the cost of computing above 3-size candidates smaller relatively to that of all 2-size candidates.

Effect of min_PI. Observe Fig. 5.9(g)–(i). Firstly, we note that the execution time of all algorithms goes up generally as *min_PI* decreases. The reason is that the computing cost of any candidate reduces in any possible world since *min_PI* is larger. The impact of *min_PI* on MA is especially significant because of the pruning by Lemmas 5.4 and 5.5. Secondly, we note that the number of 3-size candidates decreases as *min_PI* decreases on the three synthetic data sets. But the larger features which contain more spatial instances go into 3-size candidates after *min_PI* < 0.5.

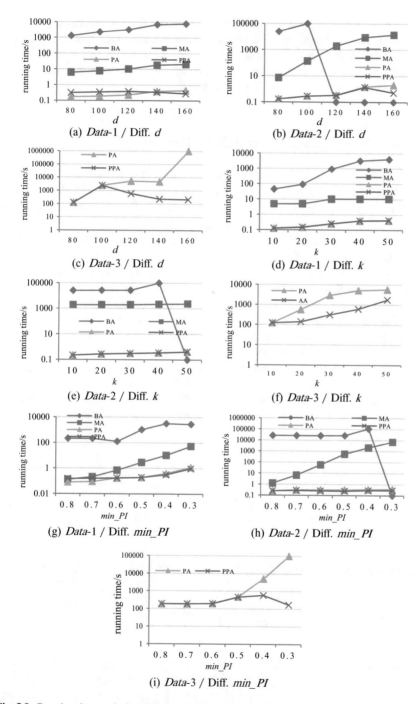

Fig. 5.9 Running time analysis, where (**a**) Data-1 / Diff. *d*; (**b**) Data-2 / Diff. *d*; (**c**) Data-3 / Diff. *d*; (**d**) Data-1 / Diff. *k*; (**e**) Data-2 / Diff. *k*; (**f**) Data-3 / Diff. *k*; (**g**) Data-1 / Diff. *min_PI*; (**h**) Data-2 / Diff. *min_PI*; (**i**) Data-3 / Diff. *min_PI*

This can be used to explain why the run-time goes down when varying min_PI from 0.7 to 0.6 in Fig. 5.9(g), and the rapidly increasing run-times of BA and MA in Fig. 5.9(h). Lastly, we note that the cost of PA is small and less variable on the smaller data sets $data$-1 and $data$-2. On the other hand, its cost gets worse when min_PI decreases on the larger data set $data$-3.

5.7.1.3   Accuracy of the Approximation Algorithm

Besides offering efficient run time and memory cost, the approximation accuracy is the more important target for the approximately top-k probabilistic prevalent co-location mining algorithm PPA. We use equal $\frac{|AR \cap ER|}{k}$ to measure the accuracy of PPA. Note that AR means the result generated from the approximate algorithm PPA, and ER is the result generated from the exact algorithm PA. Tables 5.4–5.6 show the accuracy of PPA in the three synthetic data sets by varying d, min_PI and k, respectively. We find that the accuracy is almost 1 in our all experiments. In $data$-1, we observe that there is no false positive in any of the experiments. We also find that the accuracy of the strong skew data set $data$-2 is the worst in all three data sets. This is due to the fact that our PPA design is based on an optimization for the expected participation ratio. So, the bigger is the variance in the number of instances in features, the worse is the accuracy of PPA. On the other hand, we note that the accuracy may reduce as d increases or min_PI decreases, but it can be raised as k increases. This is due to the missing probabilistic prevalent patterns which may be found when k is larger, while the accuracy of PPA is 1 when k is less than or equal to 60 since there are then fewer of the higher sizes' co-locations in the results.

Table 5.4   Accuracy/d

d	110	130	150	170	180
$data$-1	1	1	1	1	1
$data$-2	1	1	0.9875	0.975	0.9625
$data$-3	1	1	1	0.9875	0.9875

Table 5.5   Accuracy/min_PI

min_PI	0.8	0.7	0.6	0.5	0.4	0.3
$data$-1	1	1	1	1	1	1
$data$-2	1	1	1	1	0.9875	0.975
$data$-3	1	1	1	1	1	1

Table 5.6   Accuracy/k

k	40	60	80	100	120	150
$data$-1	1	1	1	1	1	1
$data$-2	1	1	0.9875	1	1	1
$data$-3	1	1	1	1	0.99167	0.9867

5.7.1.4 Effect of ε and δ

We also study the impact of error threshold and compensation factor by varying ε from 0.1 to 0.00001 and δ from 0.02 to 0.2, respectively. Firstly, as shown in Table 5.7, the accuracies for varying ε in *data*-1 and *data*-3 are always 1. This is due to: (1) for the relatively smaller data set *data*-1, the number of generated possible worlds $l = 3\ln\left(\frac{1}{\varepsilon}\right)/\left(min\_PI^2 \times ACQ[k].Prob^2\right)$ represents all the possible worlds even with $\varepsilon = 0.1$ since the value $ACQ[k].Prob^2$) in l formula is too small; (2) for *data*-3, there are a few above 3-size co-location patterns in the top-k mining results with a setting of $k = 70$, and the computation of 2-size candidates is almost exact using the parameters' default values. The above explanations can also be verified by Fig. 5.10. Secondly, from the results of *data*-2 in Table 5.7 we can see that the missing prevalent pattern in the top-k results can be found as ε is increased. Then, the results of Table 5.8 illustrate that a reasonable value of δ can raise the accuracy of PPA. Our experimental study suggests that for typical values of k, d, and min_PI, setting ε with 0.0001 and δ with 0.02 are good enough. Finally, we find that the running time of PPA is linear on varying ε. We have only tested the run time on varying ε because the influence of δ is far less.

Table 5.7 Impact on accuracy for varying ε

ε	0.1	0.01	0.001	0.0001	0.00001
data-1	1	1	1	1	1
data-2	0.9857	1	1	1	1
data-3	1	1	1	1	1

Fig. 5.10 Effect of the error threshold on the running time

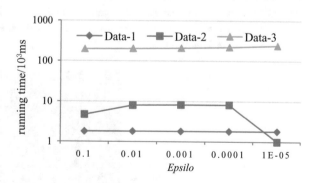

Table 5.8 Impact on accuracy for varying δ

δ	0.02	0.05	0.1	0.15	0.2
data-1	1	1	1	1	1
data-2	1	1	0.9857	0.9857	0.9857
data-3	1	1	1	1	1

5.7.2   *Evaluation on Real Data Sets*

In this section, we mainly evaluate the accuracy and efficiency of the approximate algorithm PPA in the real data sets. The real data sets come from the vegetation distribution data sets of the "Three Parallel Rivers of Yunnan protected Areas." As shown in Fig. 5.11, if we select the yellow area as the sample data, and a sample point is the 250 meter * 250 meter cell, the number of samples in the yellow area is 115*242.4 = 27876. The range of samples in the yellow area covers the 14 types of vegetations and the area of 0.25 * 115 * 0.25 * 242.4 = 1742.25 sq. km.

5.7.2.1   Running Time of Algorithms

The size of a cell affects the quality of sample data. As shown in Fig. 5.12, there are three kinds of vegetation in a 250 * 250 cell. Although we can refine cells into smaller cells, the problem is essentially unchanged beyond increasing the number of samples. The best approach is that the uncertainty of a cell value is expressed by a confidence probability. Therefore, in the data sets used in experiments, each of vegetation is a feature and a cell value is a spatial instance of the vegetation with its associated confidence probability expressing the likelihood that this cell is the specific vegetation

Table 5.9 summarizes three real data sets used in our experiments. They are all from yellow area in Fig. 5.11. The difference is the size of cells. A 1000 * 1000 cell is selected in *real*-1, a 500 * 500 cell is for *real*-2 and the 250*250 cell is for *real*-3.

In the following, we report the accuracy of mining results on *real*-1 and *real*-2 by using the results of *real*-3 as the benchmark, because a cell in *real*-2 and *real*-1 corresponds to 4 cells and 16 cells in *real*-3, respectively. Then, we present the run time of PPA over *real*-1, *real*-2, and *real*-3. We see that PPA provides high approximation quality for minor computational effort. Finally, we analyze the scalability of PPA as well. The default values of the parameters are *min_PI*=0.4, $d = 1$, $\varepsilon = 0.0001$, and $\delta = 3$.

Fig. 5.11 The location of the vegetation samples

Fig. 5.12 There are three distinct vegetations in a 250 * 250 cell

Table 5.9 Characteristics of the three real data sets

Name	$|F|$	Total No. of instances	(Max, Min)	Size of a cell
real-1	14	3089	(632, 9)	1000 * 1000
real-2	14	9098	(2048,20)	500 * 500
real-3	14	27,876	(6621,50)	250 * 250

Table 5.10 Accuracy in real data sets

Accuracy	$k = 10$	$k = 15$	$k = 20$	$k = 25$
real-1	1	14/15	18/20	23/25
real-2	1	1	1	1
real-3	1	1	1	1

Approximation quality vs. run time. Faced with the real data sets in Table 5.9, even the polynomial algorithm PA can do nothing with it due to the exponential complexity of PA. We note that as the cells become smaller, the uncertainty of the data lessens, the data size rises sharply, and the computational complexity becomes too high. However, the approximate algorithm PPA can achieve good accuracy when the cell size is enlarged. Table 5.10 reports the accuracy of the top-k mining results on *real*-1, *real*-2 based on *real*-3, and Fig. 5.13 is the run time of the corresponding mining processes. We find that PPA can mine the highly accurate results with minor computational effort. Thus, our mining algorithm which has high-quality approximation could perhaps settle the big data mining problem. In addition, we observe that the approximation quality and run time of PPA are less sensitive to the variation of k from Table 5.10 and Fig. 5.13 when varying k from 10 to 25.

Scalability. We further analyze the scalability of PPA. In Fig. 5.14, varying the number of spatial instances in the data sets from 10k to 40k, we find the run time of PPA with $k = 10/20$ are linear.

Fig. 5.13 Running time of corresponding mining in Table 5.10

Fig. 5.14 Scalability analysis in real data sets

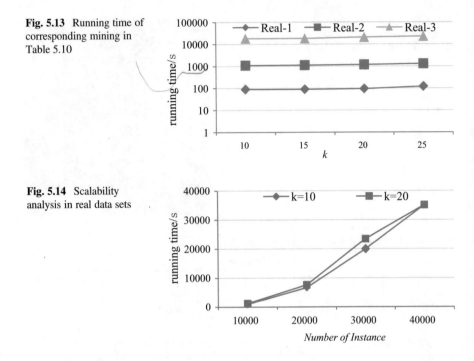

5.8   Chapter Summary

In this chapter, we studied the extraction of the **top-k** PPCPs over spatially uncertain data sets. We presented a basic framework for efficiently mining top-k PPCPs from spatially uncertain data sets with existential probabilities under the possible world semantics. The proposed novel matrix method and polynomial strategy exhibited their superiority, as was shown both theoretically and experimentally. Furthermore, based on the polynomial method, the approximate algorithm in Wang et al. (2013a) is alternated to compute the prevalence probability of a top-k candidate with minimal computational effort and the results are highly accurate.

In the next chapter, we will discuss the redundancy reduction problem of the spatial prevalent co-location patterns by further application of distribution information from co-location instances.

Chapter 6
Non-redundant Prevalent Co-location Patterns

6.1 Introduction

Spatial co-location pattern (SCP) mining is an interesting and important task in spatial data mining which discovers the sets of spatial features frequently observed together in nearby geographic space. However, the traditional framework of mining prevalent co-location patterns produces numerous redundant co-location patterns, which makes it hard for users to understand or apply.

This chapter is an attempt to address this issue by the following contributions:

1. A *semantic distance* metric between a co-location and its super-patterns is proposed, and shows it is a sub-valid distance metric.
2. A concept of *δ-covered* to estimate the redundancy degree of a SCP is defined.
3. We propose two algorithms: **RRclosed**, which follows existing redundancy reduction techniques to adopt the post-mining framework that reduces redundant SCPs from the set of closed prevalent co-locations; **RRnull**, which employs a *mine-and-reduce* framework to discover non-redundant results directly from the spatial data sets and runs much faster than the closed co-location mining algorithm in Yoo and Bow (2011a), itself a very fast closed co-location mining method.

Our performance study shows that the introduction of *δ-covered* can effectively reduce the number of closed co-locations. In addition, users can control the redundancy reduction power by adjusting the coverage measure δ ($0 \leq \delta \leq 1$).

Figure 6.1 presents the organization of this chapter. Section 6.2 discusses the needs of exploring non-redundant SCPs. In Sect. 6.3, we give the related definitions for non-redundant SCP mining. Section 6.4 presents the **RRclosed** method, and the

From Wang, L., Bao, X., Zhou, L.: Redundancy Reduction for Prevalent Co-Location Patterns, *IEEE Transactions on Knowledge and Data Engineering (TKDE)* 30(1), 142–155 (2018).

© The Author(s), under exclusive license to Springer Nature Singapore Pte Ltd. 2022
L. Wang et al., *Preference-based Spatial Co-location Pattern Mining*, Big Data
Management, https://doi.org/10.1007/978-981-16-7566-9_6

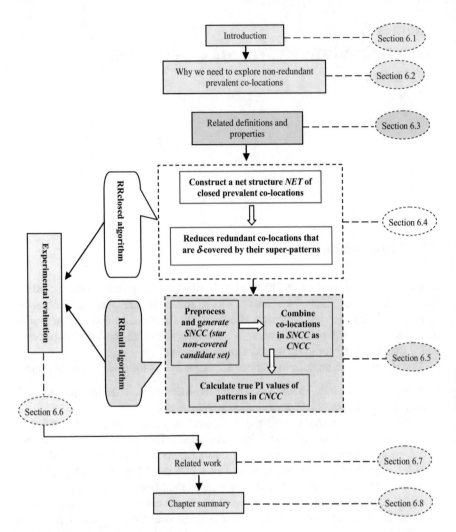

Fig. 6.1 The organization of this chapter

RRnull method is proposed in Sect. 6.5. Our performance study is presented in Sect. 6.6. The related work is discussed in Sects. 6.7 and 6.8 concludes.

6.2   Why We Need to Explore Non-redundant Prevalent Co-locations

Mining spatial co-location patterns (SCPs) is an interesting and important spatial data mining task with a broad range of applications including Earth science (Verhein & Al-Naymat, 2007), public health (Li et al., 2016), public transportation (Yu, 2016; He et al., 2018), environmental studies (Akbari et al., 2015), and et al. In the paper of Yao et al. (2017), for example, the extracted patterns in the public-service facilities of developed cities can be used to plan layouts or arrange new facilities in cities.

An *SCP* is a group of spatial features whose instances are frequently located close to each other (Huang et al., 2004). Examples of SCPs include symbiotic species, e.g., West Nile Virus and stagnant water sources in public health, and interdependent incidents, e.g., traffic jams, car accidents, ambulances, and police in public transportation.

The traditional framework of SCP mining uses the frequencies of a set of spatial features participating in a SCP to measure the prevalence (known as *participation index* (Huang et al., 2004), or *PI* for short) and requires a user-specified minimum PI threshold to find interesting SCPs. The meaning of PI is that wherever a feature in a SCP c is observed, all other features in c can be observed in its neighborhood with a probability of at least $PI(c)$. Similar to the support metric in frequent itemset mining, the PI metric satisfies the *anti-monotonicity property*. That is, if a SCP is prevalent with respect to a threshold of PI, then all of its subsets (sub-patterns) will be discovered as prevalent SCPs. Traditional frameworks generate numerous redundant SCPs which jeopardize the usability of the technique, as it then demands great effort to discern or understand the discovered knowledge.

Two major approaches have been developed to aid the user: *lossless* and *lossy* redundancy reduction. The former, using *closed prevalent co-locations* (Yoo & Bow, 2011a) (a prevalent SCP c is closed if there is no SCP c' such that $c \subset c'$ and $PI(c) = PI(c')$), concentrates too much on the PI information of SCPs so that its redundancy reduction power is quite limited. The latter, using *maximal prevalent co-locations* (Wang et al., 2009b; Yoo & Bow, 2011b) (a prevalent SCP c is maximal if there is no prevalent SCP c' such that $c \subset c'$), may significantly reduce the number of SCPs, but it loses PI information from most of the SCPs, leaving difficulties for the user. This paper presents a new, improved, redundancy reduction framework for detecting prevalent SCPs, utilizing the spatial distributed information of co-location instances while retaining some useful features of the non-redundant co-location sets.

An explanatory example is shown below.

Example 6.1   Figure 6.2(a) shows an example spatial data set, where instances of four spatial features, A, B, C and D, are denoted by the feature type and a numeric id value, e.g. A.1, and edges connecting two instances indicate spatial neighboring relationships. Figure 6.2(b) lists the co-location instances, the PRs and the PIs of all

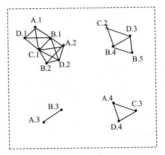

(a)   An example spatial data set

T({A,B,C,D})

A	B	C	D
A.1	B.1	C.1	D.1
A.2	B.1	C.1	D.2
A.2	B.2	C.1	D.2
2/4	2/5	1/3	2/4
	1/3		

T({A,B,C})

A	B	C
A.1	B.1	C.1
A.2	B.1	C.1
A.2	B.2	C.1
2/4	2/5	1/3
	1/3	

T({A,B,D})

A	B	D
A.1	B.1	D.1
A.2	B.1	D.2
A.2	B.2	D.2
2/4	2/5	2/4
	2/5	

T({A,C,D})

A	C	D
A.1	C.1	D.1
A.2	C.1	D.2
A.4	C.3	D.4
3/4	2/3	3/4
	2/3	

Legend: - - ► co-location; - ► row instance; co-location instance; - - - - ► PRs; - - - - ► PI

They are the same.

T({B,C,D})

B	C	D
B.1	C.1	D.1
B.1	C.1	D.2
B.2	C.1	D.2
B.4	C.2	D.3
3/5	2/3	3/4
	3/5	

T({A,B})

A	B
A.1	B.1
A.2	B.1
A.2	B.2
A.3	B.3
3/4	3/5
	3/5

T({A,C})

A	C
A.1	C.1
A.2	C.1
A.4	C.3
3/4	2/3
	2/3

T({A,D})

A	D
A.1	D.1
A.2	D.2
A.4	D.4
3/4	3/4
	3/4

T({B,C})

B	C
B.1	C.1
B.2	C.1
B.4	C.2
3/5	2/3
	3/5

T({B,D})

B	D
B.1	D.1
B.1	D.2
B.2	D.2
B.4	D.3
B.5	D.3
4/5	3/4
	3/4

T({C,D})

C	D
C.1	D.1
C.1	D.2
C.2	D.2
C.2	D.3
C.3	D.4
3/3	4/4
	1

T({A,D}) is fully contained in T({A,C,D})

(b) The co-location instances, PR values and PI values of possible co-locations in data set of Fig. 6.2a

Fig. 6.2 A motivating example, where (**a**) an example spatial data set; (**b**) the co-location instances, the PRs and the PIs of all possible SCPs in the data set

possible SCPs in the data set (the definitions of co-location instance, PR and PI are provided in Sect. 6.3).

If a minimum PI threshold is 0.3, maximal prevalent co-location mining will only report the 4-size SCP {A, B, C, D}. In contrast, the result of closed prevalent co-location mining will be {{A, B, C, D}, {A, B, D}, {A, C, D}, {B, C, D}, {A, B}, {A, D}, {B, D}, {C, D}}. However, we observe that each SCP in the set {{A, B, D}, {A, C, D}, {B, C, D}, {A, B}, {A, D}, {B, D}, {C, D}} is significantly different with respect to their PI values from {A, B, C, D}. Additionally, closed prevalent co-location mining is too prolific, as we note that the co-location instance $T(\{A, D\})$ of {A, D} is fully contained in co-location instance $T(\{A, C, D\})$ of its super-pattern {A, C, D} (as shown in the dotted boxes in $T(\{A, D\})$ and $T(\{A, C, D\})$). We say {A, D} is *covered* by {A, C, D} with respect to the distributed information of co-location instances (see Definition 6.7). Similarly, SCPs {A, B, D} and {B, D} are covered by {A, B, C, D} and {B, C, D}, respectively, and the co-location instance information of {A, C, D} and {B, C, D} covers that of {C, D}. The high-quality non-redundant result is {{A, B, C, D}, {A, C, D}, {B, C, D}, {A, B}} for this example data set.

A strategy for improving the redundancy reduction power in closed prevalent co-locations is to identify redundant SCPs according to certain similarity measures. However, there are three crucial questions which need to be answered:

1. How to measure the similarity between the SCPs?
2. How to efficiently and completely eliminate redundant SCPs and, for research purposes?
3. How to estimate the redundancy degree of SCPs?

This chapter is an attempt to offer answers to these questions. We first introduce the concept of *semantic distance* between a SCP and its super-SCPs, and then define redundant SCPs by introducing the concept of *δ-covered*, where δ $(0 \leq \delta \leq 1)$ is a coverage measure. We develop two algorithms **RRclosed** and **RRnull** to perform the redundancy reduction for prevalent SCPs. Our performance studies on the synthetic and real-world data sets demonstrate that our method effectively reduces the size of the original collection of closed co-location patterns by about 50%. Furthermore, the RRnull method runs much faster than the related closed co-location pattern mining algorithm.

6.3 Problem Definition

In this section, we first introduce a semantic distance metric to measure the similarity between the SCPs, and then the non-redundant prevalent SCP mining problem is defined formally, based on a new *δ-covered* concept, where δ $(0 \leq \delta \leq 1)$ is a coverage measure.

6.3.1 Semantic Distance

To improve the redundancy reduction power in the set of closed prevalent co-locations, we introduce a semantic distance metric to measure the similarity between two closed prevalent co-locations based on their co-location instances, which contain the neighbor relationship information of their spatial instances.

Definition 6.1 (Semantic distance, SD) Let c and c' be two closed prevalent co-locations, and $c \subset c'$. The **semantic distance** between c and c' is defined as:

$$SD(c, c') = \min_{f_i \in c} \left\{ \left(1 - \frac{| \Pi_{f_i} T(c') |}{| \Pi_{f_i} T(c) |} \right) \right\} \qquad (6.1)$$

where $\Pi_{f_i} T(c)$ is the set of distinct instances of fi in $T(c)$, and $T(c)$ is the co-location instance of c.

Let us apply the SD measure to the SCPs in Fig. 6.2 to see whether it reasonably reflects the distance between SCPs in term of redundancy. Firstly, we consider $c = \{A, D\}$ and $c' = \{A, C, D\}$. According to Definition 6.1, $|\prod_A T(c)| = |\{A.1, A.2, A.4\}| = 3$, $|\prod_D T(c)| = |\{D.1, D.2, D.4\}| = 3$, $|\prod_A T(c')| = |\{A.1, A.2, A.4\}| = 3$, $|\prod_D T(c')| = |\{D.1, D.2, D.4\}| = 3$, so $SD(c, c') = \min\{1-3/3, 1-3/3\} = 0$. This means the co-location instance information of $\{A, D\}$, which shows the prevalence information of a SCP, is fully contained in that of $\{A, C, D\}$ (i.e., when the instances of features A and D are observed in a neighborhood, the instance of feature C must occur in this neighborhood too). That is, $\{A, D\}$ is a redundant SCP relative to $\{A, C, D\}$. Secondly, let us consider $c = \{A, B\}$ and $c' = \{A, B, C, D\}$. We can calculate $SD(c, c') = \min\{1-2/3, 1-2/3\} = 1/3$, which indicates that $\{A, B\}$ have extra row instance distribution information relative to $\{A, B, C, D\}$. Finally, let us illustrate the meaning of the "min" in Eq. (6.3). We observe that $SD(\{B, D\}, \{B, C, D\}) = 0$ but $T(\{B, D\})$ has not been fully contained in $T(\{B, C, D\})$. In fact, there is no extra instance of feature D in $T(\{B, D\})$ which occurs relative to $T(\{B, C, D\})$. As far as *the distribution of co-location instances* is concerned, $T(\{B, D\})$ does not contain extra information relative to $T(\{B, C, D\})$. (Because D.3 in the row instance $\{B.5, D.3\}$ has occurred in row instance $\{B.4, C.2, D.3\}$ of $T(\{B, C, D\})$, $\{B.5, D.3\}$ is not a new distribution of row instances.) Thus we see that the SD measure captures the redundancy power between a SCP and its super-SCP.

Theorem 6.1 The semantic distance SD is a sub-valid distance metric, such that:

1. $SD(c, c') \geq 0, \forall c \subset c'$.
2. $SD(c, c') = 0, \forall c = c'$.
3. *For* $\forall c \subset c' \subset c''$, if

$$\arg_f \max \left\{ \left(\frac{|\prod_f T(c')|}{|\prod_f T(c)|} \right) : f \in c \right\} = \arg_f \max \left\{ \left(\frac{|\prod_f T(c'')|}{|\prod_f T(c')|} \right) : f \in c' \right\}.$$

then $SD(c, c') + SD(c', c'') \geq SD(c, c'')$.

Proof By the definition of SD, it is easy to verify that the first two properties are true. We prove the third statement as below.

To simplify the presentation, we define the variables:

$$x = \max_{f \in c} \left\{ \frac{|\prod_f T(c')|}{|\prod_f T(c)|} \right\}, y = \max_{f \in c'} \left\{ \frac{|\prod_f T(c'')|}{|\prod_f T(c')|} \right\}, \text{and } z$$

$$= \max_{f \in c} \left\{ \frac{|\prod_f T(c'')|}{|\prod_f T(c')|} \right\}$$

Plug in all the variables into the distance definition.

$$SD(c, c') + SD(c', c'') \geq SD(c, c'') \Leftrightarrow (1 - x) + (1 - y) \geq (1 - z) \qquad (6.2)$$

If $c \subset c'$ then every row instance of c' contains a subset of instances which is a row instance of c. So $|\prod_f T(c)| \geq |\prod_f T(c')|$ for $f \in c$.

We can assume $x = b/a$ and $y = c/b$ in Eq. (6.2) based on the condition of the third statement. Therefore,

If $z = c/a$, we have $a \geq b \geq c$ due to $c \subset c' \subset c''$.

Then, $(1 - b/a) + (1 - c/b) = (1 - (b/a - ((b - c)/b))) \geq (1 - (b/a - ((b - c)/a)))$ (by $a \geq b$) $= (1 - c/a)$.

So, Eq. (6.2) is true in this case.

Else, the values a and c in z are different from that in x and y. Since $z =$

$$\max{}_{f \in c} \left\{ \frac{\left| \prod_f T(c'') \right|}{\left| \prod_f T(c) \right|} \right\}, 1 - z \leq 1 - c/a. \text{ Eq. (6.2) is still true.}$$

Thus the third statement is true. $\square$

Remark (1) Although the SD can reasonably reflect the distance between SCPs in term of redundancy, it is sub-valid since there is a condition on the third statement in Theorem 6.1. (2) The SD can be extended to general prevalent SCPs excepting that, for a non-closed co-location c, there is a closed co-location c' such that $c \subset c'$ and $SD(c, c') = 0$. This is because from the condition $PI(c) = PI(c')$ of a non-closed co-location c, we can infer that there exists a feature f_i in c such that $PR(c, f_i) = PR(c', f_i)$, and therefore $SD(c, c') = 0$ holds.

6.3.2   δ-Covered

Based on the SD metric, we can define a covered relationship between SCPs, and then the concept of *δ-covered* is introduced further.

Definition 6.2 (Covered (or non-covered)) For an SCP c, if there exists (does not exist) an SCP c' such that $c \subset c'$ and $SD(c, c') = 0$. We say c is **covered** by c' (c is a **non-covered** SCP).

For example, SCP $\{A, D\}$ is covered by $\{A, C, D\}$ in the data set of Fig. 6.2(a). If $\{A, C, D\}$ has been in the set of closed prevalent co-locations, $\{A, D\}$ is a *redundant* CPC with respect to the distribution of co-location instances. By contrast, the SCP $\{A, B\}$ in the data set of Fig. 6.2(a) is a non-covered SCP since its row instance $\{A.3, B.3\}$ cannot be contained in any of its super-SCPs.

Obviously, we can use the covered concept to prune redundant closed prevalent co-locations in the set of closed prevalent co-locations. For example, in Fig. 6.2, if $M = 0.3$, the closed prevalent co-location set is $\{\{A, B, C, D\}, \{A, B, D\}, \{A, C, D\},$

{B, C, D}, {A, B}, {A, D}, {B, D}, {C, D}}. So closed prevalent co-locations {A, B, D}, {A, D}, and {B, D} can be pruned since they are covered by {A, B, C, D}, {A, C, D}, and {B, C, D}, respectively.

In order to achieve a more succinct compression of the non-covered prevalent SCPs, we extend the concept of covered in two ways, as follows.

First, let c' be a set of the super-SCPs of c, say $c' = \{c_1, c_2,\ldots, c_t\}$, and we then have the following extended concept of *SD*:

Definition 6.3 (Extended semantic distance, ESD) Let c be a closed prevalent co-location and $\{c_1, c_2,\ldots, c_t\}$ ($t \geq 1$) be a set of closed prevalent co-locations, and $c \subset c_i\,(1 \leq i \leq t)$. The **extended semantic distance** between c and $\{c_1, c_2,\ldots, c_t\}$ is defined as:

$$\text{ESD}(c, \{c_1, c_2, \ldots, c_t\}) = \min{}_{f_i \in c} \left\{ \left(1 - \frac{\left| \overset{t}{\underset{j=1}{\cup}} \prod_{f_i} T(c_j) \right|}{\left| \prod_{f_i} T(c) \right|} \right) \right\} \tag{6.3}$$

where $\prod_{f_i} T(c)$ is the set of distinct instances of f_i in $T(c)$, and $T(c)$ is the co-location instance of c.

Naturally, the SD in Definition 6.2 can be extended to ESD, and then more SCPs in closed prevalent co-locations could be eliminated.

Example 6.2 In Fig. 6.2, if $M = 0.3$, for {C, D} in closed prevalent co-location set, there are two closed prevalent co-locations {A, C, D} and {B, C, D}, such that $SD(\{C, D\}, \{\{A, C, D\}, \{B, C, D\}\}) = \min\left\{1 - \frac{3}{3}, 1 - \frac{4}{4}\right\} = 0$. {C, D} is covered by its super-SCP set {{A, C, D}, {B, C, D}}. That is to say, if {A, C, D} and {B, C, D} are in the closed prevalent co-location set, {C, D} is deemed to be redundant and it should be eliminated so as to further reduce the number of non-covered SCPs in the set of closed prevalent co-locations.

Accordingly, for the data set of Fig. 6.2(a), the closed prevalent co-locations set is reduced to {{A, B, C, D}, {A, C, D}, {B, C, D}, {A, B}}. We regard this as the ideal non-redundancy result, because each pattern has extra information (i.e., an extra co-location instance, see Fig. 6.2(a)).

Second, we extend the *covered* concept to *δ-covered* to further reduce the number of non-covered SCPs in the set of closed prevalent co-locations by adjusting the coverage measure δ ($0 \leq \delta \leq 1$), where δ is a user specified coverage measure threshold.

Definition 6.4 (δ-covered) A co-location c is **δ-covered** by a set of SCPs $\{c_1, c_2,\ldots, c_t\}$ ($t \geq 1$) if $c \subset c_i\,(1 \leq i \leq t)$ and $\text{ESD}(c, \{c_1, c_2,\ldots, c_t\}) \leq \delta\,(0 \leq \delta \leq 1)$.

6.3.3 The Problem Definition and Analysis

Based on the above discussion, the prevalent SCP redundancy reduction problem is formally defined as follows.

Definition 6.5 (Non-redundant prevalent SCP discovery problem) Given a spatial data set D (a collection of instances S of a set of spatial feature F), a minimum PI threshold M and a coverage measure δ, the non-redundant **prevalent SCP discovery problem** is to find a minimal set of non-covered prevalent SCPs Ω, such that for any prevalent SCP c in D, i.e., $PI(c) \geq M$, there exists a set of SCPs $\{c_1, c_2, \ldots, c_t\}$ $(t \geq 1)$ in Ω s.t. $c \subset c_i$ and $ESD(c, \{c_1, c_2, \ldots, c_t\}) \leq \delta$.

We note that the size of Ω is no less than the number of the maximal prevalent SCPs. This is because a maximal prevalent SCP can only be covered by itself. On the other hand, the size of Ω is no larger than the number of the closed prevalent co-locations since a non-closed prevalent co-location must be covered by a closed prevalent co-location.

Theorem 6.2 The δ-covered relationship is a limited partial order in the prevalent SCP set, such that:

1. c is δ-covered by c (reflexivity).
2. if c is δ-covered by c' and c' is δ-covered by c, then $c = c'$ (anti-symmetry).

3. if c is covered by c' and c' is δ-covered by $\{c_1, c_2, \ldots, c_t\}$, and $f^* =$

$$\arg_f \max \left\{ \frac{\left| \prod_f T(c') \right|}{\left| \prod_f T(c) \right|} : f \in c \right\} = \arg_f \max \left\{ \left(\frac{\left| \cup_{i=1}^t \prod_f T(c_i) \right|}{\left| \prod_f T(c') \right|} \right) : f \in c' \right\} \quad \text{then}$$

c must be δ-covered by $\{c_1, c_2, \ldots, c_t\}$ (limited-transitivity).

Proof By the definition of δ-covered, it is easy to verify that the first two properties are true. We prove the third statement here.

According to the conditions of the third statement, we have

$$SD(c, c') = 1 - \max_{f \in c} \left\{ \frac{\left| \prod_f T(c') \right|}{\left| \prod_f T(c) \right|} \right\} = 0 \text{ and}$$

$$ESD(c', \{c_1, \ldots c_t\}) = 1 - \max_{f \in c'} \left\{ \frac{\left| \bigcup\limits_{i=1}^{t} \prod_f T(c_i) \right|}{\left| \prod_f T(c') \right|} \right\} \leq \delta \Rightarrow$$

$$ESD(c, \{c_1, \ldots c_t\}) = 1 - \max_{f \in c} \left\{ \frac{\left| \bigcup\limits_{i=1}^{t} \prod_f T(c_i) \right|}{\left| \prod_f T(c) \right|} \right\}$$

$$= \left(1 - \frac{\left| \prod_{f^*} T(c') \right|}{\left| \prod_{f^*} T(c) \right|} \cdot \frac{\left| \bigcup\limits_{i=1}^{t} \prod_{f^*} T(c_i) \right|}{\left| \prod_{f^*} T(c') \right|} \right) \leq \delta. \quad \square$$

The semantic distance, a *sub-valid* distance metric, leads to the *limited-transitivity* expressed in Theorem 6.2, and it means that there may exist SCPs that do not satisfy transitivity. We call these hard SCPs.

Definition 6.6 (Hard SCP) For a prevalent SCP c, if c is covered by its super-SCP c' and c' is δ-*covered* by its super-SCP set $\{c_1, c_2, \ldots, c_t\}$, but c cannot be δ-*covered* by $\{c_1, c_2, \ldots, c_t\}$, c *is* called a **hard SCP** of c'.

For example, in Fig. 6.2, if the co-location instance of SCP $\{A, B, C, D\}$ became $\{\{A.1, B.1, C.1, D.1\}, \{A.2, B.1, C.1, D.2\}, \{A.2, B.2, C.1, \textbf{\textit{D.3}}\}\}$, the SCP $\{B, C, D\}$ was covered by $\{A, B, C, D\}$ ($\delta = 0$). But the SCP $\{B, C\}$ cannot be covered by $\{A, B, C, D\}$. Thus, $\{B, C\}$ is a hard SCP of $\{B, C, D\}$.

For a non-closed prevalent co-location c, there is a closed prevalent co-location c' such that and $c \subset c'$ and $SD(c, c') = 0$, so we have the following lemma, proof omitted.

Lemma 6.1 Given a spatial data set D, a minimum PI threshold M and a coverage measure δ, if any SCP in the "closed+hard" SCP set is δ-*covered* by SCPs in Ω, then any prevalent SCP in D can be δ-*covered* by SCPs in Ω.

Accordingly, the discovery of the non-covered prevalent SCP set Ω has to start from the largest size of closed prevalent co-locations. At the same time, hard SCPs need to be added dynamically.

For the convenience of computing ESD and identifying non-covered SCPs, we introduce a new concept and a Lemma.

Definition 6.7 (Set participation ratio) The set participation ratio *SPR* $(\{c_1, c_2, \ldots, c_t\}, f)$ of the common feature f in $\{c_1, c_2, \ldots, c_t\}$ is the fraction of instances of f that occur in $\bigcup\limits_{j=1}^{t} \prod_{f_i} T(c_j)$, that is,

$$SPR(\{c_1, c_2, \ldots, c_t\}, f_i) = \frac{\left| \overset{t}{\underset{j=1}{\cup}} \prod_{f_i} T(c_j) \right|}{\text{Total number of instances of } f_i} \qquad (6.4)$$

where $\prod_{f_i} T(c)$ is the set of distinct instances of f_i in $T(c)$, and $T(c)$ is the co-location instance of c.

For example, consider the data set in Fig. 6.2(a), and $c_1 = \{A, C, D\}$ and $c_2 = \{B, C, D\}$ in Fig. 6.2(b). Since $\prod_c T(c_1) = \{C.1, C.3\}$, $\prod_c T(c_2) = \{C.1, C.2\}$ and C has three instances, we have $SPR(\{c_1, c_2\}, C) = 3/3 = 1$.

Lemma 6.2 For any SCP c in Ω, if its super-SCP set is $\{c_1, c_2, \ldots, c_t\}$, then $\widehat{M} < 1 - \delta$ holds, where $\widehat{M} = \max_{f_i \in c} \left\{ \frac{SPR(\{c_1, c_2, \ldots, c_t\}, f_i)}{PR(c, f_i)} \right\}$.

Proof Since $c \in \Omega$, we have $ESD(c, \{c_1, c_2, \ldots, c_t\}) > \delta$. So,

$$\delta < ESD(c, \{c_1, c_2, \ldots, c_t\}) = \min_{f_i \in c} \left\{ \left(1 - \frac{\left| \overset{t}{\underset{j=1}{\cup}} \prod_{f_i} T(c_j) \right|}{\left| \prod_{f_i} T(c) \right|} \right) \right\}$$

$$= 1 - \max_{f_i \in c} \left\{ \frac{\left| \overset{t}{\underset{j=1}{\cup}} \prod_{f_i} T(c_j) \right|}{\left| \prod_{f_i} T(c) \right|} \right\} = 1 - \widehat{M},$$

where $\widehat{M} = \max_{f_i \in c} \left\{ \frac{SPR(\{c_1, c_2, \ldots, c_t\}, f_i)}{PR(c, f_i)} \right\}$.

That is, $\widehat{M} < 1 - \delta$ holds. $\square$

According to Definitions 6.4 and 6.5 and the proof of Lemma 6.2, the condition $\widehat{M} < 1 - \delta$ is an iff condition with respect to whether a SCP c remains in Ω.

Discussion:

1. The number of hard SCPs in a data set is usually hard to estimate. From a large number of experiments in Sect. 6.6, we found this number to be very small.
2. Because of the *limited-transitivity* in Theorem 6.2, the set of non-covered prevalent SCPs Ω of a spatial data set D should not be unique. Finding the optimal solution is NP-hard, so the two algorithms presented in Sects. 6.4 and 6.5 are aimed at obtaining a reduced result with respect to the original collection of closed prevalent co-locations.

6.4   The RRclosed Method

In this section, we present the RRclosed method which adopts a *post-mining* framework to implement the prevalent SCP redundancy reduction from *CPC* which is a collection of closed prevalent co-locations.

The RRclosed method consists of two phases. Phase 1 constructs a *net structure NET* of *CPC* according to the relationship of SCPs and super-SCPs in order to facilitate the next phase, and Phase 2 reduces redundant SCPs that are δ-covered by their super-SCPs.

In Phase 1, we adopt a method beginning from the largest-size SCPs of *CPC*. When inserting a size-l SCP c into *NET*, we compute $DEC(c)$, which is the collection of the super-SCPs of c, by using the intersection operation of c with $l + 1$ size SCPs in *NET*. If $DEC(c) = \phi$, $l + 2$ size SCPs are considered, until reaching the root of *NET*. For example, for the spatial data set in Fig. 6.2(a), if $M = 0.3$ then $CPC = \{\{A, B, C, D\}, \{A, B, D\}, \{A, C, D\}, \{B, C, D\}, \{A, B\}, \{A, D\}, \{B, D\}, \{C, D\}\}$. The *NET* of *CPC* is shown in Fig. 6.3.

In Phase 2, we check SCPs in *NET* starting from the largest size minus one. According to Lemma 6.2, we calculate $\widehat{M}$ of checked SCP c and prune it from *NET* if $\widehat{M} \geq (1 - \delta)$. In the realization, we can sort all features in c in the *ascending order* of the PR values, and the negative condition in Lemma 6.2 (i.e., $\widehat{M} \geq (1 - \delta)$) may be satisfied earlier. When an SCP c is pruned from *NET*, it is necessary to revise the relationships of SCPs and super-SCPs affected by c, and insert the *hard co-locations* of c into *NET*. For example, in Fig. 6.3, if $\{A, B, D\}$ is covered by its super-SCP $\{A, B, C, D\}$, its sub-SCP $\{A, B\}$ will be directly connected to $\{A, B, C, D\}$ (see the dotted line in Fig. 6.3) because $\{A, B, D\}$ is a unique super-SCP of $\{A, B\}$.

The full RRclosed algorithm is summarized in Algorithm 6.1.

Fig. 6.3 The NET of CPC for the data set in Fig. 6.2(a)

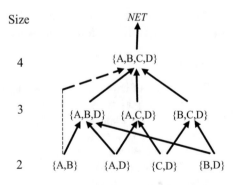

Algorithm 6.1   RRclosed

Input:

(1) A collection of closed prevalent co-locations CPC and their co-location instances;

(2) A minimum PI threshold, M;

(3) A coverage measure threshold, δ.

Output:

A set of non-covered prevalent-SCPs Ω.

Method:

//Construct a net structure representing inclusion relationships

1)   Initiate an empty net structure *NET*;

2) l_{max} =largest_size(*CPC*);

3) $l = l_{max}$;

4)   **while** ($l > 1$ or $CPC \neq \phi$) **do**

5)   **for** each *l*-size SCP *c* in *CPC*;

6)   *NET*.addRelations(*c*, DEC(*c*));

         //DEC(c) is the collection of the super-SCPs of c

7) $l=l-1$;

//Reduce the redundant SCPs

8) $l = l_{max}-1$;

9)   **while** ($l > 1$) **do**

10)   **for** each *l*-size SCP *c* in *NET*

11) $\hat{M} = \max_{f \in c} \{ \dfrac{SPR(DEC(c), f)}{PR(c, f)} \}$;   *//see Lemma 6.2*

12)   **if** $\hat{M} \geq (1-\delta)$ **then**   *//c is δ-covered*

13)   *NET*.prune(*c*);

14)   **if** $l > 2$ **then**

15)   **for** each *c'* connected only to *c* in *NET*

                 // c is the only super-SCP of c' in NET

16)   *NET*.updateRelations(*c'*, DEC(*c*));

17)   *NET*.addHard(*c*);

              // the hard SCPs of c are added into NET

18) $l=l-1$

19) $\Omega \leftarrow NET$ *//convert the structure NET into the set Ω*

20) **Output** Ω

END

The computational cost of RRclosed mainly comes from the second phase, whose *coarse* computation complexity is $O(\sum_{c \in CPC}|T(c)|^r)$, where $T(c)$ is the co-location instance of *c*, *r* is the average time of scanning $T(c)$ (some $T(c)$ may be scanned many times for calculating $\hat{M}$ in Step 11, but the average scanning time *r* is not too big, just slightly greater than 1 time unit in general). The running time of RRclosed is principally affected by the *minimum PI threshold M* and *spatial neighbor distance threshold d*, because they control $T(c)$, the number of *CPC* and the largest size of *CPC*.

However, RRclosed needs to first compute the *CPC*. To improve the computation of the set *Ω*, a new method RRnull is presented in the next section.

6.5   The RRnull Method

In this section, we introduce a new method called RRnull which pushes the redundancy (coverage) validation into the prevalent SCP mining process.

6.5.1   The Method

Computing the closed prevalent co-locations and their co-location instances is necessary for RRclosed, since the method checks coverage information based on the mined closed prevalent co-locations. To develop a much more efficient method, we introduce a lexicographic prefix-tree structure to store feature neighborhood transactions. We start with the generation of *non-covered* SCP candidates.

According to the related definitions, the coverage metrics are based on the co-location instances that contain the spatial neighbor relationships of instances in SCPs. So, we convert the input data to neighborhood transactions. The calculation of the neighbor relationship of the input data can be performed using a sweeping-based spatial join approach (Arge et al., 1998).

Definition 6.8 (Neighborhood transaction (NT)) Given a spatial instance $f.i \in S$, the **neighborhood transaction (NT)** of $f.i$ is defined as a set consisting of $f.i$ and the other spatial instances having neighbor relationships with $f.i$, i.e., $NT(f,i) = \{f.i, g.j \in S \mid NR(f.i, g.j) = true \cap f \neq g\}$, where NR is a spatial neighbor relationship.

For example, in Fig. 6.2(a), the neighbor transaction of A.1 is {A.1, B.1 C.1, D.1}, including itself as shown in Fig. 6.4(b). Note that each instance in the transaction has a neighbor relationship with the first instance, which is called a *reference* instance.

This data structure was first introduced in Yoo and Shekhar (2006) and Yoo and Bow (2011a). It gives several advantages for *non-covered* SCP mining. First, the neighborhood transactions do not lose any instances, nor lose any neighbor relationships of the original data. Second, the neighborhood transactions can be easily constructed from the neighboring instance pairs of the input data. Third, the neighborhood transactions can give the information about the upper bound value of the PI of a candidate. Finally, the feature neighborhood transactions, which are the set of distinct features in the neighborhood transactions, can be used to generate *non-covered* SCP candidates.

Definition 6.9 (Feature neighborhood transaction (FNT)) The lexicographic set of distinct features in NT is called **feature neighborhood transaction (FNT)**.

The feature neighborhood transactions relative to the neighborhood transactions in Fig. 6.4(b) are shown in Fig. 6.4(a).

The candidate generation method in Yoo and Bow (2011a) considers feature sets having possible clique relationships as candidates. However, here we consider feature sets having "*non-covered + possible clique relationships*" as candidates.

Trans. No.	Neighbor features		Trans. No.	Neighbor instances	
1	A	B,C,D	1	A.1	B.1,C.1,D.1
2	A	B,C,D	2	A.2	B.1,B.2,C.1,D.2
3	A	B	3	A.3	B.3
4	A	C,D	4	A.4	C.3,D.4
5	B	A,C,D	5	B.1	A.1,A.2,C.1,D.1,D.2
6	B	A,C,D	6	B.2	A.2,C.1,D.2
7	B	A	7	B.3	A.3
8	B	C,D	8	B.4	C.2,D.3
9	B	D	9	B.5	D.3
10	C	A,B,D	10	C.1	A.1,A.2,B.1,B.2,D.1,D2
11	C	B,D	11	C.2	B.4,D.3
12	C	A,D	12	C.3	A.4,D.4
13	D	A,B,C	13	D.1	A.1,B.1,C.1
14	D	A,B,C	14	D.2	A.2,B.1,B.2,C.1
15	D	B,C	15	D.3	B.4,B.5,C.2
16	D	A,C	16	D.4	A.4,C.3

(a) feature neighborhood transactions (*FNT*)   (b) neighborhood transactions (*NT*)

Fig. 6.4 The feature neighborhood transactions and neighborhood transactions of the data set in Fig. 6.2(a)

For this, we revise the procedure proposed in Yoo and Bow (2011a) in three ways, as follows.

Firstly, we generate feature sets for *star non-covered candidates* from FNTs using a lexicographic prefix-tree structure. This lexicographic prefix-tree is defined as follows: (1) It consists of one root labeled as a reference feature and a set of feature neighbor relationships as the children of the root, (2) each node consists of three fields: feature-type, count, and node-link, where feature-type denotes a feature that this node represents, count registers the number of neighborhood transactions represented by the portion of the path reaching this node, and node-link links to the next node in the tree carrying the same feature-type. As shown in Fig. 6.5(a), one prefix-tree per feature is built.

Definition 6.10 (Star non-covered candidate (*SNCC*) and upper participation ratio (*UPR*)) A feature set having relationships with the root node (reference feature) in a lexicographic prefix-tree is called a **star non-covered candidate (*SNCC*)** if its star participation ratio is greater than or equal to M and it has not been δ-covered by longer candidates in this prefix-tree. The star participation ratio represents the upper bound of the participation ratio of the reference features, which is the fraction of the count of reference feature in the count of neighborhood transactions of all other features in a candidate. It is called the **upper participation ratio (*UPR*)**.

SNCCs are generated using the following method.

1. Each branch in a lexicographic prefix-tree forms a SNCC if its *UPR* is greater than or equal to M.

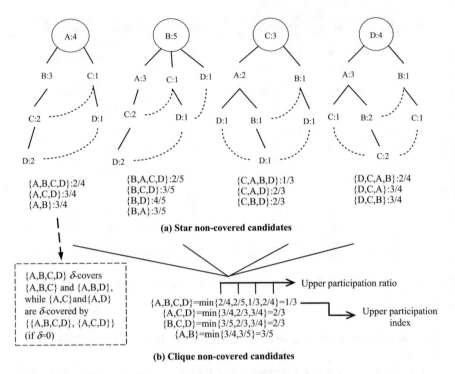

Fig. 6.5 Candidate generation, where (a) generating star non-covered candidates; (b) generating clique non-covered candidates

2. The sub-sets of the branches, which contain the root node, form SNCCs if they are not δ-*covered* by generated longer size candidates in the prefix-tree.

For example, in the prefix-tree of feature A, we can generate two candidates {A, B, C, D}: 2/4 and {A, C, D}: 3/4 from the two branches {A, B, C, D} and {A, C, D}, and if δ = 0 then the sub-set {A, B} of branch {A, B, C, D} is also a candidate {A, B}: 3/4 since $\frac{UPR(\{A,B,C,D\},A)}{UPR(\{A,B\},A)} = \frac{2}{3} < 1 - \delta$ (see Lemma 6.2). The star neighborhood information of the remaining sub-sets, which contain the root node, has been δ-covered by generated candidates. For example, the star neighborhood information of the sub-sets {A, B, C}, {A, B, D} in branch {A, B, C, D} is the same as that of {A, B, C, D}, while the star neighborhood information of the sub-sets {A, C}, {A, D} is covered by the candidates {A, B, C, D} and {A, C, D}. To form sub-sets in a branch, we conduct breadth-first enumerations in the branch set except for the root node.

Secondly, the SNCCs are combined for filtering the *clique non-covered candidates* (CNCCs).

Definition 6.11 (Clique non-covered candidate (*CNCC*) and upper participation index (*UPI*)) A size-k candidate combining from k size-k *SNCCs* in the prefix-trees is called a size-k **clique non-covered candidate (*CNCC*)**. The minimum value of k UPRs is called the **upper participation index (*UPI*)**.

For example, in Fig. 6.5(b), to be {A, B, C, D}, which is a clique non-covered candidate, four SNCCs {A, B, C, D}, {B, A, C, D}, {C, A, B, D}, and {D, A, B, C} are needed. The sub-set {B, D} is a star non-covered candidate in prefix-tree B, but {D, B} is not a star non-covered candidate in prefix-tree D. After the combining step, {B, D} is pruned.

Once a candidate is pruned, its covered sub-sets need to be generated. For example, if $M = 0.4$, the generated candidate set in the prefix-tree C would be {{C, A, D}: 2/3, {C, B, D}: 2/3, {C, D}: 3/3}. The clique non-covered candidate {A, B, C, D} cannot be formed in the combining step, as the covered sub-sets {A, B, C}: 2/4 and {A, B, D}: 2/4 of the {A, B, C, D} in the prefix-tree A need to be generated. Prefix-tree B and D are treated similarly. The process of filtering CNCCs is conducted by dynamically changing SNCCs.

Thirdly, the true PIs of candidates are computed starting from the largest size candidates. The *candidate co-location instances* of candidates are gathered by scanning NTs in Fig. 6.4(b), even though they are not the true co-location instances. True co-location instances can be filtered from the candidate instances by examining clique relationships among other instances of the candidate co-location instance, except for the first instance. For example, in Fig. 6.4(b), {A2, B2, C1, D2} is a true co-location instance of candidate {A, B, C, D}, but {A2, B1, C1, D2} is not.

For a candidate c, if $\text{PI}(c) = \text{UPI}(c)$, then c must be a non-covered co-location. Otherwise, we first need to generate the covered sub-sets of c since these sub-sets have been pruned assuming the condition $\text{UPI}(c) = \text{PI}(c)$; next, if $\text{PI}(c) < M$ then c can be pruned out; else, we need to check whether c is δ-covered by its super-SCPs or not.

Note that the UPI values of size 2 SCPs are the true PI values.

6.5.2 The Algorithm

Algorithm 6.2 shows the pseudo code of the RRnull method.

Algorithm 6.2 RRnull

Input:

(1) a feature set, $F=\{f_1,f_2,\ldots,f_n\}$;

(2) a spatial instance set, S;

(3) a spatial neighbor distance threshold, d;

(4) a minimum PI threshold, M;

(5) a coverage measure threshold, δ.

Output:

the non-covered prevalent SCP set Ω.

Method:

// Preprocess and generate star non-covered candidates

1) *NP*=find_neighbor_pairs(*S*,*d*);

2) (*NT*,*FNT*)=gen_neighbor_transactions(*NP*);

3) **for** *i*=1 to *n*

4)   *Tree$_i$* =build_prefix-tree(*f$_i$*,*FNT*);

5)   *SNCC* = gen_candi_and_cal_upr (*tree$_1$*,..,*tree$_n$*,*M*);
                //Generating star non-covered candidates with UPR

// Combining step

6) *CNCC*←size 2 candidates in *SNCC*;
                //CNCC is the set of clique non-covered candidates

7) *l* = largest size of *SNCC*;

8) **while** (*l*>2 and *SNCC* $\neq\phi$) **do**

9)   **for** *l*-size candidates in *SNCC*;

10)   *CNCC*←combine_and_cal_upi (*SNCC*);

11)   **if** *l*-size candidate *c* in *SNCC* cannot be combined

12)   **then** *SNCC* ←gen_covered_(*l*-1)-sub-sets(*c*, *SNCC*);

13)   *l*=*l*-1;

// calculate true PIs of candidates

14) *Ω*←size 2 candidates in *CNCC*;

15) *l* = largest size of *CNCC*;

16) **while** (*l*>2 and *CNCC* $\neq\phi$) **do**

17)   **for** each *l*-size candidate *c* in *CNCC*;

18)   *SI$_c$*=find_star_instances(*c*, *NT*);

19)   *CI$_c$*=filter_clique_instances(*SI$_c$*, *NT*);

20)   *PI*(*c*)=calculate_true_pi(*CI$_c$*);

21)   **if** PI(*c*)=UPI(*c*)

22)   **then** move *c* from *CNCC* to *Ω*

23)   **else** *CNCC* ←gen_covered_(*l*-1)-sub-sets(*c*, *CNCC*);

24)   **if** PI(*c*)<*M*

25)   **then** prune_candidate(*CNCC*)

26)   **else if** *c* is not covered   *//by Lemma 6.2*

27)   **then** *Ω*←*c*

28)   *l*=*l*-1;

29) **Output** *Ω*

END

Algorithm 6.2 contains three phases. The first one is to preprocess and generate *SNCC*, the second one is to combine *SNCC* as *CNCC*, and the third one is to calculate true PI values of candidates. In the second and the third phases, once a candidate can be pruned out, its covered sub-SCs need to be generated.

In Phase 1, we first find all neighboring instance pairs for a given input spatial data set. The neighborhood transactions are generated by grouping the neighboring instances per instance. Then, a prefix-tree per feature is built with the lexicographic neighborhood transactions. The set of SNCCs is generated based on the prefix-trees.

In Phase 2, the set of CNCCs is filtered by combining the SNCCs. The UPI of each candidate in *CNCC* is computed. In this phase, if candidates in *SNCC* cannot be combined, their smaller size covered sub-SCPs are generated. The combining step starts from the largest size of *SNCC*.

The third phase is to calculate the true PIs of candidates in *CNCC*. First, the star instances of a candidate are found by scanning neighborhood transactions. Then, the clique instances can be filtered from the star instances by examining a clique relationship among other instances, except for the first instance of the star instance. Next, the true PIs can be calculated based on the clique instances of candidates. For a candidate c, if $PI(c) = UPI(c)$, then the candidate can be moved from *CNCC* to the non-covered prevalent SCP set Ω. However, if $PI(c) \neq UPI(c)$, we have to do some further work as shown in Algorithm 6.2.

6.5.3 The Correctness Analysis

Although Algorithm 6.2 seems simple, it can completely eliminate redundancy and get the correct non-covered prevalent SCP set Ω, i.e., Algorithm 6.2 works. The reasons are as follows:

1. A co-location instance must be a star neighborhood instance, and it corresponds to a feature neighborhood transaction in Algorithm 6.2.
2. According to the concept of δ-covered, for a SCP c, if the all instances of one feature in $T(c)$ are δ-covered by its super-SCP, c is δ-covered. So we can introduce the SNCC and CNCC in Algorithm 6.2.
3. For the sub-SCPs δ-covered by a set of super-SCPs, because the generation of *SNCC* is based on the prefix-tree of the reference feature, if the co-location instances of the reference feature are δ-covered by its super-SCPs, then it must not appear in the *SNCC*. That is why we have Step 22 in Algorithm 6.2.
4. When $PI(c) \neq UPI(c)$, Step 23 generates $(l-1)$-size sub-SCPs covered by c, and Step 26 checks whether c is δ-covered by its super-SCPs or not.

6.5.4 The Time Complexity Analysis

Algorithm 6.2 has three main parts: generating *SNCC* (Steps 1–5), filtering *CNCC* (Steps 6–13), and calculating the true PIs (Steps 14–29). The complexity analysis of the three parts is shown as follows.

Generating *SNCC*: In order to generate *SNCC*, RRNull first generates *NT* and *FNT* (Steps 1–2), and then builds the prefix-trees for each feature (Steps 3–4). Finally, *SNCC* is generated from the prefix-trees (Step 5).

1. Generating *NT* and *FNT*: A grid-based method is used to calculate the neighborhood relationships. The whole space is divided into grids with area $d*d$ (d is the spatial neighbor distance threshold), such that every instance in a certain grid g is only compared with the instances located in 4 grids around g (east, southeast, south, and southwest). *FNT* is generated during the generation of *NT*, and a neighborhood relationship will be added to both *NT* and *FNT*, so that the computational complexity of generating *NT* and *FNT* is about: $O\left(n^2 * \frac{d^2}{A}\right) \left(\frac{d^2}{A} \ll 1\right)$, where d is the distance threshold, n is the number of instances, and A is the area of the whole space.

2. Building prefix-trees: If the number of features is m, m prefix-trees are built based on *FNT*. We note that the upper value of the number of *FNT* is n (n is the number of instances). Thus, to build m prefix-trees based on the *FNT*, the computational complexity is about: $O(size_{avg}(FNT)*|FNT|)$, where $size_{avg}(FNT)$ is the average size of the transactions in *FNT*, and $|FNT| \approx n$.

3. Generating *SNCC*: SNCCs are always found from the leaf nodes in RRnull, for example, for the first prefix-tree in Fig. 6.5(a), there are 2 leaf nodes (D: 2 and D: 1), for the leaf node D: 2, we generate an SNCC {A, B, C, D}: 2/4, remove D: 2 and the count value of the leaf node's ancestors minus the leaf node's count value of 2. Then every node with a count value 0 is removed from the prefix-tree (covered). Thus, an SNCC {A, B, C, D}: 2/4 is generated and the node C: 2 is removed. The process will continue until the prefix-tree is empty. The method performs well and the computational complexity in the worst case where only the leaf node is removed when getting a SNCC is: $O((size_{avg}(FNT))^2 * n')$, where n' is the number of branches of the all prefix-trees ($n' < n$).

In summary, the computational complexity of generating *SNCC* is about:

$$O\left(n^2 * \frac{d^2}{A}\right) + O\left((size_{avg}(FNT))^2 * n\right).$$

Filtering *CNCC*: In the process of generating *SNCC*, the participation ratio of each SNCC is stored in a hash set h wherein the key of h is the SNCC, and the value is the set of participation indexes whose first value is the minimum value of the whole set. For example, if {A, B, C, D} is generated from the first prefix-tree in Fig. 6.5(a), its participation ratio will be added to h as [key: {A, B, C, D}, value: {2/

4, 2/4}]. If the participation ratio of {A, B, C, D} calculated from the second prefix-tree in Fig. 6.5(a) is 2/5, it will be added to h as [key: {A, B, C, D}, value: {2/5, 2/4, 2/5}]. After the process of generating $SNCC$, h is used to filter $CNCC$. If the number of participation ratios of one candidate c is less than the size of c, c will be pruned. Otherwise, the UPI of c can be quickly obtained from the first element of the value attribute of c in h, and then c is regarded as a CNCC. The main cost of this process is the traverse of h, so the computational complexity of this part is about: $O(|SNCC|)$.

Calculating the true PIs: To calculate the true PI of an SCP c, the co-location instance $T(c)$ of c is needed. For each candidate c in $CNCC$, based on NT, a joinless approach is used to generate $T(c)$. The computational complexity is about: $O(|CNCC| *(size_{avg}(CNCC))^2 * l_{avg}(CNCC_{instance}))$, where $size_{avg}(CNCC)$ is the average size of the candidates in $CNCC$ (the average size of candidates in $CNCC$ is close to the average size of transactions in FNT), and $l_{avg}(CNCC_{instance})$ is the average count of the co-location instances of candidates in $CNCC$, and that in general $(l_{avg}(CNCC_{instance}) > n)$.

Combining the above analysis of the three parts in RRNull, the final computational complexity of RRNull is about: $O\left(n^2 * \frac{d^2}{A}\right) + O((size_{avg}(FNT))^2 * n) + O(|SNCC|) + O(|CNCC|*(size_{avg}(CNCC))^2 * l_{avg}(CNCC_{instance})) \approx O(|CNCC|* (size_{avg}(CNCC))^2 * l_{avg}(CNCC_{instance}))$.

Obviously, the computational complexity of RRnull is dominated by the third part.

6.5.5 Comparative Analysis

The running time of RRnull is much faster than that of closed prevalent co-location mining. The comparative analysis is as follows.

If an SCP is covered by its super-SCPs, it might be eliminated in the generating star non-covered candidates' phase, in the combining phase, or in the phase of calculating true PIs. If the eliminated SCPs were equally distributed in the three phases, about 2/3 of the co-location instances of the covered SCPs are no longer calculated. Indeed, more covered SCPs may be eliminated in advance. For the data set in Fig. 6.2(a), all covered SCPs have been eliminated before the combining step:

1. The *non-covered* condition is stronger than the *closed* condition, so the candidate set generated in Algorithm 6.2 must be smaller than that in closed prevalent co-location mining.
2. The *size* of the covered SCPs is smaller than that of their super-SCPs. We note that the smaller the size of SCPs, the larger the number of co-location instances.
3. When there are plenty of star co-location instances that are not true co-location instances, the work of generating and checking their sub-SCPs is time consuming. However, the corresponding problem also appears in closed prevalent

co-location mining. Therefore, in this case the running time of Algorithm 6.2 is
still faster than that of the closed prevalent co-location mining.

6.6   Experimental Results

In this section, we design sets of experiments to test the performance of the proposed
algorithms. We use three real data sets and a series of synthetic data sets in our
experiments. The proposed algorithms are implemented in Visual C#. All of our
experiments are performed on an Intel PC running Windows 7 with Intel Core i5
3337U @ 1.80GHz CPU and 2GB-memory.

6.6.1   On the Three Real Data Sets

This section examines the performance of the proposed algorithms on the three real
data sets. The first tests the redundancy reduction power, and the second measures
the computational performance of the proposed algorithms. A summary of the
selected three real data sets is presented in Table 6.1. Real-1 is from the rare plant
data of the Three Parallel Rivers of Yunnan Protected Areas whose instances form a
zonal distribution as shown in Fig. 6.6(a). Real-2 is a spatial distribution data set of
urban elements whose instances' distribution is both even and dense as shown in
Fig. 6.6(b). Real-3 is a vegetation distribution data set of the Three Parallel Rivers of
Yunnan Protected Areas, which has the fewest features but the most instances, its
instance distribution being various clusters as shown in Fig. 6.6(c).

1. *The Power of Redundancy Reduction*

   For each real data set, we vary the values of parameters M (the minimum PI
   threshold), d (the spatial neighbor distance threshold), and δ (the coverage
   measure threshold), respectively, to verify the redundancy reduction power of
   our method with respect to the original closed prevalent co-locations (l

Table 6.1 A summary of the three real data sets

Name	N. of features	N. of instances	(Max, min)	The distribution area of spatial instances (m^2)
Real-1	32	335	(63, 3)	80,000 × 130,000
Real-2	20	377,834	(60,000, 347)	50,000 × 80,000
Real-3	15	501,046	(55,646, 8706)	110,000 × 160,000

(Max, Min): are respectively the maximum number and the minimum number of the feature's
instances in the data sets

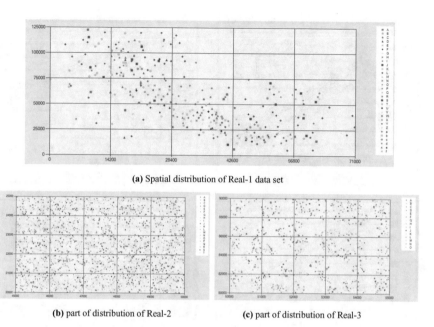

(a) Spatial distribution of Real-1 data set

(b) part of distribution of Real-2   **(c)** part of distribution of Real-3

Fig. 6.6 Spatial distribution of the three real data sets, where (**a**) is for Real-1; (**b**) is for Real-2; (**c**) is for Real-3

$S_{closed}| - |\Omega|)/|S_{closed}|$, where S_{closed} is the set of closed prevalent co-locations and Ω is the non-covered prevalent SCP set produced by Algorithm 6.1 or Algorithm 6.2. The experimental results are shown in Fig. 6.7(a) to Fig. 6.7(f).

We have the following observations: First, RRclosed and RRnull generate the same results on all real data sets; second, on all three real data sets, the redundancy reduction power is between 10% and 85%, the mean value being about 56%. On the Real-2 data set, the effect of redundancy reduction is the best, and its mean redundancy reduction power reaches 65%. This is because our redundancy reduction method is based on utilizing distributed information about co-location instances, and Real-2 is an evenly distributed data set; third, the redundancy reduction power becomes large when M is low or d is large. That is expected because there are more closed prevalent co-locations mined under lower M or larger d; fourth, as we expected, the redundancy reduction power increases when the value of δ increases. But the difference is not very big. This result illustrates that the value of δ is not the main factor that affects the redundancy reduction power. In the experiments, we set δ as 0, 0.1, 0.2, and 0.3, respectively.

The comparisons of the redundancy reduction power over different sizes of patterns are shown in Fig. 6.8(a) to Fig. 6.8(c). As can be seen, the longest closed prevalent co-locations are kept because no patterns can contain them, while for each size from maxlen-1, the number of kept SCPs is less, or even much less, than the number of closed prevalent co-locations. Usually, SCPs are reduced mostly in the middle sizes, e.g., SCPs with size 4 and size 5 in Fig. 6.8(b) are reduced the most.

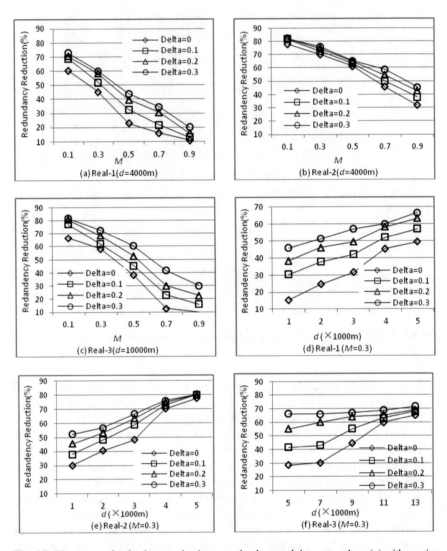

Fig. 6.7 The power of redundancy reduction over the three real data sets, where (**a**) with varying minimum PI threshold M on Real-1; (**b**) with varying minimum PI threshold M on Real-2; (**c**) with varying minimum PI threshold M on Real-3; (**d**) with varying neighbor distance threshold d on Real-1; (**e**) with varying neighbor distance threshold d on Real-2; (**f**) with varying neighbor distance threshold d on Real-3

2. *The Running Time*

The corresponding running time of the three methods, RRclosed, RRnull, and Closed which is a closed prevalent co-location mining algorithm presented in Yoo and Bow (2011a) is shown from Fig. 6.9(a) to Fig. 6.9(f). The running time of RRclosed includes the Closed procedure, which we have optimized.

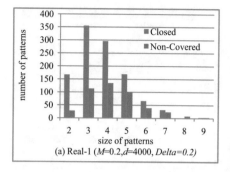

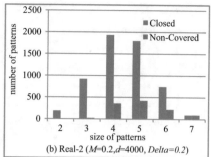

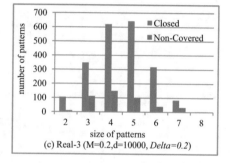

Fig. 6.8 Comparison of the redundancy reduction power over different sizes of patterns, where (**a**) on Real-1; (**b**) on Real-2; (**c**) on Real-3

   The results show that RRclosed is much slower than RRnull, especially when M is low and d large. Comparing RRnull and Closed, we observe that RRnull runs much better than Closed especially on dense data sets (a larger d makes a denser data set). This is because RRnull examines the δ-covered co-locations, while Closed examines the co-locations' closeness, and the former condition is stronger than the latter's. We further observe that RRnull runs two times faster than Closed in Real-2 when $M = 0.3$ in Fig. 6.9(b), or when $d = 3000$ m and 4000 m in Fig. 6.9(e), and three times faster in Real-2 when $M = 0.1$ in Fig. 6.9(b), or when $d = 5000$ m in Fig. 6.9(e). Because RRnull avoids identifying many candidates, it also saves much space. Finally, from the running times of RRclosed and Closed which are almost identical, we can verify that Algorithm 6.1 is efficient for redundancy reduction.

6.6.2 On the Synthetic Data Sets

This section examines the scalability of the RRnull and the RRclosed with the varying numbers of spatial instances, numbers of spatial features, neighbor distance thresholds, prevalence thresholds, and coverage measure thresholds.

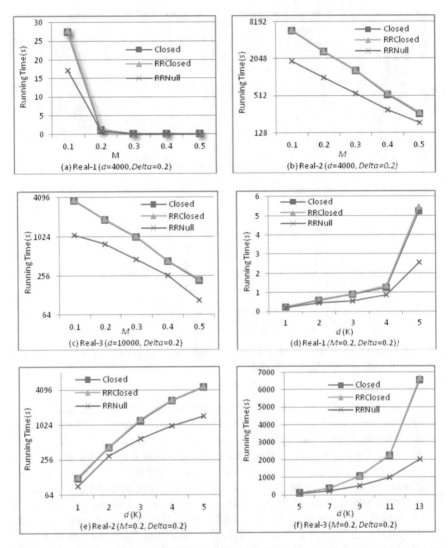

Fig. 6.9 Running time of Closed, RRclosed, and RRnull over three real data sets, where (**a**) with varying minimum PI threshold M on Real-1; (**b**) with varying minimum PI threshold M on Real-2; (**c**) with varying minimum PI threshold M on Real-3; (**d**) with varying neighbor distance threshold d on Real-1; (**e**) with varying neighbor distance threshold d on Real-2; (**f**) with varying neighbor distance threshold d on Real-3

Synthetic data sets were generated using a spatial data generator similar to Huang et al. (2004) and Yoo and Shekhar (2006). Table 6.2 describes the parameters used for the data generation in the related experiments. First, the distribution area of spatial instances was determined with $D*D$. The whole area was divided into grids

Table 6.2 Parameters and their values in experiments

Parameter	Definition	Experiment figures				
		F.6.10 (a)	F.6.10 (b)	F.6.10 (c)	F.6.10 (d)	F6.10 (e)
D	Spatial area ($D \times D$)	10,000	10,000	10,000	10,000	10,000
P	Number of ♀co-locations	20	20	20	20	20
Q	Average size of ♀co-locations	5	5	5	5	5
I	Average number of ♀co-location instances	S/100	2000	2000	2000	2000
S	Number of instances	*	200,000	200,000	200,000	200,000
F	Number of features	20	*	20	20	20
d	Spatial neighbor distance threshold	1000	1000	*	1000	1000
M	Minimum PI threshold	0.2	0.2	0.2	*	0.2
δ	Measure of coverage	0.2	0.2	0.2	0.2	*

♀: initial core co-location, *: variable values

with $d*d$ where d is the spatial neighbor distance threshold. Then, we generated P initial core patterns whose average size was Q. The feature types of each core pattern were randomly chosen from F features. An average of I instances per core pattern was generated. The total number of instances was around S. Finally, the co-location instances for each initial pattern were distributed. To locate a co-location instance, we first randomly chose a grid, and all points of the instance were then randomly located within the chosen grid.

As shown in Fig. 6.10(a) to Fig. 6.10(e), the RRnull algorithm shows scalability to large dense sets, at lower M, larger d and lower δ, and it performs better than RRclosed in all the experiments. This is because RRclosed considers feature sets having "*possible clique relationships*" as candidates, while RRnull takes "*non-covered + possible clique relationships*" as candidates. When the number of spatial instances is 500,000 as in Fig. 6.10(a), RRnull runs almost five times faster than RRclosed. We compare the number of closed prevalent co-locations, the number of RRnull candidates, and the number of non-covered co-locations over different sizes in Fig. 6.11. From the figure, we can see that the number of RRnull candidates is much lower than that of closed prevalent co-locations. Also, we can see that with the size of candidates growing, the number of RRnull candidates gets closer and closer to the final result. Clearly, checking a longer pattern costs much more time than checking a shorter one.

In addition, we notice that the trend in Fig. 6.10(b) does not increase progressively as the number of features grows. This is because we have fixed the total number of instances, so the number of instances for each feature reduces successively when the number of features grows. When the number of features exceeds 40, the number of co-location instances and the number of candidates decreases sharply.

We have further investigated the reason for speed increase of the RRnull algorithm. Table 6.3 compares the numbers of the generated candidates by RRnull and

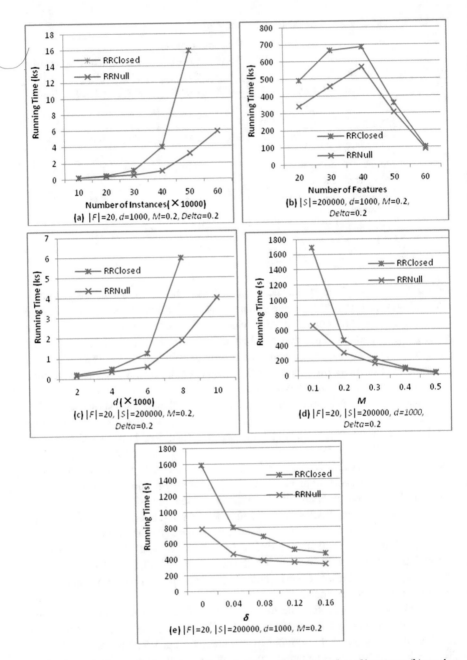

Fig. 6.10 Scalability analysis on the synthetic data sets, where (**a**) number of instances; (**b**) number of features; (**c**) neighbor distance threshold d; (**d**) minimum PI threshold M; (**e**) measure of coverage δ

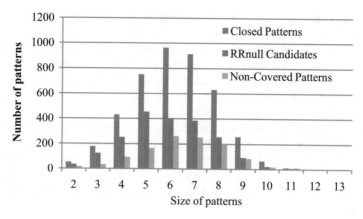

Fig. 6.11 Further analysis of the 500,000 instances in Fig. 6.10(a)

Table 6.3 Comparison of the number of candidates generated by RRnull and Closed

N. of candidates	$|S| = 500{,}000$ in Fig. 6.10(a)	$|F| = 30$ in Fig. 6.10(b)	$d = 8000$ in Fig. 6.10(c)	$M = 0.1$ in Fig. 6.10(d)	$\delta = 0$ in Fig. 6.10(e)
RRnull	2039	3201	2573	1236	1319
Closed	5285	5396	5538	2651	2944

Closed at several special places found in Fig. 6.10. We can see that RRnull identifies about 50% of the false candidates before calculating their true co-location instances.

6.7   Related Work

In Sect. 6.2, we have discussed the connection of our work with previous prevalent SCP mining, with maximal prevalent SCP mining and with closed prevalent SCP mining. A closely related work is the top-k closed SCP mining problem studied in Yoo and Bow (2011a), where the criterion of the top-k SCPs is to provide best prevalence estimation of those SCPs that are closed and not selected. This paper's approach is more sophisticated since the SCPs reduced by our method are δ-covered by their super-SCPs with respect to their distributed information about the co-location instances.

The motivation for our work is the same as that in papers (Xin et al., 2005, 2006; Yan et al., 2005; Mielikäinen & Mannila, 2003) but now our redundant SCP concept is based on spatial distribution information of co-location instances, dissimilar to the techniques used in transaction data sets. Further, our proposed new algorithms can reduce the size of the original collection of closed SCPs by about 50%.

Our work shares some common interests with the work in papers (Sengstock et al., 2012; Qian et al., 2014; Mohan et al., 2011; Celik et al., 2007; Barua & Sander, 2014) because they all take spatial distribution of co-location instances into consideration. However, our work is totally different from these works, in which the spatial instance distribution information is integrated into prevalence metrics or neighborhood distance measures. We did not change the classical prevalence metrics expressed in papers (Verhein & Al-Naymat, 2007). What we have studied is the relationship between SCPs by introducing the δ-covered concept based on the spatial distribution of co-location instances. Our purpose is to discover more succinct compression of the non-redundant SCP sets.

Recently domain-driven pattern mining has been attracting more researchers. Many efforts (Wang et al., 2013a; Wang et al., 2016b; Wang et al., 2017a; Ouyang et al., 2017; Lu et al., 2017; Wang & Wang, 2017) have been devoted into prevalent SCP mining, which have extended the prevalent SCP mining problem. We expect that the study of domain-driven prevalent SCP redundancy reduction will also prove to be significant.

6.8 Chapter Summary

This chapter discussed the non-redundant prevalent co-location pattern mining problem by applying distribution information from co-location instances. It is worth mentioning that the proposed method not only solves the redundancy reduction problem but also provides high efficiency.

It is worth mentioning that this chapter and Chap. 5 are based on co-location instance information, but Chap. 5 focuses on the PI value of SCPs, and the mining results need to be able to derive all prevalent SCPs and their PI values. Whilst this chapter focuses on mining non-redundant SCPs, that is, in terms of co-location instance distribution, the results of this chapter seek a minimum set of prevalent SCPs that can cover all co-location instances of prevalent SCPs.

In the next chapter, we will discuss to mine high-quality co-location patterns (call Dominant Spatial Co-location Patterns (Dominant SCPs)) by combining the prevalence and completeness of co-location patterns.

Chapter 7
Dominant Spatial Co-location Patterns

7.1 Introduction

It may well be that users are not only interested in identifying the prevalence of a feature set, but also its completeness, namely, the portion of co-location instances that a pattern occupies in their neighborhood. Combining the prevalence and completeness of co-location patterns, we can provide users with a set of higher quality co-location patterns called dominant spatial Cc-location patterns (Dominant SCPs). In this chapter, we focus on mining dominant SCPs, and so make the following contributions to the general field of spatial co-location mining:

1. A new relationship, called a connected neighbor relationship, is presented to divide the instances of co-location pattern into non-overlapping neighborhoods. The definitions of spatial occupancy ratio and spatial occupancy index are then proposed as new metrics to measure the completeness of co-location patterns.
2. The dominant SCP mining problem is formulated by combining prevalence and completeness metrics, and a weight parameter between occupancy and prevalence is provided to allow users to obtain their specific mining results according to different preferences. An algorithm called DSCPMA (dominant spatial co-location pattern mining algorithm) is then developed to solve the dominant SCP mining problem.
3. For improving the efficiency of DSCPMA, the properties of the upper bound of spatial occupancy for dominant SCPs are explored. Furthermore, a novel data structure, a co-location neighborhood table, is designed to store instances and a series of pruning strategies is developed to help reduce the search space.
4. The efficiency and effectiveness of the new algorithms are evaluated on a series of synthetic data sets and three real data sets. Specifically, the effect of different parameters supplied to the proposed algorithms and the proposed pruning strategies are examined by varying parameter settings on several synthetic data sets with different data densities and data scales. The algorithm's scalability is then explored by increasing the number of features and instances, respectively.

© The Author(s), under exclusive license to Springer Nature Singapore Pte Ltd. 2022
L. Wang et al., *Preference-based Spatial Co-location Pattern Mining*, Big Data Management, https://doi.org/10.1007/978-981-16-7566-9_7

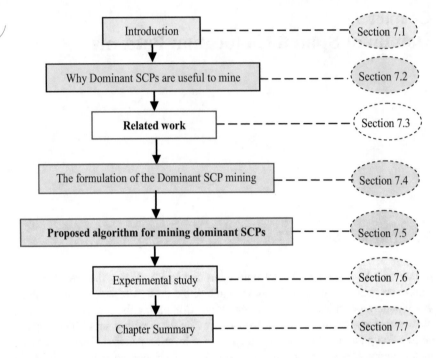

Fig. 7.1 The organization of this chapter

Experiments on three real-world data sets demonstrate the effectiveness of DSCPMA, and the practical significance of dominant SCP mining is discussed in two real-world applications.

Figure 7.1 presents the organization of this chapter. Section 7.2 discusses the reasons for developing dominant SCP mining. Section 7.3 give an overview of the related work on SCP mining and occupancy-based pattern recommendations. Section 7.4 presents the formulation of the dominant SCP mining problem. The details of DSCPMA for dominant SCP mining, especially on how to calculate the upper bounds on occupancy, are discussed in Sect. 7.5. The experimental evaluation is discussed in Sect. 7.6, and Sect. 7.7 ends this chapter with some concluding remarks.

7.2   Why Dominant SCPs Are Useful to Mine

Spatial co-location pattern (SCP) mining aims to find the groups of spatial features where their instances are located together, prevailing in the same neighborhoods (Shekhar & Huang, 2001). As a critical component of spatial association rule mining (Soltani & Akbarzadeh, 2014; Wang et al., 2005), the idea of SCP mining originates

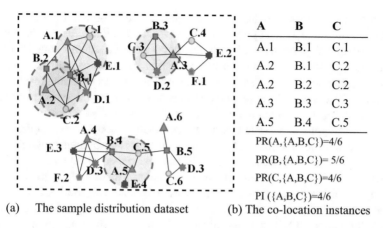

(a)   The sample distribution dataset   (b) The co-location instances

Fig. 7.2 An explanatory example, where (**a**) the sample distribution dataset; (**b**) the co-location instances

from Tobler's First Law: "Everything is related to everything else, but near things are more related to each other." An example in a real geographic space would be that the plant Matsutakes usually grows under the plant Abies Georgei Orr, giving rise to a co-location pattern {Matsutake, Abies Georgei Orr}, which may be obvious to one botanist, but not to all. SCP mining techniques have been used to discover implicit but interesting knowledge hidden in spatial data, as "hidden information" can revealed, extracted from the complex distribution of spatial objects. Extracting correlated spatial features has been used extensively in domains such as ecology (Shekhar & Huang, 2001; Huang et al., 2004), public health and service (Li et al. 2016; Yao et al., 2017; Vaezpour et al., 2016), decision-making (Zhou & Wang, 2012), location-based recommendations (Yu, 2016), etc.

In general, SCP mining process requires collecting the instance groups located in the same neighborhood and to which belong a specific group of features (i.e., co-location instance). As in previous chapters, the prevalence of this group of features is evaluated by its participation ratio (PR) and its participation index (PI) (the definitions of PR and PI are recalled in Sect. 7.4). For example, Fig. 7.2 (a) shows a simple distribution data set, where instances of six spatial features, A, B, C, D, E and F, are denoted by a vertex and marked by the feature type and an instance ID value (e.g., A.1). The edges among the instances represent neighbor relationships under a neighbor relationship R. Figure 7.2(b) lists the co-location instances, PRs and PI of {A, B, C} in the data set of Fig. 7.2(a). Setting the prevalence threshold to 0.3, for instance, gives {A, B, C} as a prevalent SCP.

The prevalence measurement perfectly reflects the strength of the co-existence of group features in a geo-space. However, a prevalence-based mining process fails to capture the completeness information of co-location instances. As shown in Fig. 7.2 (a), there are some non-pattern instances in each neighborhood of the co-location instance {A, B, C} (the green circular area) such as E1, D1, D2, E4, etc. Because a prevalence-based SCP mining identifies only the neighbor relationships between feature instances of the pattern, the co-location instance of {A, B, C} fails to provide complete instance information in the neighborhood formed by its co-located instances. In some real applications of co-location mining, users are not only interested in the prevalence of a group of co-location patterns, but also in the completeness, namely, the portion of co-location instances of pattern occupied in their neighborhood. To indicate the significance of considering both prevalence and completeness in the co-location pattern mining, we shall now describe two applications which require information about the completeness of patterns.

The first application which requires information about the completeness of patterns is that of plant diversity research. In this area, biologists require that a group of features (a pattern) is sufficiently prevalent to ensure the co-existence strength of this pattern, meanwhile the co-location instances of the pattern should occupy a portion as large as possible in their located neighborhood so that this pattern can reflect feature types in their located areas as completely as possible to ensure the biologists will not miss diversity information from this pattern. Furthermore, according to Tobler's first law, if spatial objects in a neighborhood are correlated, the instances of a co-location pattern will probably be affected by other instances, located in the same neighborhood but which do not belong to the pattern. Though biologists can frequently obtain groups of plant species co-located in different neighborhoods by the standard prevalence-based co-location mining techniques, they still need completeness information to determine whether the association among these species is limited to only these groups, or is also affected by other species.

The second application relates to urban facility planning, where city planners try to manipulate public facilities in urban areas to include the most common facility types, as well as a variety of facilities to benefit residents' lives. A prevalence metrics can support the universality of a group of facility types, but there is a need for a new measurement to reflect the completeness of this group of facilities. Moreover, due to the high-density distribution and strong autocorrelation of urban POI data, prevalence-based SCP mining techniques are likely to give mined results which may have high prevalence but no valid correlation among pattern features.

To cope with situations like the above, we introduce a new spatial occupancy metrics, defined later, which was first proposed in the paper by Tang et al. (2012). Combining the prevalence and completeness of a co-location pattern, we provide users with a set of higher quality co-location patterns called Dominant SCPs. Compared with the traditional SCPs, these types of patterns can provide users with considerably more comprehensive information.

Conducting dominant SCPs mining is challenging. Firstly, in a transaction data mining task, the completeness of a frequent pattern is generally measured by the ratio the pattern occupies to its supporting transactions. However, due to the continuity of space, the same spatial instance quite often participates in different co-location instances, possibly causing the neighborhoods formed by the co-location instances of a pattern to overlap each other. As shown in Fig. 7.2(a), for co-location pattern {A, B, C}, the neighborhoods of co-location instances: {A.1, B.1, C.1}, {A.2, B.1, C.2}, and {A.2, B.2, C.2} overlap each other. To avoid repeated calculations leading to erroneous results, we need to reduce the overlaps of the neighborhoods formed by the instances of a pattern, a first challenge. Furthermore, the measure of spatial occupancy satisfies neither monotony nor anti-monotony, so a second challenge is to combine the participation index and the measure of spatial occupancy to efficiently mine the dominant SCPs.

7.3 Related Work

Spatial co-location patterns represent frequent co-occurrences of a subset of Boolean spatial features (Shekhar & Huang, 2001). Although Boolean spatial features can be thought of as item types, there is no concept of transactions in spatial co-location pattern mining due to the continuity of the underlying space. Huang et al. (2004) proposed a notion of user-specified neighborhoods in place of transactions to specify groups of items, and also defined a prevalence measure which possesses the desirable anti-monotone property, the participation index, to measure the co-occurrence frequency of a spatial feature set; meanwhile an Apriori-like algorithm called join-base algorithm was developed to discover all prevalent SCPs. After that, in view of the large number of instance-joining operations performed by the join-base algorithm will reduce its performance on dense data sets. A series of methods were developed to improve the efficiency of join-based algorithm (Yoo et al., 2004; Yoo & Shekhar, 2006; Wang et al., 2008; Yao et al., 2016; Andrzejewski & Boinski, 2018; Bao & Wang, 2019). However, the effectiveness of SCP mining was limited by the large number of mined results, which users found hard to understand or to apply in real applications. Further studies on improving the effectiveness of SCP mining mainly included data-driven methods and domain-driven methods. Data-driven methods focus on mining co-location pattern on various different data types such as co-location mining on uncertain data (Wang et al., 2013a), fuzzy objects (Ouyang et al., 2017; Wang et al., 2019c, 2019e), extended objects (Bembenik et al., 2017), spatio-temporal data (Akbari et al., 2015; Huang et al., 2008; Wang et al., 2020), and co-location condensed representation (Wang et al., 2018a). The co-location condensed representation included lossy condensation using maximal co-location mining methods (Wang et al., 2009b; Yao et al., 2016; Bao & Wang, 2019; Mohan et al., 2011) and lossless condensation used closed co-location mining methods (Wang et al., 2018b; Yoo & Bow, 2011a). Domain-driven co-location pattern mining became widely studied due to new and interesting measures and domain constraints (Flouvat et al., 2015) which could fulfil the need of various domains such as mining co-location patterns with high utility (Wang et al., 2017a), co-location patterns with dominant features (Fang et al., 2017), regional co-location patterns (Mohan et al., 2011; Qian et al., 2014), dynamic co-location patterns (Hu et al., 2020), co-location patterns with specific relationships (Lu et al., 2017, 2018), etc.

The concept of occupancy was proposed by Tang et al. (2012) as an interesting new measure and constraint, aiming to capture the completeness of a pattern in market-basket mining. Occupancy is applied to measure the degree to which the pattern occupies its supporting transactions. Then, Zhang et al. (2015) extended the occupancy measure to sequence data for mining qualified sequence patterns. Gan et al. (2019) introduced the occupancy concept into high utility pattern mining and proposed a measure called utility occupancy to measure the contribution of a pattern within a transaction. Shen et al. (2016) combined user preferences in terms of frequency, utility, and occupancy to mine high utility occupancy patterns. As each object may have different importance in these real-world applications, Zhang et al. (2017) incorporated weights into occupancy and produced highly qualified patterns with both frequency and weight occupancy. Compared to traditional maximal patterns which used an absolute size of a pattern as a constraint, an occupancy measure can be seen as more flexible, being the relative size of a pattern to its supporting transactions. Occupancy measurement was successfully used in many real applications which require completeness information concerning mined results, such as web page-area recommendations (Tang et al., 2012), web print task recommendations (Li et al., 2013, 2014), travel route recommendations (Zhang et al., 2015), goods match recommendations (Zhang et al., 2017), etc.

The task of dominant spatial co-location pattern mining looks similar to the occupancy-based itemset mining problem but in fact is very different because of the lack of a transaction concept in spatial data sets. Firstly, the measure of occupancy in spatial data is different from that of frequent itemset mining work. The traditional occupancy measure in frequent itemset mining work is based on a transaction concept where the transactions are independent of each other. However, instances of spatial features are inherently embedded in continuous space and share a variety of spatial relationships (e.g., neighbor relationship) with each other. Thus, we have developed a new spatial occupancy measure for spatial co-location pattern mining, detailed later. Secondly, the goal of dominant SCP mining is different from that of transaction data mining. Traditional occupancy-based transaction data mining sets out to find patterns which are frequent and occupy a large portion of its supporting transactions. However, dominant SCP mining aims to find a set of co-location patterns which are complete in their neighborhoods as well as truly correlated among features. Thirdly, the technique for mining dominant SCPs differs from that of transaction data mining. The dominant SCP mining framework is based on neighborhoods in space rather than on transactions in market-basket data, so a new algorithm and a new data structure needed to be developed for dominant SCP mining. Further, the spatial occupancy metric does not satisfy monotonic or anti-monotonic properties, so new pruning methods need be explored to improve the efficiency of dominant SCP mining.

7.4   Preliminaries and Problem Formulation

In this section, we first give some preliminaries relating to the traditional SCP mining framework, and we then formally propose the connected neighbor relationship, giving formal definitions of spatial occupancy ratio and index. We can then measure

Table 7.1   List of notations frequently used throughout the chapter

Variable	Explanation
$F = \{f_1, f_2 \ldots, f_n\}$	A set of n spatial features
$c_k = \{f_1, f_2 \ldots, f_k\}$	A k-size co-location pattern
$o_i \ (\in S)$	A spatial instance in spatial instance set S
$l_i \ (\in T(c_k))$	A co-location instance in table instance $T(c_k)$
tp_i	A co-location instance class of c_k
ip_i	A instance class of c_k
pn_i	A neighborhood set of instance class ip_i,
$IN(o_i)$	A set of neighborhood of o_i
$T(c_k)$	A set of co-location instance of c_k
$RN(l)$	A set of co-location instance neighbor of l
$TN\ (c_k)$	Table instance neighbor set of c_k:
$PR(c_k, f_i)$	Participation ratio of feature f_i in c_k
$PI(c_k)$	Participation index of c_k
$TP(c_k)$	A set of co-location instance classes of c_k
$CIP(c_k)$	A set of instance classes of c_k
$PN(c_k)$	A neighborhood set of c_k
$OR(c_k, ip_i)$	Spatial occupancy ratio of instance class ip_i in c_k
$OI(c_k)$	Spatial occupancy index of c_k
$Quality(c_k)$	Quality value of c_k

the completeness of a co-location pattern and so, finally, we formulate the dominant SCP mining problem which includes prevalence and occupancy. The main notations used in this chapter are listed in Table 7.1.

7.4.1   Preliminaries

Given a set of spatial features $F = \{f_1, f_2 \ldots, f_n\}$, and a set of their spatial instances $S = S_1 \cup S_2 \cup \ldots \cup S_n$, where S_i ($1 \leq i \leq n$) is a set of instances of feature f_i, and a reflexive and symmetric neighbor relationship R over S, where a Euclidean metric is used for R with a distance threshold d, two spatial instances are neighbors if the Euclidean distance between them is not greater than d. A k-size **co-location pattern** $c_k = \{f_1, f_2 \ldots, f_k\}$ is a subset of F ($c_k \subseteq F$), whose instances frequently form cliques under R. A set of instances which includes the instances of all features in c_k and forms a clique is called a **co-location instance** or row instance of c_k. A collection of all co-location instances $T(c_k)$ is called a **table instance of c_k**.

For example, as shown in Fig. 7.2(a), for a co-location pattern {A, B, C}, {A.1, B.1, C.1} is a co-location instance, and the table instance of {A, B, C} is shown in Fig. 7.2(b). It is worth mentioning that a single feature can be seen as a 1-size co-location pattern and that its table instance is the set of all instances of this feature.

The prevalence of a k-size co-location c_k is measured by its participation ratio and its participation index as follows.

Definition 7.1 (Participation ratio and Participation index) Given a co-location pattern $c_k = \{f_1, f_2 \ldots, f_k\}$, and a spatial instance set S, the **Participation ratio** for feature type f_i in c_k is the fraction of instances of f_i that participate in $T(c_k)$. The participation ratio is defined as: $PR(c_k, f_i) = |\pi_{f_i}(T(c_k))| / |T(\{f_i\})|$, where π is the relational projection operation. The **participation index** $PI(c_k)$ of c_k is the minimum participation ratio $PR(c_k, f_i)$ of all features f_i in c_k: $PI(c_k) = \min_{i=1}^{k}(PR(c_k, f_i))(f \in c_k)$.

Definition 7.2 (Prevalent co-location pattern) Given a user-specified prevalence threshold min_prev, c is prevalent if $PI(c) \geq min\_prev$.

For example, as shown in Fig. 7.2(b), $PI(\{A, B, C\}) = 4/6$, and supposing $min\_prev = 0.3$, then $\{A, B, C\}$ is a prevalent co-location pattern.

Lemma 7.1 Anti-monotone property. Following Shekhar and Huang (2001) the participation ratio and participation index are monotonically non-increasing as the size of co-locations increases.

7.4.2 Definitions

The definition of participation index is used to capture the prevalence of co-location patterns. In this subsection, we firstly propose the concepts of a connected neighbor relationship and a connected neighborhood to divide the instances of a co-location pattern into non-overlapping neighborhood sets, and then give suitable definitions of spatial occupancy and dominant SCPs.

Definition 7.3 (Instance neighborhood) Given a set of spatial features $F = \{f_1, f_2 \ldots, f_n\}$, and a set of instances S, where o_i is an instance of feature f_i, the neighborhood of o_i is a set which is defined as:

$$IN(o_i) = \{o_j \in S | o_i = o_j \vee (f_i \neq f_j \wedge R(o_i, o_j))\} \qquad (7.1)$$

where $f_j \in F$ is feature type of o_j and R is a neighbor relationship.

Definition 7.4 (Co-location Neighborhood) Given a k-size co-location pattern $c_k = \{f_1, f_2, \ldots, f_k\}$, for each co-location instance (row instance) $l = \{o_1, o_2, \ldots, o_k\}$ of c_k, the co-location neighborhood of l is defined as the set of spatial instances:

$$RN(l) = \cap_{i=1}^{k} IN(o_i)(o_i \in l) \qquad (7.2)$$

Table 7.2 Table instance neighborhoods of {A, B, C}

		RN_1	A.1, B.1, C.1, D.1, E.1
Pn1		RN_2	A.2, B.1, C.2
		RN_3	A.2, B.2, C.2
Pn2		RN_4	A.3, B.3, C.3, D.2
Pn3		RN_5	A.5, B.4, C.5

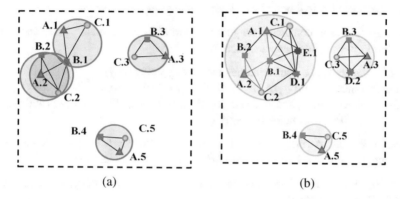

Fig. 7.3 Sample distribution data sets of {A, B, C}. (**a**) Co-location instances of {A, B, C}. (**b**) Instance partition neighborhoods of {A, B, C}

Correspondingly, for the table instance $T(c_k) = \{l_1, l_2, \ldots, l_h\}$, the *table instance neighborhood* is the collection of co-location neighborhoods of c_k: $TN(c_k) = \{RN(l_1), RN(l_2), \ldots, RN(l_h)\}$.

Example 7.1 Figure 7.2's $TN(\{A, B, C\})$ is listed in Table 7.2.

With these definitions of co-location instance and co-location instance neighborhood, it seems feasible to imitate the traditional occupancy definition and regard each co-location instance as an item set, and the neighborhood of this co-location instance as a supporting transaction. However, a transaction is disjoint in the sense of not sharing instances whereas co-location instances always overlap in space because an instance may be shared by multiple co-location instances, and so lead to duplicate counting of instances in same locations. As shown in Fig. 7.3(a), it can be easily seen that the co-location instances {A.1, B.1, C.1}, {A.2, B.1, C.2}, {A.2, B.2, C.2} overlap in space. How to avoid the instance overlap but not lose any neighbor relationship contributing to form co-location instances is a crucial task of dominant SCP mining. To solve this problem, we develop a partitioning strategy which replaces clique-based neighbor relationships by an equivalence relationship, so the instance of a pattern can be partitioned into a set of equivalence classes to form disjoint neighborhoods of co-location patterns.

Definition 7.5 (Connected neighbor relationship) Given a set of spatial instances S, for any instances o_p and o_q in S, if there exists at least a path $\{o_p, o_{v1}, \ldots, o_q\}$ from

o_p to o_q [i.e., there is a set of neighbor relationship pairs $(o_p, o_{v1}), (o_{v1}, o_{v2}), \ldots, (o_{vm}, o_q)$], o_p and o_q satisfy a connected neighbor relationship, denoted as $CR(o_p, o_q)$:

$$CR(o_p, o_q) \Leftrightarrow \{R(o_p, o_{v1}), R(o_{v1}, o_{v2}), \ldots, R(o_{vm}, o_q)\} \qquad (7.3)$$

For a set of spatial instances $O = \{o_1, \ldots, o_t\}$ $(t \geq 2)$, if every instance pair in O are connected neighbors, O is called a *Connected Neighborhood*.

Theorem 7.1 The connected neighbor relationship is a logical equivalence relationship in the spatial instances, such that:

1. An instance o_p is a connected neighbor of o_p (reflexivity)
2. For instances o_p and o_q $(o_p, o_q \in S)$, $CR(o_p, o_q) \Leftrightarrow CR(o_q, o_p)$ (symmetry)
3. For instances o_p, o_q and o_r $(o_p, o_q, o_r \in S)$, if they satisfy $CR(o_p, o_q)$ and $CR(o_q, o_r)$, then $CR(o_p, o_r)$ holds (transitivity)

Proof It is easy to verify that the first two properties are true by the concept of a connected neighbor relationship. We prove the third statement below.

According to the definition of connected neighbor relationship, if o_p, o_q and o_r satisfy $CR(o_p, o_q)$, then:

$$CR(o_p, o_q) \Leftrightarrow \{R(o_p, o_{v1}), R(o_{v1}, o_{v2}), \ldots, R(o_{vm}, o_q)\}$$

$$CR(o_q, o_r) \Leftrightarrow \{R(o_q, o_{h1}), R(o_{h1}, o_{h2}), \ldots, R(o_{hn}, o_r)\}$$

$$\{R(o_p, o_{v1}), R(o_{v1}, o_{v2}), \ldots, R(o_{vm}, o_q), R(o_q, o_{h1}), R(o_{h1}, o_{h2}), \ldots, R(o_{hn}, o_r)\}$$
$$\Leftrightarrow CR(o_p, o_r)$$

Thus, also considering the first two properties above, the theorem holds.

Lemma 7.2 Given a co-location table instance $T(c_k) = \{l_1, l_2, \ldots, l_h\}$, for any co-location instance $l_i = \{o_1, o_2, \ldots, o_k\}$ $(l_i \in T(c_k))$, all instances in l_i belong to an equivalence class under the connected neighbor relationship.

Proof Given two instances o_p and o_q $(o_p, o_q \in l_i)$, since the co-location instance is formed by clique neighbor relationship, there exists $\{R(o_p, o_q)\}$. According to Theorem 1, it follows that $R(o_p, o_q) \Leftrightarrow CR(o_p, o_q)$, so that o_p and o_q are connected neighbors. Consequently, all instances of l_i belong to an equivalence class under the connected neighbor relationship.

Lemma 7.3 Given a co-location table instance $T(c_k) = \{l_1, l_2, \ldots, l_h\}$, for two co-location instances l_i and l_j $(l_i, l_j \in T(c_k))$, if $l_i \cap l_j \neq \varnothing$, then all instances of $l_i \cup l_j$ must belong to an equivalence class under the connected neighbor relationship.

Proof Assume $l_i \cap l_j = \{o_p\}$, then according to Theorem 7.1, any instance in l_i and l_j can be connected by o_p. Thus, all instances in $l_i \cup l_j$ must belong to an equivalence class under the connected neighbor relationship.

Definition 7.6 (Co-location instance partition) Given a k-size co-location pattern $c_k = \{f_1, f_2, \ldots, f_k\}$, its table instance $T(c_k) = \{l_1, l_2, \ldots, l_h\}$ can be divided into a set of equivalence classes under a connected neighbor relationship: $TP(c_k) = \{tp_1, tp_2, \ldots, tp_m\}$($tp_i \neq \varnothing$, $tp_i \cap tp_j = \varnothing$, $1 \leq i < j \leq m$) and is called the *co-location instance partition* of c_k, where $tp_i = \{l_1, l_2, \ldots, l_t\}$($tp_i \subseteq T(c_k)$, $t \leq h$) is an equivalence class of $T(c_k)$. Correspondingly, the *instance partition classes of co-location pattern* are defined as the collection: $CIP(c_k) = \{ip_1, ip_2, \ldots, ip_m\}$, where $ip_i = \{l_1 \cup l_2 \cup, \ldots, \cup l_t\}$ is the set of distinct instances of tp_i.

The instance equivalence classes of a co-location pattern c_k satisfy that:

1. All instances in an equivalence class of c_k are connected neighbors to each other.
2. Two instances o_p and o_q ($o_p \in ip_i, o_q \in ip_j, i \neq j$) which belong to different equivalence classes of c_k cannot satisfy the connected neighbor relationship.
3. Any instance of $T(c_k)$ must belong to, and only belong to, one of the instance equivalence classes of c_k.

Note that $TP(c_k)$ is the collection of row-instances, and $CIP(c_k)$ is the collection of instances.

Example 7.2 From Table 7.2, and according to Lemmas 7.2 and 7.3, the co-location instance partition of TP ($\{A, B, C\}$) = $\{\{l_1, l_2, l_3\}, \{l_4\}, \{l_5\}\}$, CIP ($\{A, B, C\}$) = $\{\{A.1, A.2, B.1, B.2, C.1, C.2\}, \{A.3, B.3, C.3\}, \{A.5, B.4, C.5\}\}$, all instance partitions and their neighbors of $\{A, B, C\}$ are as shown in Fig. 7.3(b), and represented by yellow circular areas. As shown in Fig. 7.3(b), we represent a connected neighbor relation of co-location pattern $\{A, B, C\}$ by solid lines.

Definition 7.7 (Instance partition neighborhood of a co-location pattern) Given a k-size co-location pattern $c_k = \{f_1, f_2, \ldots, f_k\}$, the co-location partition of the co-locaton pattern $TP(c_k) = \{tp_1, tp_2, \ldots, tp_m\}$, the instance partition set $CIP(c_k) = \{ip_1, ip_2, \ldots, ip_m\}$, then for an instance partition class ip_i ($ip_i \subseteq CIP(c_k)$), the neighborhood of ip_i is defined as the set:

$$pn_i = \bigcup_{l_x \in tp_i} RN(l_x) \tag{7.4}$$

The instance partition neighborhood of a co-location pattern is defined as the collection of neighborhoods of the instance partition class of c_k: $PN(c_k) = \{pn_1, pn_2, \ldots, pn_m\}$.

Example 7.3 According to Example 7.2, $TP(\{A, B, C\}) = \{\{l_1, l_2, l_3\}, \{l_4\}, \{l_5\}\}$, $PN(\{A, B, C\}) = \{pn_1, pn_2, pn_3\}$, $pn_1 = RN(l_1) \cup RN(l_2) \cup RN(l_3) = \{A.1, A.2, B.1, B.2, C.1, D.1, E.1\}$, $pn_2 = \{A.3, B.3, C.3, D.2\}$, $pn_3 = \{A.5, B.4, C.5\}$. As shown in

Fig. 7.3(b), the areas of the co-location pattern neighborhoods of {A, B, C} are marked by a yellow circle.

According to Definitions 7.6 and 7.7, all instances of a pattern can be assigned into disjoint subsets under the connected neighbor relationship, so solving the instance overlap problem under the traditional neighbor relationship. Notice that although the instance partition classes are disjoint, their neighborhood sets are allowed to share the same neighbor instances.

Definition 7.8 (Occupancy ratio and occupancy index) Given a spatial co-location pattern c_k, if the instance partition set of c_k: $CIP(c_k) = \{ip_1, ip_2, \ldots, ip_m\}$, and if the neighbor set $PN(c_k) = \{pn_1, pn_2, \ldots, pn_m\}$, then the spatial occupancy ratio of ip_i in $CIP(c_k)$ can be defined as follows:

$$OR(c_k, ip_i) = \frac{|ip_i|}{|pn_i|} \tag{7.5}$$

The spatial *Occupancy Index* of c_k is the minimum spatial occupancy ratio $OR(c_k, ip_i)$ in all instance partition classes $CIP(c_k) = \{ip_1, ip_2, \ldots, ip_m\}$ of c_k:

$$OI(c_k) = \min_{i=1}^{m}\{OR(c_k, ip_i)\}(ip_i \in IP(c_k)) \tag{7.6}$$

The minimum occupancy ratio (occupancy index) is intended to capture the worst-case of the completeness, and evaluate as accurately as possible the influence of non-pattern features on the co-location pattern to ensure there exists true correlation among the pattern features.

Example 7.4 Let $c = \{A, B, C\}$, then according to Example 7.2 and Example 7.3, $OR(c, ip_1) = |\{A.1, A.2, B.1, B.2, C.1, C.2\}|/|\{A.1, A.2, B.1, B.2, C.1, C.2, D.1, E.1\}| = 0.75$, and $OI(c) = \min\{0.75, 0.75, 1\} = 0.75$.

According to Definition 7.8, the completeness of a co-location pattern can be measured by counting those instances directly participating in the pattern, and comparing the count of how many instances are left in the neighborhood of pattern. Thus, with the definition of participation index and spatial occupancy index, we can obtain a set of co-location patterns which are both prevalent and complete under the threshold constraints. To suit different application domains, a quality metric is proposed which allows users to obtain a sorted result by flexibly combining these two factors.

Definition 7.9 (Quality) Given a co-location pattern c_k, a weight parameter ω, the quality of c_k is defined as follows:

$$Quality(c_k) = \omega PI(c_k) + (1 - \omega)OI(c_k) \tag{7.7}$$

Example 7.5 Suppose weight parameter $\omega = 0.4$, then the quality value of co-location pattern {A, B, C}: Quality ({A, B, C}) = 0.4*0.66 + 0.6*75 = 0.65.

7.4.3   Formal Problem Formulation

By considering both the prevalence and the completeness metrics of a co-location pattern, we can provide a high-quality co-location patterns, the dominant SCPs. The following is the problem formulation for mining dominant SCPs.

Definition 7.10 (Dominant spatial co-location pattern (dominant SCP)) Given a set of spatial features F, a set of their spatial instances S, a neighbor relationship R, a prevalence threshold min_prev ($0 \leq min\_prev \leq 1$), a spatial occupancy threshold min_occ ($0 \leq min\_occ \leq 1$), then a co-location pattern c_k is a dominant SCP if it satisfies the following conditions: (1) $PI(c_k) \geq min\_prev$, (2) $OI(c_k) \geq min\_occ$.

The problem of *dominant SCP mining (DSCPM)* is to discover the complete set in which each SCP satisfies both min_prev and min_occ conditions and to sort the result by the quality value (Definition 7.9).

Example 7.6 Suppose $min\_prev = 0.3$, $min\_occ = 0.3$, weight parameter $\alpha = 0.4$, then for co-location pattern $\{A, B, C\}$ in Fig. 7.2, $PI(\{A, B, C\}) = 0.66 > min\_prev$, $OI(\{A, B, C\}) = 0.75 > min\_occ$, so $\{A, B, C\}$ is a dominant SCP with quality value 0.65.

7.4.4   Discussion of Progress

This chapter's goal is to find a set of dominant SCPs which are not only prevalent but also complete. As spatial data lacks an explicit transaction concept, a series of operations has been developed for measuring the completeness of co-location patterns, differing from the traditional definition of occupancy. These new operations transform the occupancy of the traditional transaction into one of spatial occupancy. Firstly, we proposed an equivalence relationship called a connected neighbor relationship to solve the instance overlap problem in co-location instances. Then we gave the equivalence partition of co-location instances under the connected neighbor relationship. Next, we collected the neighbors for each co-location instances into an equivalence class. By means of these operations, we developed a spatial occupancy ratio and an occupancy index for evaluating the completeness of a co-location pattern. Their definitions allowed us to formulate the dominant SCPs mining problem. Although similar to an occupancy metric measuring transaction data, a spatial occupancy metric also does not satisfy monotonic or anti-monotonic properties, so the next section will explore two upper bounds of spatial occupancy to improve the efficiency of dominant SCP mining.

In addition, readers may be interested in the difference between our work and maximal co-location pattern mining. These two works are quite different in both mining purpose and methods. Maximal co-locations aim to find a set of long-size prevalent co-location patterns which can infer all prevalent co-location patterns, and use the size of co-location patterns as a measure. However, dominant SCP mining aims to find a set of co-location patterns which are both prevalent in the space and complete in their located neighborhoods. We use the ratio of the number of instances in a partition to all instances in the partition neighborhoods as a measure of occupancy ratio, and use the minimum occupancy ratio as an occupancy index to evaluate the completeness of a co-location pattern. Although high occupancy seems to imply a longer size of co-location patterns, a maximal co-location pattern may still have lower occupancy when there are a large number of neighbors in its co-location neighborhoods. Furthermore, by considering spatial occupancy and prevalence as measures of interest, the mined results of dominant SCPs may be more useful in real-world applications, which we will illustrate in Sect. 7.6.

7.5   Proposed Algorithm for Mining Dominant SCPs

7.5.1   Basic Algorithm for Mining Dominant SCPs

We first develop a basic algorithm for mining dominant spatial co-location patterns (DSCPMA).

Algorithm 7.1 DSCPMA

Input: *(1) S: A spatial data set; (2) F: a feature set; (3) d: a distance threshold; (4) min_prev: a prevalence threshold; (5) min_occ: an occupancy threshold; (6)ω: A weight parameter*

Output: *A set of dominant spatial co-location patterns: DSCP*

Method:

//preprocess and generate instance neighbors

1) NI=find_ins_neighbors (S, d)

2) $P_1 = F$, $k = 2$, $DSCP = \varnothing$;

3)   **While** $(P_{k-1} \neq \varnothing)$

4) C_k =gen_candi_co-location(k, P_{k-1})//*Lemma 1*

5)   **For each** $c_k \in C_k$:

    //generate table instance neighborhood of c_k

6) $T(c_k)$ = gen_table_ins (NI, c_k);

7)   **If** *(calculate $PI(c_k)$) ≥min_prev:*

8) $P_k \leftarrow c_k$

9) $TN(c_k)$ =find_co-location_neighbors$(T(c_k), NI)$

    //divide equivalence classes of table instance of c_k and corresponding instance set (Theorem 1)

10)   Initialize $TP(c_k) \leftarrow T(c_k)$

11) $CIP(c_k)$=divide_table_instance$(TP(c_k))$

12) $PN(c_k)$=find_neighbor $(CIP(c_k))$

13) $OI(c_k)$=calculate_occ $(CIP(c_k), PN(c_k))$

14)   **If** $(OI(c_k) \geq min\_occ)$:

15) $Q(c_k)$=cal_quality$(\omega, OI(c_k), PI(c_k))$

16) $DSCP \leftarrow$ sort_by_quality$(c_k, Q(c_k))$

17) $k = k + 1$

18)   **Output** *DSCP*

The workings of this algorithm can be summarized as follows:

1. *Materializing the input spatial data into the instance neighborhood model we gave in Definition 7.4 (Step 1).* This process can be seen as a variant of the star neighborhood instance model in Yoo ang Shekhar (2006).
2. *Generate candidate dominant SCPs (Steps 2–4):* We initialize all features to 1-size prevalent co-locations by the definition of a participation index. A k-size $(k > 1)$ candidate is generated from the $(k − 1)$-size prevalent co-location pattern set P_{k-1} (Lemma 7.1). The candidates will be pruned if any $k − 1$ sub-patterns are not prevalent (Step 4).
3. *Prevalence filtering (Steps 5–8):* The 2-size candidate co-location instances can be directly obtained from instance neighborhoods of the first feature instances for each co-location instance since our neighbor relationship is symmetric. For 3 or more size, we need to check the clique relationship between instances before we generate the table instance (Step 6). Next we calculate the participation ratio and participation index of candidates, and if the participation index is greater than *min_prev,* we add this candidate to the k-size prevalent pattern set P_k (Steps 7–8).
4. *Occupancy filtering (Steps 9–13):* According to Definition 7.5, we can divide the equivalence classes of a table instance of a candidate co-location pattern and so obtain the corresponding instance partition set (Theorem 7.1). This process is presented in Algorithm 7.2 which uses a recursive strategy to divide table instances (Step 11). Then we gather the neighborhood of each instance partition class (Step 12) to calculate the occupancy ratio and index of the candidate, and so select dominant SCPs (Step 13).
5. *Sorting dominant SCPs by quality* (Steps 15–16): We can calculate the quality value of a dominant SCP by a weight parameter, and insert this dominant SCP in the dominant SCP set *DSCP* by descending order of quality value.

Algorithm 7.2 divide_table_instance($TP(c_k)$)

Method:

1)	*Flag=***True**
2)	**For** each pair of tp_i, $tp_j \in TP(c_k)$
3)	**if** ($tp_i \cap tp_j \neq \emptyset$):
4)	*Flag=***False**
5)	delete tp_i, tp_j from $TP(c_k)$
6)	$TP(c_k) \leftarrow$ Union(tp_i, tp_j)
7)	**if** (*Flag*):
8)	$CIP(c_k) \leftarrow$ collection of instances in $TP(c_k)$
9)	**Return** $TP(c_k)$, $CIP(c_k)$
10)	**else:**
11)	divide_table_instance($TP(c_k)$)

7.5.2 Pruning Strategies

Algorithm 7.1 gives a straightforward solution to the dominant SCP mining problem. In this subsection, we explore two upper bounds of spatial occupancy index to help in pruning the dominant SCPs search space, and a new data structure is designed to improve the efficiency of dominant SCP mining with prevalence and completeness filters.

1. *Co-location Neighborhood Table*

   To facilitate the dominant SCP mining process and reduce the redundant information, a new data structure called a *Co-location Neighborhood Table* is designed to store the co-location instance neighbors of co-location patterns. Based on this new data structure, we can build a mapping relationship between features to speed up both the prevalence and the completeness calculation processes.

Definition 7.11 (Co-location neighborhood table) Given a k-size co-location pattern c_k, a co-location neighborhood table (*CNT*) of co-location pattern c_k is organized by three components:

1. The table instance neighborhood (Definition 7.4) $TN(c_k) = \{RN(l_1), RN(l_2), \ldots, RN(l_h)\}$ with row index.
2. The feature types in $TN(c_k)$ include the pattern feature set $c_k = \{f_1, f_2 \ldots, f_k\}$ and the neighbor feature set of c_k: $NF(c_k) = \{f_{k+1}, \ldots, f_o\}$.
3. The instance count of each feature participating in $CNT(c_k)$.

   As shown in Fig. 7.4, the parameter k in the grids lists the co-location instances, and those instances that are the neighbors of a co-location instance are grouped by

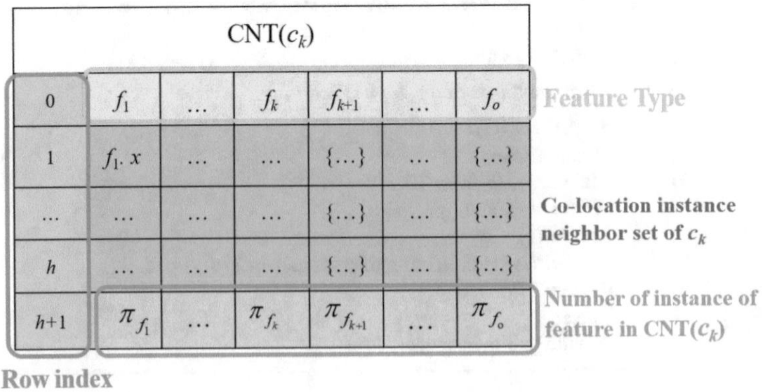

CNT(c_k)							
0	f_1	...	f_k	f_{k+1}	...	f_o	Feature Type
1	$f_1 . x$	...	...	$\{...\}$	...	$\{...\}$	
...	...	...	...	$\{...\}$	...	$\{...\}$	Co-location instance neighbor set of c_k
h	...	...	...	$\{...\}$	...	$\{...\}$	
h+1	π_{f_1}	...	π_{f_k}	$\pi_{f_{k+1}}$	...	π_{f_o}	Number of instance of feature in CNT(c_k)

Row index

Fig. 7.4 Co-location neighborhood table

their feature types and stored as an enumeration set structure, since instances that belong to the same neighbor feature are always of size greater than size-1.

Next, we will show how this new data structure helps to facilitate both the prevalence and completeness filtering.

2. *Prevalence Filter*

The $CNT(c_k)$ contains all information of those $k + 1$ size candidate co-location patterns which are prefixed by c_k. Thus, we can directly find all $k + 1$ size candidates which are prefixed by c_k by combining c_k and its neighbor features in $CNT(c_k)$, and then filter candidates by testing the participation ratio of the neighbor feature in $CNT(c_k)$:

Pruning strategy 1 According to Lemma 7.1, given a neighbor feature set of a k-size co-location pattern $NF(c_k)$, for any $k + 1$ size candidate $c_{k+1} = c_k \cup f (f \in NF)$, if $|\pi_f(CNT(c_k))| / |T(f)| \leq min\_prev$, then the c_{k+1} candidate can be pruned.

To calculate the participation ratio/index of all the $k + 1$ size candidates without generating their table instances, we also build a mapping relationship between the features.

Firstly, from definitions in other literature (Wang et al., 2015a), two set information functions can be given to describe the relationship between features and co-location neighborhoods:

$$\alpha_{f_i} : 2^{TN} \rightarrow 2^{S_i}, \alpha_{f_i}(TN') = \{\pi_{f_i}(RN_x) | RN_x \in TN'\}(TN' \subseteq TN) \qquad (7.8)$$

$$\beta_{f_i} : 2^{S_i} \rightarrow 2^{TN}, \beta_{f_i}(S_i') = \{RN_x | \pi_{f_i}(RN_x) \in S_i'\}(S_i' \subseteq S_i) \qquad (7.9)$$

Based on the two information functions (7.8) and (7.9), a feature mapping function is given as follows.

Definition 7.12 (Feature mapping function) Given a k-size prevalent co-location $c_k = \{f_1, f_2 \dots, f_k\}$, features f_i and f_j in $CNT(c_k)$ can be mapped as follows:

$$\varphi_{f_i \rightarrow f_j}(S_i') = \alpha_{f_j}\left(\beta_{f_i}(S_i')\right) \qquad (7.10)$$

For example, the instance subset of neighbor feature C in $CNT(\{A, B\})$ is $\pi_C(CNT(\{A, B\})) = \{C.1, C.2, C.3, C.5\}$, and the instances of feature A which are located in the same row as the C instances are:

$$\varphi_{C \rightarrow A}(\{C.1, C.2, C.3, C.5\}) = \alpha_A(\beta_C\{C.1, C.2, C.3, C.5\})$$
$$= \alpha_A(\{l_1, l_3, l_4, l_5, l_7\}) = \{A.1, A.2, A.3, A.5\}.$$

According to Definition 7.12, given a neighbor feature set of a k-size co-location pattern $NF(c_k)$, for any $k + 1$ size candidate $c_{k+1} = c_k \cup f$ $(f \in NF(c_k))$, then the participation index of c_{k+1} can be calculated directly as:

$$PI(c_k \cup f) \mid = \min^{f_j \in c_k} \left\{ |\varphi_{f_j \to f}(\pi_f(CNT(p_{k-1})))| / |T(\{f_j\})| \right\} (f \in NF(c_k)).$$

Based on Definition 7.12, we can prune the search space of prevalent co-location patterns and simply calculate all those $k + 1$ size candidates which are prefixed by c_k from $CNT(c_k)$ directly, without generating their table instances.

3. *Occupancy Filter*

Although the occupancy index metric does not satisfy monotonicity or anti-monotonicity, we can still explore the upper bound of the occupancy index metric to reduce the search space when mining dominant SCPs.

Lemma 7.4 (Upper bound of occupancy index) Given a k-size co-location pattern $c_k = \{f_1, f_2, \ldots, f_k\}$, its instance partition set $CIP(c_k) = \{ip_1, ip_2, \ldots, ip_m\}$, and co-location pattern neighborhood $PN(c_k) = \{pn_1, pn_2, \ldots, pn_m\}$, there exists an upper bound of $OI(c_k)$: $OI(c_k) \leq \frac{\sum_i^m |ip_i|}{\sum_i^m |pn_i|}$ $(ip_i \in CIP(c_k), pn_i \in PN(c_k))$.

Proof We will prove by induction that for all $m \in Z_+$

(*) $OI(c_k) = \min_{i=1}^m \left\{ OR\left(\frac{|ip_i|}{|pn_i|}\right) \right\} = \min_{i=1}^m \left\{ \frac{|ip_i|}{|pn_i|} \right\} \leq \frac{\sum_i^m |ip_i|}{\sum_i^m |pn_i|}$ holds

1. Base case: When $m = 1$, we have $\frac{|ip_1|}{|pn_1|} = \frac{|ip_1|}{|pn_1|}$, both sides are equal and (*) holds for $m = 1$.

2. Induction: Let $n \in Z_+$ be given and suppose (*) is true for $m = n$, we have:

$$\min_{i=1}^{n+1} \left\{ \frac{|ip_i|}{|pn_i|} \right\} = \min \left\{ \min_{i=1}^n \left\{ \frac{|ip_i|}{|pn_i|} \right\}, \frac{|ip_{n+1}|}{|pn_{n+1}|} \right\} \text{(by recurrence for } m)$$

Assuming that $\min_{i=1}^n \left\{ \frac{|ip_i|}{|pn_i|} \right\} = \frac{|ip_j|}{|pn_j|} (1 \leq j \leq n)$, there are two situations:

(2.1) when $\min_{i=1}^n \left\{ \frac{|ip_i|}{|pn_i|} \right\} \leq \frac{|ip_{n+1}|}{|pn_{n+1}|}, \frac{|ip_j|}{|pn_j|} \leq \frac{|ip_{n+1}|}{|pn_{n+1}|}$ and $\frac{|ip_j|}{|pn_j|} \leq \frac{\sum_i^n |ip_i|}{\sum_i^n |pn_i|}$

$$\Rightarrow |ip_j| * |pn_{n+1}| \leq |pn_j| * |ip_{n+1}| \quad \text{and} \quad |ip_j| * \sum_i^n pn_i \leq |pn_j| * \sum_i^n ip_i$$

$$\Rightarrow |ip_j| * \left(|pn_{n+1}| + \sum_i^n pn_i\right) \leq |pn_j| * \left(|ip_{n+1}| + \sum_i^n ip_i\right)$$

$$\Rightarrow \frac{|ip_j|}{|pn_j|} \leq \frac{\left(|ip_{n+1}| + \sum_i^n ip_i\right)}{\left(|pn_{n+1}| + \sum_i^n pn_i\right)} = \frac{\sum_i^{n+1} ip_i}{\sum_i^{n+1} pn_i}$$

Thus, $\min_{i=1}^m \left\{ \frac{|ip_i|}{|pn_i|} \right\} \leq \frac{\sum_i^m ip_i}{\sum_i^m pn_i}$ holds

(2.2) When $\frac{|ip_{n+1}|}{|pn_{n+1}|} \leq \min_{i=1}^n \left\{ \frac{|ip_i|}{|pn_i|} \right\}$

$$\frac{|ip_{n+1}|}{|pn_{n+1}|} \leq \frac{\sum_i^n ip_i}{\sum_i^n pn_i} \Rightarrow |ip_{n+1}| * \sum_i^n pn_i \leq |pn_{n+1}| * \sum_i^n ip_i$$

$$\Rightarrow |ip_{n+1}| * \sum_i^n pn_i + |ip_{n+1}| * |pn_{n+1}| \leq |pn_{n+1}| * \sum_i^n ip_i| + |ip_{n+1}| * |pn_{n+1}|$$

$$\Rightarrow |ip_{n+1}| * \left(\sum_i^n pn_i + |pn_{n+1}|\right) \leq |pn_{n+1}| * \left(\sum_i^n ip_i + |ip_{n+1}|\right)$$

$$\Rightarrow \frac{|ip_{n+1}|}{|pn_{n+1}|} \leq \frac{\sum_i^n ip_i + |ip_{n+1}|}{\sum_i^n pn_i + |pn_{n+1}|} = \frac{\sum_i^{n+1} ip_i}{\sum_i^{n+1} pn_i}$$

Then $\min_{i=1}^{n+1} \left\{ \frac{|ip_i|}{|pn_i|} \right\} = \frac{|ip_{n+1}|}{|pn_{n+1}|} \leq \frac{\sum_i^{n+1} ip_i}{\sum_i^{n+1} pn_i}$ holds.

According to (2.1) and (2.2), (*) holds for $m = n + 1$ and the proof of the induction step is completed. By the principle of induction (*) is true and the pruning strategy 1 is valid.

Pruning strategy 2 Given a k-size co-location pattern $c_k = \{f_1, f_2, \ldots, f_k\}$, a set of instance partition $CIP(c_k) = \{tp_1, tp_2, \ldots, tp_m\}$, and a spatial occupancy threshold min_occ. According to Lemma 7.4, the upper bound of spatial occupancy index $Upp\_occ(c_k) = \frac{\sum_i^m |ip_i|}{\sum_i^m |pn_i|}$, so if $Upp\_occ(c_k) \leq min\_occ$, then this candidate can be pruned.

Based on $CNT(c_k)$, $Upp\_occ(c_k)$ can be simply calculated as: $Upp\_occ(c_k) =$

$$\frac{\sum\limits_{1 \leq i \leq k} |\pi_{f_i}(CNT(c_k))|}{\sum\limits_{1 < j < mk+1 \leq i \leq o} |\pi_{f_i}(tp_j)|} \quad (f_i \in c_k)$$

According to Lemma 7.4, candidates can be pruned by Pruning strategy 2 before the process of generating an instance partition neighborhood. However, the table instance dividing process still takes a large amount of computation. Further filtering of the candidates before the instance partition process would be useful, so we also develop a loose upper bound to the occupancy index.

Lemma 7.5 (Loose upper bound of occupancy index) Given a k-size co-location pattern $c_k = \{f_1, f_2, \ldots, f_k\}$, its instance partition $CIP(c_k) = \{ip_1, ip_2, \ldots, ip_m\}$, and partition neighborhood $PN(c_k) = \{pn_1, pn_2 \ldots, pn_m\}$, there exist a loose upper bound of $OI(c_k)$:

$$OI(c_k) \leq \frac{\text{Number of distinct instances of } IP(c_k)}{\text{Number of distinct instances of } PN(c_k)}$$

Proof According to Lemma 7.4:

$$OI(c_k) \leq \frac{\sum_i^m |ip_i|}{\sum_i^m |pn_i|} \; (ip_i \in CIP(c_k), pn_i \in PN(c_k))$$

1. Due to the instance partition $CIP(c_k) = \{ip_1, \ldots, ip_m\}$ are disjoint partitions under the connected neighbor relationship: $\sum_i^m |ip_i| =$ the number of instances of c_k.
2. As neighboring instances may participate in one or more sub-neighborhoods of c_k, if no any neighboring instance belongs to two or more sub neighborhoods of c_k, then the number of neighboring instances of $c_k = \sum_i^m |pn_i|$; otherwise the number of neighboring instances of $c_k < \sum_i^m |pn_i|$.

Pruning strategy 3 According to Lemma 7.5, given a k-size co-location pattern $c_k = \{f_1, f_2, \ldots, f_k\}$ and a spatial occupancy threshold *min_occ*, the loose upper bound of spatial occupancy index c_k can be simply calculated as:

$$Loose\_Upp\_Occ(c_k) = \frac{\sum\limits_{1 \leq i \leq k} \left| \pi_{f_i}(CNT(c_k)) \right|}{\sum\limits_{1 \leq j < k \leq m} \left| \pi_{f_j}(CNT(c_k)) \right|} \; (f_i, f_j \in CNT(c_k))$$

If $Loose\_Upp\_occ(c_k) \leq min\_occ$, this candidate can be pruned.

7.5.3   An Improved Algorithm

With the new data structures and the three pruning strategies, an improved algorithm for dominant SCP mining can be developed, denoted DSCPMA (IA), which improves the generation of candidates, their prevalence filter, and their completeness filter processes. This improved algorithm is presented in Algorithm 7.3.

1. *Generating candidate co-location patterns:* for a prevalent co-location patter p_{k-1}, its candidate k-size co-locations which extend from p_{k-1} can be selected from the $CNT(p_{k-1})$. According to pruning strategy 1, we filter the $k + 1$ size candidates by testing the participation ratio of each extended feature, obtained directly from $CNT(p_{k-1})$.

2. *Prevalence filter*: We calculate the participation index of a k-size candidate co-location combined with a feature extended from $CNT(p_{k-1})$. According to Definition 7.11, we can calculate the participation index of k-size candidate co-locations without generating table instances of candidates.
3. *Completeness filter:* With pruning strategy 3, the candidate c_k can be filtered by its loose upper bound. The pruning strategy 2 then helps to prune the search space of candidate dominant SCPs and so avoid the cost of generating instance partitions for the candidate whose upper bound of spatial occupancy is less than min_occ.

Algorithm 7.3 Improved Algorithm of DSCPMA

Input: (1) S: A spatial data set; (2) F: a feature set; (3) d: a distance threshold; (4) min_prev: a prevalence threshold; (5) min_occ: an occupancy threshold; (6) ω: A weight parameter

Output: *A set of dominant spatial co-location patterns: DSCP*

Method:

1) NI=find_ins_neighbors (S, d)
2) $P_1 = F, k = 2, DSCP = \varnothing$;
3)   **While** $(P_{k-1} \neq \varnothing$)
4)   **For each** $f \in Neighbor\_Feature(CNT(p_{k-1}))$
5) $c_k = p_{k-1} \cup f$

//prevalence filter and pruning strategy 1

6)   **If** $(\,|\,\pi_f(CNT(p_{k-1}))\,|\,/\,|\,\pi_f(T(\{f\}))\,|\,{\geq} min\_prev)$:

7) $PI(c_k)$=calculate_PI$(CNT(p_{k-1}), f)$
8)   **If** $(PI(c_k) \geq min\_prev)$:
9) $P_k \leftarrow c_k$
10) $CNT(c_k)$=generate_CNT$(CNT(p_{k-1}), f)$

//completeness filter and pruning strategy 2,3

11)   **If** $(Loose\_Upp\_Occ\,(c_k) > min\_occ)$:
12) $TP(c_k)$ =select_table_instance$(CNT(c_k))$
13) $CIP(c_k)$=divide_table_instance$(TP(c_k))$
14)   **If** $(Upp\_Occ(c_k) > min\_occ)$:
15) $PN(c_k)$=find_neighbor $(CIP(c_k), CNT(c_k))$
16) $OI(c_k)$=calculate_occ $(CIP(c_k), PN(c_k))$
17)   **If** $(OI(c_k) \geq min\_occ)$:
18) $Q(c_k)$=cal_quality$(\omega, OI(c_k), PI(c_k))$
19) $DSCP \leftarrow$ sort_by_quality$(c_k, Q(c_k))$
20)   **Output** $DSCP$

7.5.4   Comparison of Complexity

In this section, the two algorithms Basic_ DSCPMA (BA) and Improved_ DSCPMA (IA) are compared. Both algorithms involve five phases: (1) materializing spatial data into instance neighborhood model, (2) generating candidate co-location patterns, (3) selecting SCPs, (4) selecting dominant SCPs, and (5) sorting dominant SCPs by quality value. The greatest fraction of computation time is devoted to Phases 2–4.

1. *Generating candidate process:* In BA, this process is only pruned according to Lemma 1, so avoiding generating unnecessary table instances. In IA, for a prevalent co-location p_{k-1}, a co-location neighborhood table *of p_{k-1}* is used to store the information needed to prune and filter all k size candidates c_k which are extended by p_{k-1}, but without generating table instances. This process saves the storage space of unnecessary co-location candidates and their table instances.

2. *Prevalence filter process:* In IA, for each candidate co-location $c_k = p_{k-1} \cup f_i$, the participation ratio of f_i can be directly obtained from $CNT(p_{k-1})$, and the participation ratio of other features in c_k can be calculated by a mapping function, so it only costs $O(m)$, m being the number of rows where there exist extended features as co-location instance neighbors. Thus, in the improved algorithm, we save computation space and time, both for generating table instances and for calculating participation indexes of candidate co-locations.

3. *Completeness filter process:* we calculate the upper bound of spatial occupancy to prune the search space, based on the last row of the co-location neighborhood table which stores the projection of features participating in the table instance, so the upper bound can be directly calculated. The cost of the pruning strategies we have developed is a constant time consumption. However, the strategies can help prune the search space of dominant SCPs in the three main mining processes. The next section shows this improvement, as we present the efficiency of the algorithm on different data sets.

7.6 Experimental Study

In this section, we show the results of extensive experiments to evaluate the proposed algorithms from multiple perspectives on both synthetic and real data sets. All the algorithms are implemented in Visual C#. All of our experiments are performed on a 2.4GHZ, 8GB-memory and Intel Core i7 computer.

7.6.1 Data Sets

We use three real-world data sets and a series of synthetic data sets in our experiments to evaluate the efficiency and effectiveness of the algorithms.

1. *Synthetic data generation:* The synthetic data sets are randomly generated in a given range according to the Poisson distribution function for simulating the distribution of space instances in real geographical space. The distribution range

of spatial instances, $D*D$, was divided into grids of $d*d$ where d is the spatial neighbor distance threshold. Dataset-1, Dataset-2, and Dataset-3 were generated in a 1000×1000 space, Dataset-4 is generated in a 2000×2000 space, and Datasets $5 \sim 12$ is generated in $100{,}000 \times 100{,}000$ spaces. Note that although Dataset-2 contains fewer instances than Dataset-3, Dataset-2 has a higher density than Dataset-3 due to a smaller distribution range.

2. *Real-world data:* A summary of the three real-world data sets is presented in Table 7.3. Real-1 data set is a spatial distribution data set of Beijing POI (Point Of Interest) data, which contains around 26,546 instances and 16 features. As shown in Fig. 7.5(a), the distribution of its instances is even and dense and the number of instances is quite different for different features. The Real-2 data set is rare plant data from the "Three Parallel Rivers of Yunnan Protected Areas," which contains 32 features and only 355 instances with a zonal distribution as shown in Fig. 7.5 (b). Real-3 is another vegetation distribution data set of the Three Parallel Rivers of Yunnan Protected Areas, which contains 25 features and 13,350 instances with a block distribution as shown in Fig. 7.5(c). Table 7.3 lists the details and default parameters of all the real data sets used in our experiments.

7.6.2 Efficiency

This subsection examines the efficiency of the two algorithms, basic-dominant DSCPMA (BA), and improved-DSCPMA (IA), on a series of synthetic data sets with several workloads, i.e., different distance thresholds, different minimum prevalence thresholds, different minimum occupation thresholds, and different weight parameters.

The effect of prevalence threshold: The running time comparison of BA and IA at four different minimum prevalence thresholds (*min_prev*) on four data sets is shown in Fig. 7.6. The results of BA and IA are represented by solid and dotted lines, respectively. Different colors represent the results with different data sets; e.g., BA-1 presents the performance of BA on Dataset-1. For each data set, the running times of both BA and IA decrease as *min_prev* increases. Note that for Dataset-1, 2, 3, the running time of BA and IA is similar at *min_prev* $= 0.6$ and BA is more efficient than IA at *min_prev* $= 0.8$. This is because a high *min_prev* constraint leads to the generation of fewer prevalent patterns and most of those are short-size patterns. As the pruning strategies make no contribution to the 2-size co-locations, the pruning strategies with IA consume even more computation time than with BA. For Dataset-1 and Dataset-2, the efficiency decreases as the number of features increases, so the running time of Dataset-2 is longer than that of Dataset 1. The running time of Dataset-3 is much longer than that of Dataset-4, indicating that the efficiency is mainly affected by the data density. Compared to the influence of the number of instances and the number of features on the algorithms, data density has a more significant effect on the algorithms. For Dataset-3, the effect of *min_prev* on algorithm performance is particularly evident since low threshold and dense data leads to huge numbers of high-size candidates, and so the pruning strategies perform

Table 7.3 The experimental data sets and default parameters

dataset	Instance amount	Feature amount	Spatial area ($D*D$)	Default distance threshold	Default *min prev*	Default *min occ*	Default *Weight* α
Dataset-1	20,000	20	1000 × 1000	10	0.2	0.1	0.5
Dataset-2	20,000	50	1000 × 1000	10	0.2	0.1	0.5
Dataset-3	40,000	25	1000 × 1000	10	0.2	0.1	0.5
Dataset-4	40,000	25	2000 × 2000	10	0.2	0.1	0.5
Dataset-5	100,000	30	100,000 × 10,0000	400	0.2	0.1	0.5
Dataset-6	100,000	40	100,000 × 100,000	400	0.2	0.1	0.5
Dataset-7	100,000	50	100,000 × 100,000	400	0.2	0.1	0.5
Dataset-8	100,000	60	100,000 × 100,000	400	0.2	0.1	0.5
Dataset-9	200,000	30	100,000 × 100,000	400	0.2	0.1	0.5
Dataset-10	300,000	30	100,000 × 100,000	400	0.2	0.1	0.5
Dataset-11	400,000	30	100,000 × 100,000	400	0.2	0.1	0.5
Dataset-12	500,000	30	100,000 × 100,000	400	0.2	0.1	0.5
Real-1	26,546	16	20,000 × 12,000	40	0.2	0.1	0.5
Real-2	13,350	25	5000 × 80,000	230	0.2	0.2	0.5
Real-3	335	32	8000 × 13,000	6000	0.2	0.2	0.5

better. The lower *min_prev* is, the more effective the pruning strategies are, especially on dense data sets.

The effect of distance threshold: Fig. 7.7 presents the comparison of running times of BA and IA on Datasets-1, 2, 3, 4 with respect to their variations of distance threshold, respectively. The effect of higher distance thresholds on algorithm performance is especially obvious, indicating that the performance of the algorithms is mainly affected by the data density. For Dataset-1 and Dataset-2, the running times are similar at $d = 12$, meaning that when the distance threshold is lower, there is little difference in the efficiency of BA and IA. As the distance threshold continues to increase, the performance of IA algorithm becomes progressively more efficient than BAs due to the series of pruning strategies in IA efficiently avoiding the generation of complete neighbor tables for all candidates, and then repeatedly partitioning the pattern space. The running time on Dataset-3 is much more than the running time on

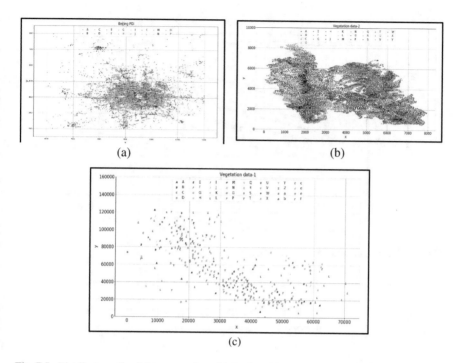

(a)   (b)

(c)

Fig. 7.5 Distribution of real data sets, where (**a**) Real-1; (**b**) Real-2; (**c**) Real-3

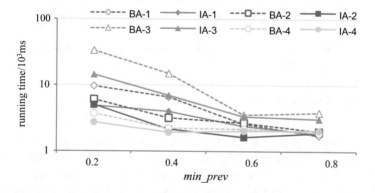

Fig. 7.6 The variation of *min_prev* on different data sets

Dataset-4 which indicates that the developed algorithm is sensitive to the density of data, although the number of instances has little influence on the algorithms.

The effect of co-location occupancy threshold: Fig. 7.8 shows the respective running time of the BA and IA algorithms on the four Datasets-1, 2, 3, 4 with respect to variations of the occupancy threshold (*min_occ*). Comparing the running time on the four data sets, it is obvious the running time does not fluctuate greatly with the increase of occupancy threshold on each data set. This is because the

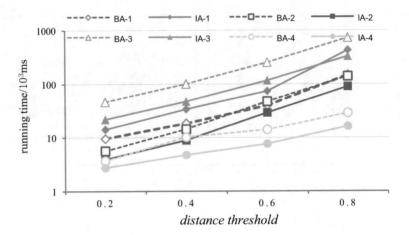

Fig. 7.7   The variation of distance on different data sets

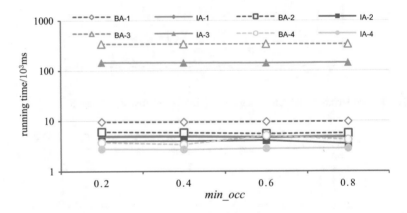

Fig. 7.8   The variation of *min_occ* on different data sets

occupancy index does not satisfy monotonicity or anti-monotonicity. If the participation index of a co-location is no less than *min_prev*, even though the occupancy index of this co-location is less than *min_occ*, its super co-locations still need be calculated. For each data set, then, IA is more efficient than BA since IA can filter many candidates by using two upper bounds and reducing the computational requirement of the pattern area partitioning process. For Dataset-1 and Dataset-2, the efficiency of computation on Dataset-1 is better than on Dataset-2 because the number of features in Dataset-2 is more than in Dataset-1, yet the difference in efficiency is not obvious. The results from Dataset-3 and Dataset-4 indicate that the efficiency improvement is particularly evident for the performance of IA on dense data sets.

The scalability of proposed algorithms. This subsection examines the scalability of BA and IA in several scenarios, i.e., different numbers of spatial instances, and

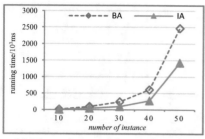
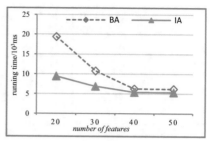

(a) The variation of the number of instance

(b) The variation of the number of features

Fig. 7.9 The scalability of proposed algorithms

different numbers of spatial features on the synthetic Datasets 5–12. The running time of BA exceeds the time limit (2,400,000 ms > 40,000 h) when the number of spatial instances reaches 500,000, and the running time for IA exceeds the time limit (1,240,000 ms > 26,000 h) as shown in Fig. 7.9(a). That means IA is more efficient than BA as the instances increase. Figure 7.9(b) shows the running time of both BA and IA on different numbers of features. As the number of features increases, the running time decreases, because, as the number of features grows, more time is spent on the prefix-trees of features. When the number of features reaches 20, the running time drops because the data set is too sparse to have larger-size prevalent patterns if the total number of spatial instances is fixed.

7.6.3 Effectiveness

As we discussed in Sect. 7.6.2, the parameter prevalence threshold (i.e., *min_prev*) and distance threshold (i.e. d) are the main factors affecting the efficiency of the developed algorithms. In this subsection, we will discuss the parameters which affect the effectiveness of the algorithms and explain the practical application of dominant SCP mining on real data sets. Three real-world data sets are used in our experiments to demonstrate the effectiveness of our algorithm. Compared to the synthetic data, mining results on real data sets are generally more reliable and meaningful.

The concept of spatial occupancy can be regarded as an interesting new measure and constraint. Since, according to the definition of a dominant SCP, a dominant SCP needs to meet prevalence and spatial occupancy constraints, it can be easily inferred that the mining results of dominant SCPs where *min_occ* = 0 are the same as traditional prevalent spatial co-location patterns (SCPs) under the same *min_prev* and d. Thus, we conduct experiments by changing the prevalence threshold (i.e., *min_prev*), the occupancy threshold (i.e., *min_occ*), and weight (i.e. ω) to reveal the effect of parameter settings on the results of dominant SCP mining.

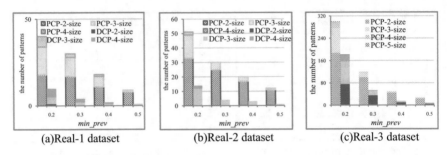

Fig. 7.10 The variation of *min_prev* on real-world data sets, where (**a**) on Real-1; (**b**) on Real-2; (**c**) on Real-3

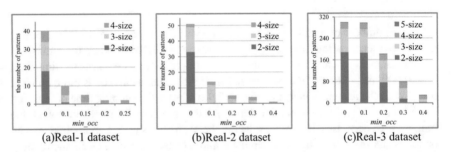

Fig. 7.11 The variation of *min_occ* on real-world data sets, where (**a**) on Real-1; (**b**) on Real-2; (**c**) on Real-3

The effect of min_prev on dominant SCP and SCP mining results. As the experiments show in Fig. 7.10, we set *min_occ* = 0 to obtain the SCPs on three real data sets, and we set *min_occ* = 0.1 to obtain dominant SCP results on the Real-1 and Real-2 data sets. We set *min_occ* = 0.2 to obtain dominant SCP results on the Real-3 data set, and the other default parameters are shown in Table 7.3. In Fig. 7.10, we present the mining results of SCPs and dominant SCPs with different *min_prev* and record the number of patterns of different size for each mining result. It can be seen that on each data set, the number of dominant SCPs and SCPs both decrease with an increase of *min_prev* and that the number of SCP mining results are much more than those of the dominant SCP mining results under same *min_prev*. It is worth noting that as *min_prev* increases, the proportion of short-size patterns in the SCP results becomes higher and higher. For each data set, the number of both the higher size and smaller size dominant SCPs are less, and the proportion of middle-size dominant SCPs is the largest.

The effect of min_occ on dominant SCP mining results. Figure 7.11 presents the mining results of dominant SCPs with different *min_occ* under the same prevalence threshold where *min_prev* = 0.2, and the other default parameters are as shown in Table 7.3. For each data set in the experimental results shown in Fig. 7.11, the SCP mining result is represented by a stacked column where *min_occ* = 0, and a different color represents a different pattern size. It can be seen that for each data set, the

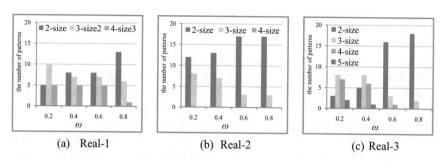

Fig. 7.12 The variation of *weight* on real data sets, where (**a**) on Real-1; (**b**) on Real-2; (**c**) on Real-3

number of dominant SCPs decreases rapidly with the increasing of *min_occ*, especially for the shorter size patterns. To the contrary, as *min_occ* increases, long size patterns keep being retained in the dominant SCP results. This retention indicates even though the spatial occupancy metric is not strictly monotonic, the longer a pattern size is, the higher its spatial occupancy index may be. The experimental results shown in Fig. 7.11 can further explain the differences between the SCP and dominant SCP mining results in Fig. 7.10. For each data set, even though some high-size patterns are filtered by the prevalence threshold constraints, most of those of short size are also filtered by the spatial occupancy threshold.

The effect of ω on dominant SCP mining results. Figure 7.12 shows the change of dominant SCP mining results using different weights (i.e., changing ω). According to Definition 7.9 in Sect. 7.4, the weight parameter ω only participates in the quality value calculation part of the dominant SCP mining process. Thus, it can only affect the sorted representation of the dominant SCP results rather than affect the collection of mining results. In the experiment shown in Fig. 7.12, we select only the top-20 quality-valued dominant SCPs to observe the effect of the weight on the dominant SCP mining sorting results where *min_prev* = 0.2, *min_occ* = 0.1. For each data set, as ω increases, the proportion of longer-size dominant SCPs in the top-20 mining results decreases and the proportion of shorter-size dominant SCPs in the mining results increases. Also, under the same *min_prev* and *min_occ*, the top-20 dominant SCP results are similar to the top-20 SCP results with a high ω. For example, the proportion of patterns of different sizes in the dominant SCP result where ω = 0.8 in Fig. 7.12(a) is similar to the SCP results in Fig. 7.11(a), and the proportion of patterns of different sizes in the dominant SCP result where ω = 0.2 in Fig. 7.12 (c) is similar to the dominant SCP results in Fig. 7.11(c) where *min_occ* = 0.3. Evidently, the higher the ω, the more prevalence metrics contribute to the quality of the dominant SCPs. That indicates that the role of ω is in adjusting the contribution of spatial occupancy and prevalence to the quality of dominant SCP as well as sorting the dominant SCP mining results.

7.6.4 Real Applications

For the experimental results shown in Figs. 7.13 and 7.14, we discussed the effect of
prevalence threshold, spatial occupancy threshold, and the quality weight on the
dominant SCP mining results, respectively. Now, we consider the dominant SCP
and SCP mining results, respectively, on real-world data sets and explore the
practical significance in real applications of dominant SCP mining.

The biodiversity analysis application of dominant SCP: Table 7.4 lists the result
of the top-5 quality-valued dominant SCPs and Table 7.5 lists the top 5 PI-valued
SCPs on data set Real-3 (i.e., vegetation data). Compared with the dominant SCP

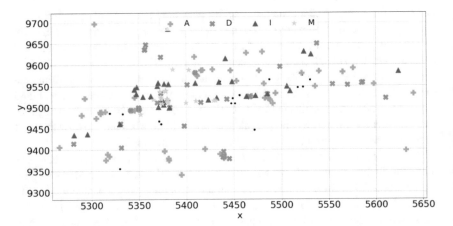

Fig. 7.13 The distribution of {Pterocarya delavayi Franch(A), Magnolia sieboldii(D), Anisodus
acutangulus(I), Hemsleya lijiangensis(M)}

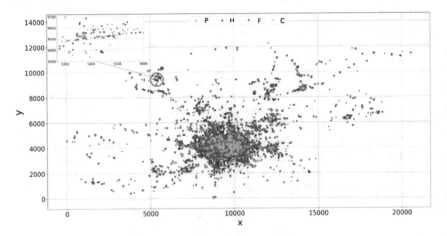

Fig. 7.14 The distribution of {Chinese Food (F), Hotel(H), Parking Lot (P), Clothing Store(C)}

Table 7.4 The results of TOP-5 dominant SCPs on Real-3 data set

	Dominant SCPs	PI	OCI	Q
1	{Pterocarya delavayi Franch, Magnolia sieboldii, Anisodus acutangulus, Hemsleya lijiangensis}	0.33	0.54	0.44
2	{Golden buckwheat, Glycyrrhiza yunnanensis, Anisodus acutangulus}	0.58	0.27	0.42
3	{Triosteum himalayanum Wall, Golden buckwheat, Glycyrrhiza yunnanensis, Hemsleya lijiangensis}	0.42	0.42	0.42
4	{Psammosilene tunicoides, Metanemone ranunculoides}	0.5	0.33	0.42
5	{Davidia involucrata Baill, Anisadenia pubescens Griff, Trillium tschonoskii Maxim, Saussurea gossypiphora}	0.26	0.54	0.4

Table 7.5 The results of TOP-5 SCPs on Real-3 data set

	SCPs	PI
1	{Magnolia sieboldii, Anisodus acutangulus}	0.78
2	{Magnolia sieboldii, Hemsleya lijiangensis}	0.69
3	{Triosteum himalayanum Wall, Hemsleya lijiangensis}	0.67
4	{Golden buckwheat, Glycyrrhiza yunnanensis}	0.67
5	{Davidia involucrata Baill, Pterocarya delavayi Franch}	0.65

Table 7.6 The results of TOP-5 dominant SCPs on Real-1 data set

	Dominant SCPs	PI	OCI	Q
1	{Chinese Food, Hotel, Parking Lot, Clothing Store}	0.29	0.29	0.29
2	{Chinese Food, Hotel, Hostel, Parking Lot}	0.4	0.12	0.26
3	{Chinese Food, Coffee shop, Parking Lot}	0.42	0.11	0.26
4	{Chinese Food, Hostel, Parking Lot, Clothing Store}	0.29	0.2	0.24
5	{Coffee shop, Parking Lot, Clothing Store}	0.26	0.17	0.22

mining results, the top-5 SCPs are shorter-size patterns, while longer size patterns come from the dominant SCPs as that process considers both completeness and prevalence of a pattern. For example, the distribution of the co-location pattern {Pterocarya Delavayi Franch, Magnolia Sieboldii, Anisodus Acutangulus, Hemsleya Lijiangensis} is shown in Fig. 7.13. It can be seen that in the areas of the co-location instances, the pattern instances are densely distributed, and occupy a large fraction of all instances in the neighborhoods. This observation indicates that the mining methods developed in this chapter should find qualified dominant SCPs. Further, the occupancy measurement solves the problem that botanists cannot rule out, by prevalence alone, the effects and interference of other features in their distribution area. For example, the dominant SCP {Psammosilene Tunicoides, Metanemone Ranunculoides} is a 2-size dominant spatial co-location pattern, meaning that this pattern is both prevalent and complete, and the plant co-existence relationship is strictly limited to these two.

Application of dominant SCPs to Urban Facility Planning: Table 7.6 lists the result of top-5 quality-valued dominant SCPs and Table 7.7 lists top-5 PI-valued

Table 7.7 The results of TOP-5 SCPs on Real-1 data set

	SCPs	PI
1	{Chinese Food, Hotel, Parking Lot}	0.78
2	{Hotel, Parking Lot}	0.76
3	{Chinese Food, Hotel,}	0.75
4	{Chinese Food, Hotel, Parking Lot}	0.64
5	{Coffee Shop, Clothing Store}	0.56

SCPs for the Real-1 (i.e., Beijing POI) data set. Compared to the dominant SCP mining results, the top-5 SCPs are generally shorter-size patterns, and the information contained in these patterns is either common sense or not representative. The dominant SCP mining results, however, provide comprehensive co-location patterns with more pattern information for users. For example, the distribution of the co-location pattern {Chinese Food, Hotel, Parking Lot, Clothing Store} is shown in Fig. 7.14. It is easily seen that the co-location instances of this pattern are widely distributed in the data set, indicating that the pattern appears prevalently in space. As shown in the diagram enlarged in the upper left corner in Fig. 7.14, that pattern's co-location instances occupy a large portion of their located neighborhood and the pattern is indeed a dominant spatial co-location pattern which is both prevalent and complete.

These demonstration scenarios show the effectiveness of the DSCPMA algorithm for mining both POI data and plant data, and could be further applied in other application areas similar to urban planning and biodiversity analysis application.

7.7   Chapter Summary

Most studies on the spatial co-location pattern mining take the prevalence of co-locations as the measure of interest. However, in some real-world applications, users are not only interested in the prevalence of co-location patterns, but also focus on their completeness. In this chapter, we have introduced a new spatial occupancy metric to evaluate the completeness of co-location patterns, using the ratio of the co-location instances occupied in their instance neighbor set and have formulated the problem of dominant SCP mining by considering both completeness and prevalence. For solving the co-location instance overlap in space, we developed a connected neighbor relationship to partition the co-location instances into instance partition sets. We also developed an efficient algorithm, DSCPMA, to discover the dominant SCPs, and then explored the use of two upper bounds of the spatial occupancy index and a compact data structure to develop three pruning strategies for pruning the DSCP search space. Finally, we evaluated the efficiency and effectiveness of the algorithms on a series of synthetic data sets and three real-world data sets. The mined results on two real-world applications demonstrate that dominant SCP mining is practical and produces significant results.

So far, we have considered the prevalence and the completeness of SCPs, but the importance or value of each feature in SCPs has not been distinguished and studied. In the next chapter, we will incorporate utility into the SCP mining through the concept of pattern utility, and discuss a spatial high utility co-location pattern mining problem.

Chapter 8
High Utility Co-location Patterns

8.1 Introduction

In our previous chapters on spatial co-location pattern mining, the importance of different features was regarded as the same. However, in many spatial databases the importance of the different features is not the same. What's more, previous work on spatial co-location pattern mining has focused on the participation ratio of each spatial feature whereby the selection of interesting patterns is generally based on a frequency framework. This ignores some interesting but low prevalence patterns, as well as unfortunately mining a lot of prevalent but not interesting patterns.

This chapter starts to remedy the situation by including the following:

1. By incorporating utility into spatial pattern mining through the concept of pattern utility, a general framework for high utility spatial co-location pattern (high utility SCP) mining is defined.
2. We define a concept of extended pattern utility ratio, and of partial extended pattern utility ratio, and also present an extended pruning algorithm (EPA) and a partial pruning algorithm (PPA) to prune down the number of candidates as well as obtain a complete set of high utility SCPs. Both EPA and PPA should improve the mining performance and accelerate the generation of high utility SCPs under different parameter-driven environments.
3. Using synthetic and real-world databases, substantial experiments show that, as expected, EPA and PPA effectively and efficiently identify high utility SCPs.

Figure 8.1 presents the organization of this chapter. We first discuss why we need to discover high utility SCPs in Sect. 8.2, and Sect. 8.3 gives the related work. Then the formal problem definition for mining high utility SCPs is presented in Sect. 8.4.

From Yang, S., Wang, L., Bao, X., et al.: A framework for mining spatial high utility co-location patterns. In: *Proceedings of the 12th International Conference on Fuzzy Systems and Knowledge Discovery (FSKD 2015)*, IEEE, Zhangjiajie, China, pp. 595–601 (2015).

© The Author(s), under exclusive license to Springer Nature Singapore Pte Ltd. 2022
L. Wang et al., *Preference-based Spatial Co-location Pattern Mining*, Big Data Management, https://doi.org/10.1007/978-981-16-7566-9_8

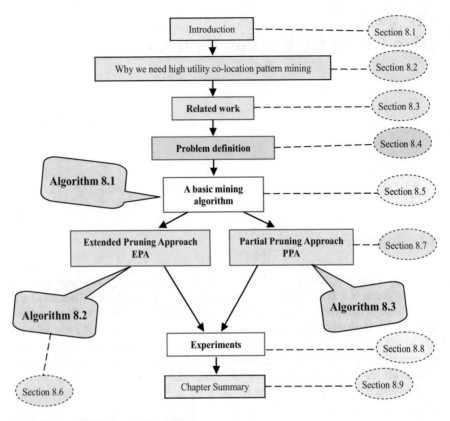

Fig. 8.1 The organization of this chapter

Section 8.5 gives a basic mining algorithm for high utility SCPs. In Sect. 8.6, we present an extended pruning algorithm based on the property of extended pattern utility ratio. A partial pruning approach is described in Sect. 8.7. Experimental results and evaluations are shown in Sect. 8.8. Finally, we conclude this chapter in Sect. 8.9.

8.2   Why We Need High Utility Co-location Pattern Mining

A spatial co-location pattern (SCP) is a set of spatial features whose instances are frequently co-located in the same region. For example, West Nile Virus often appears in regions with poor mosquito control and the presence of birds. SCP mining is an important task of spatial data mining.

In SCP mining, different features all have the same importance. However, we know intuitively that the importance of different features is not the same in many spatial databases. A related problem is that previous work on SCP mining

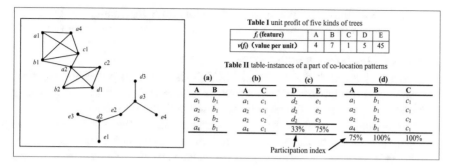

Fig. 8.2 A specific example to illustrate the problem

concentrated on the participation ratio of each spatial feature has ignored interesting but low prevalence SCPs, as well as mining a lot of prevalent SCPs of no real interest to the user.

For instance, in location-based services (LBS), various services provided by a mobile telecoms operator bring different profits, and each service has a number of service points in different geographical locations. Here, the services are equivalent to spatial features, and the service points are equivalent to spatial instances. For a telecoms operator, point of service A might bring a profit of $v(A)$ per month, while point of service B brings $v(B)$, where $v(A) >> v(B)$. The combination of services generating a huge profit, i.e., which contains A, may be ignored if the combination/ pattern appears infrequently and we are using a method based on frequency to mine interesting co-location service combinations/patterns. It could be that the service combination with a low profit, i.e., which contains B, is selected only because it appears frequently.

We can see this effect clearly in Tables II(c) and II(d) in Fig. 8.2 where, with a method based on prevalence, the participation index of $\{A, B, C\}$ is 75% and $\{D, E\}$ is 33.3%. But, according to Table I in Fig. 8.2, the sum of values of the instances of $\{D, E\}$ is $1 \times 5 + 3 \times 45 = 140$ and those of $\{A, B, C\}$ is $3 \times 4 + 2 \times 7 + 2 \times 1 = 28$. Obviously, from the view of economic profit, $\{D, E\}$ is more significant than $\{A, B, C\}$. On the one hand, the classic prevalence-based method often finds many SCPs, most of which are not informative enough for businesses, such as $\{A, B, C\}$. On the other hand, a lot of SCPs are ignored as their prevalence values are low. So, for the first time, we incorporate utility into the SCP mining framework, to ensure that high utility SCPs are mined.

In general, the challenges of mining high utility SCPs lie in two aspects.

1. **How to identify and measure high utility SCPs**

    Conventional techniques often ignore the differences between the utility of different features, as they often only pay attention to whether SCPs are prevalent or not. Measures based on prevalence are often not suitable for mining high utility SCPs.

Our contributions. We incorporate utility into the mining of SCPs and propose a new measure, pattern utility, by which a user can determine an SCP's interest.

2. **How to mine the high utility SCPs**

We consider an SCP as high utility SCP, if and only if its pattern utility ratio is higher than a minimum pattern utility ratio threshold. In classic SCP mining based on a prevalence framework, the downward closure property, also named anti-monotonicity, plays a key role in pruning down the number of eligible candidates. This is because the value of such a measure, such as the participation ratio, decreases with an increasing size of SCPs. Through examples, we will show that the downward closure property does not work in utility-based SCP mining, implying that most of the existing algorithms based on prevalence cannot be directly transferred from prevalent SCP mining to high utility SCP mining.

Our contributions. First, we propose a basic algorithm for mining high utility SCPs. It is complete but inefficient. Second, we define a new concept, extended pattern utility ratio. We then show that the extended pattern utility ratio is an upper bound of the pattern utility ratio. Based on this property, we develop two pruning methods, expressed in an extended pruning algorithm (EPA) and in a partial pruning algorithm (PPA). Compared with the basic algorithm, in which a pattern utility ratio threshold is applied to the mining process, both EPA and PPA should be more efficient. From our experimental analysis, it can be seen that EPA and PPA are both efficient in environments with differing parameters.

8.3 Related Work

8.3.1 *Spatial Co-location Pattern Mining*

The problem of mining spatial association rules based on spatial relationships was first discussed in Koperski and Han (1995). Statistically meaningful interest measures were proposed in Shekhar and Huang (2001) for SCP mining, and a join-based SCP mining algorithm was presented in Huang et al. (2004). Join-less SCP mining algorithm was introduced in Yoo and Shekhar (2006), using an instance-lookup scheme for identifying co-location instances. Some studies (Yang et al., 2018a, 2018b) were conducted to explore the MapReduce-based approach and to address the problem of mining SCPs from massive spatial databases.

There exists some other interesting work on mining different kinds of SCPs. Maximal SCP mining was studied in Wang et al. (2009b) and Yao et al. (2016). Research on closed SCP mining was presented in Yoo and Bow (2011a) and Wang et al. (2018b). Wang et al. (2018a) proposed non-redundant SCPs which are subsets of prevalent SCPs where each SCP cannot cover any other one by considering their row-instances. The problem of interactively extracting user-preferred SCPs was studied in Bao et al. (2021) and Wang et al. (2018c).

High utility SCP mining was first presented in Yang et al. (2015). Their algorithm is a size-order traversal algorithm that would show a less obvious pruning effect when it traverses low-size SCPs compared to when it traverses high-size SCPs. Based on the concept of high utility SCPs in Yang et al. (2015), the problem of incrementally mining high utility SCPs was studied in Wang et al. (2016) and Wang et al. (2019d). Differing from the work in Yang et al. (2015), Wang et al. (2017a) takes instances with utilities as study objects and combines the intra-utility ratio and the inter-utility ratio into a utility participation index for identifying high utility SCPs.

8.3.2   Utility Itemset Mining

Utility itemset mining was first discussed in Yao et al. (2004). Every item in the itemset is associated with an additional value, called the internal utility which is a numeric quantity related to the item. A UMining algorithm was proposed by Yao et al. (2006) which uses an estimation method to prune the search space. Although it is shown to have good performance, it cannot capture the complete set of high utility itemsets since some high utility patterns may be pruned during the process. The two-phase algorithm presented in Liu et al. (2005) efficiently prunes down the number of candidates, through the transaction-weighted downward closure property. Also the algorithms (Tseng et al., 2010, 2013; Song et al., 2016) have been developed for efficient mining high utility itemsets, and the concise and lossless representation of high utility itemsets have also been studied (Tseng et al., 2015, 2016; Duong et al., 2016).

An incremental mining algorithm (Lin et al., 2012) for efficiently mining high utility itemsets was proposed to handle the environment of intermittent data. Ahmed et al. (2011) introduced frequency affinity based on utility to mine high utility itemsets, items inside of which have strong correlations. UP-Growth proposed in Tseng et al. (2010) enhanced the mining performance in utility mining by maintaining the information of high utility itemsets with a UP-tree. Shie et al. (2010) applied utility mining to data stream environments. A generic framework was proposed in Yin et al. (2012) for mining high utility sequential patterns by combining utility with sequence. Ahmed et al. (2009) and Hong et al. (2012) maintained high utility patterns in an incremental environment by avoiding multiple scans of the databases.

8.4   Problem Definition

In this section, we describe the basic concepts of high utility SCP mining. Definitions 8.1–8.4 relate to concepts of traditional SCP mining and high utility itemsets mining as preliminaries, while Definitions 8.5–8.12 relate to the concepts presented in this chapter for high utility SCP mining.

We can divide the data in a spatial database into various spatial features, similar to the items in a traditional transaction database. Figure 8.2 shows five spatial features, A-E, each of which has many instances. For example, a_1 and a_2 are instances of feature A.

Definition 8.1 (Neighbor Relationship R) Let a and b be an instance of feature A and B, respectively, and the neighbor relationship R between them expressed by a Euclidean distance metric. In this chapter, with a threshold value d, we define the neighbor relationship R: two spatial instances are neighbors if they satisfy the Euclidean distance between them not exceeding d, i.e., $R(a, b) \Leftrightarrow (distance(a, b) \leq d)$. When two spatial instances of diverse features satisfy the neighbor relationship R, we connect them with a line in the spatial diagram, such as in Fig. 8.2.

Definition 8.2 (Size) Let $F = \{f_1, \ldots, f_n\}$ be the feature set of spatial database S. A co-location is a subset of F and a co-location is called a k-co-location, i.e., its size is k, if there are k features in the SCP.

For example, the SCP $c = \{A, B, C\}$ is a 3-co-location.

Definition 8.3 (Row instance and table instance) A row instance I of an SCP c is a set of instances including instances of all the features in c and which forms a clique relationship with R, but without repeating the feature types of instances in I. The set of all row instances of c is called a table instance of c, denoted as $T(c)$.

For example, in Fig. 8.2, $\{a_1, b_1, c_1\}$ is a row instance of SCP $\{A, B, C\}$ since the feature type of a_1 is A, the feature type of b_1 is B, and the feature type of c_1 is C, and $R(a_1, b_1)$, $R(b_1, c_1)$, and $R(a_1, c_1)$ hold.

Definition 8.4 (External utility) The external utility is used to describe the importance (e.g., price) of different feature. We denote the external utility of a feature $f_i \in F$ as $v(f_i)$.

For example, in location-based services, the profit brought by a service point is the external utility of the service. From a different environment, forestry, the unit economic profit of a kind of tree is the external utility of the tree. Indeed, Table I in Fig. 8.2 is a table of external utilities for differing kinds of tree.

Definition 8.5 (Internal utility) The quantity of different instances of feature f_i appearing in the table-instance of c is internal utility of f_i in c, defined as $q(f_i, c) = |\prod_{f_i} T(c)|$, where $\prod$ is the projection operation. If $c = \{f_i\}$, then $q(f_i, \{f_i\})$ means the quantity of all instances of feature f_i in S.

For example, in Fig. 8.2, Tables II(c) and II(d) show the table instances of SCP $\{D, E\}$ and $\{A, B, C\}$, respectively. Thus the internal utility of D in $\{D, E\}$ is $q(D,$

{D, E}) = $|\prod_D T(\{D, E\})| = 1$, and the internal utility of A in {A, B, C} is q (A, {A, B, C}) = $|\prod_A T(\{A, B, C\})| = 3$.

From Definitions 8.4 and 8.5, we can see that the external utility $v(f_i)$ of a feature f_i is the value of an instance of f_i, while the internal utility $q(f_i, c)$ of f_i in an SCP c is the number of different instances of f_i in the table-instance of c. We can immediately define the utility of f_i in c as in Definition 8.6.

Definition 8.6 (Utility of a feature in an SCP) Given a k-co-location $c = \{f_1, ..., f_k\}$, we define the product of the external utility and the internal utility of f_i in c as the utility of f_i in c, denoted as

$$v(f_i, c) = v(f_i) \times q(f_i, c) \tag{8.1}$$

For example, the utility of A in {A, B, C} is $v(A, \{A, B, C\}) = v(A) \times q$ (A, {A, B, C}) = $4 \times 3 = 12$, and the utility of B in {A, B, C} is $v(B, \{A, B, C\}) = v(B) \times q$ (B, {A, B, C}) = $7 \times 2 = 14$. Note that if $c = \{f_i\}$, then $v(f_i, \{f_i\}) = v(f_i) \times q(f_i, \{f_i\})$ means the total utility of all instances of feature f_i in S.

Definition 8.7 (Pattern utility) Given a k-co-location $c = \{f_1, ..., f_k\}$, the pattern utility of c is the sum of the utilities of all features in c. The formal definition is as follows:

$$u(c) = \sum_{f_i \in c} v(f_i, c) \tag{8.2}$$

For example, the pattern utility of {A, B, C} is $u(\{A, B, C\}) = v(A, \{A, B, C\}) + v(B, \{A, B, C\}) + v(C, \{A, B, C\}) = 12 + 14 + 1 \times 2 = 28$.

Definition 8.8 (Total utility of database) Given a spatial database S and the feature set $F = \{f_1, ..., f_n\}$, the total utility of data set S is the sum of total utilities of all features, denoted as:

$$U(S) = \sum_{f_i \in F} v(f_i, \{f_i\}) \tag{8.3}$$

For example, according to the data set S in Fig. 8.2, the total utility of S is $U(S) = v(A, \{A\}) + v(B, \{B\}) + v(C, \{C\}) + v(D, \{D\}) + v(E, \{E\}) = 4 \times 4 + 7 \times 2 + 1 \times 2 + 5 \times 3 + 45 \times 4 = 227$.

In a spatial database, we call a co-location a high utility SCP if its pattern utility is high enough. How high the pattern utility of an SCP should be such that it is considered as a high utility SCP is problematic and needs a threshold somehow specified by the user.

Definition 8.9 (Pattern utility ratio) Given a spatial database S and an SCP c, the total utility of S is $U(S)$, and the pattern utility of c is $u(c)$. The pattern utility ratio of

c is defined as $\lambda(c) = u(c)/U(S)$, the ratio of the utility of c to the total utility of S. In other words, $\lambda(c)$ indicates the percentage of the utility that c contributes to S. A large $\lambda(c)$ indicates that c is more valuable in S and of more interest to the user.

For example, according to Table II(d) in Fig. 8.2, the pattern utility ratio of {A, B, C} is $\lambda(\{A, B, C\}) = u(\{A, B, C\})/U(S) = 28/227 = 12.3\%$.

Definition 8.10 (Pattern utility ratio threshold) The pattern utility ratio threshold is a constant between 0 and 1, denoted as ξ ($0 \leq \xi \leq 1$), which is generally specified by users. We consider an SCP c as a high utility SCP if $\lambda(c) \geq \xi$.

8.5   A Basic Mining Approach

Our goal is to mine all the high utility SCPs in databases, the λ of which are above ξ. A basic approach is designed as three steps: First, identify table instances of all the SCPs; second, calculate the pattern utility ratios of them; third, compare them with ξ in order to judge which of the SCPs are high utility SCPs.

SCPs of size 1 cannot generate rules such as $(A) \rightarrow (B, C)$, as there is only one feature in them and so they are not considered further. Given a spatial database S with n features, the approach (we call it Algorithm 8.1) needs to obtain table instances of all $2^n - n - 1$ SCPs, except for SCPs of size 1, and calculate the λ of them. This approach, which tests all SCPs of size 2 and above, is complete. Unfortunately, it is also inefficient, as the calculations of table instances of all SCPs are horrendous. Therefore, we hope there is an upper bound of λ, comparing it with ξ could prune low utility SCPs without calculating their table-instances and λ. We might hope λ is anti-monotonic, similar to the participation ratio in prevalence-based traditional SCP mining methods. Unfortunately, neither λ nor u is anti-monotonic. The following example illustrates this situation.

With the example in Definition 8.7, we obtain $u(\{A, B, C\}) = 28$, $u(\{A, B\}) = v(A, \{A, B\}) + v(B, \{A, B\}) = 4 \times 4 + 7 \times 2 = 30$, and $u(\{A, C\}) = v(A, \{A, C\}) + v(C, \{A, C\}) = 4 \times 3 + 2 \times 1 = 14$. So $u(\{A, B, C\}) < u(\{A, B\})$ while $u(\{A, B, C\}) > u(\{A, C\})$. This demonstrates that that the pattern utility u is neither monotonic nor anti-monotonic, and so neither is λ.

8.6   Extended Pruning Approach

In this section, we present an extended pruning algorithm based on the property of extended pattern utility ratio which will prune low utility SCPs.

8.6.1   Related Definitions

Definition 8.11 (Single feature table instance of SCP) We define a single feature table instance of an SCP as the set of instances of feature f appearing in all subsets of an SCP c, denoted as $\text{Tas}(f, c)$. In other words, if the feature f belongs to SCP c, we then get all the subsets of c which contain f, in order to get the projections of table instances of them on f. The intersection of these projections is $\text{Tas}(f, c)$ whose formal definition is

$$\text{Tas}(f,c) = \bigcap_{c' \subset c \wedge f \in c' \cap c} \left(\prod_f T(c') \right) \tag{8.4}$$

Furthermore, the quantity of instances of f appearing in all subsets of c are denoted as

$$qas(f,c) = |\text{Tas}(f,c)| \tag{8.5}$$

And the utility of f appearing in all subsets of c is denoted as

$$vas(f,c) = v(f) \times qas(f,c) \tag{8.6}$$

For example, according to Fig. 8.2, the SCP {A, B, C} has {A, B}, {A, C} and {A} as three subsets which contain feature A. $\prod_A T(\{A\})$ is equal to the table instance of {A}, which is $\{a_1, a_2, a_3, a_4\}$. $\prod_A T(\{A, B\})$ is $\{a_1, a_2, a_3, a_4\}$ and $\prod_A T(\{A, C\})$ is $\{a_1, a_2, a_4\}$. Therefore, $\text{Tas}(A, \{A, B, C\}) = \{a_1, a_2, a_4\}$, $qas(A, \{A, B, C\}) = 3$, and $vas(A, \{A, B, C\}) = v(A) \times qas(A, \{A, B, C\}) = 4 \times 3 = 12$.

Theorem 8.1 If $c' \subset c$ and $f \in c' \cap c$, then $v(f, c) \leq v(f, c')$.

Proof As f is a common feature of c and c', if an instance o of feature f appears in $T(c)$, then it must appear in $T(c')$. So the number of instances of f in $T(c)$ is no more than that in $T(c')$, i.e., $q(f, c) \leq q(f, c')$. Therefore, according to Definition 8.6, the utility of feature f in co-location c is no more than that in c', i.e., $v(f, c) \leq v(f, c')$. $\square$

Theorem 8.2 The utility of feature f in SCP c is no more than $vas(f, c)$.

Proof Given an SCP c, which contains feature f, suppose c' is any subset of c, which also contains f. As f is a common feature of c and c', if an instance o of feature f appears in $T(c)$, then it must appear in $T(c')$ and must also appear in $\prod_f T(c')$. In general, the instance o must appear in $\text{Tas}(f,c) = \bigcap_{c' \subset c \wedge f \in c' \cap c} \left(\prod_f T(c') \right)$. That is to say, the quantity (internal utility) of instances of f in c is no more than $qas(f, c)$, i.e., $q(f, c) \leq qas(f, c)$. Therefore, according to Definition 8.6, the utility of feature f in SCP c is no more than $vas(f, c)$, i.e., $v(f, c) \leq vas(f, c)$. $\square$

In order to reduce the cost of computing, by adding a positive integer variable s, we extend Tas(f, c) to Tss(f, c, s), meaning the set of instances of f appearing in some subsets of c. i.e.,

$$\text{Tss}(f, c, s) = \bigcap_{c^s \subset c \wedge f \in c^s \cap c} \left(\prod_f T(c^s) \right) \tag{8.7}$$

where c^s is one of top-s subsets of c, which are ordered by size in descending order and then in lexicographical order. For example, $\text{Tss}(A, \{A, B, C, D\}, 4) = \bigcap_{c^4 \subset c \wedge f \in c^4 \cap c} \left(\prod_f T(c^4) \right)$, where c^4 is $\{A, B, C\}$, $\{A, B, D\}$, $\{A, C, D\}$ and $\{A, B\}$.

Accordingly, we extend qas (f, c) to qss $(f, c, s) = |\text{Tss}(f, c, s)|$, and extend vas$(f, c)$ to vss$(f, c, s) = v(f) \times qss(f, c, s)$.

Theorem 8.3   The utility of feature f in SCP c is no more than $vss(f, c, s)$.

Proof   Obviously, Tas$(f, c) \subset$ Tss(f, c, s), which means qas $(f, c) \le qss$ (f, c, s). Therefore, $vas(f, c) \le vss(f, c, s)$. As v $(f, c) \le vas(f, c)$ according to Theorem 8.2, the inequality v $(f, c) \le vss(f, c, s)$ is true. □

Definition 8.12 (Extended pattern utility ratio)   Given a feature set $F = \{f_1, \ldots, f_n\}$, and a SCP c. We define the extended pattern utility ratio of c as the sum of $\lambda(c)$ and the ratio of $\sum_{f_i \in f - c} vss(f_i, c \cup f_i, s)$ to $U(S)$. The formal definition is:

$$\text{EPUR}(c) = \lambda(c) + \sum_{f_i \in f - c} vss(f_i, c \cup f_i, s) / U(S) \tag{8.8}$$

Theorem 8.4   If c is a subset of c', then the pattern utility ratio of c' is no more than the extended pattern utility ratio of c.

Proof $\lambda(c') = u(c')/U(S) = \sum_{f_i \in c'} v(f_i, c')/U(S) = (\sum_{f_i \in c} v(f_i, c') + \sum_{f_i \in c' - c} v(f_i, c'))/U(S)$. According to Theorem 8.1, $\sum_{f_i \in c} v(f_i, c') \le \sum_{f_i \in c} v(f_i, c) = u(c)$. According to Theorem 8.1 and Theorem 8.3, $\sum_{f_i \in c' - c} v(f_i, c') \le \sum_{f_i \in c' - c} v(f_i, c \cup f_i) \le \sum_{f_i \in c' - c} vss(f_i, c \cup f_i, s) \le \sum_{f_i \in F - c} vss(f_i, c \cup f_i, s)$. Therefore, $\lambda(c') \le \text{EPUR}(c)$. □

8.6.2   Extended Pruning Algorithm (EPA)

EPUR(c) is an upper bound of $\lambda(c')$, where c' is any superset of c. Therefore, if EPUR $(c) < \xi$, c can be pruned from candidates, as all supersets of c are low utility SCPs.

Using this property, we propose an extended pruning algorithm (EPA), described as follows:

Algorithm 8.1 EPA

Inputs:

$F= \{f_1,...,f_n\}$: a set of spatial features

S: a set of spatial instances

V: a two-dimensional table for external utility of each $f_i \in F$

R: a spatial neighbor relationship

s: a parameter standing for fineness level of pruning

ξ: a utility ratio threshold

Output:

A set of all high utility SCPs with pattern utility ratio $\lambda \geq \xi$

Variables:

k: co-location size

C_k: a set of size k candidate co-locations

$T(c)$: the table instance of pattern c

U_k: a set of size k high utility co-locations

$vss(f_i, c, s)$: the utility of f_i appearing in the top s subsets of c.

$EPUR(c)$: the extended pattern utility ratio of c

Method:

1). $U(S)=$get_database_utility(S,F,V);

2).   for $i \in \{2,...,n\}$ do $C_i =\varnothing$, $U_i=\varnothing$;

3). $k=2$;

4).   while $(k \leq n)$

5).   if $k=2$ then do $C_k=$gen_neighborhoods(S, F, R);

6).   else do $C_k=$gen_candidate_colocations(C_{k-1});

7).   for $c \in C_k$ do

8).   if $k>2$ then do $T(c) =$gen_table_instance(C_{k-1});

9). $u(c)=$get_pattern_utility$(V, T(c))$; $\lambda(c)=u(c)/U(S)$;

10).   if $\lambda(c) \geq \xi$ then put c into U_k;

11).   else do for $f_i \in F-c$ do

12).   calculate $vss(f_i, c, s)$;

13).   calculate $EPUR(c)$;

14).   if $EPUR(c)<\xi$ then remove c from C_k;

15). $k=k+1$;

16). return $\cup (U_2, ..., U_k)$;

Initialization (Steps 1–5)

Given an input spatial data set and a neighbor relationship R, we first calculate $U(S)$ according to Definition 8.8. We initialize C_i and U_i, where i is from 2 to n. Then we generate C_2 and the table instances of each SCP c in C_2 by finding all the neighboring instance pairs using a geometric method such as plane sweep (Arge et al., 1998).

The generation of candidates (Steps 6–8)

The $T(c)$ of each c whose size is 2, is implicitly generated in step 5. For $k > 2$, size k candidate co-locations and their table instances are generated from size k-1 candidates through the joinless algorithm approach of Yoo and Shekhar (2006).

Calculating the pattern utility ratio (Steps 9–10)

We calculate $u(c)$ and $\lambda(c)$, according to Definitions 8.7 and 8.9. If and only if $\lambda(c) \geq \xi$, the co-location c is considered as a high utility SCP and put into the set of high utility SCPs.

Pruning low utility patterns with EPUR (Steps 11–14)

If c is a low utility co-location, we further check whether its supersets could be pruned. By calculating vss and EPUR, if $EPUR(c) < \xi$, we can prune all supersets of c, by removing c from the candidate set. In particular, the value of s in $vss(f_i, c, s)$ will highly influence the efficiency of pruning. With a higher s, we obtain lower vss and EPUR, which helps to increase the chances of pruning. However, calculating vss leads to more costly computing. Further considerations about s will be discussed in Sect. 8.7.

In EPA, if the SCP c is a low utility pattern, whether its supersets will be pruned depends on whether the $EPUR(c)$ is low enough. However, when the size of c is low (e.g. 2 or 3-co-location), the number of row-instances of c is generally high, which may lead to the vss and EPUR of c being too high.

Therefore, when we check a low-size SCP c, many low utility supersets will be missed by EPA, as $EPUR(c)$ is too high, ($EPUR(c) > \xi$). So we need another approach which will be efficient when it prunes the low utility supersets of a low size SCP.

8.7   Partial Pruning Approach

8.7.1   Related Definitions

Definition 8.13 (Partial extended pattern utility ratio) Given two SCPs c and c', where $c \subset c'$, we define the partial extended pattern utility ratio of c in c' as the sum of $\lambda(c)$ and the ratio of $\sum\limits_{f_i \in c'-c} vss(f_i, c \cup f_i, s)$ over $U(S)$. Here, $vss(f_i, c \cup f_i, s)$ is the utility of f_i appearing in the top-s subsets of $c \cup f_i$. The formal definition is

$$\text{PEPUR}(c, c') = \lambda(c) + \sum_{f_i \in c'-c} vss(f_i, c \cup f_i, s)/U(S) \tag{8.9}$$

Theorem 8.5 If c is a subset of c', then the pattern utility ratio of c' does not exceed the partial extended pattern utility ratio of c in c'.

Proof $\lambda(c') = u(c')/U(S) = \sum\limits_{f_i \in c'} v(f_i, c')/U(S) = \left(\sum\limits_{f_i \in c} v(f_i, c') + \sum\limits_{f_i \in c'-c} v(f_i, c') \right)$

$/U(S)$. According to Theorem 8.1, $\sum\limits_{f_i \in c} v(f_i, c') \le \sum\limits_{f_i \in c} v(f_i, c) = u(c)$. According to

Theorems   8.1   and   8.3, $\sum\limits_{f_i \in c'-c} v(f_i, c') \le \sum\limits_{f_i \in c'-c} v(f_i, c \cup f_i) \le$

$\sum\limits_{f_i \in c'-c} vss(f_i, c \cup f_i, s)$. Therefore, $\lambda(c') = (\sum\limits_{f_i \in c} v(f_i, c') + \sum\limits_{f_i \in c'-c} v(f_i, c'))/$

$U(S) \le (u(c) + \sum\limits_{f_i \in c'-c} vss(f_i, c \cup f_i, s))/U(S) = \lambda(c) + \sum\limits_{f_i \in c'-c} vss(f_i, c \cup f_i, s)/$

$U(S) = \text{PEPUR}(c, c')$, i.e., $\lambda(c') \le \text{PEPUR}(c, c')$. The implication is that if $\text{PEPUR}(c, c') < \xi$, then c' can be pruned as a low utility SCP. $\square$

To make sure the pattern c is a low utility pattern, we first sort the f in descending order by $vss(f, c \cup f, s)$. We can then define the relationship between same level patterns.

Definition 8.14 (Same level patterns and their relationship) Given two k-co-location patterns c_k and c_k'. When $c \subset c_k' \cap c_k$, we say c_k and c_k' are same level patterns about c. Moreover, if the vss of each f in $c_k'-c$ is less than or equal to that of each f in corresponding position in $c_k - c$ and $c_k' \ne c_k$, we say c_k' is lower than c_k, i.e., $c_k' < c_k$.

For example, Given three SCPs, $c = \{f_5, f_8\}$, $c_5 = \{f_3, f_5, f_7, f_8, f_{10}\}$, $c_5' = \{f_3, f_5, f_8, f_9, f_{12}\}$, then we say $c_5' < c_5$, because $c_5-c = \{f_3, f_7, f_{10}\}$, and $c_5'-c = \{f_3, f_9, f_{12}\}$. Here, f in the patterns is sorted in the descending order of vss. It is important to note that if there is $c_5'' = \{f_3, f_5, f_6, f_8, f_{12}\}$, we cannot say either $c_5'' < c_5$ or $c_5'' > c_5$. This is because $c_5 - c = \{f_3, f_7, f_{10}\}$ and $c_5'' - c = \{f_3, f_6, f_{12}\}$, and $vss(f_{10}, c \cup f_{10}, s) > vss(f_{12}, c \cup f_{12}, s)$ while $vss(f_7, c \cup f_7, s) < vss(f_6, c \cup f_6, s)$.

Obviously, if c_k and c_k' are the same level SCPs about c and $c_k' < c_k$, then PEPUR $(c, c_k') < \text{PEPUR}(c, c_k)$, because $\sum\limits_{f_i \in c_k'-c} vss(f_i, c \cup f_i, s) < \sum\limits_{f_i \in c_k-c} vss(f_i, c \cup f_i, s)$.

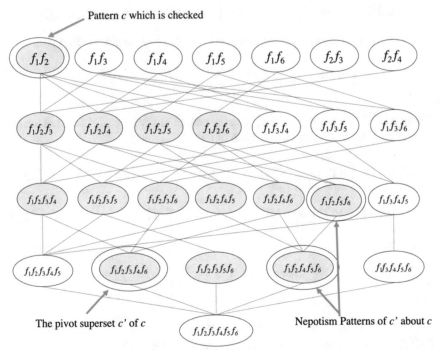

Fig. 8.3 The rule of partial pruning algorithm

Therefore, if PEPUR(c, c_k) < ξ, then PEPUR(c, $c_k{'}$) < ξ when c_k is pruned, but c_k is a superset of c, so all other k-supersets of c which are less than c_k should be pruned too. For example, in Fig. 8.3, features have been sorted by vss in descending order, where $c = \{f_1, f_2\}$, $c_4 = \{f_1, f_2, f_3, f_4\}$. We can see that $\{f_1, f_2, f_3, f_5\}$, $\{f_1, f_2, f_3, f_6\}$, $\{f_1, f_2, f_4, f_5\}$, $\{f_1, f_2, f_4, f_6\}$ and $\{f_1, f_2, f_5, f_6\}$ are the same level patterns of c_4, and less than c_4. So, if $\lambda(c) < \xi$, and PEPUR(c, c_4) < ξ, then we can prune all of them including c_4.

Definition 8.15 (Sub-pattern, max-size sub-pattern, highest utility max-size sub-pattern) Suppose c_i and c_k are supersets of c, and $c_i \subset c_k$. Then we say that c_i is a *sub-pattern* of c_k about c. When the size $i = k - 1$, we say that c_i is a *max-size sub-pattern* of c_k about c. Suppose c_{k-1} is a max-size superset of c_k about c, and $f_i = c_k - c_{k-1}$. If f_i is the feature whose vss is the least in $c_k - c$, then we say c_{k-1} is the *highest utility max-size sub-pattern* of c_k about c.

For example, if $c = \{f_3, f_9\}$, $c_5 = \{f_1, f_3, f_5, f_7, f_9\}$, $c_4 = \{f_1, f_3, f_5, f_9\}$, then c_4 is the highest utility max-size sub-pattern of c_5 about c because $f_7 = c_5 - c_4$ and f_7 is the least in $c_5 - c$. Here f is sorted in the descending order of vss.

Obviously, when c' is a sub-pattern of c_k about c, $\text{PEPUR}(c, c') < \text{PEPUR}(c, c_k)$, because $\sum_{f_i \in c'-c} vss(f_i, c \cup f_i, s) < \sum_{f_i \in c_k - c} vss(f_i, c \cup f_i, s)$. Therefore, if PEPUR $(c, c_k) < \xi$, then $\text{PEPUR}(c, c') < \xi$, that is to say, if c_k is pruned, all of its sub-patterns about c should be pruned, too. For example, in Fig. 8.3, $c = \{f_1, f_2\}$, $c_4 = \{f_1, f_2, f_3, f_4\}$. We can see that $\{f_1, f_2, f_3\}$ and $\{f_1, f_2, f_4\}$ are sub-patterns of c_4 about c. So, if $\lambda(c) < \xi$, and $\text{PEPUR}(c, c_4) < \xi$, then we can prune $\{f_1, f_2, f_3\}$, $\{f_1, f_2, f_4\}$ and c_4.

Notice that if c_{k-1} is the highest utility max-size sub-pattern of c_k about c, then c_{k-1} has the most same-level patterns which are less than it.

Definition 8.16 (Nepotism pattern) Given patterns c and c', and $c \subset c'$, we define sub-patterns of c' about c and their same level patterns less than them as nepotism patterns of c'.

According to Theorem 8.5, Definitions 8.14 and 8.15, if $\text{PEPUR}(c, c') < \xi$, then c' and the nepotism patterns of it should be pruned, even if $\text{EPUR}(c) > \xi$. For example, in Fig. 8.3, all of the gray patterns are nepotism patterns of $\{f_1, f_2, f_3, f_4, f_6\}$ about $\{f_1, f_2\}$.

Definition 8.17 (Pivot superset) When c is a low utility pattern, in order to prune more other low utility SCPs, we hope to find a superset c_k' of c, which meets the following conditions:

1. $\text{PEPUR}(c, c_k') < \xi$, which ensures c_k' can be pruned.
2. The nepotism patterns of c_k' about c should be as many as possible.

There are two aspects relating to condition (2) to consider:

(a) c_k' should be as high as possible for a fixed k. This is because when k is fixed, the higher c_k' is, the more same-level patterns of c_k' there are, which are lower than c_k'. Moreover, the higher c_k' is, the higher the highest utility max-size sub-pattern of c_k' is. This aspect should ensure that there are as many nepotism patterns of c_k' as possible in a horizontal direction.
(b) k should be as high as possible. The higher the k, the more varied is the size of the sub-patterns of c_k'. This aspect should ensure there are as many nepotism patterns of c_k' as possible in a vertical direction.

However, we must decide how to choose the pivot superset c_k' from so many supersets of c and how to ensure that the chosen pivot superset c_k' can meet those two conditions.

Condition (1) is easy. With inequality PEPUR(c, c_k') $< \xi$, we get $\sum\limits_{f_i \in c_k'-c} vss(f_i, c \cup f_i, s) < (\xi\text{-}\lambda(c)) \times U(S)$.

For a given c, the right side of the inequality is constant. We denote it as

$$M_c = (\xi - \lambda(c)) \times U(S)$$

So, Condition (1) is equal to $\sum\limits_{f_i \in c_k'-c} vss(f_i, c \cup f_i, s) < M_c$.

As mentioned earlier, in order to meet Condition (2), there are two aspects to be considered: (a) the pivot superset should be as high as possible in its size. (b) k should be as high as possible. However, aspect (a) and aspect (b) contradict to each other when Condition (1) is true. The contradiction occurs because a higher c_k' generally means a higher vss of the features of c_k', which must lead to a lower k, as the inequality $\sum\limits_{f_i \in c_k'-c} vss(f_i, c \cup f_i, s) < M_c$ does not allow there to be too many features in c_k'.

Therefore, we compromise and convert the problem into a kind of subset sum problem, which can be described as follows: If c is a low utility pattern, we can find the subset G of F-c. The sum of the vss of all features in G is no more than, but is the nearest to M_c. $c_k' = G \cup c$ is called pivot superset. For example, $\{f_1, f_2, f_3, f_4, f_6\}$ is the pivot superset of $\{f_1, f_2\}$. By dynamic programming, the subset sum problem can be solved within pseudo polynomial time.

For the patterns that cannot be pruned, we get their table instances through a star neighborhood set, then calculate their pattern utility ratios to judge whether they are high utility SCPs or not.

8.7.2   Partial Pruning Algorithm (PPA)

PPA is described as follows:

Algorithm 8.2 PPA

Inputs:

$F=\{f_1,...,f_n\}$: a set of spatial features

S: a set of spatial instances

V: a two-dimensional table for the external utility of each $f_i \in F$

R: a spatial neighbor relationship

s: a parameter standing for the fineness level of pruning

ξ: a utility ratio threshold

Output:

A set of all high utility SCPs with pattern utility ratio $\lambda \geq \xi$

Variables:

$SN=\{SN_{f1},...,SN_{fn}\}$: a set of feature f_i star neighborhoods

k: colocation size

C_k: a set of size k candidate SCPs

Cp_k: a set of size k pruned SCPs

T_c: the table instance of pattern c

U_k: a set of size k high utility SCPs

Method:

3) $U(S)$=get_database_utility(S,F,V);

4) SN=gen_star_neighborhoods(F,S,R);

5)   for $i \in \{2,...,n\}$ do $Cp_i=\varnothing$,$C_i=\varnothing$,$U_i=\varnothing$;

6) k=2;

7)   **while** ($k \leq n$)

8) C_k=gen_candidate_colocations(F,Cp_k);

9)   **for** $c \in C_k$ **do**

10) T_c=gen_tableinstance(SN);

11) $u(c)$=get_pattern_utility(V,T_c); $\lambda(c)$ =$u(c)/U(S)$;

12)   **if** $\lambda(c) \geq \xi$ **then** put c into U_k

13)   **else do**

14) M_c=(ξ-$\lambda(c)$)$\times U(S)$;

15)   **for** $f_i \in F$-c **do**

16)   calculate $vss(f_i, c \cup f_i, s)$;

17)   sort(F-c, $vss(f_i, c \cup f_i, s)$);

18) c'=subset_sum_problem (F,c,M_c); j=| c' |;

19)   **while** ($c' \neq c$) **do**

20)   put c' and every $c'_t < c'$ into Cp_j

21) c'=c'_s; j=j-1;

22) k=k+1;

23)   **for** $m \in \{2,...,n\}$ **do** output U_m

Generate *SN* (Step 2)

Use a geometric method to find all neighbor instance pairs, then convert the spatial data set into a joinless star neighborhood set (Yoo & Shekhar, 2006).

Initialization and generate *Ck* (Steps 3–6)

Step 3 initializes C_k, Cp_k, T_c, U_k as empty sets. The method gen_candidate_colocations in Step 6 is used to generate C_k by Cp_k and the combinations of features in F.

Verify high utility SCPs (Steps 7–10)

For each pattern c in Ck, calculate the table instance of c from the joinless star neighborhood set. If $\lambda(c) \geq \xi$, then put it into the set of high utility SCPs.

Verify the pivot superset and prune the nepotism patterns (Steps 12–19)

If $\lambda(c) \leq \xi$, then find its pivot superset c' to prune more low utility patterns. First, calculate M_c, then Steps 13–15 sort features in F-c by *vss* in descending order. The method *subset_sum_problem* in Step 16 is used to solve the subset sum problem and find the pivot superset c', where j is the number of features in c'. Steps 17–19 are used to prune nepotism patterns of c' by incrementally looping by size.

8.8   Experiments

The algorithms EPA and PPA were implemented in C# of Visual Studio 2013. All experiments were conducted on a desktop computer with Intel Core 5 CPU of 2.30GHz, 4GB memory and Windows 7.

We used a synthetic data set and a real plant data set in the experiments. The synthetic data set was randomly generated and the real plant data set was collected from "Three Parallel Rivers of Yunnan Protected Areas," where the spatial range is 1000*1000 and the number of spatial features is 15 ($|F| = 15$).

8.8.1   Differences Between Mining Prevalent SCPs and High Utility SCPs

We set the number of all instances from 5000 to 20,000. With the same parameters of $d = 25$, $\xi = 20\%$, we compare results of mining by a prevalence-based method (the joinless algorithm) and a utility-based method (the basic approach of Algorithm 8.1). As Table 8.1 shows, the SCPs which frequently appear are not always high utility SCPs, and vice versa. That means the method used for mining frequently appearing SCPs is not appropriate for mining high utility SCPs.

Table 8.1 The number of SCPs mined by using joinless and Algorithm 8.1

$d = 25, \xi = 20\%$	5000	10,000	15,000	20,000
Number of high utility patterns	43	201	427	1395
Number of prevalently appearing patterns	155	482	1711	6057
Number of repeated patterns	29	79	239	848
Ratio of repeated patterns to high utility patterns	67.4%	39.3%	56.0%	60.8%
Ratio of repeated patterns to prevalently appearing patterns	18.7%	16.4%	14.0%	14.0%

8.8.2 Effect of the Number of Total Instances n

We compared the performance of EPA and the basic algorithm. In Fig. 8.4(a), $d = 20$, $s = 4$, $\xi = 15\%$ and we see that, due to the increasing number of total instances, the distance calculations among instances are more frequent and the cost of the join operation is increased, so the running times of both algorithms are increased. As the function of EPUR is to prune down a lot of low utility patterns, the performance of EPA outweighs that of the basic algorithm.

8.8.3 Effect of the Distance Threshold d

In Fig. 8.4(b), $n = 10,000$, $s = 4$, $\xi = 25\%$. The performance of EPA is still better than that of the basic algorithm, as there is a pruning strategy in EPA. Similarly, total running time increases as d increases because a big value of d means more instances could generate cliques, which brings more join operations.

8.8.4 Effect of the Pattern Utility Ratio Threshold ξ

In Fig. 8.5(a), $n = 10,000$, $s = 4$, $d = 35$. With an increase of ξ, more low utility patterns are pruned in the earlier stages of the running process, helping to enhance the efficiency of EPA. In particular, if $\xi = 0$, EPA would degenerate to the state below that of the basic algorithm, as there is the extra cost of calculating intersections in vss, which is part of EPA.

8.8.5 Effect of s in vss

In Fig. 8.5(b), $n = 10,000$, $d = 30$, $\xi = 15\%$. As s passes a certain point, with an increasing s, the running time of EPA does not decrease and the performance of EPA

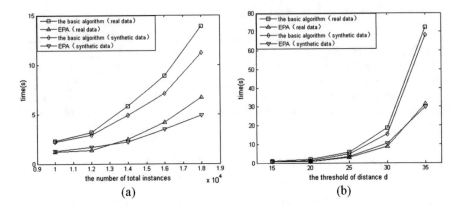

Fig. 8.4 Effects of total number of total instances n and the distance threshold d, where (**a**) vary the number of instances; (**b**) vary the distance threshold

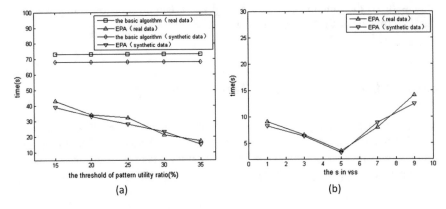

Fig. 8.5 Effect of the pattern utility ratio threshold ξ and the s in vss, where (**a**) vary the pattern utility ratio threshold ξ; (**b**) vary the s in vss

becomes worse. This is because a large value of s brings about a large cost from calculating the intersections in *vss*.

8.8.6   Comparing PPA and EPA with a Different Utility Ratio Threshold ξ

The major difference in time cost between PPA and EPA appears when the utility ratio threshold changes. In Fig. 8.6, $n = 15,000$, $s = 4$, $d = 30$. When EPA checks low size and low utility patterns, *vss* and EPUR are too high, because the number of instances of a low size pattern is generally large. Therefore, when ξ is low, it is difficult for EPA to show its advantage, as many low utility patterns are missed when EPA checks these low size patterns. However, PPA is more adaptable when ξ is low

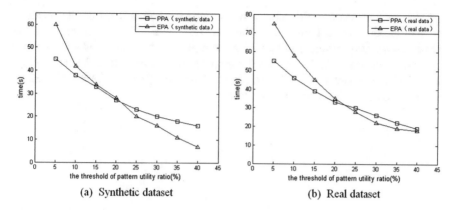

Fig. 8.6 Effects of the pattern utility ratio threshold ξ in PPA and EPA; where (**a**) synthetic dataset; (**b**) real dataset

as it can prune a lot of those low utility patterns missed by EPA when checking low size patterns. So when ξ is low, PPA is more efficient than EPA.

When ξ increases to an extent, though, more low utility patterns can be pruned by EPA at an earlier stage. That leads to an improved efficiency of EPA. Meanwhile, the efficiency of PPA is also improved, because M_c increases with the increase of ξ, leading to more nepotism patterns being pruned. However, as the calculating subset sum problem brings an extra time cost, the increase of efficiency of PPA is not as obvious as for EPA. Overall, the efficiency of EPA is better than PPA, but only as ξ increases to a certain extent. With the parameters given above, the inflection point of ξ is 40%, when running these two algorithms with a real dataset.

8.9 Chapter Summary

In this chapter, we incorporated utility into the framework of SCP mining, and developed two algorithms, EPA and PPA, for mining high utility SCPs.

The EPA algorithm performs efficiently and effectively in most cases, as proved through experiments. However, in EPA, if a pattern c is a low utility SCP, whether or not its supersets can be pruned depends on EPUR(c). Therefore, we defined the new concept of PEPUR, which helps to find low utility supersets while checking low-size patterns. In addition, the new concepts of nepotism patterns and pivot superset are defined in this chapter, and we used them to find as many as possible low utility patterns that were missed by EPA. A series of experiments showed that the problems of mining frequently appearing patterns and of mining high utility patterns are completely different. Experiments also showed the effects of various parameters on the efficiency of methods based on utility. The efficiencies of EPA and PPA running with the same parameters were analyzed.

This chapter has made developments on the assumption that different features have different utilities. However, in the real world, even different instances of the same feature have different utilities. For example, the fresh apple is always more expensive than stale one. The grown oak is always more worthy than the oak sapling. So in the next chapter, we will explore the problem of mining high utility SCPs based on a utility difference between instances.

Chapter 9
High Utility Co-location Patterns with Instance Utility

9.1 Introduction

In this chapter, we present a new measure for mining interesting high utility spatial co-location patterns (high utility SCPs) from spatial data sets with instance-specific utilities. Differing from the developments of the last chapter, this chapter makes the following contributions to the mining process:

First, we take instances with their associated utilities as study objects, and consequently the importance of features and instances is treated differently.

Second, we propose a new measure to identify interesting high utility SCPs in spatial data sets with instance-specific utilities.

Third, we present a basic algorithm to mine the high utility SCPs with instance utility. In order to reduce the computational cost, some pruning strategies are given.

Finally, extensive experiments on synthetic and real-world data sets verify that the proposed methods are both effective and efficient.

Figure 9.1 presents the organization of this chapter. Section 9.2 discusses the needs of taking the utility value of each instance into account in SCP mining. Related work is presented in Sect. 9.3. Section 9.4 gives the related concepts for mining high utility SCPs from spatial data sets with instance-specific utilities, and a basic mining algorithm is presented in Sect. 9.5. In Sect. 9.6, the new pruning strategies are detailed. Experimental results and evaluation are shown in Sect. 9.7 and the conclusions are given in Sect. 9.8.

From Wang, L., Jiang, W., Chen, H., et al.: Efficiently mining high utility co-location patterns from spatial data sets with instance-specific utilities. In: *Proceedings of the 22nd International Conference on Database Systems for Advanced Applications (DASFAA 2017)*, LNCS 10178, Suzhou, China, pp. 458–474 (2017).

© The Author(s), under exclusive license to Springer Nature Singapore Pte Ltd. 2022
L. Wang et al., *Preference-based Spatial Co-location Pattern Mining*, Big Data Management, https://doi.org/10.1007/978-981-16-7566-9_9

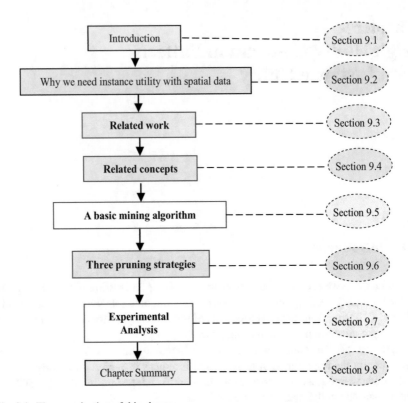

Fig. 9.1 The organization of this chapter

9.2 Why We Need Instance Utility with Spatial Data

In recent years, spatial data has been rapidly generated and the size of spatial data sets is getting continues to increase. For example, currently NASA's Earth Observing System generates more than 1 TB of spatial data per day. As the number of mobile devices increases, so data associated with location information increases faster and faster. The vast amounts of this spatial data contain potentially valuable information which can help us make important decisions, but only if the interesting patterns in the data can be extracted, or mined. A lot of researches have already taken place on spatial data mining, including spatial association rule analysis, spatial clustering, spatial classification, and so on.

In spatial data, if the distance between two spatial instances is no more than a given distance threshold, then the two instances are said to satisfy the *neighbor relationship*. Traditional spatial co-location pattern (SCP) mining aims at finding the subsets of spatial features whose instances are frequently located in neighborhoods. A *row instance* of an SCP c represents a subset of instances, which includes an instance of each feature in c and forms a clique under the neighbor relationship. All the row instances of an SCP c make up its *table instance* denoted as $T(c)$. A

Fig. 9.2 An example
spatial data set

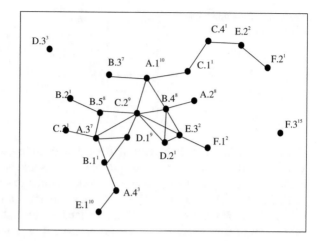

participation index (PI) is used to evaluate the prevalence of SCPs, similar to the support measures in association rules mining (ARM). The *PI* of an SCP c is defined as $PI(c) = \min_{f_i} \in c\{PR(c, f_i)\}$, where $PR(c, f_i)$ is the *participation ratio* (PR) of feature f_i in an SCP c, that is $PR(c, f_i) = \frac{|\pi_{f_i}T(c)|}{\text{Number of instances of } f_i}$, where π is the relational projection operation with duplication elimination. Participation ratio is used to evaluate the prevalence of features, and the participation index, which is the measure of interest normally used in traditional SCP mining, measures the prevalence of SCPs.

Mining SCPs is very significant in the real world. For example, botanists have found that there are orchids in 80% of the area where the middle-wetness green-broad-leaf forest grows. A mobile service provider may be interested in those mobile service patterns frequently requested by geographically neighboring users. Other applications include Earth science, public health, biology, transportation, etc.

In most previous studies, the importance of all features and instances are treated similarly. However, often there exist differences between features and even instances belonging to the same feature. For instance, the economic value of rosewood is much greater than that of ordinary pine. What's more, the value of different sizes of rosewood is also different. So, only checking the prevalence of SCPs may be insufficient for identifying really interesting patterns. Traditional SCP mining suffers from not finding some low prevalence but highly interesting patterns (Yang et al., 2015), but finding many prevalent patterns which just reflect common sense and are worthless to users.

Here, we use an example to illustrate the problem. Figure 9.2 shows the locations of instances of six kinds of plants (features), and each instance is denoted by the plant type and a numeric id, e.g., A.1, and edges among instances indicate neighboring relationships. The superscript of each instance represents its utility value, which can easily be considered as its price. Table 9.1 gives the total utility value of each kind of plant which is the sum of utility value of all instances belonging to the plant type.

Table 9.1 Total utility value of each plant in Fig. 9.2

Features	Instances	Total utility values
A	$A.1^{10}, A.2^8, A.3^7, A.4^3$	28
B	$B.1^1, B.2^1, B.3^7, B.4^8, B.5^8$	25
C	$C.1^1, C.2^9, C.3^1, C.4^1$	12
D	$D.1^9, D.2^1, D.3^3$	13
E	$E.1^{10}, E.2^2, E.3^2$	14
F	$F.1^2, F.2^1, F.3^{15}$	18

From Fig. 9.2, according to the traditional SCP mining, for the co-location {A, B, C}, $PI(\{A, B, C\}) = 1/4$ and if the prevalence threshold is 0.3, {A, B, C} would be regarded as a non-interesting SCP. However, according to $T(\{A, B, C\}) = \{\{A.1^{10},$ $B.4^8, C.2^9\}, \{A.3^7, B.5^8, C.2^9\}\}$, the utility value of feature A's instances in {A, B, C} is 17, which accounts for 17/28 of total utility value of A. Similarly, the proportion of B is 16/25 and C is 9/12. So the utility of each feature in {A, B, C} accounts for a large proportion of the total utility, suggesting that {A, B, C} may well be an interesting pattern. However, as to the pattern {E, F}, $PI(\{E, F\}) = 2/3$, $T(\{E, F\}) = \{\{E.2^2, F.2^1\}, \{E.3^2, F.1^2\}\}$. The proportion of E is only 4/14 and F is only 3/18 so the utility of each feature in {E, F} is less than 30%. In comparison to {A, B, C}, {E, F} is probably non-interesting to the user.

Therefore, we see that traditional measures may not find interesting SCPs because the utilities of features and instances are ignored. In this chapter, we remedy that situation by focusing on mining high utility SCPs from spatial data sets with instance-specific utilities.

9.3 Related Work

The problem of mining spatial association rules was first discussed in Koperski and Han (1995). The participation index for prevalent SCP mining and join-based algorithm was presented in Shekhar and Huang (2001) and Huang et al. (2004). A lot of existing work about prevalent SCP mining is based on the participation index which satisfies the downward closure property. The join-less algorithm was introduced in Yoo and Shekhar (2006), using a novel model to materialize spatial neighbor relationships and an instance-lookup scheme to reduce the computational cost of identifying table instances. An efficient algorithm based on iCPI-Tree was proposed in Wang et al. (2009a). In order to mine SCPs with rare features, a new prevalence measure, the maximal participation ratio, was proposed in Huang et al. (2006). A new general class of measures of interest based on the spatial distribution of SCPs and information entropy was proposed in Sengstock et al. (2012). Probabilistically prevalent SCP mining was introduced in Wang et al. (2013a) to find SCPs in the context of uncertain data. Wang et al. (2010) studied co-location rule mining on interval data and defined new related concepts based on a semantic proximity neighborhood. An optimal candidate generation method was proposed in Lin and

Lim (2009). The SCP mining to deal with complex spatial relationships was introduced in Verhein and Al-Naymat (2007).

Research on high utility pattern mining was first discussed in Yao et al. (2004), where the utility of each item consists of an *internal utility* and an *external utility*. The internal utility represents the quantity of items in transactions and the external utility is the unit profit values of items. But the utility of itemsets doesn't satisfy the downward closure property which is used to improve mining efficiency, and so a two-phase algorithm for the fast mining of high utility itemsets was proposed in Liu et al. (2005). Ahmed et al. (2011) introduced a novel framework to mine interesting high utility patterns with strong frequency affinities. An incremental mining algorithm for efficiently mining high utility itemsets was proposed to handle intermittent data environments in Hong et al. (2012). UP-Growth proposed in Tseng et al. (2010) enhanced mining performance by maintaining the information of high utility itemsets with a UP-tree. A novel algorithm named GUIDE and a special data structure named TMUI-tree were proposed for mining temporal maximal utility itemsets from data stream environments (Shie et al., 2010). Yin et al. (2012) introduced an efficient algorithm named USpan to mine high utility sequences from large-scale data with very low minimum utility.

There are more and more studies on SCP mining and high utility itemsets mining, but rarely is there literature about high utility SCP mining (Yang et al., 2015; Wang et al., 2016b, 2019d). Similar to the work of Yao et al. (2004), Yang et al. (2015) divided the utility of features in an SCP into *external utility* and *internal utility*. The external utility represents the unit profile and the internal utility represents the quantity of different instances of features in a table instance. The utility of a feature in an SCP is equal to the product of external and internal utilities. A framework for mining high utility SCPs was thus proposed (Yang et al., 2015). By following the definitions in Yang et al. (2015), Wang et al. (2016a, 2016b, 2019c, 2019d) discussed the problem of updating high utility SCP mining on evolving spatial databases.

In some real-world data, the utilities of features are different from each other and even instances belonging to the same feature may have an obvious difference in their utilities. Furthermore, in some cases, the data set does not map into a model of external and internal utility. Considering the complexity of real-world data, there exist two major challenges in high utility SCP mining from spatial data sets with instance-specific utilities. One is how to define the measure of interest reasonably so as to judge high utility SCPs with instance utility, and the other is how to efficiently mine high utility SCPs with instance utility. This chapter tackles both these challenges.

9.4 Related Concepts

In the real world, the importance of each instance may be different, so we take the instances with utilities as study objects and assume the utilities reflect their importance. The related concepts for mining high utility SCPs are given in this section, and Table 9.2 summarizes notations frequently used throughout the chapter.

Definition 9.1 (Spatial instance with utility value) Given a set of spatial features F and a set of their instances S, let spatial instance $f_i.j^v \in S$ be the j-th instance of feature $f_i \in F$. The utility value of $f_i.j^v$ is expressed by the superscript v and we denote the utility of spatial instance $f_i.j^v$ as $u(f_i.j) = v$.

According to Definition 9.1, every instance may have a distinct utility, even if they belong to the same feature. Using our rosewood example, the feature A may represent the rosewood in general. $A.1^{1000}$ is a 100-year-old rosewood and worth \$1000, i.e., $u(A.1) = 1000$. $A.2^{25}$ is a 10-year-old rosewood, which is worth \$25, i.e. $u(A.2) = 25$.

The **total utility** of a feature $f_i \in F$ is the sum of utilities of its instances, denoted as $u(f_i) = \sum_{j=1}^{m} u(f_i \cdot j)$, where m is the number of instances belonging to f_i. For example, the total utility of feature A in Fig. 9.2 is $u(A) = u(A.1) + u(A.2) + u(A.3) + u(A.4) = 10 + 8 + 7 + 3 = 28$.

Definition 9.2 (Utility of feature in SCP) Given a size k SCP $c = \{f_1, f_2, \ldots, f_k\}$, we define the sum of utilities of instances belonging to feature $f_i \in c$ in table instance $T(c)$ as the utility of f_i in c, denoted as:

$$u(f_i, c) = \sum_{f_i.j \in \pi_{f_i}(T(c))} U(f_i \cdot j) \qquad (9.1)$$

where π is the relational projection operation with duplication elimination.

Table 9.2 Summary of notation

Notation	Definition	Notation	Definition
F	Set of spatial features	$u(f_i)$	Utility of feature f_i
f_i	i-th spatial feature	$u(f_i, c)$	Utility of feature f_i in co-location c
S	Set of features' instances	$IntraUR(f_i, c)$	Intra-utility ratio of f_i in c
$f_i.j^v$	j-th instance with utility v of f_i	$InterUR(f_i, c)$	Inter-utility ratio of f_i in c
c	A co-location pattern	$UPR(f_i, c)$	Utility participation ratio of f_i in c
k	Size of c	$UPI(c)$	Utility participation index of c
R	A spatial neighbor relationship	w_1	Weighted value of $IntraUR$ in computing UPR
$T(c)$	Table instance of c	w_2	Weighted value of $InterUR$ in computing UPR
$u(f_i.j)$	Utility of instance $f_i.j$	M	A UPI threshold

For example, for $c = \{A, B, C\}$ in Fig. 9.2, $T(c) = \{\{A.1^{10}, B.4^8, C.2^9\}, \{A.3^7, B.5^8, C.2^9\}\}$. The utility of A in c is $u(A, c) = u(A.1) + u(A.3) = 10 + 7 = 17$.

Definition 9.3 (Intra-utility ratio) Given a size k SCP $c = \{f_1, f_2, \ldots, f_k\}$, the intra-utility ratio of feature f_i in c is defined as the proportion of f_i's utility in c to its total utility as follows:

$$IntraUR(f_i, c) = \frac{u(f_i, c)}{u(f_i)} \tag{9.2}$$

$IntraUR(f_i, c)$ indicates the direct utility of feature f_i in SCP c, which can be regarded as its direct influence on c.

For example, for $c = \{A, B, C\}$ in Fig. 9.2, $T(c) = \{\{A.1^{10}, B.4^8, C.2^9\}, \{A.3^7, B.5^8, C.2^9\}\}$. The intra-utility ratio of each feature in c is calculated as:

$$IntraUR(A, c) = \frac{u(A.1) + u(A.3)}{u(A)} = 17/28, IntraUR(B, c) = \frac{u(B.2) + u(B.5)}{u(B)}$$

$$= 16/25, IntraUR(C, c) = \frac{u(C.2)}{u(C)} = 9/12.$$

Definition 9.4 (Inter-utility ratio) Given a size k SCP $c = \{f_1, f_2, \ldots, f_k\}$, the inter-utility ratio of feature f_i in c is defined as:

$$InterUR(f_i, c) = \frac{\sum_{f_j \in c, j \neq i} u(f_j, c)}{\sum_{f_j \in c, j \neq i} u(f_j)} \tag{9.3}$$

The inter-utility ratio is regarded as the influence of feature f_i on other features in SCP c, which is an indirect influence of f_i on c. In an SCP, some instances of features often co-occur in neighborhoods. Thus, in an SCP $c = \{f_1, f_2, \ldots, f_k\}$, any change of feature $f_i \in c$ probably impacts the utility of other features in c. For example, in location-based services the sales of service A might promote the sales of service B. So, we use the inter-utility ratio to indicate the effect of a feature on other features in an SCP. In Fig. 9.2, the effect of feature A in SCP $\{A, B, C\}$ on other features B and C is computed as: $InterUR(A, c) = \frac{u(B,c) + u(C,c)}{u(B) + u(C)} = 25/37$.

We split the influence of feature f_i into two parts to evaluate an SCP c comprehensively and reasonably. One part is the influence of its utility in c, denoted as $IntraUR(f_i, c)$, the other part being the indirect influence of f_i on c, denoted as $InterUR(f_i, c)$.

Definition 9.5 (Utility participation ratio, UPR) Given a size k SCP $c = \{f_1, f_2, \ldots, f_k\}$, the weighted sum of $IntraUR(f_i, c)$ and $InterUR(f_i, c)$ is defined as the utility participation ratio of feature f_i in c, denoted as $UPR(f_i, c)$. Note that $UPR(f_i, c) = w_1 \times IntraUR(f_i, c) + w_2 \times InterUR(f_i, c)$, where $0 \leq w_1, w_2 \leq 1$ and

$w_1 + w_2 = 1$, w_1 representing the weighted value of $IntraUR(f_i, c)$ and w_2 representing that of $InterUR(f_i, c)$.

The w_1 and w_2 in Definition 9.5 are expected to be assigned specific values by the application user and can be used to adjust the effects of $IntraUR$ and $InterUR$. For example, in supermarket sales, if we are more concerned about promoted sales of different goods, $w_1 \le w_2$ may be reasonable. Usually, w_1 and w_2 satisfy $w_1 \ge w_2$.

For example, in Fig. 9.2, if we suppose $w_1 = 0.7$ and $w_2 = 0.3$, then the UPR of each feature in $c = \{A, B, C\}$ is computed as:

$$UPR(A, c) = 0.7 \times IntraUR(A, c) + 0.3 \times InterUR(A, c)$$
$$= 0.7 \times (17/28) + 0.3 \times (25/37) = 0.628.$$

$$UPR(B, c) = 0.7 \times IntraUR(B, c) + 0.3 \times InterUR(B, c)$$
$$= 0.7 \times (16/25) + 0.3 \times (26/40) = 0.643.$$

$$UPR(C, c) = 0.7 \times IntraUR(C, c) + 0.3 \times InterUR(C, c)$$
$$= 0.7 \times (9/12) + 0.3 \times (33/53) = 0.711.$$

Definition 9.6 (Utility participation index, UPI) Given a size k SCP $c = \{f_1, f_2, \ldots, f_k\}$, We define the minimum utility participation ratio among all features in c as the utility participation index of c, i.e., $UPI(c) = \min\{UPR(f_i, c), f_i \in c\}$.

A SCP c is a **high utility SCP** if and only if $UPI(c) \ge M$ holds, where M is a UPI threshold given by the user.

The UPI measure extends the traditional PI measure based on prevalence only. If the utilities of instances and the influence between features in an SCP are ignored, UPI is equal to the traditional PI.

Prevalent patterns may not be high utility patterns and the high utility patterns may not be prevalent as well, which can be proved by SCPs $\{E, F\}$ and $\{A, B, C\}$ in Fig. 9.2. If $w_1 = w_2 = 0.5$ and $M = 0.3$, $UPI(\{E, F\}) = 0.226$ and $PI(\{E, F\}) = 0.667$, while $UPI(\{A, B, C\}) = 0.628$ and $PI(\{A, B, C\}) = 0.25$. Because of the full consideration into the difference of each instance, our measure of interest is more reasonable. However, different from the traditional measures of interest, UPI does not satisfy the downward closure property which has been found to be a very efficient pruning strategy for mining prevalent SCPs. Therefore, finding all high utility SCPs directly is time-consuming. For example, for $c = \{A, D\}$ in Fig. 9.2, $T(c) = \{\{A.3^7, D.1^9\}\}$. Given $w_1 = w_2 = 0.5$, we can get $UPI(\{A, D\}) = 0.471$. But the super pattern $c' = \{A, C, D\}$ of c, $T(c') = \{\{A.3^7, C.2^9, D.1^9\}\}$, and $UPI(\{A, C, D\}) = 0.485$. So, we have the inequality $UPI(c') > UPI(c)$.

9.5   A Basic Algorithm

In this section, we present a basic algorithm for mining the high utility SCPs defined in Sect. 9.4. The basic algorithm has three phases. The first phase is to materialize the spatial neighbor relationships. The spatial data set is converted into the star neighborhood partition model in Yoo and Shekhar (2006). The second phase is to generate candidate high utility SCPs and compute their table instances. The third phase is to compute the UPI of each candidate and find high utility SCPs. The second and third phases are repeated by incrementing the co-locations' size. Algorithm 9.1 shows the pseudocode of the basic algorithm.

Algorithm 9.1 Basic Algorithm

Input:

$F=\{f_1, f_2, \ldots, f_n\}$: a set of spatial features;

S: a set of spatial instances;

R: a spatial neighbor relationship;

w_1: the weighted value of *IntraUR*;

w_2: the weighted value of *InterUR*;

M: the UPI threshold

Output:

A set of all SCPs with UPI $\geq M$

Steps:

1) $SN = gen\_star\_neighborhoods(F, S, R)$;
2) $H_1 = F$; $k=2$;   //H_k: a set of size k high utility SCPs
3) **While** (not empty H_{k-1} and $NonH_{k-1}$) **do**
                     //$NonH_k$: a set of size k non-high utility SCPs
4) $C_k=gen\_candi\_colocations(H_{k-1}, NonH_{k-1})$;
                     //C_k: a set of size k candidate co-locations
5) $CTI_k=gen\_table\text{-}instances(C_k, SN)$;
                     //CTI_k: a set of table instances of size k candidates
6) $Compute\_UPI(C_k, w_1, w_2)$;
7) $H_k=select\_utility\_colocations(C_k, CTI_k, M)$;
8) $NonH_k=C_k - H_k$;
9) $k=k + 1$;
10) **End do**
11) **Return** $\cup \{H_1, H_2, \cdots, H_{k-1}\}$

Initialization (Steps 1–2): Given a spatial data set and a spatial neighbor relationship, we need to find all neighboring instance pairs using a geometric method such as mesh generation or plane sweep (Yoo & Shekhar, 2006). The star neighborhoods can be generated from the neighbor instance pairs in lexicographical order (Yoo & Shekhar, 2006). After generating the star neighborhood set (SN), we initialize all size 1 co-locations to a utility participation index of 1.0, which means all size 1 co-locations are high utility SCPs. We then add all size 1 co-locations into H_1.

Generating candidate co-locations (Step 4): A size k ($k \geq 2$) candidate high utility SCPs in C_k is generated from a size k-1 co-location c in H_{k-1} or $NonH_{k-1}$ as well as a new feature f_s which is not included in c and which is greater than all features of c in lexicographical order, i.e., $C_k = \{c' | c' = c \cup \{f_s\}, \forall c \in H_{k-1} \cup NonH_{k-1}, f_s > \forall f_i \in c\}$.

The size 2 candidates in C_2 can be generated from the star neighborhood set directly.

Calculating the UPIs of candidates (Steps 5–6): The size 2 co-locations' table instances can be gathered from the star neighborhood set directly. For size k ($k > 2$) co-locations, their table instances need to be extended by the size k-1 co-locations' table instances. For example, the table instance of co-location {A, B, C} can be generated from the table instance of co-location {A, B}. Then, we can compute the UPI of each candidate co-location according to Definitions 9.5 and 9.6.

Identifying high utility SCPns (Steps 7–8): We can filter high utility SCPs by the UPIs of candidates and the given UPI threshold M. Then the high utility SCPs are added into H_k and the non-high utility SCPs are added into $NonH_k$.

Steps 3–10 are repeated by incrementing the size of k.

In Fig. 9.2, if $w_1 = w_2 = 0.5$ and $M = 0.5$, we can get the high utility SCPs {A, B}, {A, C}, {A, B, C}, {B, C}, {B, D}, {C, D}, and {C, E}. The algorithm developed so far, the basic algorithm tests all possible patterns, computes their UPIs accurately and is complete and correct, but it is inefficient. In the next section, we give some needed pruning strategies to improve the efficiency of the basic algorithm.

9.6   Pruning Strategies

In this section, we introduce some pruning strategies which promote the efficiency of the basic algorithm. Similar to traditional SCP mining, the most time-consuming component in mining high utility SCPs is to generate the table instances of candidate patterns. Traditional SCP mining based on PI can efficiently find all prevalent SCPs due to the downward closure property, but there is no a similar method to find all high utility SCPs due to the non-existence of the downward closure property. In order to improve the efficiency of the basic algorithm, then, we have to identify early in the mining process some non-high utility candidate co-locations, but without generating their table instances. The following pruning strategies are used to facilitate this early pruning of non-high utility candidate patterns.

Lemma 9.1 For $n_1 \geq m_1 > 0$, $n_2 \geq m_2 > 0$, there exists the following inequality:

$$\frac{m_1 + m_2}{n_1 + n_2} \leq \max\left\{\frac{m_1}{n_1}, \frac{m_2}{n_2}\right\}$$

Proof Given $n_1 \geq m_1 > 0$, $n_2 \geq m_2 > 0$. If $\frac{m_1}{n_1} \geq \frac{m_2}{n_2}$, then there exists $\frac{m_1+m_2}{n_1+n_2} - \frac{m_1}{n_1} = \frac{m_2 n_1 - m_1 n_2}{n_1(n_1+n_2)} \leq 0$. So, $\frac{m_1+m_2}{n_1+n_2} \leq \frac{m_1}{n_1}$ holds.

Similarly, if $\frac{m_2}{n_2} \geq \frac{m_1}{n_1}$, then $\frac{m_1+m_2}{n_1+n_2} \leq \frac{m_2}{n_2}$.

Therefore, $\frac{m_1+m_2}{n_1+n_2} \leq \max\left\{\frac{m_1}{n_1}, \frac{m_2}{n_2}\right\}$ holds. $\square$

Corollary 9.1 For k ($k > 1$) pairs m_i and n_i ($i = 1, 2, \ldots, k$), if $n_i \geq m_i > 0$, there exists the following inequality: $\frac{\sum_{i=1}^{k} m_i}{\sum_{i=1}^{k} n_i} \leq \max_{i=1}^{k}\left\{\frac{m_i}{n_i}\right\}$.

Definition 9.7 (Non-high utility feature set) Given a size k co-location $c = \{f_1, f_2, \ldots, f_k\}$, the set of all features in c whose *UPR* is less than the *UPI* threshold M we call the non-high utility feature set of c.

For example, for $c = \{A, B, D\}$ in Fig. 9.2, if $M = 0.4$ and $w_1 = w_2 = 0.5$, then $UPR(A, c) = 0.257$, $UPR(B, c) = 0.215$ and $UPR(C, c) = 0.422$. The non-high utility feature set of c is $\{A, B\}$.

Theorem 9.1 If c_1 and c_2 are two non-high utility SCPs, and they have one and only one common feature f_i and it is also a non-high utility feature, then the pattern $c = c_1 \cup c_2$ must be a non-high utility SCP, i.e., $c = c_1 \cup c_2$ can be pruned.

Proof Because f_i is a non-high utility feature in c_1 and c_2, we have:

$$UPR(f_i, c_1) = w_1 \frac{u(f_i, c_1)}{u(f_i)} + w_2 \frac{m_1}{n_1} < M \tag{9.4}$$

where $m_1 = \sum_{f_j \in c_1, j \neq i} u(f_j, c_1)$ and $n_1 = \sum_{f_j \in c_1, j \neq i} u(f_j)$. And

$$UPR(f_i, c_2) = w_1 \frac{u(f_i, c_2)}{u(f_i)} + w_2 \frac{m_2}{n_2} < M \tag{9.5}$$

where $m_2 = \sum_{f_j \in c_2, j \neq i} u(f_j, c_2)$ and $n_2 = \sum_{f_j \in c_2, j \neq i} u(f_j)$.

For the co-location $c = c_1 \cup c_2$, the UPR of f_i in c satisfies:

$$UPR(f_i, c) = w_1 \frac{u(f_i, c)}{u(f_i)} + w_2 \frac{m_1 + m_2}{n_1 + n_2} \tag{9.6}$$

due to f_i being the unique common feature in c_1 and c_2.

According to Definition 9.2 and the concept of table instance, we have $u(f, c) \leq u(f, c')$ if f is the common feature in co-locations c and c', and $c' \subseteq c$.

According to Lemma 9.1, $\frac{m_1+m_2}{n_1+n_2} \le \max\left\{\frac{m_1}{n_1}, \frac{m_2}{n_2}\right\}$.

Therefore, we can infer $UPR(f_i, c) < M$ by (9.4), (9.5) and (9.6), and so decide that $c = c_1 \cup c_2$ is a non-high utility co-location. $\square$

For example, for $c_1 = \{A, B, D\}$ and $c_2 = \{B, E\}$ in Fig. 9.2, if $w_1 = w_2 = 0.5$ and $M = 0.5$, $T(c_1) = \{\{A.3^7, B.1^1, D.1^9\}\}$ and $T(c_2) = \{\{B.4^8, E.3^2\}\}$. The UPRs of common feature B in c_1 and c_2 are $UPR(B, c_1) = 0.215 < M$ and $UPR(B, c_2) = 0.231 < M$, respectively $UPR(B, c_2) = 0.231 < \lambda$, which satisfy the conditions of Theorem 9.2. So, $c_1 \cup c_2 = \{A, B, C, D\}$ must be a non-high utility SCP and can be pruned.

According to the Theorem 9.1 and Corollary 9.1, we can infer Corollary 9.2.

Corollary 9.2 For size 2 non-high utility SCPs $c_1, c_2, \ldots, c_k$ $(k > 1)$, if they have a common non-high utility feature f, then the pattern $c = c_1 \cup c_2 \cup \ldots \cup c_k$ must be a non-high utility SCP, i.e., c can be pruned.

When the spatial data set is sparse or the UPI threshold M is high, there often are large amounts of size 2 non-high utility SCPs, so we can prune a large number of higher size non-high utility SCPs by combining those size 2 non-high utility SCPs.

In Fig. 9.2, if $w_1 = w_2 = 0.5$ and $M = 0.5$, the size 2 non-high utility SCPs are $\{A, E\}$, $\{B, E\}$, $\{D, E\}$ and $\{E, F\}$. As E is a non-high utility feature, Corollary 9.2 enables us to prune $\{A, B, E\}$, $\{A, D, E\}$, $\{A, E, F\}$, $\{B, D, E\}$, $\{B, E, F\}$, $\{D, E, F\}$, $\{A, B, D, E\}$, $\{A, B, E, F\}$, $\{A, D, E, F\}$, $\{B, D, E, F\}$, and $\{A, B, D, E, F\}$.

According to Definition 9.2, for a size k co-location $c = \{f_1, f_2, \ldots, f_k\}$ and $f_i \in c$, then $u(f_i, c) \le u(f_i, c')$ holds, where c' is an arbitrary size $k - 1$ sub-pattern of c including f_i. We call the minimum of the utilities of those f_i in size $k - 1$ sub-patterns of c which include f_i as the upper bound utility of f_i in c, the $upbound\_u(f_i, c)$.

For example, for $c = \{A, B, C\}$ in Fig. 9.2, the upper bound utility of feature A in c is $upbound\_u(A, c) = \min\{u(A, \{A, C\}), u(A, \{A, B\})\} = \min\{17, 28\} = 17$.

Lemma 9.2 Given a size k co-location $c = \{f_1, f_2, \ldots, f_k\}$ and its size $k + 1$ super-pattern $c' = c \cup \{f_{k+1}\}$, the upper bound of $UPI(c')$ is computed as follows:

$$\min\left\{w_1 \frac{u(f_i, c)}{u(f_i)} + w_2 \frac{\sum_{f_j \in c, j \ne i} u(f_j, c) + upbound\_u(f_{k+1}, c')}{\sum_{f_j \in c, j \ne i} u(f_j) + u(f_{k+1})}, 1 \le i \le k\right\}$$

Proof If $c = \{f_1, f_2, \ldots, f_k\}$ and $c' = c \cup \{f_{k+1}\}$, then for any feature $f_i \in c$, the inequality $u(f_i, c') \le u(f_i, c)$ holds.

So, we have $UPR(f_i, c') \le w_1 \frac{u(f_i, c)}{u(f_i)} + w_2 \frac{\sum_{f_j \in c, j \ne i} u(f_j, c) + upbound\_u(f_{k+1}, c')}{\sum_{f_j \in c, j \ne i} u(f_j) + u(f_{k+1})}$.

Based on Definition 9.6, we can infer that:

$$UPR(c') \le$$

$$\min\left\{w_1 \frac{u(f_i,c)}{u(f_i)} + w_2 \frac{\sum_{f_j \in c, j \ne i} u(f_j,c) + upbound\_u(f_{k+1},c')}{\sum_{f_j \in c, j \ne i} u(f_j) + u(f_{k+1})}, 1 \le i \le k\right\}. \quad \Box$$

Theorem 9.2 Given a size k non-high utility SCP $c = \{f_1, f_2, \ldots, f_k\}$ and its size $k+1$ super-pattern $c' = c \cup \{f_{k+1}\}$, if there is a non-high utility feature $f_i \in c$ which satisfies $\frac{\sum_{f_j \in c, j \ne i} u(f_j,c)}{\sum_{f_j \in c, j \ne i} u(f_j)} > \frac{upbound\_u(f_{k+1},c')}{u(f_{k+1})}$, then c' is a non-high utility SCP, i.e., c can be pruned.

Proof For a non-high utility SCP $c = \{f_1, f_2, \ldots, f_k\}$ and $c' = c \cup \{f_{k+1}\}$, if f_i is a non-high utility feature in c and M is the UPI threshold, we have

$$UPR(f_i,c) = w_1 \frac{u(f_i,c)}{u(f_i)} + w_2 \frac{m}{n} < M \tag{9.7}$$

where $m = \sum_{f_j \in c, j \ne i} u(f_j,c)$ and $n = \sum_{f_j \in c, j \ne i} u(f_j)$.

According to Lemma 9.2, the UPR of f_i in c' satisfies the following inequality:

$$UPR(f_i,c') \le w_1 \frac{u(f_i,c)}{u(f_i)} + w_2 \frac{m + upbound\_u(f_{k+1},c')}{n + u(f_{k+1})}$$

According to Lemma 9.1, we have

$$\frac{m + upbound\_u(f_{k+1},c')}{n + u(f_{k+1})} \le \max\left\{\frac{m}{n}, \frac{upbound\_u(f_{k+1},c')}{u(f_{k+1})}\right\}$$

If $\frac{m}{n} > \frac{upbound\_u(f_{k+1},c')}{u(f_{k+1})}$, the following inequality holds:

$$UPR(f_i,c') \le w_1 \frac{u(f_i,c)}{u(f_i)} + w_2 \frac{m}{n}$$

Based on Inequality (9.7), we can infer that $UPR(f_i, c') < M$. So, c' must be a non-high utility SCP. $\Box$

For example, for $c = \{B, C, D\}$ in Fig. 9.2, if $w_1 = w_2 = 0.5$ and $M = 0.5$, c is a non-high utility SCP because $T(c) = \{\{B.4^8, C.2^9, D.2^1\}\}$, $UPR(B, c) = 0.36$, $UPR(C, c) = 0.493$ and $UPR(D, c) = 0.268$. For the super-pattern $c' = \{B, C, D, E\}$ of c, $upbound\_u(E, c') = \min\{u(E, \{B, C, E\}) + u(E, \{B, D, E\}) + u(E, \{C, D, E\})\} = \min\{2, 2, 2\} = 2$. As to the feature B in $\{B, C, D\}$, we have

$$\frac{u(\mathrm{C}, c) + u(\mathrm{D}, d)}{u(\mathrm{C}) + u(\mathrm{D})} = \frac{9 + 1}{12 + 13} > \frac{upbound\_u(\mathrm{E}, c')}{u(\mathrm{E})} = \frac{1}{14}$$

So, based on the results of computing the size 3 SCPs, we can infer that the size 4 SCP {B, C, D, E} must be a non-high utility SCP.

Theorem 9.1, Corollary 9.2 and Theorem 9.2 become the three pruning strategies to identify some non-high utility SCPs early in the mining process.

9.7   Experimental Analysis

This section verifies the effect and efficiency of the basic algorithm and of the algorithm with pruning strategies on both synthetic and real data sets. The algorithms are implemented in Java 1.7 and run on a windows 8 operating system with 3.10GHz Intel Core i5 CPU and 4GB memory.

9.7.1   Data Sets

We conducted the experiments on synthetic data sets and on a plant data set of the "Three Parallel Rivers of Yunnan Protected Areas.". Synthetic data sets were generated using a spatial data generator similar to Huang et al. (2004) and Yoo and Shekhar (2006), and the utilities of instances were assigned randomly between 0 and 20. In the plant data sets, we computed the utilities of plant instances according to the plant price associated with that size and kind of plant. The efficiency of the basic algorithm and of the algorithm with pruning strategies are examined on both data sets.

9.7.2   The Quality of Mining Results

This chapter aims at finding the high utility SCPs whose instances are frequently located together in geographic space and which have high utilities, so we take the criterion $Q(c) = \sum_{f \in c} u(f, c) / \sum_{f \in c} u(f)$ to evaluate the quality of a mined SCP c.

To show that the UPI measure of interest is reasonable we compare the quality of mining results identified by different measures of interest. These are the traditional participation index measure (PI), the traditional pattern utility ratio (PUR) proposed in Yang et al. (2015) and the UPI proposed here.

In the experiments which produce Fig. 9.3, we take the number of spatial features $|F|$ as 15, the total number of instances $|S|$ as 10,000, the neighboring distance threshold d as 30, and $w_1 = 0.9$, $w_2 = 0.1$. Figure 9.3(a) shows the sum of the

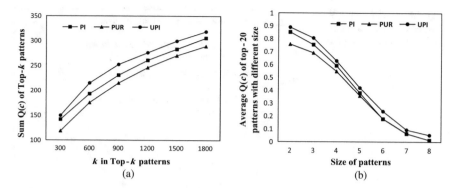

Fig. 9.3 Testing the quality of mining results for (**a**) the sum of quality of top-k interesting patterns;
(**b**) the average of quality of top-20 interesting patterns with different sizes

quality of the top-k interesting SCPs identified by the PI, PUR and UPI measures.
Figure 9.3(b) shows the average quality of top-20 interesting patterns identified by
the three measures over different sizes. The results show that our UPI measure can
identify higher quality SCPs, and it can extract top SCPs with higher average utility.

9.7.3 Evaluation of Pruning Strategies

On synthetic and real data sets, we evaluated the effect of pruning strategies with
several workloads, e.g., different numbers of instances, neighbor distance thresholds, UPI thresholds, and pruned rate.

1. *Influence of the number of instances*
   We compared the running time of the basic algorithm and the algorithm with
   pruning strategies on the synthetic and real data sets. We set $|F| = 20$, $d = 20$,
   $M = 0.3$, $w_1 = w_2 = 0.5$, and measured the running time of two algorithms as
   the number of instances increased, as shown in Fig. 9.4. The performance of the
   algorithm with pruning strategies is better than the basic algorithm on both the
   synthetic and real data sets. Compared with synthetic data sets, the neighbor
   relationships of real data sets are relatively fewer, which results in fewer row
   instances being computed explaining why the runtime of the algorithms on the
   real data set was less than that on the synthetic data set in our experiments.
2. *Influence of the distance threshold d*
   In the experiment producing Fig. 9.5, we set $|F| = 20$, $|S| = 10,000$, $M = 0.3$,
   $w_1 = w_2 = 0.5$. We compared the running time of two algorithms by changing the
   distance threshold d, and we can see that the algorithm with pruning strategies
   was still faster than the basic algorithm. However, both algorithms may have a
   huge time-cost associated with increases in d. This is because, as d increases there

Fig. 9.4 The influence of
the number of instances over
synthetic and real data sets

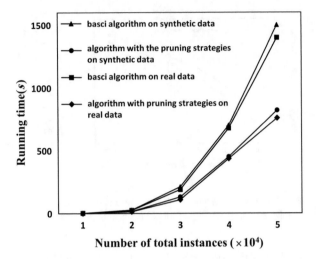

Fig. 9.5 The influence of
distance thresholds over
synthetic and real data sets

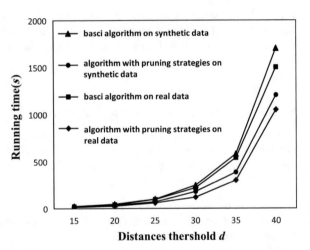

are more cliques formed, resulting in huge numbers of row instances having to be
computed and more time consumed.

3. *Influence of the UPI threshold M*

We set $|F| = 20$, $|S| = 10,000$, $d = 15$, $w_1 = w_2 = 0.5$ in this experiment. The
running time of two algorithms with the changes of the UPI threshold M is shown
in Fig. 9.6. With an increase of M, more non-high utility co-locations are pruned
early, which improves the efficiency of the algorithm with pruning strategies.

4. *Pruned rate*

In order to examine the efficiency of the three pruning strategies (Theorem 9.1,
Corollary 9.2, and Theorem 9.2), we counted the number of candidates pruned by
each pruning strategy, respectively. In this experiment, we set $|F| = 15$, $|S| = 4000$, $d = 20$, $M = 0.3$, $w_1 = w_2 = 0.5$, and we randomly generated

Fig. 9.6 The influence of
the UPI threshold M over
synthetic and real data sets

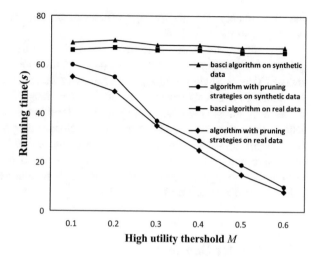

legend:
—▲— basci algorithm on synthetic data
—●— algorithm with pruning strategies on synthetic data
—■— basci algorithm on real data
—◆— algorithm with pruning strategies on real data

x-axis: **High utility thershold M**
y-axis: **Running time(s)**

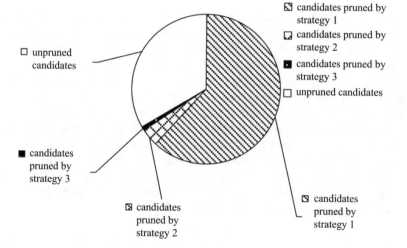

☒ candidates pruned by strategy 1
▨ candidates pruned by strategy 2
■ candidates pruned by strategy 3
☐ unpruned candidates

Fig. 9.7 The proportion of candidates pruned by each strategy

5 different data sets whose size is similar to each other. We independently ran the algorithm with pruning strategies on the five different data sets and computed the average proportion of the candidates pruned by each strategy. The proportions are shown in Fig. 9.7.

The results show that the pruning strategies are very efficient. However, it seems the efficiency of pruning strategies need not be further improved, for two reasons. First, the process of pruning candidates costs some time. Second, some pruned co-locations may be used to generate the table instances of super co-locations, so we might have to generate the table instances of pruned co-locations, which would have a negative effect on the algorithm. Fortunately, these effects rarely occurred in the experiments and the average efficiency of the pruning strategies we have developed so far is obvious.

In addition, the basic algorithm and the algorithm with pruning strategies presented in this paper convert spatial data sets into the star neighborhood partition model (Yoo & Shekhar, 2006). Algorithms in both papers store spatial neighbor relationships and table instances of current candidates. Therefore, the memory cost of our algorithms is similar to the join-less algorithm in Yoo and Shekhar (2006). Due to the non-existence of the downward closure property, the scalability of the basic algorithm requires improvement. From Figs. 9.4, 9.5, 9.6, and 9.7, we can see that the pruning strategies significantly reduce the overall runtime of the basic algorithm, although in some extreme cases less so. Further improvement of algorithm scalability is left for future work.

9.8   Chapter Summary

Different from the last chapter, we take the instances with utilities as study objects which more closely reflect the real world and a new measure of interest is proposed in this chapter. We combine the intra-utility ratio and the inter-utility ratio into a utility participation index for identifying high utility SCPs, which is comprehensive and reasonable. Because the utility participation index does not satisfy the downward closure property, we developed some effective pruning strategies to improve the efficiency of finding high utility SCPs. The experiments on synthetic and real data sets show that these pruning strategies significantly reduce the overall runtime of the basic algorithm. Although the algorithm with pruning strategies is better than the basic algorithm, it also shows less improvement in some extreme cases.

All SCP mining is instigated by users and users rarely want a black box process. To better satisfy user preferences, Chap. 10 proposes an interactive probabilistic post-mining method to discover user-preferred SCPs.

Chapter 10
Interactively Post-mining User-Preferred Co-location Patterns with a Probabilistic Model

10.1 Introduction

We have seen that spatial co-location pattern (SCP) mining is an important task in spatial data mining. However, traditional mining frameworks often produce too many prevalent patterns of which only a small proportion may be truly interesting to end users, which is an unsatisfactory situation. This chapter proposes an interactive probabilistic post-mining method to discover user-preferred SCPs by iteratively involving user feedback and probabilistically refining user-preferred SCPs.

The chapter's work proceeds as follows:

1. A framework of interactively post-mining SCPs is developed which helps users effectively discover preferred SCPs according to their specific interests. In the framework, we introduce a *probabilistic model* method to measure the user's subjective preference for an SCP. To further improve the method, two effective computation methods for the distribution probabilities of 2-size SCPs are developed which involve some adjusting factors.

2. We develop a simple and effective algorithm to implement the post-mining process. In this algorithm, an initially selected sample of SCPs is based on their prevalence, and the selection of subsequent sample SCPs is based on their probability related to the user feedback. Two optimization strategies for selecting sample SCPs are also devised to further improve the efficiency of the interactive process.

3. We set up an experimental environment called *Simulator* to simulate user feedback. With Simulator, we evaluate the performance of the developed algorithms on both synthetic and real data sets and show that the proposed approaches are effective in discovering user-preferred SCPs.

From Wang, L., Bao, X., Cao, L.: Interactive Probabilistic Post-mining of User-preferred Spatial Co-location Patterns. In: *Proceedings of the 34th IEEE International Conference on Data Engineering (ICDE 2018)*, IEEE Press, Paris, French, pp. 1256–1259 (2018).

© The Author(s), under exclusive license to Springer Nature Singapore Pte Ltd. 2022
L. Wang et al., *Preference-based Spatial Co-location Pattern Mining*, Big Data Management, https://doi.org/10.1007/978-981-16-7566-9_10

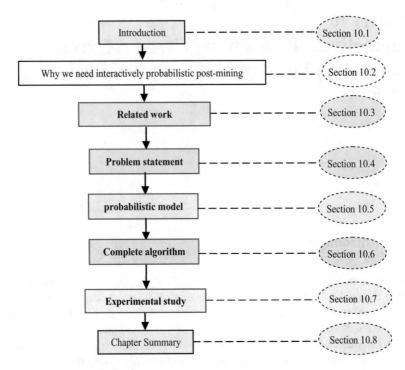

Fig. 10.1 The organization of this chapter

Figure 10.1 presents the organization of this chapter. Section 10.2 discusses why we may need an interactive probabilistic post-mining method to discover user-preferred SCPs. Section 10.3 is the related work. Section 10.4 presents the problem statement. Section 10.5 discusses the probabilistic model which discovers the preferred result set for a user, and the complete algorithm is shown in Sect. 10.6. The experimental evaluation is conducted in Sect. 10.7. Section 10.8 ends this chapter with some conclusive remarks.

10.2   Why We Need Interactive Probabilistic Post-mining

The extraction of spatial co-location patterns (SCPs) is a rising and promising field in spatial data mining. An SCP is composed of a set of spatial features frequently observed together within geographical neighborhoods (Shekhar & Huang, 2001; Zhang et al., 2004). SCP mining yields important insights for various applications such as Earth science (Verhein & Al-Naymat, 2007), public transportation (Yu, 2016), and air pollution (Akbari et al., 2015). Examples of SCPs include symbiotic species, e.g., the Nile Crocodile and Egyptian Plover in ecology (Huang et al., 2004), and interdependent incidents, e.g., traffic jams caused by car accidents and the relevant ambulance and police actions (Yu, 2016).

Typically, SCP mining methods use the frequencies of a set of spatial features participating in an SCP to measure a pattern's prevalence (known as *participation index, PI* for short) and require a user-specified minimum prevalence threshold, *min_prev,* to filter prevalent SCPs (Shekhar & Huang, 2001; Zhang et al., 2004; Huang et al., 2004). However, determining an appropriate *min_prev* is not trivial for users. To avoid missing interesting SCPs, very low thresholds are often set, resulting in a large number of prevalent SCPs of which only a small proportion is interesting. This problem is further exacerbated by the *downward closure* property that holds for the *PI* measure, whereby all of the 2^l subsets of each l-size prevalent SCP are included in the result set. Consequently, a huge number of prevalent SCPs are often generated, but only a small number of them may satisfy user preferences. User preferences are often subjective, and a pattern preferred by one user may not be favored by another, and so cannot be measured by objective-oriented *PI* measures. Therefore, it is necessary and advantageous to involve user preferences and filter user-preferred SCPs.

For example, in the field of the environment and vegetation protection, to study the influence of vegetation distribution on the environment one can mine the prevalent SCPs of vegetation distribution data in a region. Similarly, a user who studies urban air quality will be interested in SCPs that include vegetation which regulates the climate and purifies the air. However, a user paying attention to soil and water conservation probably would not think these co-locations are intriguing co-location patterns at all, and would prefer to reanalyze the data with their own interests in mind.

Similar ideas have been explored in the studies of interesting frequent itemset mining (Xin et al., 2009; Bhuiyan & Hasan, 2016). These works follow a common interactive process: a limited number of sample patterns selected from candidate patterns are fed to the user at the beginning of each iteration, the user then feeds back his/her preferences on the sample patterns, then candidate patterns are updated by learning models according to the user's feedback, and new samples are selected for the next iteration. For example, Xin et al. (2009) proposed a framework to learn user prior knowledge from interactive feedback. In their work, users needed to rank the supplied sample frequent itemsets, and the user prior knowledge was learned from the interactive feedback of a *log-linear model* or *biased belief model.* Bhuiyan and Hasan (2016) proposed an interactive pattern discovery framework named PRIIME which identifies a set of interesting patterns for a specific user without requiring any prior input concerning measures of interest in patterns from the user. In their work, a softmax classification-based iterative learning algorithm that used a limited amount of interactive feedback from the user was proposed to learn the user prior knowledge. However, both of these two frameworks suggest adopting *Jaccard distance,* based on transactions, to measure a patterns' interest and to select sample patterns for the user. Their frequent itemsets, however, are generated from transactions. Because there are no transactions or concept-like transactions in spatial data, SCPs are generated from a list of instances with locations and so a Jaccard distance is

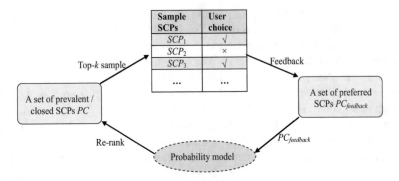

Fig. 10.2 A framework for interactively post-mining user-preferred co-locations

irrelevant. Also Bhuiyan et al. (2012) and Boley et al. (2013) on interactively post-mining frequent itemsets use transactions in their calculations, so that work similarly cannot be applied to the post-mining of SCPs.

There is a limited amount of work on the post-mining of SCPs. Utilizing ontology, where ontology was used to estimate the semantic similarity between two SCPs, Bao et al. (2015), Bao and Wang (2017), and Bao et al. (2021) proposed an approach to identify user-preferred SCPs by explicitly constructing reasonably precise background knowledge, but its construction makes it hard to use.

This chapter develops a framework to discover user-preferred SCPs by iteratively involving user feedback and probabilistically quantifying user preferences for co-locations. We assume that a set of candidate co-location patterns (i.e., prevalent co-locations or closed co-locations) has already been mined so our goal here is to help the user effectively post-mine preferred SCPs. Rather than requiring the user to explicitly construct the prior knowledge beforehand, we merely ask them to choose preferred SCPs from a small set of sample SCPs.

Our proposed framework for interactively post-mining user-preferred SCPs is shown in Fig. 10.2.

Our system takes a set PC of prevalent or closed SCPs as input. First, the top-k (e.g., $k = 5$, in prevalence value order) prevalent SCPs in PC are presented to the user as sample co-location patterns, and the system then asks the user for their preferences. The user chooses a set of preferred SCPs from the sample co-location patterns and so the first set $PC_{feedback}$ of selected SCPs is collected. Based on $PC_{feedback}$, the prevalent SCPs in PC are estimated for their subjective preferences by a *probabilistic model*, and ranked by their estimated preferences, where the estimation relates their probability to the user feedback. Then the top-k co-locations (in estimated subjective preference order) are fed to the user again. After several rounds of the interactive process, as shown in Fig. 10.2 the system produces a refined output that is close to the user preferences for SCPs.

The probabilistic model is a content-based model, which can calculate the probabilities of preference-related SCPs. It has the advantage that the results can be ranked in a descending order of their relative probabilities. This is the approach to similar applications widely used in uncertainty reasoning (Baral et al., 2002), information retrieval (Cai & Chen, 2016), and data mining (Zhang et al., 2008; Wang et al., 2013a, 2013b).

10.3 Related Work

In Sect. 10.2, we mentioned the connection of our work with some previous related works. In this section, we discuss the work related to this chapter in a more comprehensive and detailed way.

The problem of SCP mining was first introduced by Morimoto (Morimoto, 2001), where a *support* metric was defined as the number of instances of an SCP and was used to measure the prevalence of an SCP. Shekhar and Huang (2001) proposed using *minimum participation ratio* (called *participation index*) as the interest measures that are more statistically meaningful. An extended version of the work in Shekhar and Huang (2001) was presented in Huang et al. (2004). Zhang et al. (2004) enhanced the SCP in Shekhar and Huang (2001) and proposed an approach to find spatial star, clique, and generic patterns. Approaches to reduce expensive join operations used for finding co-location instances in Shekhar and Huang (2001) and Huang et al. (2004) were proposed in Yoo and Shekhar (2006) and Xiao et al. (2008). The work in Wang et al. (2009b), Yoo and Bow (2011b), and Yao et al. (2017) studied the problem of maximal SCP mining. The concept of *maximal SCPs* is based on a lossy condensed representation, which can infer the original collection of interesting SCPs, but not their PI values. The introduction of *closed SCPs* created a lossless condensed representation (Yoo & Bow, 2011a; Wang et al., 2018b), which could infer not only the original collection of prevalent SCPs but also their PI values. The redundancy reduction problem of prevalent SCPs determined by applying distribution information from co-location instances was studied in Wang et al. (2018a).

Since the pattern of a user's interest strongly depends on the user knowledge and preferences, post-mining interesting patterns involving user feedback have been studied extensively in traditional frequent itemset mining, for example, in Xin et al. (2009), Bhuiyan and Hasan (2016), Bhuiyan et al. (2012), and Boley et al. (2013). Although these studies achieved satisfactory results, again they cannot be directly applied to the interactive post-mining of SCPs due to the lack of transaction concepts in spatial data sets. In these itemset mining papers, transactions are used to calculate the distance between two patterns P_1 and P_2, $(D(P_1, P_2) = 1 - \frac{T(P_1) \cap T(P_2)}{T(P_1) \cup T(P_2)}$, where $T(P)$ is the set of transactions containing pattern P).

Limited work is available on discovering interesting SCPs by involving user feedback. Bao et al. (2016) and Bao and Wang (2017) proposed an interactive approach, OICM (ontology-based interesting co-location miner), to find interesting SCPs, but the ontology-based method requires users to explicitly construct a reasonably precise background knowledge, which is found to be difficult in many real applications. To overcome this drawback, our proposed probabilistic model is simple but results in a good outcome, namely that it can help the user effectively discover his/her preferred SCPs according to his/her specific preferences. We took the first step of introducing an interactive probabilistic post-mining method to discover user-preferred SCPs in Wang et al. (2018c). We extend that work here. The extended contents include more detailed application background analysis, theoretical analysis of the proposed method, complete experimental evaluation, etc.

10.4   Problem Statement

We first present the concepts and preliminaries for SCP mining. We then discuss the subjective preference measure of the users. Finally, the problem is formally stated so that solutions can be developed.

10.4.1   Basic Concept

In a spatial database, let F be a set of n **features** $F = \{f_1, f_2, \ldots, f_n\}$, S be a set of *instances* of F, where each **instance** is a triple <feature type, instance ID, location>, and R be a **neighbor relationship** over locations of instances, where R is symmetric and reflexive. With a distance threshold value d, we define the neighbor relationship R: two spatial instances are neighbors if they satisfy the condition that the Euclidean distance between them does not exceed d, i.e., $R(a, b) \Leftrightarrow (distance(a, b) \leq d)$.

A **spatial co-location pattern (SCP)** c is a subset of the feature set F. The number of features in c is called the **size** of c. For $F = \{A, B, C\}$, $\{A, B\}$ is a SCP of size 2.

In SCP mining, the participation index (PI) proposed by Huang et al. (2004) is commonly adopted to characterize how frequently the instances of different features in an SCP are neighbors.

A SCP c is a **prevalent SCP**, if its participation index PI is no less than a given prevalence threshold *min_prev*, i.e., $PI(c) \geq min\ prev$.

PI measures the prevalence strength of an SCP. Wherever a feature in a SCP c is observed, all other features in c can be observed in the feature's neighborhood with a probability $PI(c) \geq min\ prev$. The PI measure satisfies the **anti-monotonicity property** (*downward closure property*), i.e., $PI(c) \geq PI(c')$ for any $c \subset c'$, enabling level-wise search (like Apriori) (Huang et al., 2004). This kind of search has good performance when the given threshold, *min_prev*, is high and the neighborhood relations of spatial data are sparse. However, an Apriori-based SCP discovery algorithm has to examine all of the 2^k subsets of each size k feature set and generates numerous irrelevant patterns.

Lossless ccondensed representations are the diminished descriptions of prevalent SCP collections such that it is possible to infer the original collection of prevalent

SCPs and their PI values by inference methods. The introduction of *closed SCPs* enables a lossless condensed representation to be created. A prevalent SCP c is **closed** if there is no SCP c' such that $c \subset c'$ and $PI(c) = PI(c')$ (Yoo & Bow, 2011a; Wang et al., 2018b).

10.4.2   Subjective Preference Measure

We assume that a set PC of prevalent or closed SCPs has already been mined, which will form the input to our system. Each co-location $c \in PC$ consists of the *features* in c and its participation index ($PI(c)$), which indicates the prevalence of c. In PC, we suppose that there is a set PC_I of ideal SCPs of interest to the user, so that PC_I is the preferred co-location set and $PC_{II} = PC - PC_I$ is the non-preferred co-location set.

In traditional prevalent SCP mining the value $PI(c)$ ($c \in PC$) is an objective interest measure. In practice, though, it is not possible that objective interest can be substituted for subjective preference. PC might contain a large number of mined prevalent SCPs, which may not be actionable or useful for users, since they may just be general knowledge, or their prevalence may have been enhanced by the instances' autocorrelation, or they are just regarded as irrelevant by the user.

In our approach the user feedback (the selected SCPs) is combined into a set of user-preferred SCPs, denoted as $PC_{feedback}$. The set $PC_{feedback}$ is updated whenever the system obtains user feedback. In the interactive process, we use a similarity measure $SIM(c, PC_{feedback})$ between an SCP c in PC and the selected SCPs $PC_{feedback}$ to evaluate the degree of subjective preference of any SCP c which has not yet been judged.

10.4.3   Formal Problem Statement

The problem of *post-mining user-preferred SCPs through interactive feedback* can be stated as follows. Given a set of prevalent or closed SCPs, can the system return the ideal SCPs of user preference, according to user feedback about preferred SCPs, but at the same time minimize the user efforts in providing feedback?

Due to the uncertainties of the user's ideal preferences, in this chapter, we use a *classic probabilistic model* method to model the prior knowledge of the user. The basic idea of this method is that, given a set PC of prevalent or closed SCPs, there will exist a set PC_I of ideal preference SCPs in PC for a user. Clearly, the system does not know the characteristics of the set PC_I at the beginning of the interactive process and it needs to make a guess. According to this guess, the system will identify a result set PC_I as an initial hit. Then the user or system judges the initial result PC_I. Based on this feedback, the system can optimize and improve the initial result PC_I incrementally in the interactive process until, after repeated interactions, the resultant PC_I should be close to the user's ideal preference result set.

The essence of the above probabilistic model is to estimate the similarity measure $SIM(c, PC_{feedback})$ between the selected SCPs $PC_{feedback}$ per user feedback and an SCP c in the set of prevalent or closed co-locations PC, whose preference level has not yet been judged.

10.5   Probabilistic Model

In this section, we discuss the probabilistic model which will help discover the preferred result set PC_I for a user.

10.5.1   Basic Assumptions

The basic assumptions of the probabilistic model are:

1. A user-preferred SCP c contained in PC is not related to other SCPs in PC. In other words, that an SCPn is preferred by a user is only because of itself, and not due to the existence of other SCPs in PC.
2. The subjective preference of an SCP is binary; i.e., there is only "prefer" or "not prefer," so an SCP either belongs to the user ideal preference set PC_I or it does not.

10.5.2   Probabilistic Model

Assume, for a user, there exists a preferred co-location set PC_I and also a non-preferred co-location set PC_{II} in the prevalent or closed co-location set PC. After obtaining a set $PC_{feedback}$ of user feedback, the similarity $SIM(c, PC_{feedback})$ between an SCP c in PC and the set $PC_{feedback}$ per user feedback is defined as the ratio of the probability of c being user-preferred to the probability of c not being user-preferred, i.e.,

$$SIM\left(c, PC_{feedback}\right) = \frac{P(PC_I|c)}{P(PC_{II}|c)} \qquad (10.1)$$

where $P(PC_I|c)$ represents the probability that c is preferred by the user and $P(PC_{II}|c)$ represents the probability that c is not preferred by the user.

Since the values of $P(PC_I|c)$ and $P(PC_{II}|c)$ cannot be computed directly, they need to be estimated with known values. Assume there is an initial guess about the user's ideal preference set PC_I, then Eq. (10.1) can be converted by the Bayes' rule:

$$SIM\left(c, PC_{feedback}\right) = \frac{P(c|PC_I) \times P(PC_I)}{P(c|PC_{II}) \times P(PC_{II})} \qquad (10.2)$$

where $P(c \mid PC_I)$ represents the probability that PC_I contains c; $P(c \mid PC_{II})$ represents the probability that PC_{II} contains c, and $P(PC_I)$, and $P(PC_{II})$ represents the prior probabilities that any SCP in PC belongs to PC_I or PC_{II}, respectively.

Given a set of prevalent or closed SCPs PC, the two values $P(PC_I)$ and $P(PC_{II})$ are related only to the user and, as we only need be concerned about the relative values in computing SIM, Eq. (10.2) can be simplified to:

$$SIM\left(c, PC_{feedback}\right) = \frac{P(c|PC_I)}{P(c|PC_{II})} \qquad (10.3)$$

Since an SCP is a set of spatial features which are frequently observed together in nearby geographic space, 1-size SCP mining is meaningless, unlike the situation in transactional databases. The set of 2-size SCPs is the basis for mining all higher-size SCPs, because the measurement of co-location prevalence can be based on the clique relationship of instances. Hence, the probability that PC_I or PC_{II} contains c can be calculated by the distribution of each 2-size SCP c_i in PC_I and PC_{II}:

$$P(c|PC_I) = \prod_{i=1}^{m} P(c_i|PC_I)^{w_i(c)} P(\overline{c}_i|PC_I)^{(1-w_i(c))} \qquad (10.4)$$

$$P(c|PC_{II}) = \prod_{i=1}^{m} P(c_i|PC_{II})^{w_i(c)} P(\overline{c}_i|PC_{II})^{(1-w_i(c))} \qquad (10.5)$$

where n is the number of features in F, m represents the number of 2-size SCPs in F, and $m = n(n-1)/2$. We define $w_i(c) \in \{0, 1\}$ such that $w_i(c) = 1$ when the i-th 2-size SCP c_i in F is contained in $PC_{feedback}$ and c at the same time; otherwise $w_i(c) = 0$, and $\overline{c}_i$ represents "not containing 2-size SCP c_i."

Equation (10.4) can now be interpreted as follows: when the 2-size SCP c_i is in $PC_{feedback}$ and c at the same time, i.e., $w_i(c) = 1$, the probability that an SCP in PC_I contains c_i is regarded as a contribution to the probability that PC_I contains c. In the contrary situation, when the 2-size SCP c_i is not contained in either $PC_{feedback}$ or c, the probability that any SCP in PC_I does not contain c_i is also regarded as a contribution. The interpretation of Eq. (10.5) is similar.

There are two reasons why we use 2-size SCPs c_i ($1 \le i \le m$, $m = n(n-1)/2$, and n is the number of features in F) to judge the contribution:

1. The 2-size SCP contained in the SCP c is the minimum unit of the combination of features in c.
2. The user preference for an SCP c implies that there exists a combination of features in c preferred by the user.

Based on Eqs. (10.4) and (10.5), Eq. (10.3) can be converted to:

$$SIM\left(c, PC_{feedback}\right) = \frac{\prod_{i=1}^{m} p(c_i|PC_I)^{w_i(c)} P(\overline{c}_i|PC_I)^{(1-w_i(c))}}{\prod_{i=1}^{m} p(c_i|PC_{II})^{w_i(c)} P(\overline{c}_i|PC_{II})^{(1-w_i(c))}} \tag{10.6}$$

From the meanings of $P(c_i|PC_I)$ and $P(\overline{c}_i|PC_I)$, we have $P(c_i|PC_I) + P(\overline{c}_i|PC_I) = 1$. Similarly, $P(c_i|PC_{II}) + P(\overline{c}_i|PC_{II}) = 1$ holds. We take these relations into Eq. (10.6) and by taking logarithms, convert it to:

$$SIM\left(c, PC_{feedback}\right) = \sum_{i=1}^{m} w_i(c) \log_{10} \frac{p(c_i|PC_I)(1 - P(c_i|PC_{II}))}{p(c_i|PC_{II})(1 - P(c_i|PC_I))}$$
$$+ \sum_{i=1}^{m} \log_{10} \frac{1 - p(c_i|PC_I)}{1 - p(c_i|PC_{II})} \tag{10.7}$$

In Eq. (10.7), the expression $\sum_{i=1}^{m} \log_{10} \frac{1-p(c_i|PC_I)}{1-p(c_i|PC_{II})}$ is not related to the SCP c, so Eq. (10.7) can be further simplified to:

$$SIM\left(c, PC_{feedback}\right) = \sum_{i=1}^{m} w_i(c) \log_{10} \frac{p(c_i|PC_I)(1 - P(c_i|PC_{II}))}{p(c_i|PC_{II})(1 - P(c_i|PC_I))} \tag{10.8}$$

Equation 10.8 enables us to compute the similarity between any SCP c in the candidates and $PC_{feedback}$ by Eq. (10.8), and rank them by the values $SIM(c, PC_{feedback})$. However, as mentioned before, the user preference set PC_I is not known initially, so we need a method to calculate the probabilistic values $p(c_i | PC_I)$ and $p(c_i | PC_{II})$.

A simple method for calculating the probabilistic values $p(c_i | PC_I)$ and $p(c_i | PC_{II})$ is that:

$$\begin{cases} p(c_i|PC_I) = 0.5 \\ p(c_i|PC_{II}) = n_i/N \end{cases} \tag{10.9}$$

where n_i and N represent the number of SCPs containing 2-size SCP c_i and the number of total SCPs in PC respectively. We can then calculate the $SIM(c, PC_{feedback})$ for each c in PC by Eq. (10.8) and rank them by the values $SIM(c, PC_{feedback})$ as the initial result.

The explanation of Eq. (10.9) is that the initial value of the probability that an SCP in PC_I contains a 2-size pattern c_i is put at 0.5, and the initial value of the probability that an SCP in PC_{II} contains a 2-size pattern c_i is put at n_i/N, since N is the number of total SCPs in PC, and n_i is the number of SCPs containing a 2-size pattern c_i. Obviously, the larger the n_i, the larger the probability $p(c_i|PC_{II})$.

We use V to represent the top-r SCPs in the initial result (r is a pre-specified threshold), V_i to represent the set of SCPs in V that contains a 2-size SCP c_i, and the number of SCPs in V_i is denoted r_i. In order to improve the computational result and help minimize the user efforts in providing feedback, Eq. (10.9) for calculating the probabilistic values $p(c_i | PC_I)$ and $p(c_i | PC_{II})$ can be improved. After obtaining user feedback information, we can use two improved methods (Eqs. (10.10) and (10.11)) for calculating $p(c_i \mid PC_I)$ and $p(c_i \mid PC_{II})$:

$$\begin{cases} p(c_i|PC_I) = (r_i + 0.5)/(r + 1) \\ p(c_i|PC_{II}) = (n_i - r_i + 0.5)/(N - r + 1) \end{cases} \tag{10.10}$$

$$\begin{cases} p(c_i|PC_I) = (r_i + n_i/N)/(r + 1) \\ p(c_i|PC_{II}) = (n_i - r_i + n_i/N)/(N - r + 1) \end{cases} \tag{10.11}$$

where r and r_i are adjustment factors added to the formula based on the feedback principle.

The explanation of Eqs. (10.10) and (10.11) is that we have considered r SCPs that are user-preferred, because r is the number of the top-r SCPs in the initial result. Thus, there are $N - r$ candidates left in PC_{II}, and as r_i is the number of SCPs containing the 2-size SCP c_i in the top-r SCPs, we can build the basic formula $((n_i - r_i)/(N - r))$ of Eqs. (10.10) and (10.11). To be less arbitrary, we use n_i/N instead of 0.5 in Eq. (10.11).

Note that Eq. (10.9) needs to be used at the beginning of the interactive process before using Eq. (10.10) or (10.11).

10.5.3 Discussion

In essence, the probabilistic model is a kind of decision-making process handling uncertainty. Its advantages include:

1. It has a strict theory foundation, based on mathematics and deduction.
2. It has an inherent correlation feedback mechanism and adopts a rigorous decision-making method.
3. It incurs a very small user burden in the interactive process, particularly as the results can be sorted in the descending order of the SIM values (the probability related to the user preference).
4. It supports a strategy for top-k SCP selection from the SIM values for repeatedly feeding to the user.

However, the probabilistic model also has some limitations, as below:

1. It is difficult to accurately estimate the values $p(c_i \mid PC_I)$ and $p(c_i \mid PC_{II})$, and to partition the prevalent co-location set into the user ideal interest set PC_I and the non-interest set PC_{II} at the beginning of the interactive process.
2. The weights of 2-size SCPs are assumed to be just two values. The difference of the 2-size patterns' weights in different SCPs, or with a different user choice set of $PC_{feedback,}$ is not considered, leading to results which do not reflect some of the known uncertainty.

3. It assumes that the user interests in particular SCPs are independent of each other in the probabilistic model, so there is no consideration of possible relationships between them.

Overall, the probabilistic method we have been describing theoretically seems a simple, yet effective method for interactively post-mining user-preferred SCPs, but it has to be proved, which we will do later in this chapter.

10.6   The Complete Algorithm

In this section, we first give the complete algorithm for post-mining user-preferred SCPs interactively based on the probabilistic model introduced in Sect. 10.5. Then two optimization strategies are presented to improve the efficiency of the interactive process. Finally, we make a computational complexity analysis of the algorithm.

10.6.1   The Algorithm

We have discussed the probabilistic model method to measure the SIM value of an SCP and the user-preferred sample SCPs. In Algorithm 10.1 we outline the complete algorithm for pattern ranking with user feedback.

Algorithm 10.1: Post-mining User-preferred SCPs Interactively

Input: A set of n spatial features, $F=\{f_1, f_2, ..., f_n\}$;
$\qquad$ A set of prevalent / closed SCPs, PC;
$\qquad$ Number of sample SCPs for feedback, k;
$\qquad$ Number of iterations of feedback, $iter$;
$\qquad$ Number of top-r SCPs from the values $SIM(c, PC_{feedback})$, r;

Output: *Ranked Co-location List.*

Method:
1) $\psi = $Sort$(PC, PIs)$;
2) **for** $(i=0; i<iter; i++)$
3) $\qquad$ $PC_{feedback}$ = Present top-k in ψ to request user feedback;
4) $\qquad$ $PC=PC - PC_{feedback}$;
$\qquad\qquad$ //remove the k selected patterns from PC
5) $\qquad$ $\Omega = \Omega + PC_{feedback}$; // Ω is the user feedback set
6) $\qquad$ $Cal\_SIM(PC, \Omega)$; //calculate the similarity $SIM(c, \Omega)$ between a SCP c in
$\qquad\qquad$ PC and the set Ω by Formula (10.8)
7) $\qquad$ $\psi= $Sort$(PC, SIMs)$;
$\qquad\qquad$ //re-rank SCPs in PC by their values of similarity
8) **Return** $\Omega + \psi$

The algorithm takes the entire collection of prevalent or closed SCPs as input. Users can also specify the number of iterations they would like to provide as feedback and how many SCPs they would like to judge at each round. The algorithm works as follows.

The input prevalent or closed SCPs' set PC is sorted by its participation index (PI) values (Line 1). Line 3 presents the top-k SCPs (with their current ranking) to get the user feedback. Line 4 removes the user's selected SCPs from PC so that their similarities will not be calculated, and they will not be selected again in the following iterations. Line 5 collects the user feedback in Ω. Line 6 calculates the similarity $SIM(c, \Omega)$ between an SCP c in PC and the set Ω of the user feedback by using Eq. (10.8). The remaining SCPs in PC are re-ranked according to their SIM values (Line 7). After the algorithm repeats *iter* times, the ranked results are output.

10.6.2 Two Optimization Strategies

1. *Maintaining a minimum prevalence value for selecting top-k co-locations*
   Line 1 (sort) of Algorithm 10.1 is for selecting the top-k SCPs in PC according to their PIs, so we propose a simple and efficient method to reduce its computational complexity. During the top-k selection, we first use a minimum prevalence value θ in the top-k result set and, after we obtain at least k SCPs in the result set, we use θ to determine whether an SCP can be included in the top-k result set or not. We can also prune all those super-sets of an SCP which cannot be included in the top-k result set according to the anti-monotonicity property of PI (Huang et al., 2004). In the worst case, the computational complexity of sorting s SCPs is $O(s\log_2 s)$, and the computational complexity of the optimization strategy is only $O(ks)$ (where k is generally between 5 or 10, and s is the number of SCPs in PC). In practice, the improvement effect becomes clearer if we deal with the SCPs of PC in the ascending order of sizes.
2. *A Value-based partition method for selecting top-r SCPs*
   For selecting top-r SCPs in PC per the values $SIM(c, PC_{feedback})$, which are used in Line 7 + Line 3 or in the computation of Eq. (10.10) or (10.11), we propose a new value-based partition method as follows.

Procedure SELECT (r, PC)

begin

1) Choose a SCP c randomly from PC;

2) Let S_1, S_2, and S_3 be the sub-sets of SCPs in PC, respectively greater than, equal
   to, and less than the value $SIM(c, \Omega)$;

3) **case**

4) $: |S_1| > r$: **return** (SELECT (r, S_1))

5) $: |S_1| + |S_2| \geq r$: **return** (S_1 followed by S_2);

6)   : **else: return** (S_1 followed by S_2, and followed by SELECT $(r - |S_1| - |S_2|, S_3)$)

7) **endcase**

end

SELECT imitates the *order statistics* method and is an $O(s)$ expected computational time algorithm (s is the number of SCPs in PC).

10.6.3   The Time Complexity Analysis

The main cost of Algorithm 10.1 comprises two parts: getting top-k SCP in ψ (it is in Algorithm 10.1 that is a set of the input prevalent or closed SCPs' set PC is sorted by its participation index (PI) values) in order to ask for the user feedback and calculating the similarity $SIM(c, \Omega)$.

In getting the top-k SCPs, by using procedure SELECT, the cost is about $O(s)$ expected time or $O(s^2)$ in the worst case (s is the number of SCPs in PC), and the cost of getting top-k SCPs according to their PIs for the first time is $O(ks)$.

In the calculation of the similarity $SIM(c, \Omega)$, if using Eq. (10.9) to calculate the probabilistic values $p(c_i \mid PC_I)$ and $p(c_i \mid PC_{II})$, the cost is at most $O(m \times s)$ at each iteration (round), where m is the number of 2-size SCPs in F and $m = \frac{n(n-1)}{2}$ (n is the number of features in F). The cost of Eq. (10.9) is at most $O(m \times s)$, and once it has been calculated in the first round, only minor changes are needed in subsequent calculations. If using Eq. (10.10) or (10.11), we incur extra cost to calculate n_i and r_i at each round. The cost of Eq. (10.10) or (10.11) is about $O(m \times s + s^2)$ in the worst case at each round. Thus, the worst computational cost of calculating the similarity $SIM(c, \Omega)$ becomes $O(m \times s + s^2)$ at each round when using Eq. (10.10) or (10.11).

In summary, the cost of Algorithm 10.1 is at most $O(m \times s \times iter)$ when using Eq. (10.9), or $O((m \times s + s^2) \times iter)$ when using Eq. (10.10) or (10.11), where $iter$ is the number of feedback iterations, m is the number of 2-size SCPs in F, and s is the number of SCPs in PC.

10.7   Experimental Results

We conducted comprehensive experiments to evaluate the proposed approach from multiple perspectives on both real and synthetic data sets. All the algorithms are implemented in C# and they are all memory-based. All the experiments are performed on a Windows 10 system with 4.0GB memory and a 3.30GHz CPU.

10.7.1   Experimental Setting

We set up an experimental environment, called Simulator, to simulate user feedback. Its basis is that a user may consider an SCP interesting because he/she prefers some of the spatial features co-located in the pattern. Hence, we randomly generate some spatial features' combinations and deem them to be thought of as having some rules that can be used to select preference SCPs. A target co-location set which is used to simulate user prior knowledge can be generated based on these rules. Since our goal is to discover user-preferred SCPs interactively and rank the results, our accuracy measure favors high-rank SCPs in the results. If top-l (*learned_set*) be the top-l results reported by the ranking *learned* from the interactive feedback, and *target_set* be the results in the *target* SCPs constructed by our Simulator, then the accuracy measure is defined as follows:

$$\text{Accurary} = \frac{|top - l(learned\_set) \cap target\_set|}{l} \tag{10.12}$$

where l is given $t/5$, $2t/5$, $3t/5$, $4t/5$ or t ($t = |target\_set|$) in the experiments. It is obvious that the accuracy values in Eq. (10.12) are the percentages of the top-l ranked SCPs in the *target_set*.

10.7.2   The Simulator

The Simulator generates a set of *target* (user-preferred) SCPs, *target_set*, and simulates user feedback. It is based on the hypothesis that a user prefers a pattern because some preferred combinations of spatial features co-occur in this pattern. Thus, given a set of prevalent or closed SCPs, *PC*, and its spatial feature set F, the pseudo code of Simulator is shown below.

Procedure SIMULATOR(*PC, F*)

Input: A set of *n* spatial features, $F=\{f_1, f_2, ..., f_n\}$;
          A set of prevalent/closed SCPs, *PC*;

Output: User-preferred SCPs, *target_set*.

Method:
      // *Generating user-prefered rules (some features' combinations)*
1)   *maxRuleCount* = $\lfloor \sqrt{|F|} \rfloor$;

2)   *maxRuleSize* = $\lfloor |F|/2 \rfloor$;

3)   *RuleCount* = random(1, *maxRuleCount*);
4)   **For** (*i*=0; *i*<*RuleCount*; *i*++)
5)   *RuleSize* = random(2, *maxRuleSize*);
6)   *Rules*.add(generateRandomRule(*RuleSize*));
      // *Generating target_set (simulated preference co-location set)*
7)   *result*.add(*Rules*);
8)   **for (each** co-location *c* **in** *PC*)
9)   *countHash* = generateHashSet(*c, Rules*);
10) **for** (*i*=*RuleCount*; *i*>0; *i*--)
11)   *result*.add(getCo-locations(*countHash,i*))

12)   **If** (*result*.count $\geq |F|^2 / 2$) **then break**;

13) **return** *result*

The Simulator contains two main stages, explained below.

Stage 1 is to generate user-preferred rules. Lines 1 and 2 initialize the maximum values of the number and the size of rules. Then the features' combinations (rules) are generated in Lines 3–6 randomly.

Stage 2 is to select a simulated preference co-location set (*target_set*) based on the rules generated in Stage 1 from the set of prevalent or closed SCPs *PC*. At first, each rule is a user-preferred pattern which is added into *target_set* (Line 7). Then, the count values of SCPs in *PC* are computed and stored in a hash structure <count, list of co-locations> (Lines 8–9). The count of an SCP *c* is the number of rules contained in *c*, which is used to measure the similarity of the SCP *c* with the rules. Finally, the SCPs with larger counts are added to *target_set* (Lines 10–12). Line 12 is used to control the number of generated SCPs in *target_set*.

Figure 10.3 illustrates the process of Simulator. Suppose a closed co-location set *PC* is shown in the first (left) column in Fig. 10.3, and it randomly generates 3 (suppose *RuleCount* = 3) features' combinations (or rules), listed in the second column in Fig. 10.3. Then the three rules {A, B}, {C, E} and {B, C, F} will be added into *target_set*, and a hash table will be created to store SCPs and their count values. For example, {A, B, C, E} contains the 2 rules AB and CE. Finally, *target_set* can be generated based on the hash table.

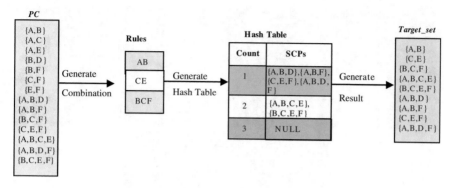

Fig. 10.3 An example of simulator

Table 10.1 A summary of the three real data sets

Name	N. of features	N. of instances	(Max, Min)	The distribution area of spatial instances (m²)
Real-1	32	335	(63, 3)	110,000 × 160,000
Real-2	20	377,834	(60,000, 347)	50,000 × 80,000
Real-3	15	501,046	(55,646, 8706)	110,000 × 160,000

(Max, Min): are respectively the maximum number and the minimum number of the feature's instances in the data sets

10.7.3 Accuracy Evaluation on Real Data Sets

Using the Simulator discussed above, our first task is to examine the accuracy of the results learned from the interactive feedback. We use three real data sets with different distributions in the experiments. A summary of the three real data sets is presented in Table 10.1. Real-1 is from the rare plant data of the Three Parallel Rivers of Yunnan Protected Areas whose instances form the zonal distribution shown in Fig. 10.4a, which has a small quantity of instances. Real-2 is a spatial distribution data set of urban elements whose instances' distribution is both even and dense as shown in Fig. 10.4b, and which also has a large quantity of features as well as instances. Real-3 is a vegetation distribution data set of the Three Parallel Rivers of Yunnan Protected Areas, which has the fewest features but the most instances of the three data sets, and its instance distribution presents various clusters as shown in Fig. 10.4c. The experimental settings for these real data sets can be found in Table 10.2, and each experiment was performed 10 times to obtain an average accuracy.

1. **On Real-1**

   The first experiment is run on the Real-1 data set. By setting the parameters shown in Table 10.2, we mine 3984 prevalent SCPs and 1259 closed SCPs. The

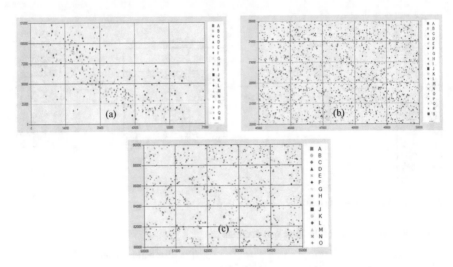

Fig. 10.4 Spatial distribution of the three real data sets ((**a**) part of the distribution of Real-1; (**b**) part of the distribution of Real-2; (**c**) part of the distribution of Real-3)

Table 10.2 Experimental parameters and their values in the experiments on real data sets

		Experiment figure		
Parameter	Definition	F.5/6/7a,d	F.5/6/7b,e	F.5/6/7c,f
min_prev	Prevalence threshold	0.1	0.1	0.1
iter	Number of iterations of feedback	*	10	10
k	Number of sample co-locations for feeding to user	10	*	10
l	Number to get top-*l*(*learned_set*) for accuracy measure in experiments	t (l *target_set*l)	t (l *target_set*l)	*
r	Number to get top-*r* co-locations under the values SIM	0.5* lPCl	0.5* lPCl	0.5* l PCl

*: Variable values

accuracy estimation of our algorithm with different parameters on Real-1 is shown in Fig. 10.5. In these figures F-9, F-10, and F-11 mean using Eqs. (10.9), (10.10) and (10.11) respectively, to calculate the probabilistic values $p(c_i \mid PC_I)$ and $p(c_i \mid PC_{II})$ and so calculate the similarity of an SCP c with $PC_{feedback}$, by Eq. (10.8). From Fig. 10.5 we can observe that both F-10 and F-11 have better accuracy than F-9 because F-10 and F-11 add adjusting factors in computing $p(c_i \mid PC_I)$ and $p(c_i \mid PC_{II})$. The accuracy of F-11 is a little better than F-10 because of the more reasonable probabilistic values. The accuracies estimated with closed SCPs are better than those with prevalent SCPs because closed SCPs are a form of compression of prevalent SCPs, which can aid the effective discovery of interesting SCPs. From Fig. 10.5(a and d) we find that, as *iter* increases, the accuracy increases, and this is because each iteration supplies

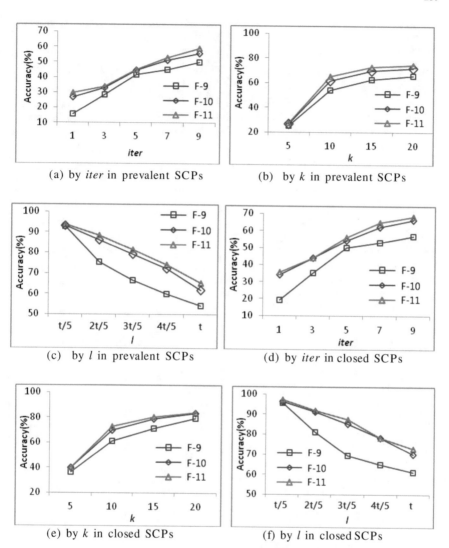

Fig. 10.5   Accuracy evaluation on Real-1

new samples to the user, and the new feedback from the user updates the SIM values of SCPs in *PC*, bringing them closer and closer to the user's real preference. Figure 10.5(b and e) show that a larger k causes a higher accuracy because more samples can be fed to the user per iteration. Figure 10.5(c and f) demonstrate that a smaller l can reach higher accuracy because the SCPs in the front of *target_set* have been already chosen by the user.

2. *On Real-2*

In this subsection, we examine the learned accuracy on the Real-2 dataset. With the settings shown in Table 10.2, 298,845 prevalent SCPs and 247,698

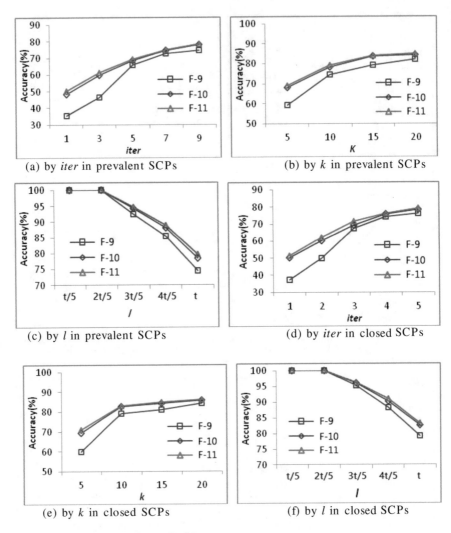

Fig. 10.6 Accuracy evaluation on Real-2

closed SCPs are discovered, and the accuracy estimation of our algorithms with different parameters on Real-2 is shown in Fig. 10.6. The main observations are similar to Real-1, although the accuracy estimated for Real-2 is higher than that for Real-1 with the same parameter values, but the accuracy gap between prevalent SCPs and closed SCPs is not as obvious as Real-1, because the compression of Real-2's closed SCPs is much lower than that of Real-1, which makes a smaller gap between them. Note that in Fig. 10.6(c and f) when $l \leq 2\ t/5$, the accuracy reaches as high as 100%, meaning that the top 40% of learned SCPs on Real-2 are fully preferred by the user.

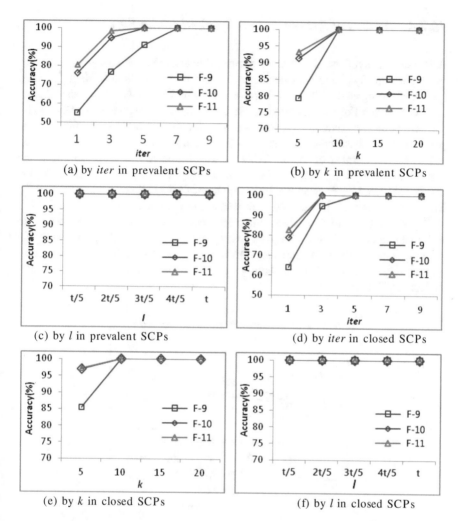

Fig. 10.7   Accuracy evaluation on Real-3

3. *On Real-3*

From the Real-3 data set, 568 prevalent SCPs and 196 closed SCPs are discovered. The accuracy estimation on Real-3 is shown in Fig. 10.7. Figure 10.7 (a and d) show that the accuracy can reach 100% within a few rounds; even in Fig. 10.7b, only 5 rounds are required to reach 100% accuracy. The reason for the high accuracy in Real-3 is that there are as few as 15 features in it, and the smaller number of features makes it easier to find the combinations preferred by a user. The cluster distribution means closed SCPs have better compression, in turn making the accuracy with closed SCPs much higher than for prevalent SCPs with the same parameter settings. Thus, in Real-3, the probabilistic model is able to return the ideal preference SCPs according to the user's feedback and the chapter's objectives have been largely achieved for this real data set.

10.7.4 *Accuracy Evaluation on Synthetic Data Sets*

In this section, synthetic data sets are generated to test the accuracy and efficiency of our algorithm. Synthetic data sets are generated by using a spatial data generator similar to Huang et al. (2004), where the average number of instances of each feature is 10,000 with a Poisson distribution, the neighborhood distance is 10,000, and all the instances are randomly located within a frame size 500000 * 500000. The prevalence threshold *min_prev* is set as 0.1, the number of iterations of feedback *iter* as 10, the number of sample SCPs for user feedback k is set as 15 and r (the number to get top-r SCPs under the values $SIM(c, PC_{feedback})$) is set as half of the number of closed SCPs generated by the synthetic data set. Each experiment uses the Simulator introduced in Sect. 10.7.2 to perform the accuracy test.

Figure 10.8 shows the algorithm's accuracy and efficiency with respect to different numbers of features. In order to get a more accurate result, each experiment with the same number of features is performed 10 times to get the average accuracy and running time. Note that Simulator generates a different *target_set* (a set of user-preferred SCPs) each time.

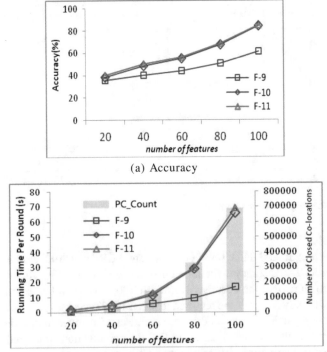

(a) Accuracy

(b) Running time of F-9, F-10 and F-11 per round and the number of closed SCPs (PC_Count)

Fig. 10.8 Evaluations on synthetic data sets with different number of features

We observe the following results:

1. As the number of features increases and the data set gets denser, Fig. 10.8a shows that the accuracy in a dense data set is higher than that in a sparse data set. This is because dense data sets can generate longer-size SCPs which have a greater chance of containing the preferred combination of features (rules), which means that preferred SCPs can be selected more easily in each round, further improving the accuracy of our algorithm.

2. As the number of features increases, F-10 and F-11 show much better accuracy than F-9 in Fig. 10.8a, and the gap inaccuracy between F-10/F-11 and F-9 also increases. This is because the adjusting factors added in F-10 and F-11 play a bigger role as the data set gets bigger. Note that in this experiment there are about 1,000,000 spatial instances with 100 features.

3. Figure 10.8b shows the average running time of F-9, F-10 and F-11 per round and the number of closed SCPs (PC_Count). It can be seen that F-9 has a much higher efficiency than either F-10 or F-11. When the number of closed SCPs reaches almost 700,000, F-9 only takes less than 20 s, and this is because F-9 only needs to calculate n_i, which can be updated based on the value from the last round. For example, if $n(AB) = 14$, meaning that there are 14 candidates containing AB, if ABC is selected as a preferred SCP, $n(AB)$ should be updated to 13. F-10 and F-11 calculate not only n_i but also r_i, although r_i cannot be updated as can n_i. In each round the top-r SCPs based on SIM values may change greatly, meaning that r_i has to be recalculated in each round, thus increasing the running time. However, even with 100 features (1,000,000 spatial instances and almost 700,000 closed co-locations), the running time per round is only around 70 s.

Overall, although F-10 and F-11 have better accuracies than F-9, they need more running time. Taking effectiveness and efficiency into consideration, the three formulas have their advantages in different situations. If a user cannot wait to find the preferred SCPs, she/he can choose to use the F-9 formula which has high efficiency and also has a useful result. If a user wants a more precise result, she/he can use F-10 or F-11.

10.7.5 Sample Co-location Selection

In this subsection, we test the effectiveness of various learning strategies to select sample co-locations for feedback. The Real-2 data set is used to perform the evaluation because it has the most features, and so well demonstrates the learning effectiveness of the various strategies.

The selection strategy proposed and used so far in this paper is that, in the first round, the samples are selected based only on PI, and in the following rounds, the samples are selected based on the subjective preference order (i.e., the order of the similarity $SIM(c, PC_{feedback})$ between a co-location pattern c in PC and the set $PC_{feedback}$ of the user feedback). We denote this strategy as St_3.

Fig. 10.9 Effect of sample
co-locations selection

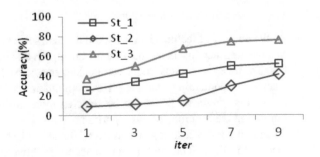

We have further designed two sample selection strategies to compare them with the sample selection strategy St-3:

1. The strategy denoted as St_1 is to select sample co-locations by using their participation index PI values and user feedback so that in the first round the samples are selected only based on PI, and in the following rounds the co-locations containing feedback and having higher PI are selected first.
2. Strategy (St_2) uses long co-locations first so that, in the first round, the samples are selected only based on the size of co-locations, and in the following rounds those co-locations containing feedback and having longer size are selected first. We denote this strategy as St_2.

The setting of this experiment is the same as that used to get Fig. 10.6d, using Eq. (10.9) and with closed SCPs generated from the Real-2 data set. Each experiment was performed ten times to get the average accuracy. Figure 10.9 shows that sample selection strategy has an important effect on the accuracy, and that the sample selection strategy St_3, as initially proposed in this chapter, has the highest accuracy.

10.8   Chapter Summary

Existing SCP mining methods generally produce many prevalent SCPs of which only a small proportion are of real interest to a user. In this chapter, we have developed a framework of interactive post-mining of SCPs which will help a user effectively discover those prevalent SCPs which are of particular interest to the user. In the framework, we introduce a probabilistic model to measure the user's subjective interest in an SCP. The performance of the proposed approach is tested on various data sets, showing that the approach is effective in discovering user-preferred SCPs. This gives the user useful information containing subjective preferences, but the user still needs to assess the relative importance of the returned SCPs.

Problems such as SCPs' compression, summary, selection, and ordering essentially measure the similarity between SCPs and so, in the next and last chapter of this book, we will develop and investigate similarity metrics between any two SCPs.

Chapter 11
Vector-Degree: A General Similarity Measure for Co-location Patterns

11.1 Introduction

Similarity measures between spatial co-location patterns (SCPs) are used to solve problems such as pattern compression, pattern summarization, pattern selection, and pattern ordering. A lot of recent research has produced various similarity measures, all providing a more concise set of SCPs. Unfortunately, these measures suffer from various weaknesses; e.g., some measures can only calculate the similarity between super-patterns and sub-patterns, while others require additional domain knowledge. In this chapter, we develop a general similarity measure for any two SCPs:

1. We propose a new representation model of SCPs based on maximal cliques in spatial data sets, ensuring that the spatial information about the instances of the pattern can be saved without loss.
2. We provide two materializing methods for the proposed representation model, which we call the 0–1 vector and the key-value vector. We also discuss the characteristics of our materialization methods and the complexity of the materialization process.
3. Based on the two materialization methods, we propose a general similarity measure that can calculate the similarity degree of any two SCPs without adding extra domain information. We analytically prove our similarity is reasonable and versatile, by comparing it with existing similarity measures.
4. Finally, the similarity is used to group SCPs by a hierarchical clustering algorithm. The experimental results on both synthetic and real-world data sets show the effectiveness and efficiency of these methods.

From Wu P., Wang L.*, and Zhou M.: Vector-Degree: A General Similarity Measure for Co-Location Patterns. In: Proc. of *the 2019 IEEE International Conference on Big Knowledge (ICBK 2019),* IEEE Press, Beijing, China, pp. 281–288 (2019).

© The Author(s), under exclusive license to Springer Nature Singapore Pte Ltd. 2022
L. Wang et al., *Preference-based Spatial Co-location Pattern Mining*, Big Data
Management, https://doi.org/10.1007/978-981-16-7566-9_11

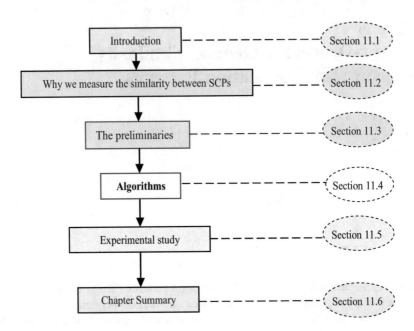

Fig. 11.1 The organization of the chapter

Figure 11.1 presents the organization of this chapter. Section 11.2 discusses why we measure the similarity between two SCPs. We use a toy example to explain the precise problem to be solved and present the preliminaries for solving the problem in Sect. 11.3. Section 11.4 details the implementation. The experimental results and analysis are presented in Sect. 11.5, and Sect. 11.6 summarizes the chapter.

11.2 Why We Measure the Similarity Between SCPs

Spatial co-location pattern (SCP) mining has a wide range of applications such as smart city planning (Yao et al., 2017), environmental criminology (Yue et al., 2017), public health (Li et al., 2016), location-based services (Yu, 2016), and so on. Traditional mining frameworks, however, produce too many SCPs, so it makes sense to reduce the number of SCPs provided to users. Besides the methods described in this book numerous others have worked on this issue with different techniques including pattern compression (Yoo & Bow, 2012; Silvestri et al., 2015; Bao & Wang, 2017; Wang et al., 2018a, 2018b), pattern ordering (Yuan et al., 2016), pattern summarization (Liu et al., 2015; Yang et al., 2018a), and so on. All these prior works have in common that a similarity measure between SCPs is considered one of the fundamental problems. Yoo and Bow (2011a) proposed a covered relationship to measure the similarity between a super-pattern and its sub-pattern whereby if a sub-pattern is covered by its super-pattern, the two patterns are deemed

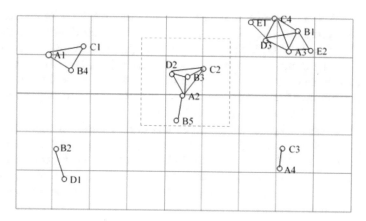

Fig. 11.2 A toy example

similar. Two looser relationships are proposed in Wang et al. (2018b) and Silvestri et al. (2015), respectively, where they define the similarity based only on information about the participation index (a definition of participation index is provided in Sect. 11.3). Wang et al. (2018a) first proposed a semantic distance measure to evaluate the strength of dissimilarity between SCPs, and presented a δ-covered relationship between two SCPs, where δ a coefficient that controls how loose is the covered relationship. Feature distance was defined in Liu et al. (2015), calculating the distance between SCPs having the same features. Bao and Wang (2017) proposed a similarity measure based on ontology information. An interactive post-mining method was presented which reduced mining results by incorporating user-preferred information, detailed in Wang et al. (2018c). Unfortunately, all these similarity measures suffer from various weaknesses, the principal ones being:

1. *Poor generality.* Existing similarity measures only consider the relationship between two specific SCPs. For example, if P_α, P_β are two SCPs, and if $P_\alpha \not\subset P_\beta$ and $P_\beta \not\subset P_\alpha$, then the covered relation between P_α and P_β cannot be calculated (Yoo & Bow, 2011a). For this similarity measure, if the feature distance between P_α and P_β is 1, then the similarity is 0 when $P_\alpha \cap P_\beta = \varnothing$. However, if instances of P_α and P_β often appear in the same cluster, can we be sure there really no relationship between P_α and P_β?

2. *Lack of quantitative analysis.* Some measures can only answer whether P_α has a relationship with P_β, but not the degree of relevance of P_α to P_β. For instance, we can only answer whether P_α possesses a δ-covered relationship with P_β in Wang et al. (2018a), not the strength of that relationship.

Thus, although previous works have done a good job of condensing the representation of SCPs, none of the developed methods quantitatively measure the similarity between any two SCPs.

In the context of spatial data, a spatial occurrence (a row instance) of an SCP is essentially a clique. Consider the example data set in Fig. 11.2, where $P_\alpha = \{A, B,$

C}, $P_\beta = \{$B, C, D$\}$ are two SCPs. The row instance {A3, B1, C4} carries all the features in P_α corresponding to an occurrence of P_α (for detailed definitions see Sect. 11.3), while {B1, C4, D3} is a row instance of P_β, and both {A3, B1, C4} and {B1, C4, D3} belong to the same maximal clique {A3, B1, C4, D3}. This provides us with the evidence of that there exists a similarity relationship between P_α and P_β. Intuitively, the more there are row instances of SCPs belonging to the same maximal cliques, the more similar we expect the SCPs to be.

As the maximal clique is the minimum unit of SCP information, we have now developed a novel lossless representation, the maximal clique vector, to efficiently represent the spatial information of an SCP. The correctness and the completeness of a maximal clique vector representation have been analyzed. An advantage of this development is that a vector space composed of multiple vectors can act as the input to the post-mining of SCPs.

The core work contained in a maximal clique vector representation will be the enumeration of maximal cliques and the generation of vectors. To effectively build a representational model, an ordered maximal clique enumeration method and two materializations of the representation model have been developed. Maximal clique enumeration is a fundamental problem in graph databases and there is recent work that investigates this problem in the context of spatial databases (for instance, Bao & Wang, 2019; Zhang et al., 2019; Al-Naymat, 2008). Bao and Wang (2019) proposed two efficient schemas, an instances-driven schema and a neighborhood-driven schema, both using tree structures to find cliques. An efficient algorithm, Grid-Clique, was proposed by Al-Naymat (2008) to generate maximal cliques from Sloan Digital Sky Survey data. Zhang et al. (2019) proved, though, that we may have $2^{\lfloor \frac{m}{2} \rfloor}$ maximal spatial cliques for m instances, and hence there is no polynomial time solution for this problem in the worst case. Learning from this previous work we have developed a depth-first method to mine order maximal cliques based on grid structures in the context of star neighborhood relationships. Its scalability has been tested on several synthetic datasets, and is presented in Sect. 11.5.

11.3 Preliminaries

11.3.1 *Spatial Co-location Pattern (SCP)*

In a spatial dataset D, different kinds of real objects can be regarded as features, and the occurrence of a feature is deemed an instance. Let F be a set of n features, and I be a collection of instances of F. I arranged in lexicographic order. R is a neighbor relationship over I, such that two instances, i and i' are neighbors, that is, $R(i, i')$, if the Euclidean distance between them is not greater than a distance threshold given by the user. An SCP is a subset of set F.

A clique is a set of instances in which any two instances satisfy R. A maximal clique is a clique all of whose supersets are not a clique. A row instance of an SCP P_α

is a clique under R that contains the instance of all features in P_α, and the row instance RI_α represents a common occurrence of feature instances in P_α. In addition, the set of row instances of P_α is called table instance TI_α of P_α, that is, $RI_\alpha \in TI_\alpha$.

Definition 11.1 Let f be a feature, P_α be an SCP, and $f \in P_\alpha$. The **participation ratio** for f in P_α is the fraction of instances of f participating in TI_α, that is:

$$PR(f, \alpha) = \frac{\text{Number of distinct instances of } f \text{ in } TI_\alpha}{\text{Number of instances of } f} \tag{11.1}$$

The participation index of P_α is the minimum participation ratio among all features f in P_α, i.e., $PI(\alpha) = \min_{f \in P_\alpha}\{PR(f, \alpha)\}$.

Traditional mining frameworks usually employ participation indexes to compute the prevalence of SCPs. An SCP is prevalent if its participation index is no less than a given PI threshold. The collection of prevalent SCPs is denoted as $\Sigma = \{P_\alpha, P_\beta, P_\gamma, \ldots\}$.

11.3.2 A Toy Example

Figure 11.2 shows 5 features $F = \{A, B, C, D, E\}$ and several instances which are marked as small circles, and denoted by the feature type and a numeric id value, e.g., A1. Edges in Fig. 11.2 are generated by calculating the distance between instances, and if two instances satisfy the neighbor relationship, an edge will be created. A clique is a set having instances that are close to each other, such as $\{B3, C2, D2\}$. However, $\{B3, C2, D2\}$ is not a maximal clique because it has a superset $\{A2, B3, C2, D2\}$ that is a clique.

Note that the spatial neighbor relationship R can be usefully materialized as star neighborhood partition model (Yoo & Shekhar, 2006), and the star neighbors of an instance i, denoted as $i.\mathbf{stars} = \{i' | i < i' \text{ AND } R(i, i')\}$ (see Table 11.1).

Instance	Star neighbors	Instance	Star neighbors
A1	B4, C1	B5	
A2	B3, B5, C2, D2	C1	
A3	B1, C4, D3, E2	C2	D2
A4	C3	C3	
B1	C4, D3, E2	C4	D3, E1
B2	D1	D1	
B3	C2, D2	D2	
B4	C1	D3	E1

Table 11.1 Star Neighborhood

11.3.3   Problem Statement

The core problem of grouping SCPs meaningfully is how to quantify the similarity of the various SCPs. Any similarity measure should take the spatial information into count, preferably quantitatively. Once the similarity can be measured, the SCPs grouping problem can be solved by a clustering algorithm. This chapter develops a new measure, vector-degree, based on the observation that the spatial information of an SCP can be represented by maximal cliques of features in the SCPs.

11.4   The Method

In this section, the new representation of SCPs is presented, and the similarity measure between SCPs is introduced, leading to an improved clustering algorithm to meaningfully group SCPs.

11.4.1   Maximal Cliques Enumeration Algorithm

Following the work in Wang et al. (2009b), we develop a method, GenClique, to mine ordered maximal cliques based on the star neighbor concept. The GenClique algorithm is divided into two parts: the generation of ordered cliques (Algorithm 11.2) and the filtering of ordered cliques (Line 4 in Algorithm 11.1). Observation 1 (below) provides the means of generating the ordered cliques. Two filtering strategies are provided in Verification 1 and Verification 2.

Definition 11.2 Let i_CL be an ordered clique in which the first instance is i, and all ordered cliques with their first instance i are denoted as i_CLs.

For example, in Fig. 11.2, clique {A2, B3, C2, D2} is a A2_CL because the first instance in the clique is A2.

Observation 1 Let i be any instance of an ordered clique, then the instances to the right of i in the ordered clique form a subset of the star neighbors of i.

For example, in Fig. 11.2, the instance set to the right of B3 in clique {A2, B3, C2, D2} is {C2, D2}, and {C2, D2} is a subset of the star neighbors of B3, while {B3, C2, D2} is a subset of the star neighbors of A2. In the other word, the clique is the result of A2.stars ∩ B3.stars ∩ C2.stars ∩ D2.stars, where A2.stars ∩ B3.stars is essentially equal to the intersection of instances that ranked to the right of B3 in A2. stars and B3.stars. Therefore, a clique can be obtained by constantly finding the intersection of star neighbors. The generating process of A2_CLs, which contains five cliques, is explained in Fig. 11.3, where the order in which the cliques are produced is indicated by numbers.

Algorithm 11.1: GenClique(*Stars*, *I*)

Input: *Stars*: star neighbors, *I*: the instance set
Output: all maximal cliques
Variables: *clique* : an order clique started with *i*, that is, *i*_CL
i.stars: the star neighborhood of instance *i*
Method:
(1) **for** all instance *i* in *I*
(2) { *clique*.Add(*i*);   //trying to extend *i* to find *i*_CLs
(3) GenOneClique (*i*, *clique*, Stars, *i*.stars);
(4) Filtering( );}

To generate A2_CLs, we search the star neighbors of A2 at the beginning, and inspect the intersection level by level within a depth-first search until the intersection is null. Then we search back to the next instance in the last intersection until all star-neighborhood instances are checked. Algorithms 11.1 and 11.2 show the pseudocodes.

Taking Fig. 11.3 as an example, we call the function GenOneClique (A2, *clique*, Stars, A2.stars) in Line 3 of Algorithm 11.1 to generate A2_CLs. To work through this function, let i' be an instance of the A2.stars, e.g., B2, i'. rights be the set of instances that are on the right side of i' in the A2.stars, e.g., {B5, C2, D2}, and then i'.stars ∩ i'. rights = {C2, D2} is the input for the next layer of search. With a depth-first search, take an instance of the intersection, e.g., D2 and continue the above

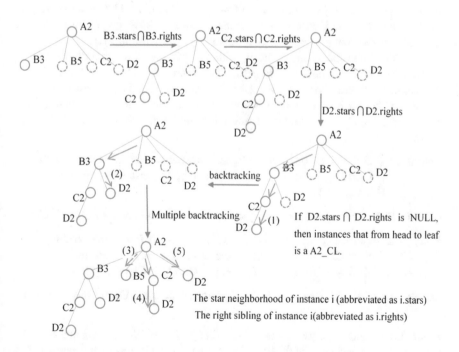

Fig. 11.3 The process of generating A2_CLs

search until the intersection is empty, so getting a clique, e.g., {A2, B3, D2}. An orderly search of all intersections produces A2_CLs.

Algorithm 11.2: GenOneClique (*i*, *clique*, *Stars*, *Q*)

Input: *i*: an instance. *clique*: an order clique started with *i*. *Stars*: star neighbors, *Q*
The intersection set of instances

Output: *i*_CLs

Variables: *i*′.rights : the set of instances that are on the right side of *i*′ in the *Q*

NQ: *Q*∩*i*′.rights

Method:

(1) **for** all instance *i*′ in *Q*

(2) { *clique*.Add(*i*′);

(3) *NQ* = *i*′.stars ∩ *i*′.rights

(4) **if** *NQ*== ∅ **then** output(*clique*); //found a *i* CL

(5) **else** GenOneClique(*i*, *clique*, *Stars*, *NQ*);
    //recursive backtracking

(6) *clique*.Remove(*i*′);}

We need to be clear about the **order** of the clusters generated by Algorithm 11.1. Let cl_1, cl_2 be two cliques generated by Algorithm 11.1. If $cl_1 \subset cl_2$, then cl_2 was searched before cl_1 (for a detailed proof, see Lemmas 11.1 and 11.2 below). For example, {A2, C2, D2} was searched before {A2, D2} in Fig. 11.3. Alternatively, if $cl_1 \not\subset cl_2$ and $cl_2 \not\subset cl_1$, then we search for these cliques in lexicographic order. We let $cl_1 <_O cl_2$ express that cl_1 was searched before cl_2 by Algorithm 11.1.

In the first three statements of the algorithm GenClique, through multiple calls of the GenOneClique method, we can get *i*_CLs, where $i \in I$. However, not all *i*_CLs are maximal cliques. For example, {A2, B3, D2} in Fig. 11.3 is not a maximal clique. To check whether a clique is maximal, a filtering function is called in Step 4 of Algorithm 11.1, the function being based on Verifications 1 and 2 as given below.

Definition 11.3 Let **FTs**$_i$ be a set of cliques whose first instance is before *i*, that is, $FTs_i = \{i' \_ CLs| i' < i\}$. In addition, let $i + 1$ be the instance following *i*, then $FTs_{i+1} = FTs_i \cup i \_ CLs$.

Lemma 11.1 Any super set of a clique *i*_CL is included in either FTs$_i$ or *i*_CLs.

Proof The super set of an *i*_CL is $i \_ CL \cup i' \_ CL$. If $i = i'$, then the super set $(i \_ CL \cup i' \_ CL) \in i \_ CLs$. Otherwise if $i' < i$, then the super set $(i \_ CL \cup i' \_ CL) \in FTs_i$, or if $i < i'$, then $(i \_ CL \cup i' \_ CL) \in i \_ CLs$. □

Lemma 11.2 Any super set of *i*_CL is produced before *i*_CL by the GenClique method.

Proof Let cl_1 and cl_2 be two cliques, $cl_1, cl_2 \in i \_ CLs$ and $cl_1 \subset cl_2$. Let i' and i'' be the first different instances of the two cliques, then i'' must be less than i', because $i' <$

Fig. 11.4 A full search tree

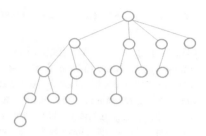

i''. In cl_2, instances that follow i'' (including i'') are a $i''\_CL = i''$. stars $\cap\, i''$. rights, that is, $i' \notin i''\_CL$ when $i' < i''$. When $i'' < i'$, according to Line 1 of Algorithm 11.2, cl_2 is produced before cl_1. On the other hand, Line 1 of Algorithm 11.1 guarantees that all the cliques in FTs_i are searched before i_CLs. Combined with Lemma 11.1, Lemma 11.2 is thus proved. $\square$

Verification 1 According to Lemma 11.2, all supersets of an i_CL are produced before i_CL by the GenClique method. In other words, we check if all pre-searched cliques before i_CL are not supersets of i_CL. If not, i_CL is a maximal clique.

Verification 2 To inspect whether a clique is a maximal clique, we divide the space into a grid structure and place each clique into its particular grid cell. The grid cell size is $d \times d$, where d is a distance threshold given by the user. The superset of a clique can then only exist in the content of the nine neighbor cells, as Fig. 11.2 depicts, and the number of checked cliques is cut down. The efficiency of the process will depend on the density of the grid.

The filtering function calls these two verifications and removes all non-maximal cliques in i_CLs, where $i \in I$. At last, we get all our verified maximal cliques, now denoted $VE(i\_CLs)$. Similarly, FTs_i is called $VE(FTs_i)$ after verification. The verification process does not change the order in which cliques are generated, so Lemma 11.2 is still valid after any verification.

Algorithm complexity analysis. Figure 11.4 generates the worst case of search tree, a full tree, for an instance containing 4 star neighbors. The numbers of nodes of the four sub-trees from right to left in the search tree are 2^0, 2^1, 2^2 and 2^3, respectively. Therefore, in the worst case, the instance containing 4 star neighbors has a search space of $2^4 - 1$. This indicates that the time complexity of the algorithm is related to the number of star neighbors in each instance. Assuming that the data is divided into G grids according to the distance threshold in Fig. 11.2, each grid averages $\lceil m/G \rceil$ instances, so the number of star neighbors of one instance will not exceed $9 \times \lceil m/G \rceil$. Thus the time complexity is $O(2^{9 \times \lceil m/G \rceil})$. The verification function of Line 4 in Algorithm 11.1 verifies whether the generated clique is a maximal clique. Assuming that each instance has T maximal cliques, its worst case verification is of $9 \times \lceil m/G \rceil \times T$ maximal cliques and its complexity will not exceed $O(9 \times \lceil m/G \rceil \times T \times L)$, where L is the average size of the maximal cliques.

11.4.2   A Representation Model of SCPs

Conforming to the definition of row instances, an occurrence of an SCP P_α is mapped to a clique in spatial data sets. Immediately we can see that the more row instances of SCPs that belong to the same clique, the more similar the SCPs are. A maximal clique is a clique that does not belong to any other clique by the definition of maximal cliques and we have now developed a new representation of SCPs based on maximal cliques. Observation 2 analyzes the claim that this representation, based on maximal cliques, is a lossless representation, while Lemma 11.3 discusses the characteristics of the representation.

Observation 2 Any row instance RI_α of an SCP P_α in a spatial data set D must be contained in a maximal clique of D.

Suppose that there exists a row instance RI_α not contained in any maximal clique, that is, $RI_\alpha \not\subseteq cl_x$, $1 \leq x \leq h$, where h is the number of maximal cliques in D produced by Algorithm GenClique. According to the definition of row instances, RI_α is a clique. That is, the clique is not contained in any maximal clique, which is a false proposition. By implication, any row instance is contained in a maximal clique. On the basis of Observation 2, then a maximal clique vector representation is a lossless representation that carries all the instance information of its SCPs.

Lemma 11.3 Let il be the last instance of the first feature in SCP P_α, then any maximal clique that contains any row instance of P_α can only appear in VE(il_CLs) $\cup$VE(FTs$_{il}$).

Proof Let if be the first instance of the first feature in SCP P_α. Then any row instance of P_α should be a i_CL, where $if \leq i \leq il$. Let i' _ CL be any clique that contains i_CL, and, by Lemma 11.1, i' _ CL is included in either FTs$_i$ or i_CLs. Also $i' \leq i$. If i' _ CL is a maximal clique, then it is included in VE(FTs$_i$)$\cup$VE(i_CLs). Otherwise, any clique that contains i' _ CL is included in either FTs$_{i'}$ or i' _ CLs. Because $i' \leq i$, both FTs$_{i'} \subseteq$ FTs$_i$ and i' _ CLs $\subseteq$ FTs$_i$ are true. Therefore, any clique that contains i' _ CL is included in either FTs$_i$ or i_CLs. That is, any maximal clique that contains i' _ CL is included in VE(FTs$_i$) $\cup$ VE(i_CLs). So, any maximal clique that contains i_CL is also included in VE(FTs$_i$) $\cup$ VE(i_CLs) because $if \leq i \leq il$, FTs$_i \subseteq$ FTs$_{il}$, and i _ CLs $\subseteq$ FTs$_{il}$ is true. Hence, any maximal clique that contains any row instance of P_α can only appear in VE(il_CLs) $\cup$ VE(FTs$_{il}$), and Lemma 11.3 is proved.

Two materializations of the representation of the 0–1 maximal clique vector and the key-value maximal clique vector, are developed as follows.

0–1 maximal clique vector. According to Observation 2, if we list all of the maximal cliques of D, then for each row instance of a SCP P_α, we can find a maximal clique that contains the row instance. Therefore, let $v(\alpha)$ be the 0–1 maximal clique vector of P_α, $v(\alpha) \in \mathfrak{R}^h$ where h denotes the number of maximal cliques in D:

$$v(\alpha) = < \mu(cl_1, \alpha), \mu(cl_2, \alpha), \ldots, \mu(cl_h, \alpha) > \tag{11.2}$$

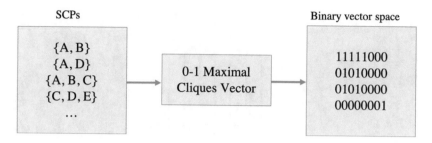

Fig. 11.5 Binary vector space

Table 11.2 All maximal cliques in Fig. 11.2

	Maximal cliques
A1_CLs	A1, B4, C1
A2_CLs	A2, B3, C2, D2/A2, B5
A3_CLs	A3, B1, C4, D3/A3, B1, E2
A4_CLs	A4, C5
B2_CLs	B2, D1
C4_CLs	C4, D3, E1

$$\mu(cl_i, \alpha) = \begin{cases} 1, & \exists RI_\alpha \in TI_\alpha \text{ AND } RI_\alpha \subseteq cl_x \\ 0, & \text{otherwise} \end{cases} \tag{11.3}$$

If cl_x is a maximal clique, where $x = 1, 2, \ldots, h$ and RI_α is a row instance of P_α and TI_α is the table instance of P_α, then $\mu(cl_x, \alpha) = 1$ if there are P_α occurrences in the maximal clique cl_x.

A vector space, composed of multiple vectors corresponding to SCPs $\Sigma = \{P_\alpha, P_\beta, P_\gamma, \ldots\}$, can act as input to the post-mining of SCPs. The process is shown in Fig. 11.5.

Observation 3 By Lemma 11.3, let $|v_0(\alpha)|$ be the number of 0 s (zeroes) in the 0–1 maximal clique vector of P_α, and then:

$$|v_0(\alpha)| \geq h - |\text{VE}(il\_\text{CLs})| - |\text{VE}(\text{FTs}_{il})| = h - |\text{VE}(\text{FTs}_{il+1})|$$

Let $|v_1(\alpha)|$ be the number of 1 in the 0–1 vector of P_α, and then $|v_1(\alpha)| \leq |\text{VE}(\text{FTs}_{il+1})|$.

Eight maximal cliques are shown in Table 11.2 and the 0–1 maximal clique vector is represented by a vector of magnitude 8. Table 11.3 lists five of the SCPs as examples where each column corresponds to a maximal clique, and each row is the 0–1 maximal clique vector of an SCP.

Key-value maximal clique vector. According to Observation 3, it can be seen that a 0–1 vector contains a lot of zeroes and the calculations need to traverse the whole vector. Therefore, a new materialization, a key-value maximal clique vector,

Table 11.3 Binary clique vector

	A1_CLs	A2_CLs		A3_CLs		A4_CLs	B2_CLs	C4_CLs
	A1B4C1	A2B3C2D2	A2B5	A3B1C4D3	A3B1E2	A4C5	B2D1	C4D3E1
{A,B}	1	1	1	1	1	1	0	0
{A,D}	0	1	0	1	0	0	0	0
{A,B,D}	0	1	0	1	0	0	0	0
{C,D,E}	0	0	0	0	0	0	0	0
{A,B,C,D}	0	1	0	1	0	0	0	0

has been developed to improve the retrieval efficiency. Let $\widetilde{v}(\alpha)$ be the key-value maximal clique vector of P_α:

$$\widetilde{v}(\alpha) =<< i,\widetilde{v}(i,\alpha) > , \; < i',\widetilde{v}(i',\alpha) > , \; \ldots, \; < i'',\widetilde{v}(i'',\alpha) >> \qquad (11.4)$$

where $\widetilde{v}(\alpha)$ is composed of several key-value pairs, let $< i,\widetilde{v}(i,\alpha) >$ be a key-value pair in $\widetilde{v}(\alpha)$, then the key in the pair is the instance i, $i \in I$, and the value $\widetilde{v}(i,\alpha)$ is the set of numeric ids that correspond to the ordered maximal clique containing a row instance of P_α, that is, $\widetilde{v}(i,\alpha) = \{x | \exists RI_\alpha \in TI_\alpha \text{ AND } RI_\alpha \subseteq cl_x, cl_x \in \text{VE}(i\_\text{CLs})\}$. Key-value pairs are constructed only when $\widetilde{v}(i,\alpha) \neq \varnothing$.

Taking $P_\alpha = \{A, B\}$ in Table 11.3 for example, the key-value maximal clique vector $\widetilde{v}(\alpha) = << A1,\widetilde{v}(A1,\alpha) > , \; < A2,\widetilde{v}(A2,\alpha) > , \; < A3,\widetilde{v}(A3,\alpha) >> = << A1, \{1\} > , < A2, \{2,3\} > , < A3, \{4,5\} > >$.

Where $<A2, \{2,3\}>$ shows that there are two maximal cliques, it is clear that cl_2, $cl_3 \in \text{VE}(A2\_\text{CLs})$ and cl_2, cl_3 contain row instances of P_α.

By Lemma 11.3, let il be the last instance of the first feature in the co-location pattern P_α, and i be the instance where $il<_o i$, then none of the row instances of P_α will be contained in i_CLs. The generation process for the key-value maximal cliques vector of an SCP P_α is shown in Algorithm 11.3.

The algorithm takes the entire collection of maximal cliques and an SCP as input. The algorithm checks the input and then works as follows. First, Line 4 is a pruning step based on Lemma 11.3. Then, Line 5 confirms whether the maximal clique contains a row instance of P_α. If the maximal clique $\text{VE}(i\_\text{CL})$ contains any row instance of P_α, we add 1 to the count value (Line 6). If the key instance i is not included in Dic (Line 7), the key-value pair is added, and then the maximal clique is added to the set value $list_i$ corresponding to the key i.

Algorithm 11.3: Genvector (P_α ,CLs)

Input: P_α : a SCP. *CLs*: all VE(i_CLs), where $i \in I$

Output: *Dic*: key-value $<i, list_i >$ maximal cliques vector of P_α

Count: number of key-value pairs of P_α

$list_i$: the set value corresponding to the key i in *Dic*.

Variables: il: the last instance of the first feature in P_α

Method:

```
count=0;
(1) for all maximal cliques VE(i_CL) in CLs
(2) {//calculate <i, listᵢ> pair
(3) if  il<ₒ i  then break; // pruning by Lemma 11.3
(4) if VE(i_CL).Contain( Pₐ ) then
(5)      count++;
(6)      if !Dic.ContainKey(i) then
(7)           Dic.Create(i, listᵢ)// The initial value of listᵢ is null
(8)      Dic[i].Add(i_CL);}
```

It is worth noting that in order to improve efficiency, in Line 5, we do not need to check row instances of P_α, provided we confirm that all the features of P_α in the maximal clique VE($i\_$CL) are included. That is, if the set of features of VE($i\_$CL) contains the set of features of P_α, the maximal clique VE($i\_$CL) contains row instances of P_α, and vice versa. This means the computational time spent is reduced to $O(\|P_\alpha\|)$, where $|P_\alpha|$ is the length of the pattern P_α.

Time complexity analysis of Algorithm 11.3: With a hash structure, the time complexity of the three operations on Lines 7, 8, and 9 is $O(1)$, and the number of executions for the entire loop is $O(|$VE($il\_$CLs) $\cup$ VE(FTs$_{il}$)$|)$, so the total time complexity is $O(|P_\alpha| * |$VE($il\_$CLs) $\cup$ VE(FTs$_{il}$)$|)$.

11.4.3   Vector-Degree: the Similarity Measure of SCPs

Definition 11.4 Let P_α, P_β, P_γ be three SCPs in Σ, let $v(\alpha)$, $v(\beta)$, $v(\gamma) \in \mathfrak{R}^h$ be their 0–1 maximal clique vectors. Let $sim(v(\cdot), v(\cdot))$ be a **similarity** function of two SCPs such that P_α is more similar to P_β than to P_γ by $sim(v(\cdot), v(\cdot))$ when $sim(v(\alpha), v(\beta)) > sim(v(\alpha), v(\gamma))$.

Another measure, cosine similarity, has been widely used to compute the similarity between vectors. Formally, the cosine similarity is defined as:

$$sim(v(\alpha), v(\beta)) = \frac{\sum_{j=1}^{h} \mu(cl_j, P_\alpha) \times \mu(cl_j, P_\beta)}{\sqrt{\sum_{j=1}^{h} \mu^2(cl_j, P_\alpha)} \times \sqrt{\sum_{j=1}^{h} \mu^2(cl_j, P_\beta)}} \qquad (11.5)$$

In the definition, if $v(\alpha) = v(\beta)$, then $sim(v(\alpha), v(\beta)) = 1$. Let $1 - sim(v(\alpha), v(\beta))$ be the distance between P_α and P_β. Let $\tilde{v}(\alpha)$, $\tilde{v}(\beta)$ be key-value maximal clique vectors

of P_α and P_β. Then, $sim(\tilde{v}(\alpha), \tilde{v}(\beta)) = \sum_{i=i', i, i' \in I} \left| \frac{\tilde{v}(i,\alpha) \cap \tilde{v}(i',\beta)|}{\sqrt{\sum_{i \in I} \lceil \tilde{v}(i,\alpha) \rceil} \times \sqrt{\sum_{i' \in I} \lceil \tilde{v}(i',\beta) \rceil}} \right|$.

Meanwhile, the upper bound of $sim(\tilde{v}(\alpha), \tilde{v}(\beta))$ is $\dfrac{\min\left\{ \sum_{i \in I} \lceil \tilde{v}(i,\alpha) \rceil, \sum_{i' \in I} \lceil \tilde{v}(i',\beta) \rceil \right\}}{\sqrt{\sum_{i \in I} \lceil \tilde{v}(i,\alpha) \rceil} \times \sqrt{\sum_{i' \in I} \lceil \tilde{v}(i',\beta) \rceil}}$.

The comparison of vector-degree with other similarity definitions is shown in Table 11.4. Similarity measures that require additional parameters or additional input information are not in the comparison in Table 11.4. Each column in Table 11.4 corresponds to a similarity measure, and each row is two SCPs from Fig. 11.2 which are to be measured for similarity. "-" in Table 11.4 indicates that similarity cannot be calculated. In general, vector-degree has the best versatility and

Table 11.4 The comparison with other similarity measures

	Covered relationship	Semantic similarity	Feature similarity	Vector degree
{A,B},{C,D}	–	–	–	0.63
{A,B},{A,C}	–	–	0.75	0.67
{B,C},{A,B,C}	Y	1	1	1
{B,C},{A,B,C, D}	N	0.67	0.67	0.82

can calculate the similarity of any two SCPs, feature similarity (Liu et al., 2015) comes second in versatility, and semantic similarity third. For the SCPs {A, B} and {C, D}, all the similarity measures except vector-degree fail to calculate their distance. In fact, in Fig. 11.2, they have two sets of instances appearing in the same maximal clique. For the SCPs {A, B} and {A, C}, the feature similarity measure treats {A2, B5} and {A2, C2} as evidence of their similarity although the two instance sets do not form a clique. The covered relationship similarity measure provided by Yoo and Bow (2011a) is interesting because it indicates that all the cliques in which these two SCPs are located are the same, so we can use it as the minimum standard of similarity and we will further compare it with vector-degree in the part of this chapter dealing with experiments.

11.4.4 Grouping SCPs Based on Vector-Degree

We can use an agglomerative hierarchical clustering method to group SCPs effectively based on the vector-degree.

For every SCP P_α, let a_α be the average distance between P_α and the other SCPs of the cluster to which P_α belongs. Let b_α be the minimum average distance from P_α to all the clusters that do not contain P_α. A silhouette coefficient can be used to evaluate the quality of clustering, i.e., $s_{avg} = \frac{1}{m} \sum_{P_\alpha \in \Sigma} \frac{b_\alpha - a_\alpha}{\max\{a_\alpha, b_\alpha\}}$.

Hierarchical clustering merges the two clusters with the minimum average distance.

11.5 Experimental Evaluations

The evaluation has been conducted on both real and synthetic data sets. First, the reason for using a vector-degree similarity measure is confirmed by comparing it with the covered relationship on both real and synthetic data sets. Then, the effectiveness and efficiency of our clustering algorithms based on 0–1 vector and key-value vector are discussed. The two materialization methods are compared and, finally, the scalability of the method is tested on multiple synthetic data sets.

All algorithms were implemented in C# and conducted on a Windows platform with a 3.70GHZ machine and 16GB RAM.

11.5.1 Data Sets

In our experiments we use both synthetic and real data sets. The real data set is extracted from POI data sets from Beijing with its category and location in a $20,000 \times 16,000$ size spatial area. The synthetic data sets are generated as follows. First, we generate several sets of maximal cliques with different distance thresholds d. Second, we randomly sample a certain number of SCPs to create a grouping problem. The spatial density is controlled by the D1 × D2 size frame; see Table 11.5 for details.

Figure 11.6 shows the number of maximal cliques mined by Syn1 and Syn2 at different distance thresholds. The data distribution of the real data set is shown in Fig. 11.7.

11.5.2 Results

1. *Effectiveness*

   In this section, we study the algorithm's effectiveness by verifying whether the SCP pairs that satisfy a covered relationship are contained in the same group. The comparison is shown in Table 11.6. To obtain all SCPs that satisfy the relationship; we set the prevalence threshold to zero for the first and second data sets. The number of SCPs that satisfy the covered relationship are recorded by the number of closed pattern pairs. In the third data set, the prevalence threshold is not zero, so the mined results, i.e., 360 co-location patterns, have a certain correlation. After grouping, the degree of separation between the groups is relatively small, so their silhouette coefficient is lower than that of the other two groups. In all three data sets, the number of covered relationship patterns pairs assigned to the two groups is 0.

2. *Effect of the number of maximal cliques*

   Synthetic data set Syn1 produces 570, 930, 1634, 8182 maximal cliques. We sampled 20 groups of 400 SCPs and computed their silhouette coefficients by our

Table 11.5 Data sets

	Real data set	Synthetic data sets	
name	Real1	Syn1	Syn2
D1 × D2	20,000 × 16,000	5000 × 5000	20,000 × 20,000
Number of instances	23k	300	5k
Number of features	16	15	25

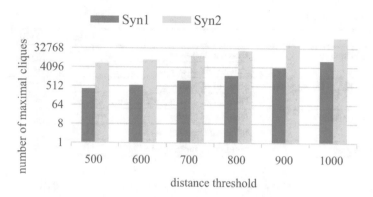

Fig. 11.6 The number of maximal cliques mined by Syn1 and Syn2 at different distance thresholds

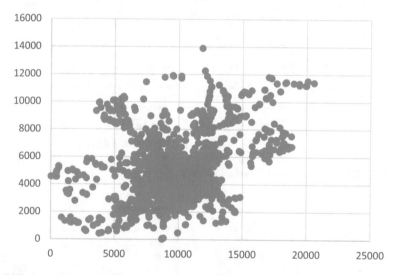

Fig. 11.7 Data distribution of the real data set

method, and then calculated the average silhouette coefficient. The other groups were calculated in the same way. The results are shown in Fig. 11.8. When the number of maximal cliques is relatively small, i.e., 570 in Fig. 11.8, the patterns are rarely contained in the same maximal cliques, especially the higher-size patterns, so their silhouette coefficient values are low, meaning that the SCPs are not well distinguished. What is also interesting from Fig. 11.8 is that if the maximal clique number is greatly enlarged, more and more SCPs are included in the same maximal clique, and so the maximal clique carries less information and has a lower coefficient. It can also be seen that this mining method on the set of patterns from 400 to 1600 is relatively smooth.

Table 11.6 Comparison

		Real1	Syn1	
Input information	Distance threshold	20	600	600
	Prevalence threshold	0	0	0.2
Mining patterns information	Number of patterns	539	5933	360
	Number of closed pattern pairs	130	4965	22
Clustering results	Number of cluster	129	1556	148
	Silhouette coefficient	0.76	0.80	0.27
Effectiveness	Number of misassignments	0	0	0

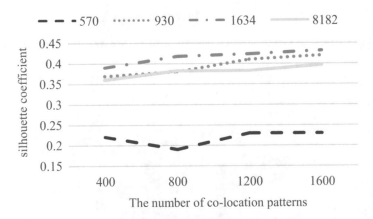

Fig. 11.8 Effect of the number of maximal cliques

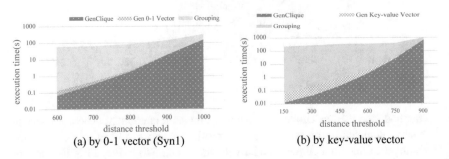

(a) by 0-1 vector (Syn1)   (b) by key-value vector

Fig. 11.9 Effect of distance threshold

3. *Performance*

The most time-consuming aspect of performance is the formation of the maximal clique vectors and grouping. We can divide the execution time into three parts, mining maximal cliques, forming vectors, and grouping, and observe the time consumption of each part. Figure 11.9(a) shows the variation of the runtime of the three parts over the synthetic data set Syn1 as the distance threshold increases based on a 0–1 vector. The number of randomly generated

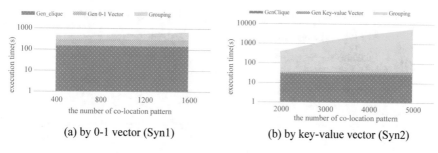

(a) by 0-1 vector (Syn1)   (b) by key-value vector (Syn2)

Fig. 11.10 Effect of the number of patterns

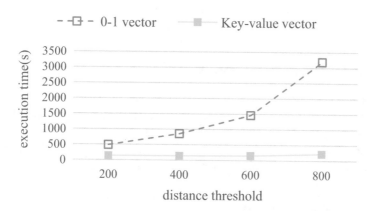

Fig. 11.11 Running times (Syn2)

patterns to be grouped is 1200. Figure 11.9(b) shows the time consumption of each part when grouping 2000 random patterns from Syn2 with the key-value vector. It can be seen from both Fig. 11.9(a) and (b) that, as the distance threshold increases and the number of maximal clique increases, the time for generating the maximal cliques increases rapidly, whereas the time spent in the clustering part is relatively stable. In particular, the vector generation portion takes much less time than the other two parts and so is almost invisible on the figures.

Figure 11.10(a) shows the time consumption of the three parts with the increase of the number of SCPs, in which the number of maximum cliques is 8182 from Syn1. Figure 11.10(b) shows the effect when the distance threshold is 750 in Syn2. In general, as the number of modes increases, the time spent in the grouping part rises slowly.

4. *Comparison of 0–1 vector with key-value vector*

Figure 11.11 shows the results on 1200 SCPs chosen randomly from Syn2. According to Fig. 11.11, the run times of both vector methods increase as the distance increases (i.e., the number of maximal cliques increases). The time consumed by the 0–1 vector increases much faster than that of the key-value vector.

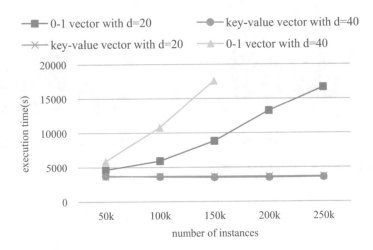

Fig. 11.12 Scalability test on the synthetic data set

5. *Scalability test*

   We generated synthetic data sets with sizes {50k, 100k, 150k, 200k, 250k} all within a spatial frame 20,000 × 20,000. The distance threshold d was set to 20 and 40. Figure 11.12 shows the results, and we can see that our method, especially the key-value vector method, can scale to large data sets.

11.6   Chapter Summary

In this chapter, we studied the problem of grouping SCPs. We developed a novel general representation model of SCPs to flexibly calculate the similarity between any SCPs. To prove how useful and effective the representation model is we conducted extensive experiments over both real and synthetic data sets. The experimental results demonstrated that our solution is effective. There are still many challenges worthy of further research, for example, parallel computation for the generation of maximal cliques.

References

Ahmed, C. F., KTanbeer, S., & Jeong, B. S. (2009). Efficient tree structures for high utility pattern mining in incremental databases. *IEEE Transactions on Knowledge and Data Engineering (TKDE), 21*(12), 1708–1721.

Ahmed, C. F., Tanbeer, S. K., Jeong, B. S., et al. (2011). A framework for mining interesting high utility patterns with a strong frequency affinity. *Information Sciences, 181*(21), 4878–4894.

Akbari, M., Samadzadegan, F., & Weibel, R. (2015). A generic regional spatio-temporal co-occurrence pattern mining model: a case study for air pollution. *Journal of Geographical Systems, 17*(3), 249–274.

Al-Naymat, G. (2008). Enumeration of maximal clique for mining spatial co-location patterns. In: *Proceedings of the IEEE International Conference on Computer Systems and Applications (AICCSA)*, Doha, Qatar, pp. 126–133

An, S., Yang, H., Wang, J., Cui, N., & Cui, J. (2016). Mining urban recurrent congestion evolution patterns from GPS-equipped vehicle mobility data. *Information Sciences, 373*, 515–526.

Andrzejewski, W., & Boinski, P. (2015). Parallel GPU-based plane-sweep algorithm for construction of iCPI-Trees. *Journal of Database Management, 26*(3), 1–20.

Andrzejewski, W., & Boinski, P. (2018). Efficient spatial co-location pattern mining on multiple GPU. *Expert Systems with Applications, 93*(3), 465–483.

Andrzejewski, W., & Boinski, P. (2019). Parallel approach to incremental co-location pattern mining. *Information Sciences, 496*, 485–505.

Arge, L., Procopiuc, O., Ramaswamy, S., et al. (1998). Scalable sweeping-based spatial join. In: *Proceedings of* VLDB 1998, pp. 570–581

Bao, X., Gu, T., Chang, L., et al. (2021). Knowledge-based interactive postmining of user-preferred co-location patterns using ontologies. *IEEE Transactions on Cybernetics, 99*, 1–14.

Bao, X., Wang, L. (2017). Discovering interesting co-location patterns interactively using ontologies. In: *Proceedings of the International Conference on Database Systems for Advanced Applications (DASFAA Workshops)*, Springer, Suzhou, China, pp.75-89

Bao, X., & Wang, L. (2019). A clique-based approach for co-location pattern mining. *Information Sciences, 490*, 244–264.

Bao, X., Wang, L., Chen, H. (2016). Ontology-based interactive post-mining of interesting co-location patterns. In: *Proceedings of the 18th Asia-Pacific Web Conference (APWEB)*, Springer, Suzhou, China, pp. 406–409

Bao, X., & Wang, L. (2017). Discovering interesting co-location patterns interactively using ontologies. In *Proceedings of DASFAA Workshops 2017, LNCS 10179* (pp. 75–89). Springer.

Baral, C., Tran, N., Tuan, L. (2002). Reasoning about actions in a probabilistic setting. In: *Proceedings of the 18th national conference on Artificial intelligence (AAAI)*, pp. 507–512

© The Author(s), under exclusive license to Springer Nature Singapore Pte Ltd. 2022
L. Wang et al., *Preference-based Spatial Co-location Pattern Mining*, Big Data Management, https://doi.org/10.1007/978-981-16-7566-9

Bartolini, I., Ciaccia, P., Patella, M. (2012). Getting the best from uncertain data: the correlated case. In: *Proceedings of the 20th Italian Symposium on Advanced Database Systems (SEBD)*, pp. 43-50

Barua, S., & Sander, J. (2011). SSCP: Mining statistically significant co-location patterns. In *Proceedings of the 12th International symposium on spatial and temporal databases (SSTD)* (pp. 2–20). Springer.

Barua, S., & Sander, J. (2014). Mining statistically significant co-location and segregation patterns. *IEEE Transactions on Knowledge and Data Engineering (TKDE), 26*(5), 1185–1199.

Bembenik, R., Jóźwicki, W., & Protaziuk, G. (2017). Methods for mining co–location patterns with extended spatial objects. *International Journal of Applied Mathematics and Computer Science, 27*(4), 681–695.

Beskales, G., Soliman, M., & Ilyas, I. (2008). Efficient search for the top-k probable nearest neighbors in uncertain databases. In *Proceedings of the VLDB Endowment* (pp. 326–339).

Bhuiyan, M. (2016). Generic frameworks for interactive personalized interesting pattern discovery. In *Proceedings of the International Conference on Big Data (BDIOT)* (pp. 606–615).

Bhuiyan, M., & Hasan, M. A. (2016). PRIIME: A generic framework for interactive personalized interesting pattern discovery. In *Proc. International Conference on Big Data* (pp. 606–615). IEEE Press.

Bhuiyan, M., Mukhopadhyay, S., & Hasan, M. (2012). Interactive pattern mining on hidden data: a sampling-based solution. In *Proceedings of the 21st International conference on Information and knowledge management (CIKM)* (pp. 95–104). ACM Press.

Boley, M., Mampaey, M., et al. (2013). One click mining: Interactive local pattern discovery through implicit preference and performance learning. In: *Proceedings of the SIGKDD workshop on interactive data exploration and analytics (SIGKDD workshop)*, ACM, pp. 27–35

Cai, F., & Chen, H. (2016). A probabilistic model for information retrieval by mining user behaviors. *Cognitive Computation, 8*(3), 494–504.

Cai, J., Liu, Q., Deng, M., et al. (2018). Adaptive detection of statistically significant regional spatial co-location patterns. *Computers, Environment and Urban Systems, 68*, 53–63.

Cao, L. (2010). Domain-driven data mining: Challenges and prospects. *IEEE Transactions on Knowledge and Data Engineering, 22*(6), 755–769.

Cao, L. (2015). Coupling learning of complex interactions. *Information Processing & Management, 51*(2), 167–186.

Celik, M., Kang, J., & Shekhar, S. (2007). Zonal co-location pattern discovery with dynamic parameters. In *Proceedings of the 7th IEEE International Conference on Data Mining (ICDM)* (pp. 433–438). IEEE Press.

Chan, H. K., Long, C., Yan, D., et al. (2019). Fraction-Score: A new support measure for co-location pattern mining. In *Proceedings of the IEEE International Conference on Data Engineering (ICDE 2019)* (pp. 1514–1525). IEEE Press.

Chang, X., Ma, Z., Lin, M., et al. (2017). Feature interaction augmented sparse learning for fast kinect motion detection. *IEEE transactions on image processing, 26*(8), 3911–3920.

Chang, X., Ma, Z., Yang, Y., et al. (2016). Bi-level semantic representation analysis for multimedia event detection. *IEEE transactions on cybernetics, 47*(5), 1180–1197.

Cheng, J., Zhu, L., Ke, Y., et al. (2012a). Fast algorithms for maximal clique enumeration with limited memory. In: *Proceedings of the ACM SIGKDD International Conference on Knowledge Discovery and Data Mining*, pp. 1240-1248

Cheng, W., Shie, B., Tseng, V., et al. (2012b). Mining top-k high utility itemsets. In *Proceedings of the 18th ACM SIGKDD international conference on Knowledge discovery and data mining (KDD)* (pp. 78–86). ACM Press.

Deng, M., Cai, J., Liu, Q., et al. (2017). Multi-level method for discovery of regional co-location patterns. *International Journal of Geographical Information Science, 31*(9), 1846–1870.

Duan, J., Wang, L., Hu, X., et al. (2018). Mining spatial dynamic co-location patterns. *Filomat, 32*(5), 1491–1497.

Duong, Q. H., Liao, B., Fournier-Viger, P., et al. (2016). An efficient algorithm for mining the top-k high utility itemsets using novel threshold raising and pruning strategies. *Knowledge-Based Systems, 104*, 106–122.

Eppstein, D., Löffler, M., Strash, D. (2010). Listing all maximal cliques in sparse graphs in near-optimal time. *Lecture Notes in Computer Science (Including Subseries Lecture Notes in Artificial Intelligence and Lecture Notes in Bioinformatics), LNCS 6506* (PART 1): 403–414

Eppstein, D., & Strash, D. (2011). Listing all maximal cliques in large sparse real-world graphs. *Lecture Notes in Computer Science (Including Subseries Lecture Notes in Artificial Intelligence and Lecture Notes in Bioinformatics). LNCS, 6630*, 364–375.

Estivill-Castro, V., & Murray, A. T. (1998). Discovering associations in spatial data—An efficient medoid based approach. In *Proceedings of PAKDD* (pp. 110–121). Springer.

Estivill-Castro, V., & Lee, I. (2001). Data mining techniques for autonomous exploration of large volumes of georeferenced crime data. In *Proceedings of the Sixth Int'l Conf. Geocomputation* (pp. 1–11).

Fang, Y., Wang, L., Wang, X., et al. (2017). Mining co-location patterns with dominant features. In: *Proceedings of the 18th International Conference on Web Information Systems Engineering (WISE). LNCS, 10569*, 183–198.

Flouvat, F., N'guyen Van Soc, J., Desmier, E., et al. (2015). Domain-driven co-location mining. *Geoinformatica, 19*(1), 147–183.

Gan, W., Lin, J., Fournier-Viger, P., et al. (2019). HUOPM: High-utility occupancy pattern mining. *IEEE transactions on cybernetics, 50*(3), 1195–1208.

Ge, Y., Yao, Z., & Li, H. (2021). Computing co-location patterns in spatial data with extended objects: a scalable buffer-based approach. *IEEE Transactions on Knowledge and Data Engineering, 33*(2), 401–414.

He, Y., Wang, L., Fang, F., et al. (2018). Discovering congestion propagation patterns by co-location pattern mining. In *Proceedings of the Asia Pacific Web (APWeb) and Web-Age Information Management (WAIM) Joint Conference on Web and Big Data (APWeb-WAIM)., LNCS 11268* (pp. 46–55). Springer.

Hong, T., Lee, C., & Wang, S. (2012). An incremental mining algorithm for high average-utility itemsets. *Expert Systems with Applications, 39*(8), 7173–7180.

Hu, X., Wang, G., Duan, J. (2020). Mining maximal dynamic spatial colocation patterns. *IEEE transactions on neural networks and learning systems*, 1–11

Hua, M., Pei, J., Zhang, W., et al. (2008). Ranking queries on uncertain data: a probabilistic threshold approach. In *Proceedings of the 2008 ACM International conference on Management of data (SIGMOD)* (pp. 673–686). ACM Press.

Huang, Y., Pei, J., & Xiong, H. (2006). Mining co-location patterns with rare events from spatial data sets. *GeoInformatica, 10*(3), 239–260.

Huang, Y., Shekhar, S., & Xiong, H. (2004). Discovering colocation patterns from spatial data sets: a general approach. *IEEE Transactions on Knowledge and data engineering, 16*(12), 1472–1485.

Huang, Y., Zhang, L., & Yu, P. (2005). Can we apply projection based frequent pattern mining paradigm to spatial co-location mining? In *Proceedings of the 9th Pacific-Asia Conference on Knowledge Discovery and Data Mining (PAKDD)* (pp. 719–725). Springer.

Huang, Y., Zhang, L., & Zhang, P. (2008). A framework for mining sequential patterns from spatio-temporal event data sets. *IEEE Transactions on Knowledge and Data Engineering, 20*(4), 433–448.

Huang, Y., & Zhang, P. (2006). On the relationships between clustering and spatial co-location pattern mining. In *Proceedings of the 18th IEEE International Conference on Tools with Artificial Intelligence (ICTAI)* (pp. 513–522). IEEE Press.

Khan, K., Dolgorsuren, B., Anh, T., et al. (2017). Faster compression methods for a weighted graph using locality sensitive hashing. *Information Sciences, 421*, 237–253.

Koperski, K., & Han, J. (1995). Discovery of spatial association rules in geographic information databases. In *Proceedings of the 4th International Symposium, Large Spatial Databases(SSD)* (pp. 47–66).

Lei, L., Wang, L., & Wang, X. (2019). Mining spatial co-location patterns by the Fuzzy Technology. In *Proceedings of the IEEE International Conference on Big Knowledge (ICBK)* (pp. 129–136). IEEE Press.

Li, J., Adilmagambetov, A., Jabbar, M., et al. (2016). On discovering co-location patterns in datasets: a case study of pollutants and child cancers. *GeoInformatica, 20*(4), 651–692.

Li, S., Zhou, J., & Xu, T. (2020). Competitive analysis for points of interest. In *Proceedings of KDD 2020, Virtual Event* (pp. 1265–1274). ACM Press.

Li, X., Zhang, L., Chen, E., et al. (2013). Mining frequent patterns in print logs with semantically alternative labels. In *Proceedings of the International Conference on Advanced Data Mining and Applications (ADMA)* (pp. 107–119). Springer.

Li, X., Zhang, L., Luo, P., et al. (2014). Mining user tasks from print logs. In *Proceedings of the 2014 International Joint Conference on Neural Networks (IJCNN)* (pp. 1250–1257). IEEE Press.

Li, Y., & Shekhar, S. (2018). Local co-location pattern detection: A summary of results. In *Proceedings of the10th International Conference on Geographic Information Science (GIScience)* (Vol. 114, pp. 1–15).

Lin, Z., & Lim, S. J. (2008). Fast spatial co-location mining without cliqueness checking. In *Proceedings of the ACM Conference on Information and Knowledge Management* (pp. 1461–1462). ACM Press.

Lin, Z., & Lim, S. (2009). Optimal candidate generation in spatial co-location mining. In *Proc. of SAC 2009* (pp. 1441–1445).

Lin, C. W., Lan, G. C., & Hong, T. P. (2012). An incremental mining algorithm for high utility item sets. *Expert Systems with Applications, 39*(8), 7173–7180.

Liu, B., Chen, L., Liu, C., et al. (2015). RCP mining: Towards the summarization of spatial co-location patterns. In *Proceedings of the International Symposium on Spatial and Temporal Databases (SSTD)* (pp. 451–469). Springer.

Liu, Q., Liu, W., Deng, M., et al. (2020). An adaptive detection of multilevel co-location patterns based on natural neighborhoods. *International Journal of Geographical Information Science, 35*, 1–26.

Liu, X., Ye, M., Xu, J., et al. (2010). K-selection query over uncertain data. In *Proceedings of the International Conference on Database Systems for Advanced Applications (DASFAA)* (pp. 444–459). Springer.

Liu, Y., Liao, W., & Choudhary, A. (2005). A two-phase algorithm for fast discovery of high utility item sets. In *Proceedings of the Pacific-Asia Conference on Knowledge Discovery and Data Mining (PAKDD)* (pp. 689–695). Springer.

Liu, Z., & Huang, Y. (2013). Mining co-locations under uncertainty. In *Proceedings of the 13th International Symposium on Spatial and Temporal Databases (SSTD)* (pp. 429–446). IEEE Press.

Lu, J., Wang, L., Fang, Y., et al. (2017). Mining competitive pairs hidden in co-location patterns from dynamic spatial databases. In *Proceedings of the 21st Pacific-Asia Conference on Advances in Knowledge Discovery and Data Mining (PAKDD)* (pp. 467–480). Springer.

Lu, J., Wang, L., Fang, Y., et al. (2018). Mining strong symbiotic patterns hidden in spatial prevalent co-location patterns. *Knowledge-Based Systems, 146*, 190–202.

Lu, J., Wang, L., Xiao, Q., et al. (2015). Incremental mining of co-locations from spatial database. In *Proceedings of the 12th International Conference on Fuzzy Systems and Knowledge Discovery (FSKD)* (pp. 612–617). IEEE Press.

Lu, Y., Wang, L., Chen, H., et al. (2010). Spatial co-location patterns mining over uncertain data based on possible worlds. *Journal of Computer Research and Development, 47*(Supplement), 215–221.

Lu, Y., Wang, L., & Zhang, X. (2009). Mining frequent co-location patterns from uncertain data. *Journal of Frontiers of Computer Science and Technology, 3*(6), 656–664.

Ma, Z., Chang, X., Yang, Y., et al. (2017). The many shades of negativity. *IEEE Transactions on Multimedia, 19*(7), 1558–1568.

Mielikäinen, T., & Mannila, H. (2003). The pattern ordering problem. In *Proceedings of the European Conference on Principles of Data Mining and Knowledge Discovery (PKDD)* (pp. 327–338). Springer.

Mohan, P., Shekhar, S., Shine, J., et al. (2011). A neighborhood graph based approach to regional co-location pattern discovery: A summary of results. In *Proceedings of the ACM 19th International conference on advances in geographic information systems (SIGSPATIAL)* (pp. 122–132). ACM Press.

Moosavi, S., Samavatian, M., Nandi, A., et al. (2019). Short and long-term pattern discovery over large-scale geo-spatiotemporal data. In *Proceedings of KDD 2019* (pp. 2905–2913). Anchorage.

Morimoto, Y. (2001). Mining frequent neighboring class sets in spatial databases. In *Proceedings of the 7th ACM international conference on Knowledge discovery and data mining (SIGKDD)* (pp. 353–358). ACM Press.

Ouyang, Z., Wang, L., & Wu, P. (2017). Spatial co-location pattern discovery from fuzzy objects. *International Journal of Artificial Intelligence Tools, 26*(02), 1750003.

Pei, J., Han, J., Mao, R. (2000): Closet: An efficient algorithm for mining frequent closed itemsets. In: *Proceedings of the ACM SIGMOD workshops on research issues in data mining and knowledge discovery (DMKD Workshops)*, Vol. 4(2), pp. 21-30

Phillips, P., & Lee, I. (2012). Mining co-distribution patterns for large crime datasets. *Expert Systems with Applications, 39*(14), 11556–11563.

Pietracaprina, A., Riondato, M., Upfal, E., et al. (2010). Mining top-k frequent itemsets through progressive sampling. *Data Mining and Knowledge Discovery, 21*(2), 310–326.

Qian, F., Chiew, K., He, Q., et al. (2014). Mining regional co-location patterns with kNNG. *Journal of Intelligent Information Systems, 42*(3), 485–505.

Sainju, A. M., Aghajarian, D., Jiang, Z., et al. (2018). Parallel grid-based colocation mining algorithms on GPUs for big spatial event data. *IEEE Transactions on Big Data, 6*(1), 107–118.

Schmidt, M. C., Samatova, N. F., Thomas, K., et al. (2009). A scalable, parallel algorithm for maximal clique enumeration. *Journal of Parallel and Distributed Computing, 69*(4), 417–428.

Sengstock, C., Gertz, M., & Van Canh, T. (2012). Spatial interestingness measures for co-location pattern mining. In *Proceedings of the 12th International Conference on Data Mining (ICDM) Workshops* (pp. 821–826). IEEE Press.

Shekhar, S., & Huang, Y. (2001). Discovering spatial co-location patterns: A summary of results. In *Proceedings of Advances in Spatial and Temporal Databases (SSTD)* (pp. 236–256). Springer.

Shekhar, S., Zhe Jiang, Z., et al. (2015). Spatiotemporal data mining: A computational perspective. *ISPRS International Journal of Geo-Information, 4*, 2306–2338.

Shen, B., Wen, Z., Zhao, Y., et al. (2016). Ocean: Fast discovery of high utility occupancy itemsets. In *Pacific-Asia Conference on Knowledge Discovery and Data Mining* (pp. 354–365). Springer.

Sheshikala, M., Rajeswara Rao, D., Vijaya Prakash, R. (2017). A map-reduce framework for finding clusters of colocation patterns—A summary of results. In: *Proceedings of the 7th IEEE International Advanced Computing Conference(IACC)*, pp. 129–131

Shie, B. E., Tseng, V. S., & Yu, P. S. (2010). Online mining of temporal maximal utility itemsets from data streams. In *Proceedings of the 2010 ACM Symposium on Applied Computing* (pp. 1622–1626). ACM Press.

Sierra, R., & Stephens, C. (2012). Exploratory analysis of the interrelations between co-located boolean spatial features using network graphs. *International Journal of Geographical Information Science, 26*(3), 441–468.

Silvestri, C., Cagnin, F., Lettich, F., et al. (2015). Mining condensed spatial co-location patterns. In *Proceedings of the Fourth ACM SIGSPATIAL International Workshop on Mobile Geographic Information Systems* (pp. 84–87).

Soltani, A., & Akbarzadeh, T. M. (2014). Confabulation-inspired association rule mining for rare and frequent itemsets. *IEEE Transactions on neural networks and learning systems, 25*(11), 2053–2064.

Song, W., Zhang, Z., & Li, J. (2016). A high utility item set mining algorithm based on subsume index. *Knowledge and Information Systems, 49*(1), 315–340.

Song, X., Nie, L., Zhang, L. (2015). Interest inference via structure-constrained multi-source multi-task learning. In: *Proceedings of the 24th International Joint Conference on Artificial Intelligence (IJCAI)*, pp. 2371–2377

Tang, L., Zhang, L., Luo, P., et al. (2012). Incorporating occupancy into frequent pattern mining for high quality pattern recommendation. In *Proceedings of the 21st ACM International Conference on Information and knowledge management (CIKM)* (pp. 75–84). ACM Press.

Tomita, E. (2017). Efficient algorithms for finding maximum and maximal cliques and their applications. *Lecture Notes in Computer Science (Including Subseries Lecture Notes in Artificial Intelligence and Lecture Notes in Bioinformatics)*, LNCS 10167: 3–15

Tomita, E., Yoshida, K., Hatta, T., et al. (2016). A much faster branch-and-bound algorithm for finding a maximum clique. *Lecture Notes in Computer Science (Including Subseries Lecture Notes in Artificial Intelligence and Lecture Notes in Bioinformatics)*, LNCS 9711: 215–226

Tran, V., & Wang, L. (2020). Delaunay triangulation-based spatial colocation pattern mining without distance thresholds. *Statistical Analysis Data Mining: The ASA Data Science Journal, 13*, 282–304.

Tran, V., Wang, L., & Chen, H. (2019b). Discovering spatial co-location patterns by automatically determining the instance neighbor. In *Proceedings of the 5th International Conference on Fuzzy Systems and Data Mining (FSDM)* (pp. 583–590). IOS Press.

Tran, V., Wang, L., & Chen, H. (2019c). A spatial co-location pattern mining algorithm without distance thresholds. In *Proceedings of the 2019 IEEE International Conference on Big Knowledge (ICBK)* (pp. 242–249). IEEE Press.

Tran, V., Wang, L., Chen, H., et al. (2021). MCHT: A maximal clique and hash table-based maximal prevalent co-location pattern mining algorithm. *Expert Systems with Applications, 175*, 114830.

Tran, V., Wang, L., Zhou, L. (2019a). Mining spatial co-location patterns based on overlap maximal clique partitioning. In: *Proceedings of the 2019 IEEE International Conference on Mobile Data Management (MDM)*, pp.467–472

Tseng, V. S., Shie, B., Wu, C., et al. (2013). Efficient algorithms for mining high utility itemsets from transactional databases. *IEEE Transactions on Knowledge and Data Engineering, 25*(8), 1772–1786.

Tseng, V. S., Wu, C., Fournier-Viger, P., & Yu, P. (2015). Efficient algorithms for mining the concise and lossless representation of high utility itemsets. *IEEE Transactions on Knowledge and Data Engineering, 27*(3), 726–739.

Tseng, V. S., Wu, C., Fournier-Viger, P., et al. (2016). Efficient algorithms for mining top-k high utility itemsets. *IEEE Transactions on Knowledge and Data Engineering, 28*(1), 54–67.

Tseng, V. S., Wu, C. W., & Shie, B. E. (2010). UP-Growth: an efficient algorithm for high utility itemset mining. In *Proceedings of the 16th ACM SIGKDD international conference on knowledge discovery and data mining* (pp. 253–262). ACM Press.

Vaezpour, S., Zhang, R., Wu, K., et al. (2016). A new approach to mitigating security risks of phone clone co-location over mobile clouds. *Journal of Network and Computer Applications, 62*, 171–184.

Verhein, F., & Al-Naymat, G. (2007). Fast mining of complex spatial co-location patterns using GLIMIT. In *Proceedings of the 7th IEEE International Conference on Data Mining Workshops (ICDMW)* (pp. 679–684). IEEE Press.

Wang, C., Dong, X., Zhou, F., et al. (2015a). Coupled attribute similarity learning on categorical data. *IEEE Transactions on Neural Networks and Learning Systems, 26*(4), 781–797.

Wang, J., Han, J., & Pei, J. (2003). CLOSET+: Searching for the best strategies for mining frequent closed itemsets. In *Proceedings of the 9th ACM SIGKDD International Conference on Knowledge Discovery and Data Mining* (pp. 236–245). ACM Press.

Wang, J., Wang, L., & Wang, X. (2019a). Mining prevalent co-location patterns based on global topological relations. In *Proceedings of The 20th IEEE International Conference on Mobile Data Management (MDM)* (pp. 210–215). IEEE Press.

Wang, L., Bao, X., Cao, L. (2018c). Interactive probabilistic post-mining of user-preferred spatial co-location patterns. In: *Proceedings of the 34th IEEE International Conference on Data Engineering* (ICDE 2018), Paris, French, pp. 1256–1259

Wang, L., Bao, X., Chen, H., et al. (2018b). Effective lossless condensed representation and discovery of spatial co-location patterns. *Information Sciences, 436*, 197–213.

Wang, L., Bao, X., & Zhou, L. (2018a). Redundancy reduction for prevalent co-location patterns. *IEEE Transactions on Knowledge and Data Engineering, 30*(1), 142–155.

Wang, L., Bao, X., Zhou, L., et al. (2017b). Maximal sub-prevalent co-location patterns and efficient mining algorithms. In *Proceedings of the 18th international conference on Web Information Systems Engineering (WISE).*, LNCS 10569 (pp. 199–214). Springer.

Wang, L., Bao, X., Zhou, L., et al. (2019b). Mining maximal sub-prevalent co-location patterns. *World Wide Web, 22*(5), 1971–1997.

Wang, L., Bao, Y., Lu, J., et al. (2008). A new join-less approach for co-location pattern mining. In *Proceedings of the IEEE 8th International Conference on Computer and Information Technology* (pp. 197–202). IEEE Press.

Wang, L., Bao, Y., & Lu, Z. (2009a). Efficient discovery of spatial co-location patterns using the iCPI-tree. *The Open Information Systems Journal, 3*(1), 69–80.

Wang, L., Chen, H., Zhao, L., et al. (2010). Efficiently mining co-location rules on interval data. In: *Proceedings of the 6th International Conference on Advanced Data Mining and Applications, (ADMA)*, Part I, LNCS 6440, pp. 477–488

Wang, L., Han, J., Chen, H., et al. (2016a). Top-k probabilistic prevalent co-location mining in spatially uncertain data sets. *Frontiers of Computer Science, 10*(3), 488–503.

Wang, X., Wang, L., Lu, J., et al. (2016b). Effectively updating high utility co-location patterns in evolving spatial databases. In *Proceedings of the Asia-Pacific Web and Web-Age Information Management (WAIM)* (pp. 67–81). Springer.

Wang, L., Jiang, W., Chen, H., et al. (2017a). Efficiently mining high utility co-location patterns from spatial data sets with instance-specific utilities. In: *Proceedings of the 22nd International Conference on Database Systems for Advanced Applications* (DASFAA), LNCS 10178, Suzhou, China, pp.458–474

Wang, L., Wu, P., & Chen, H. (2013a). Finding probabilistic prevalent co-locations in spatially uncertain data sets. *IEEE Transactions on Knowledge and Data Engineering, 25*(4), 790–804.

Wang, L., Wu, P., Chen, H., et al. (2013b). Mining co-locations from spatially uncertain data with probability intervals. In *Proceedings of the International Conference on Web-Age Information Management (WAIM) Workshops* (Vol. 7901, pp. 301–314). LNCS.

Wang, L., Xie, K., Chen, T., et al. (2005). Efficient discovery of multilevel spatial association rules using partitions. *Information and Software Technology, 47*, 829–840.

Wang, L., Zhou, L., Lu, J., et al. (2009b). An order-clique-based approach for mining maximal co-locations. *Information Sciences, 179*(19), 3370–3382.

Wang, M., Wang, L., Qian, Y., et al. (2019c). Incremental mining of spatial co-location Patterns based on the fuzzy neighborhood relationship. In *Proceedings of the 5th International Conference on Fuzzy Systems and Data Mining (FSDM)* (pp. 652–660). IOS Press.

Wang, M., Wang, L., & Zhao, L. (2019e). Spatial co-location pattern mining based on fuzzy neighbor relationship. *Journal of Information Science and Engineering, 35*, 1343–1363.

Wang, X., Lei, L., Wang, L., et al. (2021). Spatial co-location pattern discovery incorporating fuzzy theory, *IEEE Transactions on Fuzzy Systems* pp.1–15, https://doi.org/10.1109/TFUZZ.2021.3074074

Wang, X., Wang, L. (2017) Incremental mining of high utility co-locations from spatial database. In: *Proceedings of the International conference on Big Data and Smart Computing (BIGCOMP)*, pp. 215–222

Wang, X., Wang, L., & Chen, H. (2019d). Mining high utility co-location patterns based on feature utility ratio (in Chinese). *Chinese Journal of computers, 42*(8), 1721–1738.

Wang, X., Wang, L., Lu, J., et al. (2016b). Effectively updating high utility co-location patterns in evolving spatial databases. In *Proceedings of the Asia-Pacific Web and Web-Age Information Management (WAIM)* (pp. 67–81). Springer.

Wang, X., Wang, L., & Wang, J. (2020). Mining spatio-temporal co-location fuzzy congestion patterns from traffic datasets (in Chinese). *Journal of Tsinghua University (Science & Technology), 60*(8), 683–692.

Wang, X., Zhao, Y., Nie, L., et al. (2015b). Semantic-based location recommendation with multimodal venue semantics. *IEEE Transactions on Multimedia, 17*(3), 409–419.

Wu, C., Shie, B., Tseng, V. S., & Yu, P. S. (2012). Mining top-k high utility itemsets. In *Proc. of the KDD 2012* (pp. 78–86). ACM Press.

Wu, P., Wang, L., & Zhou, M. (2019). Vector-degree: A general similarity measure for co-location patterns. In *Proc. of the 2019 IEEE International Conference on Big Knowledge (ICBK)* (pp. 281–288). IEEE Press.

Xiao, X., Xie, X., Luo, Q., & Ma, W. (2008). Density based co-location pattern discovery. In *Proceedings of the 16th SIGSPATIAL International Conference on Advances in Geographic Information Systems (GIS)* (pp. 11–20). ACM Press.

Xin, D., Cheng, H., Yan, X., et al. (2006). Extracting redundancy-aware top-k patterns. In *Proceedings of the 12th ACM international conference on Knowledge discovery and data mining (SIGKDD)* (pp. 444–453).

Xin, D., Han, J., Yan, X., et al. (2005). Mining compressed frequent-pattern sets. In *Proceedings of the 31st international conference on Very large data bases (VLDB)* (pp. 709–720).

Xin, D., Shen, X., Mei, Q., & Han, J. (2009). Discovering interesting patterns through user's interactive feedback. In *Proc. 12th ACM SIGKDD Int'l Conf. Knowledge Discovery and Data Mining* (pp. 773–778). ACM Press.

Yan, X., Cheng, H., Han, J., et al. (2005). Summarizing itemset patterns: a profile-based approach. In *Proceedings of the 11th ACM international conference on Knowledge discovery in data mining (SIGKDD)* (pp. 314–323).

Yang, L., & Wang, L. (2020). Mining traffic congestion propagation patterns based on spatio-temporal co-location patterns. *Evolutionary Intelligence, 13*, 221–233.

Yang, P., Wang, L., & Wang, X. (2018b). A parallel spatial co-location pattern mining approach based on ordered clique growth. In *Proceedings of the International Conference on Database Systems for Advanced Applications (DASFAA 2018)* (pp. 734–742). Springer.

Yang, P., Wang, L., & Wang, X. (2020). A MapReduce approach for spatial co-location pattern mining via ordered-clique-growth. *Distributed and Parallel Databases, 38*, 531–560.

Yang, P., Wang, L., Wang, X., Fang, Y. (2018c). A parallel joinless algorithm for co-location pattern mining based on group-dependent shard. In: *Proceedings of the International Conference on Web Information Systems Engineering* (WISE 2018), LNCS 11234, Dubai, UAE, pp. 240–250

Yang, P., Wang, L., Wang, X., et al. (2019). An effective approach on mining co-location patterns from spatial databases with rare features. In *Proceedings of the 20th IEEE International Conference on Mobile Data Management (MDM)* (pp. 53–62). IEEE Press.

Yang, P., Wang, L., Wang, X., et al. (2021). Efficient discovery of co-location patterns from massive spatial datasets with or without rare features. *Knowledge and Information Systems (KAIS), 63*(6), 1365–1395.

Yang, P., Zhang, T., & Wang, L. (2018a). TSRS: trip service recommended system based on summarized co-location patterns. In *Proceedings of the Asia-Pacific Web and Web-Age Information Management Joint International Conference on Web and Big Data (APWeb-WAIM)* (pp. 451–455). Springer.

Yang, S., Wang, L., Bao, X., et al. (2015). A framework for mining spatial high utility co-location patterns. In *Proceedings of the 12th International Conference on Fuzzy Systems and Knowledge Discovery (FSKD)* (pp. 595–601). IEEE Press.

Yao, H., Hamilton, H. J., & Butz, C. J. (2004). A foundational approach to mining item set utilities from database. In *Proceedings 4th SIAM International Conference on Data Mining (SDM)* (pp. 215–221).

Yao, H., Hamilton, H. J., & Geng, L. (2006). A unified framework for utility-based measures for mining itemsets. In *Proceedings the ACM SIGKDD 2nd Workshop on Utility-Based Data Mining* (pp. 28–37). ACM Press.

Yao, X., Chen, L., Peng, L., & Chi, T. (2017). A co-location pattern-mining algorithm with a density-weighted distance thresholding consideration. *Information Sciences, 396*(2017), 144–161.

Yao, X., Chen, L., Wen, C., et al. (2018). A spatial co-location mining algorithm that includes adaptive proximity improvements and distant instance references. *International Journal of Geographical Information Science, 32*(5), 980–1005.

Yao, X., Jiang, X., Wang, D., et al. (2021). Efficiently mining maximal co-locations in a spatial continuous field under directed road networks. *Information Sciences, 542*, 357–379.

Yao, X., Peng, L., Yang, L., et al. (2016). A fast space-saving algorithm for maximal co-location pattern mining. *Expert Systems with Applications, 63*, 310–323.

Yi, K., Li, F., Kollios, G., et al. (2008). Efficient processing of top-k queries in uncertain databases with x-relations. *IEEE transactions on knowledge and data engineering, 20*(12), 1669–1682.

Yin, J., Zheng, Z., & Cao, L. (2012). Uspan: an efficient algorithm for mining high utility sequential patterns. In *Proceedings of the 18th ACM SIGKDD international conference on knowledge discovery and data mining* (pp. 660–668). ACM Press.

Yoo, J., Boulware, D., & Kimmey, D. (2014). A parallel spatial co-location mining algorithm based on MapReduce. In *Proceedings of the 2014 IEEE International Congress on Big Data (BigData Congress)* (pp. 25–31). IEEE Press.

Yoo, J., & Bow, M. (2011a). Mining top-k closed co-location patterns. In *Proceedings of the 2011 IEEE International Conference on Spatial Data Mining and Geographical Knowledge Services (ICSDM)* (pp. 100–105). IEEE Press.

Yoo, J., & Bow, M. (2011b). Mining maximal co-located event sets. In *Proceedings of the 2011 Pacific-Asia Conference on Knowledge Discovery and Data Mining (PAKDD)* (pp. 351–362). Springer.

Yoo, J., & Bow, M. (2012). Mining spatial colocation patterns: a different framework. *Data Mining and Knowledge Discovery, 24*(1), 159–194.

Yoo, J., & Bow, M. (2019). A framework for generating condensed co-location sets from spatial databases. *Intelligent Data Analysis, 23*(2), 333–355.

Yoo, J., & Shekhar, S. (2006). A joinless approach for mining spatial colocation patterns. *IEEE Transactions on Knowledge and Data Engineering, 18*(10), 1323–1337.

Yoo, J., Shekhar, S., Smith, J., et al. (2004). A partial join approach for mining co-location patterns. In *Proceedings of the 12th annual ACM international workshop on Geographic Information Systems* (pp. 241–249). ACM Press.

Yoo, J. S., Boulware, D., & Kimmey, D. (2020). Parallel co-location mining with MapReduce and NoSQL systems. *Knowledge and Information Systems, 62*(4), 1433–1463.

Yu, W. (2016). Spatial co-location pattern mining for location-based services in road networks. *Expert Systems with Applications, 46*, 324–335.

Yu, W., Ai, T., & He, Y. (2017). Spatial co-location pattern mining of facility points-of-interest improved by network neighborhood and distance decay effects. *International Journal of Geographical Information Science, 31*(2), 280–296.

Yuan, G., Wang, L., Yang, P., et al. (2016). Spatial co-location pattern ordering. In *Proceedings of the 2016 International Conference on Computer, Information and Telecommunication Systems (CITS)* (pp. 1–5). IEE Press.

Yue, H., Zhu, X., Ye, X., et al. (2017). The local colocation patterns of crime and land-use features in Wuhan, China. *ISPRS International Journal of Geo-Information, 6*(10), 307–321.

Zaki, M., & Hsiao, C. (2002). CHARM: An efficient algorithm for closed itemset mining. In *Proceedings of the 2002 SIAM international conference on data mining* (pp. 457–473).

Zhang, C., Zhang, Y., Zhang, W., et al. (2019). Efficient maximal spatial clique enumeration. In *Proceedings of the 35th International Conference on Data Engineering (ICDE)* (pp. 878–889). IEEE Press.

Zhang, J., Nie, L., Wang, X., et al. (2016). Shorter-is-better: Venue category estimation from micro-video. In *Proceedings of the 24th ACM international conference on Multimedia* (pp. 1415–1424). ACM Press.

Zhang, L., Luo, P., Tang, L., et al. (2015). Occupancy-based frequent pattern mining. *ACM Transactions on Knowledge Discovery from Data, 10*(2), 1–33.

Zhang, Q., Li, F., & Yi, K. (2008). Finding frequent items in probabilistic data. In *Proceedings of the 2008 ACM international conference on Management of data (SIGMOD)* (pp. 819–832). ACM Press.

Zhang, X., Duan, F., Zhang, L., et al. (2017). Pattern recommendation in task-oriented applications: A multi-objective perspective. *IEEE Computational Intelligence Magazine, 12*(3), 43–53.

Zhang, X., Mamoulis, N., Cheung, D. W., et al. (2004). Fast mining of spatial collocations. In *Proceedings of the 10th ACM international conference on Knowledge discovery and data mining (SIGKDD)* (pp. 384–393). ACM Press.

Zhao, J., Wang, L., Bao, X., et al. (2016). Mining co-location patterns with spatial distribution characteristics. In *Proceedings of the IEEE International Conference on Computer, Information and Telecommunication Systems* (pp. 26–30). IEEE Press.

Zhou, G., & Wang, L. (2012). Co-location decision tree for enhancing decision-making of pavement maintenance and rehabilitation. *Transportation Research Part C: Emerging Technologies, 21*(1), 287–305.

Zhu, F., Qu, Q., Lo, D., et al.: Mining top-*k* large structural patterns in a massive network. In: *Proceedings of the VLDB Endowment* 4(11), 807-818 (2011)

Zhu, L., Huang, Z., Liu, X., et al. (2017). Discrete multimodal hashing with canonical views for robust mobile landmark search. *IEEE Transactions on Multimedia, 19*(9), 2066–2079.

Zhu, L., Shen, J., Jin, H., et al. (2015a). Content-based visual landmark search via multimodal hypergraph learning. *IEEE Transactions on Cybernetics, 45*(12), 2756–2769.

Zhu, L., Shen, J., Jin, H., et al. (2015b). Landmark classification with hierarchical multi-modal exemplar feature. *IEEE Transactions on Multimedia, 17*(7), 981–993.

Zhu, L., Shen, J., Liu, X., et al. (2016). Learning compact visual representation with canonical views for robust mobile landmark search. In *International Joint Conferences on Artificial Intelligence (IJCAI)* (pp. 3959–3967).

Printed in the United States
by Baker & Taylor Publisher Services